FEB   2018.

The People vs. Democracy

THE PEOPLE VS. DEMOCRACY

Why Our Freedom Is in Danger and How to Save It

YASCHA MOUNK

 Harvard University Press

CAMBRIDGE, MASSACHUSETTS
LONDON, ENGLAND
2018

Library of Congress Cataloging-in-Publication Data
Names: Mounk, Yascha, 1982– author.
Title: The people vs. democracy: why our freedom is in danger and how
to save it / Yascha Mounk.
Description: Cambridge, Massachusetts: Harvard University Press,
2018. | Includes bibliographical references and index.
Identifiers: LCCN 2017045238 | ISBN 9780674976825 (alk. paper)
Subjects: LCSH: Democracy. | Populism. | Authoritarianism. | Human
rights. | Political participation.
Classification: LCC JC423 .M685 2018 | DDC 321.8—dc23 LC record
available at https://lccn.loc.gov/2017045238

Contents

Losing Our Illusions

THERE ARE LONG DECADES in which history seems to slow to a crawl. Elections are won and lost, laws adopted and repealed, new stars born and legends carried to their graves. But for all the ordinary business of time passing, the lodestars of culture, society, and politics remain the same.

Then there are those short years in which everything changes all at once. Political newcomers storm the stage. Voters clamor for policies that were unthinkable until yesterday. Social tensions that had long simmered under the surface erupt into terrifying explosions. A system of government that had seemed immutable looks as though it might come apart.

This is the kind of moment in which we now find ourselves.

Until recently, liberal democracy reigned triumphant. For all its shortcomings, most citizens seemed deeply committed to their form of government. The economy was growing. Radical parties were insignificant. Political scientists thought that democracy in places like France or the United States had long ago been set in stone, and would change little in the years to come. Politically speaking, it seemed, the future would not be much different from the past.

Then the future came—and turned out to be very different indeed.

Citizens have long been disillusioned with politics; now, they have grown restless, angry, even disdainful. Party systems have long seemed frozen; now, authoritarian populists are on the rise around the world, from America to Europe, and from Asia to Australia. Voters have long disliked particular parties, politicians, or governments; now, many of them have become fed up with liberal democracy itself.

Donald Trump's election to the White House has been the most striking manifestation of democracy's crisis. It is difficult to overstate the significance of his rise. For the first time in its history, the oldest and most powerful democracy in the world has elected a president who openly disdains basic constitutional norms—somebody who left his supporters "in suspense" whether he would accept the outcome of the election; who called for his main political opponent to be jailed; and who has consistently favored the country's authoritarian adversaries over its democratic allies.[1] Even if Trump should eventually be constrained by the checks on his power, the willingness of the American people to elect a would-be authoritarian to the highest office in the land is a very bad omen.

And the election of Trump is, of course, hardly an isolated incident. In Russia and Turkey, elected strongmen have succeeded in turning fledgling democracies into electoral dictatorships. In Poland and Hungary, populist leaders are using that same playbook to destroy the free media, to undermine independent institutions, and to muzzle the opposition.

More countries may soon follow. In Austria, a far-right candidate nearly won the country's presidency. In France, a rapidly changing political landscape is providing new openings for both the far left and the far right. In Spain and Greece, established party systems are disintegrating with breathtaking speed. Even in the supposedly stable and tolerant democracies of Sweden, Germany, and the Netherlands, extremists are celebrating unprecedented successes.

There can no longer be any doubt that we are going through a populist moment. The question now is whether this populist moment will turn into a populist age—and cast the very survival of liberal democracy in doubt.

———

After the fall of the Soviet Union, liberal democracy became the dominant regime form around the world. It seemed immutable in North America and Western Europe, quickly took root in formerly autocratic countries from Eastern Europe to South America, and was making rapid inroads across Asia and Africa.

One reason for liberal democracy's triumph is that there was no coherent alternative to it. Communism had failed. Islamic theocracy had precious little support outside the Middle East. China's unique system of state capitalism under the banner of communism could hardly be emulated by countries that didn't share its unusual history. The future, it seemed, belonged to liberal democracy.

The idea that democracy was sure to triumph has come to be associated with the work of Francis Fukuyama. In a sensational essay published in the late 1980s, Fukuyama argued that the conclusion of the Cold War would lead to "the end point of mankind's ideological evolution and the universalization of Western liberal democracy as the final form of human government." Democracy's triumph, he proclaimed in a phrase that has come to encapsulate the heady optimism of 1989, would mark "The End of History."[2]

Plenty of critics took Fukuyama to task for his supposed naiveté. Some argued that the spread of liberal democracy was far from inevitable, fearing (or hoping) that many countries would prove resistant to this Western import. Others argued that it was too early to foresee what kind of improvement human ingenuity might be able to dream up over the course of the coming centuries: perhaps, they ventured, liberal democracy was just a prelude to a more just and enlightened form of rule.[3]

Despite the vociferous criticism, Fukuyama's core assumption proved highly influential. Most of the people who warned that liberal democracy might not triumph around the world were just as sure that it would remain stable in the democratic heartlands of North America and Western Europe. Indeed, even most political scientists, far too careful to make sweeping proclamations about the end of history, reached much the same conclusion. Democracies in poor countries, they observed, often failed. Autocrats were regularly ousted from power even when they could offer their subjects a good standard of living. But once a country was both affluent and democratic, it proved incredibly stable. Argentina had experienced a military coup in 1975, when its gross domestic product per capita was about $14,000 in today's currency.[4] Above that threshold, no established democracy had ever collapsed.[5]

Awed by the unparalleled stability of wealthy democracies, political scientists began to conceive of the postwar history of many countries as a process of "democratic consolidation."[6] To sustain a durable democracy, a country had to attain a high level of wealth and education. It had to build a vibrant civil society and ensure the neutrality of key state institutions like the judiciary. Major political forces had to accept that they should let voters, rather than the might of their arms or the thickness of their wallets, determine political outcomes. All of these goals frequently proved elusive.

Building a democracy was no easy task. But the prize that beckoned was both precious and perennial: once the key benchmarks of democracy were attained, the political system would be stable forevermore. Democratic consolidation, on this vision, was a one-way street. Once democracy had, in the famous phrase of Juan J. Linz and Alfred Stepan, become "the only game in town," it was there to stay.[7]

So confident were political scientists in this assumption that few considered the conditions under which democratic consolidation might risk running in reverse. But recent events call this democratic self-confidence into question.

A quarter century ago, most citizens of liberal democracies were very satisfied with their governments and gave high approval ratings to their institutions; now, they are more disillusioned than they have ever been. A quarter century ago, most citizens were proud to live in a liberal democracy and strongly rejected authoritarian alternatives to their system of government; now, many are growing increasingly hostile to democracy. And a quarter century ago, political adversaries were united in their shared respect for basic democratic rules and norms; now, candidates who violate the most basic norms of liberal democracy have gained great power and influence.[8]

Just take two examples drawn from my own research: Over two-thirds of older Americans believe that it is extremely important to live in a democracy; among millennials, less than one-third do. The sinking attachment to democracy is also making Americans more open to authoritarian alternatives. Back in 1995, for example, only one in sixteen believed that army rule is a good system of government; today, one in six do.[9]

Under these radically changed circumstances, it would be foolhardy to assume that the stability of democracy is sure to persist. The first big assumption of the postwar era—the idea that rich countries in which the government had repeatedly changed hands through free and fair elections would forever remain democratic—has, all along, stood on shaky ground.

If the first big assumption that shaped our political imagination has turned out to be unwarranted, there's reason to reexamine the second big assumption as well.

Liberalism and democracy, we have long thought, make a cohesive whole. It is not just that we care both about the popular will and the rule of law, both about letting the people decide and protecting individual rights. It's that each component of our political system seems necessary to protect the other.

There is indeed good reason to fear that liberal democracy cannot survive if one of its elements is abandoned. A system in which the people get to call the shots ensures that the rich and powerful cannot trample on the rights of the lowly. By the same token, a system in which the rights of unpopular minorities are protected and the press can freely criticize the government ensures that the people can change its rulers through free and fair elections. Individual rights and the popular will, this story suggests, go together like apple and pie or Twitter and Donald Trump.

But the fact that a working system needs both elements to thrive does not mean that a system that has both will necessarily be stable. On the contrary, the mutual dependence of liberalism and democracy shows just how quickly dysfunction in one aspect of our politics can breed dysfunction in another. And so democracy without rights always runs the danger of degenerating into the thing the Founding Fathers most feared: the tyranny of the majority. Meanwhile, rights without democracy need not prove to be more stable: once the political system turns into a playground for billionaires and technocrats, the temptation to exclude the people from more and more important decisions will keep on growing.

This slow divergence of liberalism and democracy may be exactly what is now happening—and the consequences are likely to be just as bad as one would predict.

From style to substance, much divides the populists who are celebrating unprecedented successes on both sides of the Atlantic.

It is tempting, for example, to see Donald Trump as a uniquely

American phenomenon. From his brash manner to his boasts about his net worth, he is a walking caricature of the American id—the sort of figure a communist cartoonist tasked with ridiculing the archenemy might have drawn on behalf of some Soviet-era propaganda ministry. And in many ways, of course, Trump *is* very American. He emphasizes his credentials as a businessman in part because of the deep veneration for entrepreneurs in American culture. The targets of his ire, too, are shaped by the American context. Fears that liberal elites are plotting to take the people's guns away, for example, would seem peculiar in Europe.

And yet, the real nature of the threat Trump poses can only be understood in a much wider context: that of the far-right populists who have been gaining strength in every major democracy, from Athens to Ankara, from Sydney to Stockholm, and from Warsaw to Wellington. Despite the obvious differences between the populists who are on the rise in all these countries, their commonalities go deep—and render each of them a danger to the political system in surprisingly similar ways.

Donald Trump in the United States, Nigel Farage in Great Britain, Frauke Petry in Germany, and Marine Le Pen in France all claim that the solutions to the most pressing problems of our time are much more straightforward than the political establishment would have us believe, and that the great mass of ordinary people instinctively knows what to do. At bottom, they see politics as a very simple matter. If the pure voice of the people could prevail, the reasons for popular discontent would quickly vanish. America (or Great Britain, or Germany, or France) would be great again.

This begs an obvious question. If the political problems of our time are so easy to fix, why do they persist? Since the populists are unwilling to admit that the real world might be complicated—that solutions might prove elusive even for people with good intentions—they need somebody to blame. And blame they do.

The first obvious culprit often lies outside the country. So it is only logical that Trump blames America's economic problems on China. Nor should it be surprising that he preys on people's fears by claiming that the United States is being overrun by rapists (Mexicans) and terrorists (Muslims).[10] European populists see their enemies elsewhere, and most express their bile in a more circumspect manner. But their rhetoric has the same underlying logic. Like Trump, Le Pen and Farage believe that it must be the fault of outsiders—of Muslim moochers or Polish plumbers—when incomes stagnate or their identity is threatened by newcomers. And like Trump, they blame the political establishment—from Brussels bureaucrats to the mendacious media—for their failure to deliver on their outsized promises. People in the capital, populists of all stripes argue, are either in it for themselves or in cahoots with the nation's enemies. Establishment politicians, they say, have a misguided fetish for diversity. Or they root for their country's enemies. Or—simplest explanation of all—they are somehow foreign, or Muslim, or both.

This worldview breeds two political desires, and most populists are savvy enough to embrace both. First, populists claim, an honest leader—one who shares the pure outlook of the people and is willing to fight on their behalf—needs to win high office. And second, once this honest leader is in charge, he needs to abolish the institutional roadblocks that might stop him from carrying out the will of the people.

Liberal democracies are full of checks and balances that are meant to stop any one party from amassing too much power and to reconcile the interests of different groups. But in the imagination of the populists, the will of the people does not need to be mediated, and any compromise with minorities is a form of corruption. In that sense, populists are deeply democratic: much more fervently than traditional politicians, they believe that the *demos* should rule. But they are also deeply illiberal: unlike traditional politicians, they openly say that neither independent institutions nor individual rights should dampen the people's voice.

The fear that populist insurgents would undermine liberal institutions if they came to power may sound alarmist. But it is based on plenty of precedent. After all, illiberal populists have already been elected to office in countries like Poland and Turkey. In each of these places, they took strikingly similar steps to consolidate their power: they ratcheted up tensions with perceived enemies at home and abroad; packed courts and electoral commissions with their cronies; and took control of the media.[11]

In Hungary, for example, liberal democracy was a much more recent—and rather more brittle—transplant than in, say, Germany or Sweden. And yet, throughout the 1990s, political scientists were bullish on its prospects. According to their theories, Hungary had all the attributes that favored a democratic transition: it had experienced democratic rule in the past; its totalitarian legacy was more moderate than that of many other Eastern European countries; old communist elites had acquiesced to the new regime in a negotiated settlement; and the country bordered a number of stable democracies. Hungary, in the language of social science, was a "most likely case": if democracy didn't make it there, it would have difficulty making it in all the other postcommunist countries as well.[12]

That prediction seemed to hold up well enough throughout the 1990s. Hungary's economy grew. The government peacefully changed hands. Its lively civil society featured critical media, strong NGOs, and one of the best universities in Central Europe. Hungarian democracy seemed to be consolidating.[13]

Then the trouble started. Many Hungarians felt that they were getting too small a share of the country's economic growth. They saw their identity threatened by the prospect (though not the reality) of mass immigration. When a big corruption scandal enveloped the ruling center-left party, their discontent turned into outright disgust with the government. At parliamentary elections in 2010, Hungarian voters gave Viktor Orbán's Fidesz party a stomping majority.[14]

Once in office, Orbán systematically consolidated his rule. He appointed loyal followers to lead state-run television stations, to head the electoral commission, and to dominate the country's constitutional court. He changed the electoral system to benefit himself, pushed out foreign corporations to channel money to his cronies, instituted highly restrictive rules on NGOs, and attempted to shutter Central European University.[15]

There was no Rubicon, no single step that cleanly marked that the old political norms had been destroyed for good. Any one of Orbán's measures could be defended in this way or that. But, taken together, their effect slowly became unmistakable: Hungary is no longer a liberal democracy.

What, then, is it?

Over the years, Orbán has answered this question with increasing clarity. At first he presented himself as an honest democrat with conservative values. Now, he states his opposition to liberal democracy loud and clear. Democracy, he vows, should be hierarchical rather than liberal. Under his leadership, Hungary will become an "illiberal new state based on national foundations."[16]

This is a much better description of the nature of his enterprise than most outside observers have been able to muster. They tend to denounce Orbán as undemocratic. But though they are right to worry that his illiberal reforms may eventually allow him to disregard the will of the people, it is a mistake to think that all democracies must by their nature be liberal, or resemble our current political institutions.

Hierarchical democracy allows popularly elected leaders to enact the will of the people as they interpret it, without having to make allowances for the rights or interests of obstinate minorities. Its claim to being democratic need not be disingenuous. In the emerging system, the popular will reigns supreme (at least at first). What sets it apart from the kind of liberal democracy to which we are accustomed is not a lack of democracy; it is a lack of respect for independent institutions and individual rights.

The rise of illiberal democracy, or democracy without rights, is but one side of politics in the first decades of the twenty-first century. For even as ordinary people have grown skeptical of liberal practices and institutions, political elites have tried to insulate themselves from their anger. The world is complicated, they insist—and they have worked hard to find the right answers. If the people should grow so restive as to ignore the sage advice proffered by elites, they need to be educated, ignored, or bullied into submission.

Never was this attitude more starkly on display than in the early hours of July 13th, 2015. The Great Recession had saddled Greece with a vast amount of debt. Economists knew that the country would never be able to pay off everything it owed; most agreed that a policy of austerity would only serve to inflict further damage on a cratering economy.[17] But if the European Union allowed Greece to default, investors would worry that much larger countries, like Spain or Italy, might be next. And so technocrats in Brussels decided that, for the rest of the European monetary system to survive, Greece would have to suffer.

With few other options open to them, a succession of Greek governments did Brussels's bidding. But with the economy shrinking from year to year and youth unemployment spiking above 50 percent, desperate voters finally put their trust in Alexis Tsipras, a young, populist leader who promised to end austerity.[18]

When Tsipras took office, he set out to renegotiate the country's debt with its main creditors, represented by the European Commission, the European Central Bank, and the International Monetary Fund. But it quickly turned out that the so-called "troika" was unwilling to budge. Greece would have to persist in penury—or go bankrupt and leave the euro. By the summer of 2015, with a harsh bailout package on the table, Tsipras was down to two options: capitulate to the demands of the technocrats or lead Greece into economic chaos.[19]

Faced with a momentous choice, Tsipras did what might seem natural in a system that purports to let the people rule: he called a popular referendum. The backlash was swift, and it was mighty. Political leaders from all over Europe called the referendum irresponsible. German chancellor Angela Merkel insisted that the troika had made an "extraordinarily generous" offer. The media vilified Tsipras's decision.[20]

Amid high excitement, Greece went to the polls on July 5, 2015. The results were a big rebuke to the continent's technocratic elites. Despite ominous warnings about impending doom, voters were unwilling to swallow their pride. They rejected the deal.[21]

Emboldened by a clear expression of popular will, Tsipras went back to the negotiating table. He seemed to assume that the troika would meet Greece halfway. Instead, the original deal was off the table—and the new offer imposed even greater hardships.[22]

With Greece teetering on the brink of insolvency, Europe's political elite assembled in Brussels for a marathon of backroom negotiations. When Tsipras stepped in front of the cameras in the early morning of July 13, his eyes red and his face ashen, it quickly became apparent that the night had ended in his capitulation. A little over a week after he had let his people reject an unpopular bailout deal, Tsipras signed off on an agreement that was, by any reasonable measure, worse.[23] Technocracy had prevailed.

The politics of the Eurozone are an extreme example of a political system in which the people feel as though they have less and less say over what actually happens.[24] But they are far from atypical.

Unnoticed by most political scientists, a form of undemocratic liberalism has taken root in North America and Western Europe. In this form of government, procedural niceties are carefully followed (most of the time) and individual rights are respected (much of the time). But voters have long since concluded that they have little influence on public policy.

They aren't altogether wrong.

Hungary's rise of the populists and Greece's rule of the technocrats seem like polar opposites. In one case, the will of the people pushed aside the independent institutions that were meant to protect the rule of law and the rights of minorities. In the other case, the force of the markets and the beliefs of the technocrats pushed aside the will of the people.

But Hungary and Greece are just two sides of the same coin. In democracies around the world, two seemingly distinct developments are playing out. On the one hand, the preferences of the people are increasingly illiberal: voters are growing impatient with independent institutions and less and less willing to tolerate the rights of ethnic and religious minorities. On the other hand, elites are taking hold of the political system and making it increasingly unresponsive: the powerful are less and less willing to cede to the views of the people. As a result, liberalism and democracy, the two core elements of our political system, are starting to come into conflict.

Scholars have always known that liberalism and democracy could, at times, be observed in isolation from each other. In eighteenth century Prussia, an absolute monarch ruled in a comparatively liberal manner by respecting (some of) his subjects' rights and allowing (a modicum of) free speech.[25] Conversely, in ancient Athens, the people's assembly ruled in a blatantly illiberal manner, exiling unpopular statesmen, executing critical philosophers, and censoring everything from political speech to musical scores.[26]

Even so, most political scientists have long thought of liberalism and democracy as complementary. While they recognized that individual rights and the popular will may not always go together, they held fast to the belief that they are meant to. Where liberalism and democracy do meet, the story holds, they form an especially stable, resilient, and coherent amalgam.

But as the views of the people are trending illiberal and the preferences of the elites are turning undemocratic, liberalism and democracy are starting to clash. Liberal democracy, the unique mix of individual rights and popular rule that has long characterized most governments in North America and Western Europe, is coming apart at its seams. In its stead, we are seeing the rise of *illiberal democracy,* or democracy without rights, and *undemocratic liberalism,* or rights without democracy.

———

Once upon a time, there was a very happy chicken. Every day, the farmer would come to feed the chicken. Every day, the chicken would grow a little more plump and a little more complacent.

Other animals on the farm tried to warn the chicken. "You are going to die," they said. "The farmer is only trying to fatten you up."

The chicken did not listen. All its life, the farmer had come to feed it, muttering a few friendly words of encouragement. Why should things suddenly be so different?

But, sure enough, one day things did change: "The man who has fed the chicken every day throughout its life," Bertrand Russell writes in his characteristically wry tone, "at last wrings its neck instead."[27] As long as the chicken was young and thin, the farmer wanted to fatten it up; once it was fat enough for the market, it was time for it to be killed.

Russell meant to warn us against making facile predictions: If we don't understand what made things happen in the past, the story of the unsuspecting chicken reminds us, then we can't assume that they'll keep happening in the future. Just as the chicken failed to anticipate that its world might one day crumble, we too may be blind to the changes that lie ahead.

If we want to venture an educated guess about the future of democracy, we have to ask the "chicken question." Was the past stability of democracy brought about by conditions that are no longer in place?

The answer might well be yes.

There are at least three striking constants that characterized democracy since its founding but are no longer true today. First, during the period of democratic stability, most citizens enjoyed a rapid increase in their living standards. From 1935 to 1960, for example, the income of a typical American household doubled. From 1960 to 1985, it doubled again. Since then, it has been flat.[28]

This has heralded a radical change in American politics: Citizens never especially liked politicians—and yet they did, by and large, trust that elected officials would stick to their end of the deal, and that their lives would keep getting better as a result. Today, that trust and that optimism have evaporated. As citizens have grown deeply anxious about the future, they have started to see politics as a zero-sum game—one in which any gain for immigrants or ethnic minorities will come at their expense.[29]

This is exacerbating a second difference between the comparatively stable past and the increasingly chaotic present. All through the history of democratic stability, one racial or ethnic group has been dominant. In the United States and Canada, there has always been a clear racial hierarchy, with whites enjoying myriad privileges. In Western Europe this dominance went even further. Founded on a monoethnic basis, countries like Germany or Sweden did not recognize immigrants as true members of the nation. To an extent we often prefer to disregard, the functioning of democracy may have depended on that homogeneity.

Decades of mass migration and social activism have radically transformed these societies. In North America, racial minorities are finally claiming an equal seat at the table. In Western Europe, the descendants of immigrants are starting to insist that somebody who is black or brown can be a real German or Swede. But while a part of the population accepts, or even welcomes, this change, another part feels threatened and resentful. As a result, a vast rebellion against ethnic and cultural pluralism is gathering speed across the western hemisphere.[30]

A final change has conquered the whole wide world in the span of a few short decades. Until recently, mass communication remained the exclusive preserve of political and financial elites. The costs associated with printing a newspaper, running a radio station, or operating a television network were prohibitive for most citizens. This allowed the political establishment to marginalize extreme views. Politics remained comparatively consensual.

Over the past quarter century, by contrast, the rise of the internet, and particularly of social media, has rapidly shifted the power balance between political insiders and political outsiders. Today, any citizen is able to share viral information with millions of people at great speed. The costs of political organizing have plummeted. And as the technological gap between center and periphery has narrowed, the instigators of instability have won an advantage over the forces of order.[31]

We are only now starting to understand what has caused the existential crisis of liberal democracy, let alone how to fight it. But if we take the major drivers of our populist age seriously, we should recognize that we need to take action on at least three fronts.

First, we need to reform economic policy, both domestically and internationally, to temper inequality and live up to the promise of rapidly rising living standards. A more equitable distribution of economic growth, on this vision, is not just a question of distributive justice; it is a question of political stability.

Some economists have argued that we cannot have democracy, globalization, and the nation state all at the same time. And some philosophers have embraced the abandonment of the nation state, dreaming up predominantly international solutions to the economic problems we now face. But this is the wrong approach. To preserve democracy without giving up on the emancipatory potential of globalization, we need to figure out how the nation state can once again take control of its own fate.[32]

Second, we need to rethink what membership and belonging might mean in a modern nation state. The promise of multiethnic democracy, in which members of any creed or color are regarded as true equals, is nonnegotiable. Difficult though it may be for countries with a deeply monoethnic conception of themselves to embrace newcomers and minorities, such a transformation is the only realistic alternative to tyranny and civic strife.

But the noble experiment of multiethnic democracy can only succeed if all of its adherents start to emphasize what unites rather than what divides them. In the last years, a righteous impatience with the continuing reality of racial injustice has increasingly pushed some people to denounce the principles of liberal democracy as hypocritical, or even to make group rights the building block of society. This is a moral as well as a strategic mistake: The only society that can treat all of its members with respect is one in which every individual enjoys rights on the basis of being a citizen, not on the basis of belonging to a particular group.[33]

Finally, we need to learn to withstand the transformative impact of the internet and of social media. As hate speech and fake news have spread, there have been calls for social media companies— or governments—to act as censors. There are many commonsense steps Facebook and Twitter can take to make it more difficult for hate groups to exploit these platforms. But if governments or CEOs started to determine who can say what on the web, free speech would quickly go out the window. To make the digital age safe for democracy, we therefore need to shape not only what messages are spread on social media, but also how they are likely to be received.

Back when we understood democracy to be a daring, fragile experiment, we invested vast educational and intellectual resources in spreading the good news about our political system. Schools and universities knew that their most important task was to educate citizens. Writers and academics recognized that they had a big role to play in explaining and defending the virtues of liberal democracy. Over the years, this sense of mission has dissipated. Now, as liberal democracy is facing existential danger, it is high time to revive it.[34]

There are ordinary times, when political decisions influence the lives of millions of people in ways both big and small, but the basic features of a country's collective life are not at stake. Despite deep disagreements, partisans on both sides of the political battle line endorse the rules of play. They agree to settle their differences on the basis of free and fair elections, are committed to the basic norms of the political system, and accept that a loss at the ballot box makes it legitimate for their political opponent to take a turn at ruling the country.

As a result, the denizens of ordinary times recognize that every victory is provisional and that the loser of one political battle may yet live to win the war. Since they have it in their power to transform progress defeated today into justice delayed until tomorrow, they see every loss as but another reason to redouble their efforts at peaceful persuasion.

Then there are extraordinary times, when the basic contours of politics and society are being renegotiated. In such times, the disagreements between partisans on both sides grow so deep and nasty that they no longer agree on the rules of the game. To gain an advantage, politicians become willing to undermine free and fair elections, to flout the basic norms of the political system, and to vilify their adversaries.

As a result, the denizens of extraordinary times start to regard the stakes of politics as existential. In a system whose rules are deeply contested, they have good reason to fear that a victory at the polls may turn out to be forever; that a loss in one political battle may rob them of the ability to wage the larger war; and that progress defeated today may turn out to set the country on a path toward perennial injustice.

Most of us have spent the bulk of our lives in ordinary times.

When I was coming of age in Germany in the late 1990s, for example, politicians were debating important questions. Should the receipt of welfare benefits be made conditional on good behavior?[35] Would immigrants and their children be allowed to take on German citizenship without giving up their other passports? Might the state recognize same-sex partnerships in the form of civil unions?

The answers they gave to these questions would, I was convinced, deeply shape the country in the years to come. The future was wide open. On one side, there lay the vision of an open, generous, welcoming country. On the other, a closed, niggardly, stagnant one. As a member in the youth organization of a big political party, I spent a lot of my time fighting for what I believed to be right.

At that time, I barely knew the United States. So I didn't understand that even bigger questions were being discussed in America. Would millions of uninsured citizens get access to decent medical care? Could soldiers be thrown out of the army for being open about their sexuality? And should key parts of the welfare state be abolished?

The answers to these questions, too, would deeply shape the country. They would make the lives of millions of people better or worse, more authentic or more dissimulating, more prosperous or more precarious. It mattered—deeply—which path the country would take. And yet, with the benefit of hindsight, I recognize that this was the stuff of ordinary politics.

Now, by contrast, it is, each and every day, becoming clearer that we live in extraordinary times: in times, that is, in which the decisions we take will determine whether terrifying chaos spreads; whether unspeakable cruelty is unleashed; and whether a political system—liberal democracy—that has done more to spread peace and prosperity than any other in the history of humanity can survive.

The predicament in which we now find ourselves is so recent, and so scary, that nobody has managed to make real sense of it so far. Individual pieces of the puzzle are dissected every day in the newspaper, on television, sometimes even in the academy. But the more we obsess about these individual pieces, the less we see the overall picture.

In this book, I try to make sense of our new political landscape by making four distinctive contributions: I demonstrate that liberal democracy is now decomposing into its component parts, giving rise to illiberal democracy on the one side and undemocratic liberalism on the other. I argue that the deep disenchantment with our political system poses an existential danger to the very survival of liberal democracy. I explain the roots of this crisis. And I show what we can do to rescue what is truly valuable in our imperiled social and political order.

We have the immense fortune of living in the most peaceful and prosperous era of human history. Though the events of the last years may seem disorienting or even paralyzing, we retain the power to win a better future. But unlike fifteen or thirty years ago, we can no longer take that future for granted.

At the moment, the enemies of liberal democracy seem more determined to shape our world than its defenders. If we want to preserve both peace and prosperity, both popular rule and individual rights, we need to recognize that these are no ordinary times—and go to extraordinary lengths to defend our values.

PART ONE

THE CRISIS OF LIBERAL DEMOCRACY

IN 1830, the King of France sent a young engineer to England to study a sensational invention: a steam train that had just begun to ferry passengers from Manchester to Liverpool. Once he arrived, the engineer

> sat by the track taking copious notes as the sturdy little engine faultlessly pulled the world's first railway train back and forth between the two cities. After conscientiously calculating what he had observed, he reported his findings back to Paris: "The thing is impossible," he wrote. "It cannot work."[1]

It is tempting to scoff at the engineer. He is so beholden to scientific doctrine that he disregards the evidence barreling past his eyes at thirty miles an hour. But I must admit to having a soft spot for him. For it was, I think, not the mathematical equations in his notepad that led to his absurd conclusion—but his all-too-human refusal to believe that his understanding of the world might prove quite so mistaken. And so it is hardly surprising that, as one political shock has followed the next over the past months, people who might once have seemed perfectly rational and pragmatic have come to resemble the young French engineer.

Pundits and political scientists alike told us that Brits would never vote to Brexit. They did. Pundits and political scientists alike told us that Donald Trump could never get elected. He did. Pundits and political scientists alike told us that democracy would never be in danger of deconsolidating. It is.

We live in an era of radical uncertainty. The range of possible outcomes is much wider now than it seemed to be a few years ago. Prediction is a more difficult game than ever. And yet, the one prediction that has reliably misled us—the assumption that things will forever remain the way they have always been—remains the most popular, even today. "The thing is impossible," one article after another seems to conclude. "It cannot be."

If we are to avoid being as surprised by the future as we have been by the recent past, it is time to reexamine our basic assumptions. Might liberal democracies be less stable than we have assumed? And will the rise of populism lead to the decomposition of our political system?

To think clearly about the perils facing liberal democracy, we need to understand what its constitutive elements actually mean. This task is complicated by two facts.

First, the word *liberalism* has different meanings when we talk about everyday politics and when we talk about the nature of our political institutions. Much of the time, especially in the United States, "liberal" is used to indicate a person's political views: there are liberals and conservatives just as there are left-wingers and right-wingers or Democrats and Republicans. That is *not* what I mean when I talk about liberal democracy or use the word *liberal*. In this book, a liberal is somebody who is committed to basic values like freedom of speech, the separation of powers, or the protection of individual rights. In the sense in which I use the word, George W. Bush is as much of a liberal as Barack Obama, and Ronald Reagan was as much of a liberal as Bill Clinton.

Second, because democracy has such prestige, we have fallen into the bad habit of expanding its definition to all kinds of things we like. As a result, virtually all existing definitions of democracy don't bother to distinguish between three very different beasts: liberalism, democracy, and the historically contingent set of institutions to which we have become accustomed in North America and Western Europe.

The tendency to smuggle all desirable qualities into the very notion of democracy is most obviously true of philosophers who want to reserve the term for the most just regimes—those imaginary societies that would actually succeed in eradicating injustices like widespread poverty or rampant inequality. But even political scientists who have self-consciously tried to devise minimalist conceptions of democracy elide the key distinctions between liberalism, democracy, and institutions like parliaments or courts. Following the political scientist Robert Dahl, for example, "procedural minimalists" define a democracy as any system that features:

- "Free, fair and competitive elections;
- Full adult suffrage;
- Broad protection of civil liberties, including freedom of speech, press, and association; and
- The absence of nonelected 'tutelary' authorities (e.g. militaries, monarchies, or religious bodies) that limit elected officials' power to govern."[2]

Dahl's conceptual framework thus bakes the protection of liberal rights into the very definition of democracy. This makes it impossible to ask whether democracy and liberalism might be coming apart. By focusing on a particular set of historically contingent institutions, it also makes it difficult to ask whether these institutions actually allow the people to rule. In this way, the not-so-minimalist definition of democracy inflates the importance of our political institutions. Instead of recognizing them as a means toward democracy and liberalism, it seems to imagine that they are ends in themselves.[3]

I therefore use a much simpler set of definitions—one that makes fewer assumptions about the world and better captures democracy's original promise to let the people rule. In my view,

- A *democracy* is a set of binding electoral institutions that effectively translates popular views into public policy.[4]
- *Liberal* institutions effectively protect the rule of law and guarantee individual rights such as freedom of speech, worship, press, and association to all citizens (including ethnic and religious minorities).
- A *liberal democracy* is simply a political system that is both liberal and democratic—one that both protects individual rights and translates popular views into public policy.

This allows us to see that liberal democracies might become perverted in two ways. Democracies can be illiberal. This is especially likely to happen in places where most people favor subordinating independent institutions to the whims of the executive or curtailing the rights of minorities they dislike. Conversely, liberal regimes can be undemocratic despite having regular, competitive elections. This is especially likely to happen where the political system is so skewed in favor of the elite that elections rarely serve to translate popular views into public policy.

That, I fear, is precisely what has happened in many parts of the world over the past decades. Liberalism and democracy, I argue, have been glued together by a contingent set of technological, economic, and cultural preconditions. That glue is now rapidly thinning. As a result, liberal democracy—the unique mix of individual rights and popular rule that has long characterized most governments in North America and Western Europe—is coming apart. In its stead, two new regime forms are rising: *illiberal democracy,* or democracy without rights, and *undemocratic liberalism,* or rights without democracy. When the history of the twenty-first century is written, the decomposition of liberal democracy into these two component parts is likely to take center stage.

1
Democracy without Rights

IN THE FALL of 1989, the citizens of the "worker's paradise" in East Germany flocked to the streets of Leipzig and Dresden every Monday night to protest the communist regime. Their central slogan had a hopeful dignity: "Wir sind das Volk," the crowd would chant. We—not the secret police, nor the party elites—are the People.[1]

For the past three years, the people of Leipzig and Dresden have again taken to the streets. As anger against the hundreds of thousands of refugees coming into Germany over the course of 2015 rose to fever pitch, a movement that calls itself, rather grandiloquently, the "Patriotic Europeans against the Islamization of the Occident" (or PEGIDA, for short) began to protest Angela Merkel and her government's policies.[2]

By assembling every Monday night in the center of those same cities, PEGIDA was shrewdly appropriating the legacy of popular resistance for itself. Those who are opposing Merkel today, they were trying to say, are the rightful inheritors of the people who opposed the communist regime a quarter of a century ago. So when I went to observe thousands of angry citizens protest in the center of

Dresden, the distinct air of counterrevolution shouldn't have come as a shock to me. And yet it did.

Hatred of the *Lügenpresse*, the "lying press," is central to the movement's ideology, and most protestors refused to talk to me. When I tried to take a few photos, I was wordlessly shoved aside. "I'm here because I don't have a family," a producer for a local TV station, who had positioned his camera far from the crowd, told me. "Colleagues with children refuse to cover the protests. The risk of being beaten up is too high."[3]

Even so, PEGIDA's core themes—its hatred of refugees, its mistrust of the United States, and its insistence on the ethnic purity of the German people—were on full display. Few protestors were waving the black-red-golden flag of the Federal Republic, whose tricolor design invokes the universalist values of the French Revolution. Instead, most favored the so-called Wirmer flag, a dark cross against a maroon background, which has become popular in far-right circles because it is seen as a symbol for the country's Nordic roots and Christian traditions.

What the iconography of resistance lacked in subtlety, it made up for in variety: In the crowd, I also spotted Russian flags ("Putin puts his people first"), Confederate flags ("They were true rebels"), and a lone Japanese flag.

That last one puzzled me. I was not surprised to see that this crowd admired Putin's autocratic regime or his harsh treatment of minorities within Russia. I could see why protestors who hated the United States and were afraid of ethnic diversity might identify with the American South. But what did Japan have to do with anything?

I approached the man holding the sign with a little trepidation, but he was evidently delighted to explain his reasoning. Japan, he told me, has the same problem as Germany: a shrinking population. Germany has let in a lot of immigrants in the hope that they will make up the shortfall in the labor force and pay into social security systems. But all of that has been a big mistake. The Japanese, who have steadfastly refused to open their doors to newcomers, are much wiser: "Better to let your population shrink than to let a lot of foreigners in."[4]

The signs told a similar story. One declared that Merkel and other members of the government are "enemies of the German people" who are "waging a war of annihilation against us!!!" "Hey, Yankee," another read, "get the shit out of here and take your puppets with you." A third sign looked familiar at first, echoing the "REFUGEES WELCOME" flags that had been ubiquitous a few months before, when German volunteers enthusiastically greeted newly arrived refugees at train stations all over the country. It showed a crusader on horseback using his spear to repel a couple of Kalashnikov-wielding terrorists, the man clad in a traditional robe, the woman covered by a niqab. "ISLAMISTS NOT WELCOME," it announced in big letters. "STAY BACK OR WE'LL KICK YOU BACK." (Other signs, with similar motifs, read "RAPEFUGEES NOT WELCOME" or, simply, "MOHAMMED NOT WELCOME.")

But this carnival of hate was a sideshow. The protest's emotional center—its core message, and its insidious refrain—was the rendition of a slogan that had not changed in a quarter century. "Wir sind das Volk," the crowd chanted, over and over, each rendition a little more aggressive. We—not those foreigners who are flooding Germany, nor the politicians who are in cahoots with them—are the People.[5]

In the months following those protests, as authoritarian populists grabbed the spotlight across Europe and the United States elected Donald Trump, I kept thinking back to my experiences on that freezing night. So much of the angry energy that fueled these movements had been on display in the streets of Dresden that I could not help interpreting the events of 2016 and 2017 in light of what I saw there: the hatred of immigrants and ethnic minorities; the mistrust of the press and the spread of fake news; the conviction that the silent majority had finally found its voice; and, perhaps more than anything else, the hankering for somebody who would speak in the name of the people.[6]

The rapid ascent of strongman leaders who claim that they alone embody the will of the people is remarkable in historical perspective. As the political scientists Seymour Martin Lipset and Stein Rokkan observed, for much of the postwar era, the party structure in most Western European and North American countries appeared "frozen."[7] For the latter decades of the twentieth century, the main political movements represented in the parliaments of Bern, Copenhagen, Helsinki, Ottawa, Paris, Stockholm, and Washington barely changed. While their relative strength shifted from election to election, allowing the center-left to win office when the center-right had been in power for a while, and vice versa, the basic shape of the party structure was remarkably stable.[8]

Then, over the past twenty years, the party system rapidly thawed. In one country after another, political parties that had been marginal or nonexistent until a few short years ago established themselves as firm fixtures on the political scene.[9]

The first major democracy to go through this process was Italy. In the early 1990s, a massive corruption scandal pulverized the political system. Parties that had dominated Italian politics since the end of World War II disbanded or sank into the electoral abyss. The first person to exploit the ensuing void was Silvio Berlusconi, a businessman who himself faced corruption charges when he entered politics. Promising to clean up the system and make the country rich, Berlusconi swept to victory. Over the next few years, much of his government's energy was consumed by managing the fallout from his constant stream of gaffes—and keeping him out of jail. And yet he went on to dominate the country's politics for the next quarter century.[10]

At the time, Italy looked like an aberration. Over the past years, as political newcomers have risen to power and influence across Europe, it has become obvious that it was anything but.

In Greece, the Panhellenic Socialist Movement (PASOK), the major party of the center-left, and New Democracy, the major party of the center-right, traditionally took about 80 percent of the vote between them; but in January 2015, the Coalition of the Radical Left, or Syriza, stormed into office under the leadership of Alexis Tsipras, winning an unexpected majority.[11] In Spain, Pablo Iglesias, a young lecturer on political science at the Complutense University of Madrid who spent his days teaching courses like "Cinema, Political Identities, and Hegemony" founded a protest movement in the wake of the 2008 financial crisis; at the 2015 elections, Podemos got 21 percent of the vote, becoming Spain's third strongest party.[12] Even in Italy, a new generation of populists is pulling off the same feat of transformation as the old: Beppe Grillo, a popular comedian, started the Five Star Movement in 2009; as I am writing these lines, it is leading all other parties in the polls.[13]

The ascent of far-right parties has been even more striking than that of far-left parties like Syriza and Podemos. In Sweden, the Social Democratic Party has dominated politics for over a century, only occasionally ceding the government to a center-right coalition led by the Moderate Party; but in recent years, the Sweden Democrats, political upstarts with deep roots in the neo-Nazi movement, have risen rapidly, leading in some polls and taking second place in others.[14] In France, the Front National has long been a fixture of the political system. But after decades on the margins, Jean-Marie Le Pen unexpectedly beat the center-left candidate in the first round of the presidential election in 2002, qualifying for the runoff against President Jacques Chirac; in 2017, his daughter, Marine Le Pen, pulled off a similar feat, doubling the share of the vote he had received.[15]

A similar story holds true in Austria, the Netherlands, Finland,

Populist Parties

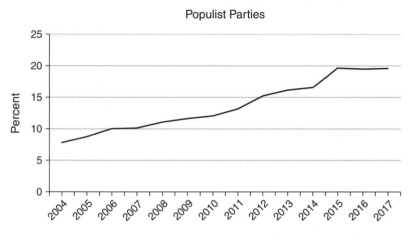

Vote share for anti-establishment parties in the European Union (EU15).

and Germany: in each of these countries, far-right populists have celebrated unprecedented successes in recent years by intoning their support of the people. In fact, the vote share of European populist parties on both the left and the right has more than doubled over the course of the past decades.[16]

My experiences in Dresden also reinforced my conviction that the standard terms of the debate about populism are misguided.

The defenders of populism have celebrated these movements as a sign of great health for our political system. "The real problem facing democracy today," Astra Taylor writes in her lament, "The Anti-Democratic Urge," is "not an excess of popular power but a lack of it."[17] "Anti-populism," Frank Furedi, a British sociologist, echoed, "is often just anti-democracy."[18]

Taylor and Furedi are right that populists often channel the voice of the people in a genuine way. But they fail to appreciate—or to mention—how deeply illiberal a lot of the energy behind the rise of populism is. When protestors in Dresden wrote that "Mohammed [is] not welcome" or chanted that "We are the People," they were posing a more fundamental challenge to respect for individual rights than people like Taylor and Furedi care to admit.

Though there is a genuinely democratic element to populism, it is also, in the long run, much more inimical to respect for the popular will than its defenders claim. As anybody who has studied Turkey, Russia, or Venezuela knows all too well, the rise of illiberal strongmen can often be a prelude to autocratic rule: once the media has been muzzled and independent institutions have been abolished, it is easy for illiberal rulers to make the transition from populism to dictatorship.

It would, then, be tempting to conclude that these new movements are diametrically opposed to democracy after all. "Populism," Ivan Krastev has put this point, channeling an emerging consensus, "is not just antiliberal, it is antidemocratic—the permanent shadow of representative politics."[19]

But this, too, obscures more than it reveals. For to say that the new crop of populists are simply antidemocratic captures neither what's distinctive about them nor what has made them so successful: Older far-right movements openly glorified fascism and advocated abolishing democracy; PEGIDA and Trump, by contrast, see elections as an opportunity for ordinary people to assert their voice. Far from seeking to abolish democracy, they are impatient for the popular will to reshape the country in its own image.

This is why the only way to make sense of these new movements is to distinguish between their nature and their likely effect. To understand the *nature* of populism, we must recognize that it is both democratic and illiberal—that it both seeks to express the frustrations of the people and to undermine liberal institutions. And to understand its likely *effect*, we must bear in mind that these liberal institutions are, in the long run, needed for democracy to survive: once populist leaders have done away with all the liberal road-

Democracy without Rights

	Liberal Democracy (e.g., Canada)	Illiberal Democracy (e.g., Poland)
	Undemocratic Liberalism (e.g., European Union)	Dictatorship (e.g., Russia)

Undemocratic

Illiberal

blocks that impede the expression of the popular will, it becomes very easy for them to disregard the people when its preferences start to come into conflict with their own.

Politics Is Simple (and Everyone Who Disagrees Is a Liar)

Over the past decades, global gross domestic product (GDP) has grown rapidly. A billion people have been lifted out of poverty. Literacy rates have skyrocketed while child mortality has fallen. Taking the world as a whole, income inequality has shrunk.[20]

But many of these improvements have been concentrated in rapidly developing countries like China. In developed economies, GDP has grown rather more slowly. And in much of the West, especially in the United States and the United Kingdom, the lion's share of that growth went to a small sliver of the elite. As a result, many middle-class people in the traditional heartlands of liberal democracy have been treading water. And while global inequality has fallen because poor countries have been growing much more rapidly than rich countries, inequality within virtually every society—both in the more stagnant economies of the affluent West and in the most dynamic economies of the global South—has markedly increased.[21]

The reasons for these developments are many. There is globalization. There is automation. There is the shift from manufacturing to services. There is the rise of a digital economy that allows for massive economies of scale, channeling vast fortunes to a few corporations and their most highly skilled workers, while offering little to everybody else.

None of these changes is beyond the purview of politics. Even today, the right policies can help to redistribute wealth and boost the living standards of ordinary citizens. But the policies that are needed to do this are far from simple, far from immediate and, all too often, far from popular. So it doesn't come as a surprise that politicians have found it increasingly difficult to sell the message that things are complicated.

Hillary Clinton's campaign, widely seen as lacking in vision by both sides of the political spectrum, is a striking example. On the left, Bill de Blasio, the mayor of New York City, lamented that he'd been "waiting to hear a vision [from Hillary]."[22] On the right, Kevin Williamson wrote that "we know what she wants to be, but not what she wants to do."[23] Both charges stuck because they had the ring of truth to them. Many voters really did feel that Clinton was more interested in reaching the White House than in enacting any particular agenda once she was there. Much of the time, I felt this way, too. And yet, I know that she has a long history of sincere public service and ran on an intricate package of policy proposals that would have made a significant difference on issues as varied as preschool education and the battle against Alzheimer's.[24]

Donald Trump, by contrast, has a long history of conning people, from the students at "Trump University" to the many contractors he never paid for services rendered.[25] Most of the policies he championed were never going to work. He capitalized on public anger about immigration by promising a wall on the Mexican border. And he capitalized on the anguish in declining manufacturing towns by promising to raise tariffs on Chinese imports. Experts kept repeating that the wall with Mexico would not stop the vast majority of undocumented immigrants, who simply overstay their visas, and that a trade war with China would not bring back the vast majority of manufacturing jobs, since those were lost to robots rather than to trade.[26] And yet, millions of voters saw the simplicity of Trump's proposals as a mark of his authenticity and determination, and the complexity of Clinton's proposals as a mark of her insincerity and indifference.

That is precisely why glib, facile solutions stand at the very heart of the populist appeal. Voters do not like to think that the world is complicated. They certainly do not like to be told that there is no immediate answer to their problems. Faced with politicians who seem to be less and less able to govern an increasingly complex world, many are increasingly willing to vote for anybody who promises a simple solution. This is why populists from India's Narendra Modi to Turkey's Recep Tayyip Erdoğan, from Hungary's Viktor Orbán to Poland's Jarosław Kaczynski, and from France's Marine Le Pen to Italy's Beppe Grillo sound surprisingly similar to each other despite their considerable ideological differences.[27]

Populist leaders' willingness to offer solutions that are so simple that they can never work is very dangerous. Once they are in power, their policies are likely to exacerbate the problems that drove public anger in the first place. It would be tempting to assume that voters, suitably chastened by the ensuing chaos, would then return their trust to establishment politicians. But the additional pain is likely to put them in an even more sour and restive mood. And as the history of many countries in Latin America shows, when one populist fails, voters are as likely to turn to another populist—or to an out-and-out dictator—as they are to return the old elites to power.[28]

In the meantime, the populists' penchant for simplicity also creates another, more immediate danger. For if the solutions to the world's problems are as obvious as they claim, then political elites must be failing to implement them for one of two reasons: either they are corrupt, or they are secretly working on behalf of outside interests.

Most of the time, populists levy both charges.

The charge that Clinton's real motivation was to make as much money as she could was a constant theme of Trump's campaign: "Hillary Clinton is an insider fighting only for her donors and her insiders. I am an outsider fighting for you," Trump said. "Follow the money . . ." he added in his ominous manner.[29]

While some of Trump's accusations were outlandish, they were not very different from the ways in which populists in other countries have long attacked mainstream politicians. In Poland, for example, Jarosław Kaczynski, in his rather more refined way, claimed that the politicians who previously led the country had been "co-opted to the socially privileged sphere," and consequently had no interest in "changing the social hierarchy."[30] In France, meanwhile, Marine Le Pen has chalked up her growing support to a rebellion against a self-interested "EU Oligarchy."[31]

Left-wing populists sing from the same songbook. In Italy, for example, Grillo loves to lambast the "political caste," a network of elites who work only for their own interests.[32] In Spain, Iglesias used similar rhetoric after Podemos took a record share of the vote in European elections in 2014: "the parties of the political caste have suffered a heavy blow. But we have not yet fulfilled our electoral goal. Tomorrow, the government of the political caste will still be in power."[33]

The money that (supposedly) is the first priority of establishment politicians has to come from somewhere, of course, and so the accusation that they are in it for themselves quickly turns into the accusation that they are puppets of big business. In the American election, the high fees that Goldman Sachs paid Hillary Clinton for her speeches made this narrative especially resonant, and Trump exploited it for all its worth: Goldman Sachs, he claimed, has "total, total control . . . over Hillary Clinton."[34]

Most populists, however, take the accusation that the leaders of the old parties are traitors one step further. They don't just claim that members of the political caste are in it for themselves, or that they are in the pocket of special interests. Rather, they claim that they harbor a special loyalty to the enemies of the people, making them more interested in advancing the interests of unpopular ethnic or religious minorities than in the fate of the majority.

Donald Trump is, once again, as pure a case of this as one is likely to find. His first real foray into politics was to claim that Barack Obama had forged his birth certificate, was not a real American, and may even be a secret Muslim. On the campaign trail, he repeated variants of the accusation over and over again—from calling Obama "the founder of ISIS" to putting his title, president, in air quotes.[35] The fact that Clinton did not have Obama's unusual name, or that she did not hail from an ethnic or religious minority, did not stop Trump from fabricating similar accusations: he called Clinton the "co-founder" of ISIS and demanded that she be "locked up" for maintaining a private email server as secretary of state.[36]

The kind of disloyalty of which establishment politicians find themselves accused varies from country to country. But while populists tailor the identity of the betrayed majority and the despised minority to the needs of their local context, the basic rhetorical structure is strikingly similar everywhere in the world.

And so, in India, Modi claims that his opponents are enemies of Hindus and has helped to create an environment in which scholars who are perceived as critical of hardline Hinduism "receive death threats and are then murdered."[37] In Turkey, Erdoğan used the coup to label any opponent of his government a supporter of terrorism,[38] arresting scores of academics and journalists.[39] And in

France and Germany and Italy, populist leaders like Marine Le Pen and Alice Weidel and Matteo Salvini claim that establishment politicians all hate the white, Christian majority. As Marion Maréchal-Le Pen, Marine's niece and a former member of the French parliament, put it, "Either we kill Islamism or it will kill us. . . . Those who choose the status quo become complicit with our enemies."[40]

I Am Your Voice (and Everybody Else Is a Traitor)

The major political problems of the day, populists claim, can easily be solved. All it takes is common sense. If jobs are moving abroad, you have to ban other countries from selling their products. If immigrants are flooding the country, you have to build a wall. And if terrorists attack you in the name of Islam, you have to ban the Muslims.

If ordinary politicians are failing to take these commonsense measures, the explanation is similarly simple. They must be self-serving. In cahoots with special interests or ethnic minorities. Politically correct. Effete. No good.

What has to happen is obvious, then. All it takes for the crisis to be solved—for the problems to go away, for the economy to boom, for the country to become great (again)—is for a faithful spokesman of the people to conquer power, to vanquish the traitors, and to implement commonsense solutions.

That spokesman is the populist—and he never tires of saying it.

It's little wonder, then, that Trump's speech at the Republican National Convention honed in on this theme over and over again. "Big business, elite media and major donors are lining up behind the campaign of my opponent because they know she will keep our rigged system in place," he said early in the speech. "They are throwing money at her because they have total control over every single thing she does. She is their puppet, and they pull the strings."[41]

Things don't have to be this bad, though. "The problems we face now—poverty and violence at home, war and destruction abroad—will last only as long as we continue relying on the same politicians who created them," he promised. To start a new day, "a change in leadership is required." This leadership, Trump vowed, would finally prioritize ordinary Americans: "The most important difference between our plan and that of our opponent is that our plan will put America First. Americanism, not globalism, will be our credo."[42]

Having prepared his audience in this way, Trump could launch his central message, which would return like a refrain throughout the speech. For too long, ordinary men and women had been forgotten. They "no longer have a voice." But, Trump claimed, he would change all of that: "I AM YOUR VOICE."[43]

This promise became the central refrain of the speech. And though it was widely ridiculed in the following days, it was a brilliant distillation of the core promise populists around the globe have offered their voters all along: Marine Le Pen ran her 2017 presidential campaign "au nom du peuple," in the name of the people. "We are the people," Erdoğan once said to his opponents. "Who are you?" Norbert Hofer, the leader of Austria's right-wing Freedom Party, echoed the same sentiment in a recent campaign appearance. "You have high society behind you," he said. "I have the people with me."[44] The promise to give expression to the unadulterated voice of the people is the central feature of populism.

The appeal to the people is as important for whom it excludes as it is for whom it includes. When populists invoke the people, they are positing an in-group—united around a shared ethnicity, religion, social class, or political conviction—against an out-group whose interests can rightfully be disregarded. In other words, they are demarcating the boundaries of the *demos,* implicitly arguing that political consideration is owed to some citizens but not to others. They are, in the apt words of Jan-Werner Müller, claiming a "moral monopoly of representation."[45]

The history of the moral monopoly of representation is as long as it is bloody. During the French Revolution, Maximilien de Robespierre came to power by opposing the monarch's claim to embody the nation—but soon started to claim that it was he alone who truly manifested the will of the people. In 1914, still thinking of himself as a socialist fighting his people's oppression by the capitalist class, Benito Mussolini founded a newspaper called *Il Popolo d'Italia,* or the People of Italy.[46]

The same rhetorical move has also been on clear display in more recent American history. This is what Sarah Palin was doing when she claimed that "the best of America is in these small towns . . . and in these wonderful little pockets of what I call the real America," implicitly contrasting "pro-America areas of this great nation" with those that are, by logical implication, "anti-America."[47] It is what Glenn Beck was doing when he wrote a book titled *The Real America: Messages from the Heart and Heartland.*[48] And of course it is what Donald Trump was expressing with characteristic bluntness when he said that "the only important thing is the unification of the people, because the other people don't mean anything."[49]

When populists are running for office, they primarily direct their ire against ethnic or religious groups whom they don't recognize as part of the "real" people. Once populists hold office, they increasingly direct their ire against a second target: all institutions, formal or informal, that dare to contest their claim to a moral monopoly of representation.

In the early phases, the war on independent institutions frequently takes the form of inciting distrust, or even outright hatred, of the free press.

Critical media outlets cover protests against the populist leader. They report on his government's failings and give voice to his prominent critics. They tell sympathetic stories about his victims. In doing so, they challenge the illusion of consensus, showing a wide audience that the populist is lying when he claims to speak for all the people.

This is what makes the press so dangerous to the populist's rule. And it is also why most populists take stringent measures against independent journalists and build up a network of loyalist media outlets that cheer their every move.

In Trump's first press conference as president-elect of the United States, he called CNN "fake news," referred to Buzzfeed as "a pile of garbage," dismissed the BBC as "another beauty," and called the press, as a whole, "dishonest."[50] On his first full day in office, he sent his press secretary out to make a series of false statements about the press's "deliberately false reporting."[51] Within his first month in office, he graduated to excluding major newspapers from a White House briefing and labeling outlets from the *New York Times* to CNN "enemies of the American people."[52]

Trump is also building his own counterprogramming. He has a very close relationship with Fox News. He has given press accreditation to fringe websites that uncritically support his agenda. And he has even launched a regular newscast on his Facebook page that feeds his fans breathless accounts of his supposed achievements.[53]

European populists, on both the left and the right, behave in very similar ways. In Poland, Kaczynski's far-right government took over the state broadcaster and attempted to bar independent reporters from the parliament.[54] In Greece, Tsipras's far-left government gave the state the power to decide who could have a voice on the air by limiting the total number of television licenses and effectively shuttering a magazine that dared to criticize the foreign secretary.[55] There is every risk that Beppe Grillo, a man who has already promised to end what he calls the political control of Italy's media, would follow suit if he were to win high office.[56]

Attacks on the free press are but the first step. In the next step, the war on independent institutions frequently targets foundations, trade unions, think tanks, religious associations, and other nongovernmental organizations.

Populists realize how dangerous intermediary institutions with a real claim to representing the views and interests of large segments of society are to the fiction that they, and they alone, speak for the people. They therefore work hard to discredit such institutions as tools of old elites or outside interests. Where this doesn't suffice, they introduce laws limiting foreign funding to weaken them financially, or use their control over the regulatory state to impede their operation.

But the greatest ire, and the most ruthless attacks, are usually reserved for state institutions that are not under the direct sway of the populist government. When public radio or television stations refuse to air government propaganda; when ethics watchdogs criticize the government; when independent electoral commissions try to ensure free and fair elections; when the military refuses to carry out illegal orders; when legislators dare to use parliament as a basis for opposition; or when the highest court of the land deems the actions of the populist unconstitutional, these crucial institutions are first tarnished with the brush of treason—and then "reformed" or abolished.

In Hungary, for instance, Orbán has systematically filled the ranks of bureaucratic institutions that had once been impartial with avid loyalists, and undermined the independence of the country's judiciary. In Venezuela, Hugo Chávez rewrote the constitution as soon as he came into power, effectively politicizing every major institution in the country.[57]

The same tactic is increasingly in evidence even in Western Europe and North America. In Great Britain, for example, there is a long tradition of deference to the judiciary. But when a court ruled that Prime Minister Theresa May needed Parliament's assent to trigger Britain's exit from the European Union, the attacks on the judiciary took on an unprecedented bitterness. Displaying the pictures of the three judges who had taken the decision in a visual style eerily reminiscent of the attacks against the German judiciary during the 1930s, the *Daily Telegraph* fulminated against the way the judgment supposedly subverted the people's will. The *Daily Mail* went a step further: pairing a similar picture with an even bigger headline, it brandished the judges as "ENEMIES OF THE PEOPLE."[58]

This perfectly captures the logic that is at work when populism turns against independent institutions. In the face of the populists' claim to be the sole representatives of the popular will, politics quickly becomes an existential struggle between the real people and their enemies. For that reason, populists on both the left and the right are likely to turn increasingly illiberal as their power grows. Over time, they come to regard anybody who disagrees with them as a traitor and conclude that any institution that stands in their way is an illegitimate perversion of the people's will. Both have to be done away with. What is left is nothing more than the populist's whim.

The People Decide (to Do Whatever They Want)

Ali Erdoğan, the president of the small Turkish community in Wangen bei Olten, had a big dream. One day, he hoped, a modest, blue-and-gold minaret—about twenty feet in height—would adorn his cultural center in northern Switzerland.

Over years of effort, he managed to raise the necessary funds and applied for a building permit. But locals quickly organized to oppose his plans. Some claimed that their views would be blocked by the minaret. Others feared that the town's cultural identity might be threatened by so ostentatious an Islamic symbol. Others still were even more forthright: minarets don't belong in Wangen bei Olten, and neither do the immigrants who want to erect them, they said. The town's Building and Planning Commission unanimously voted to reject the application.

Erdoğan did not give up so quickly, and the controversy eventually shifted from the political process to the courts—as such decisions often do these days. The Administrative Court of the Canton of Solothurn gave permission for the minaret. When locals appealed, the Federal Supreme Court finalized the decision. The minaret could be built after all.[59]

But this small victory for the rights of the Turkish community in Wangen bei Olten soon turned into a major defeat for the rights of religious minorities throughout Switzerland. Enraged by the courts' decisions, a coalition of far-right activists started to collect signatures for a popular referendum that would outlaw the building of any further minarets. "The people have said that we don't want this," Roland Kissling, the local leader of the Swiss People's Party, said. "I'm in favor of integrating immigrants—but those people just ask for too much."[60]

A majority of Kissling's compatriots agreed. On November 29, 2009, millions of Swiss voters headed to the polls to abridge Muslims' right of free worship. Political leaders, mainstream newspapers, and foreign observers all appealed to voters to respect the rights of the largest religious minority in the country. But it was in vain. When all was said and done, the motion was carried with 58 percent of the vote.[61] In the wake of the referendum, the Swiss constitution now reads: "Freedom of religion and conscience is guaranteed . . . The construction of minarets is prohibited."[62]

Ali Erdoğan got to fulfill his dream. The referendum came too late to stop his minaret. But the modest tower that now adorns a nondescript building on the outskirts of his town is the last of its kind to be built in Switzerland.

In the days after the referendum, shocked commentators all over the world called its outcome blatantly undemocratic.[63] But their misleading use of this word only shows how difficult it is to talk about the current crisis with clarity when we take democracy to mean everything and anything. After all, it is difficult to think of a more direct way to let the people rule than to let them vote on contentious issues.

That is why I prefer to say that the controversy over minarets epitomizes the disintegration of liberal democracy into two new regime forms: illiberal democracy and undemocratic liberalism.

On one side of the divide, there are the bureaucratic and technocratic institutions that uphold individual rights: The Administrative Court of the Canton of Solothurn and the Federal Supreme Court are both staffed with unelected judges. Both upheld the rights of an unpopular minority to freedom of worship. On the other side, there are the democratic institutions that allow the people to express their views: The elected members of the Building and Planning Commission and the referendum that called upon all adult citizens of Switzerland to make a final determination both served to translate popular views into public policy.

So the problem with the Swiss referendum is not that it is somehow undemocratic; it is that Swiss democracy is increasingly directing its energies against basic liberal norms.

In this, Switzerland is not alone.[64]

Since I am not in the habit of attending the rallies of far-right political parties, I expected the campaign event of the Alternative for Germany (AfD) to feel, well, exotic, I suppose. Instead, it instantly reminded me of my youth. Everything about it seemed to be inspired by the provincial German towns in which I lived for part of my childhood in the late 1980s and early 1990s.

The rally took place in a dreary sports-arena-cum-all-purpose-event-space located in a middle-class suburb of Offenburg—the kind of place made up of family homes that are not identical, exactly, but whose walls all have the same color, and whose roofs all tilt at the same angle. Except for the predictable fact that it skewed old, the audience also looked unremarkable; if a manufacturer of orthodontic products had assembled an unusually large focus group, the vibe might have been about the same. Even the party's placards looked unobtrusively commercial. Sporting blues that were a tad too blue and reds that were a tad too red, they reminded me of a PowerPoint template, or perhaps a bad subway ad.

Known for her toxic rhetoric against immigrants, Frauke Petry, then the leader of the AfD, has advocated using "verbal provocations" as a PR strategy in internal emails.[65] True to her word, she recently called on the German police to avert illegal border crossings by any means necessary, including the use of guns.[66]

When she took the stage in Offenburg, those illiberal instincts were on full display.[67] The anger at immigrants was a bit too visceral, the insistence on the inability of newcomers to become true members of the German nation a little too strident for comfort. Often accused of stoking irrational fears, she insisted that "fear and envy are an important part of politics." Germans, she said to a massive round of applause, should no longer refrain from using historically charged terms like "the Volk" with pride.

Over the course of the night, these deeply illiberal themes kept recurring. But what was just as striking, and much less widely noted in the media, is how much emphasis the party put on deepening democracy throughout the rally. Looking around the hall, I was not surprised to see placards saying that "immigration requires clear rules," or that Germany should not be "the world's paymaster." But I was baffled to spot another placard, featuring a Swiss flag: "Switzerland is in favor of referenda," it said. "We are, too."

The case for direct democracy, Petry explained early in her speech, is a core concern of the party—and one about which no journalist ever wanted to ask her. When the German Constitution was passed in 1949, she said, it promised two laws: one to elect MPs and another to allow citizens to initiate national referenda. But in the end, politicians only ever passed the law setting up elections to the Bundestag, and German citizens still lack the right to decide urgent matters for themselves. "As a result," Petry told three hundred supporters, indignation rising in her voice, "we now live in a semi-democracy."

Establishment politicians would like to keep things just the way they are. They, Petry argued, "are secretly happy that citizens have become so disenchanted with politics. After all, it means that nobody stops them from doing what they want."⁶⁸ But unlike the political establishment, her party is different. It, and it alone, wants the German people to decide its fate for itself.

That's where Germany's small neighbor comes in. Switzerland, Petry said, has a wonderful political system, precisely because it trusts its citizens to make important decisions. It's high time for Germany to do the same.

Beyond Germany's border, referenda have a newfound appeal for similar reasons. The UK Independence Party (UKIP), Podemos, Cinque Stelle, and other parties across Europe have all called for referenda. In the Netherlands, Geert Wilders presented his campaign promises for the 2017 parliamentary elections in an infamously hardline manifesto. The second of his eleven points was astoundingly simple (and thoroughly illiberal): ban the Koran. But the third point was ostensibly democratic: he sought to introduce binding referenda.⁶⁹

It's impossible to make sense of the rise of populism without facing up to the ways in which it claims the mantle of democracy.

Older far-right movements openly longed for a return to the fascist past or sought to establish a hierarchical system that would transcend democracy. In France, the founder of the Front National, Jean-Marie Le Pen, defended the Vichy Regime and dismissed the Holocaust as a "detail of history."[70] In Germany, the National Democratic Party (NPD) glorified senior Nazis like Rudolf Hess and cast doubt on the legitimacy of the country's postwar constitutional order.[71]

The successors of these movements, by contrast, don't just abstain from open sympathy for a more authoritarian system; much of the time, they portray themselves as a democratic alternative to the oligarchic establishment.

In France, Marine Le Pen expelled her father from the party when he repeated his calumnies about the Holocaust and now claims to be more democratic than the establishment parties.[72] In Germany, the AfD is (albeit reluctantly) in the process of expelling Björn Höcke because he called for a "180 degree turn in how we remember the past." The party is also doubling down on the claim that it alone stands for a truly democratic system: "they are against us," one of its slogans runs, "because we are for you."[73]

The populists' vociferous commitment to democracy is neatly summed up in the way they cheered the outcome of the 2016 American election. As Viktor Orbán put it, Trump's victory marked America's transition from "liberal non-democracy" to "real democracy."[74]

Some leading analysts of populism, like Jan-Werner Müller, have refused to acknowledge this democratic energy. The phrase "illiberal democracy," Müller argues, plays right into the hands of these regimes, reinforcing "such leaders' image as opponents of liberalism, while allowing them to continue to refer to their actions as democratic." But in truth, he claims, illiberal governments are inherently undemocratic: "if opposition parties have been hindered in making their case to the electorate, and journalists do not dare to report on the government's failures, the ballot boxes have already been stuffed."[75]

I share both Müller's anger at the damage already done by the populists and his concern about the danger they still pose. But I also fear that the refusal to acknowledge that there is something democratic about the energy that propels them to power in the first place stops us from understanding the nature of their appeal—and makes it more difficult to think carefully and creatively about how to stop them.

Rather than hoping to establish a hierarchical political system that transcends democracy, as older far-right movements often did, today's populists claim that they seek to deepen the democratic elements of our current system. That matters.

But even in cases in which the populists' democratic commitments are genuine, they still pose a danger to democracy. As Müller rightly points out, their illiberal predilections are deeply at odds with the maintenance of institutions, like free and fair elections, that stop them from running roughshod over the popular will once they become unpopular. That matters, too.

Populists claim that they are the voice of the real people. They believe that any resistance to their rule is illegitimate. And so they, all too often, give in to the temptation to silence the opposition and destroy rival power centers. It is impossible to understand their nature without acknowledging the democratic energy that is driving them—and yet it is also impossible to understand what damage they are likely to wreak without recognizing how quickly that energy can turn against the people. Unless the defenders of liberal democracy manage to stand up to the populists, illiberal democracy will always be in danger of descending into outright dictatorship.

2

Rights without Democracy

IT WAS A MOMENTOUS DAY for the peasants of the Januschau, a remote part of Eastern Prussia. For the first time in their, or their fathers', or their fathers' fathers' lives, they were called upon to vote. For centuries, they had been subjects—virtually possessions—of the Oldenburg family, with no voice and very few rights. Now, they were to partake in the incomprehensibly noble act of ruling themselves.

As they gathered around the local inn, which had hurriedly been converted into a polling station for the occasion, they saw that the new world retained not a few elements of the old. The land inspector of the Oldenburg family was handing out sealed envelopes. They contained ballots that had already been marked.

Most peasants did as they were told. They cast their first-ever ballot without knowing who it was they were voting for.

One lone rebel dared to open his envelope. He immediately attracted the inspector's fury. Striking him with a cane, he shouted, in honest indignation: "It's a secret ballot, you swine!"[1]

In most places, democracy's pretense to let the people rule was a little more serious, and the elite's hold over the electoral process a little more tenuous. Even so, this story from the dawn of democracy encapsulates the basic deal that traditional elites offered to the mass of the people at the inception of our political system: "As long as you let us call the shots, we will pretend to let you rule."

It's a deal that has proven phenomenally successful for two hundred and fifty years. Today, it is getting increasingly difficult to sustain.

Liberal democracy is all things to all people: a promise to the masses to let them call the shots; a promise to minorities to protect their rights from an oppressive majority; and a promise to economic elites that they will be allowed to keep their riches. It is this chameleonic quality that has helped to make liberal democracy uniquely stable.

At the most fundamental level, this quality depends on a tension that is central to the history of liberal democracies. The political systems of countries like Great Britain and the United States were founded not to manifest but to oppose democracy; they have retrospectively been given a democratic halo by the latter-day claim that they let the people rule. The credibility of that claim depends on what they are compared to. So long as the memory of absolute monarchy was recent, and a more directly democratic system seemed unfeasible, liberal democracies could claim to let the people rule. This held true for the century or so during which democracy enjoyed its unprecedented ideological hegemony. It no longer does. As a result, the democratic myth that has helped to make our institutions look uniquely legitimate is losing its hold.

The undemocratic roots of our supposedly democratic institutions are clearly on display in Great Britain. Parliament was not designed to let the people rule; it was a blood-soaked compromise between a beleaguered monarch and the upper echelons of the country's elite. Only when the franchise was gradually expanded over the course of the nineteenth and twentieth centuries did anybody have the idea that this system of government could possibly be thought to resemble a democracy. Even then, the widening of the franchise turned out to transform the system much less fundamentally than both the advocates and the opponents of democratic reform had predicted.[2]

Because it was founded in a more ideologically self-conscious manner, that same history is even more evident in the American case. For the Founding Fathers, the election of representatives, which we have come to regard as the most democratic way to translate popular views into public policy, was a mechanism for keeping the people at bay.

Elections were, in the words of James Madison, meant to "refine and enlarge the public views, by passing them through the medium of a chosen body of citizens, whose wisdom may best discern the true interest of their country."[3] That this radically curtailed the degree to which the people could actually influence the government was no accident: "The public voice, pronounced by the representatives of the people," Madison argued, "will be more consonant to the public good than if pronounced by the people themselves, convened for the purpose."[4]

In short, the Founding Fathers did not believe a representative republic to be second best; on the contrary, they found it far preferable to the factious horrors of a democracy. As Alexander Hamilton and James Madison made clear in Federalist No. 63, the essence of the American Republic would consist—their emphasis —"IN THE TOTAL EXCLUSION OF THE PEOPLE, IN THEIR COLLECTIVE CAPACITY, from any share" in the government.[5]

It was only in the nineteenth century, as the material and political conditions of American society changed with mass immigration, westward expansion, civil war, and rapid industrialization, that a set of entrepreneurial thinkers began to dress up an ideologically self-conscious republic in the unaccustomed robes of a born-again democracy. The very same institutions that had once been designed to exclude the people from any share in the government were now commended for facilitating government "of the people, by the people, for the people."[6]

But though America increasingly came to be seen as a democracy, reality lagged far behind. Only gradually did the United States make real improvements to its democratic process. With the ratification of the Fifteenth Amendment in 1870, "race, color, or previous condition of servitude" could no longer be used to deny citizens the right to vote (though, in practice, they often were).[7] The direct election of senators was established by the Seventeenth Amendment in 1912.[8] Finally, the Nineteenth Amendment, passed in 1920, decreed that "the right of citizens of the United States to vote shall not be denied or abridged on account of sex."[9]

These reforms did make American institutions more democratic. But the transformation of the language we use to describe the institutions of American democracy has been much more far-reaching than the transformation of the institutions themselves. And key to that transformation has been a story about the limits of democratic governance under modern conditions.

In ancient Athens, so the story went, the people—or at least those who were regarded as the people, which is to say adult male citizens—could rule directly because there were so few of them, because the territory of the state was so small, and because so many of them owned slaves who took care of their daily needs.[10] This is no longer the case. As John Adams noted, the people "can never act, consult, or reason together, because they cannot march five hundred miles, nor spare the time, nor find a space to meet."[11] Under modern conditions, direct democracy was supposedly impossible.

This realization allowed the democratic writers of the late nineteenth century to carry out a peculiar reinvention of American government. While representative institutions had been founded in self-conscious opposition to the ideal of democracy, they were now redescribed as the closest instantiation of that ideal possible under modern conditions. Thus, the founding myth of liberal democratic ideology—the improbable fiction that representative government would facilitate the rule of the people—was born.

A man who puts new wine into old bottles, warns the Gospel of Luke, is likely to come to grief: "the new wine will burst the bottles, and be spilled, and the bottles shall perish."[12] The opposite proved true for democracy. The rising tide of egalitarian sentiment during the nineteenth century should, by rights, have come into opposition with a set of avowedly aristocratic institutions. Instead, their fresh packaging gave representative institutions a new lease on life. It pleased the elites who continued to get their way on the most important issues as much as it pleased the egalitarians who came to see it as an instantiation of their aspirations.

For a long century, democracy's founding myth proved to be one of the most powerful ideological forces in the history of mankind. It was under its watch, and in the context of the miraculous transubstantiation between elite control and popular appeal which it afforded, that democracy conquered half the globe. And though it had never exactly been correct—it would, all along, have been possible to make more use of popular referenda, or to restrict the ability of representatives to deviate from the will of their constituents—it retained sufficient footing in reality to keep a hold over the democratic imagination.

That basis is now crumbling. One reason is that, with the advent of the internet, Adams's worry about the people's inability to deliberate together has come to seem quaint. It may be true that the people cannot march five hundred miles nor find a place to meet. But why should they need to? If the people truly sought to govern themselves, they could easily do so. A virtual agora could replace the physical agora of ancient Athens, allowing every citizen to debate and vote on policy proposals both big and small.

I am not suggesting that most citizens of contemporary democracies want to be intimately involved in the process of policy-making.

They don't. Nor do I believe that deliberation on a virtual agora would turn out to be civil and rational. It wouldn't. For good reason, the idea of direct democracy has many more adherents in theory than it does in practice.

But though today's citizens are no more inclined to vote and deliberate about every obscure law and regulation than were the citizens of the 1960s, or those of the 1830s, they now have a much more instinctive sense that our democratic institutions are highly mediated. To previous generations, it might have seemed natural that the people would rule through parliamentary institutions and elect their representatives by going to a polling station. But to a generation raised on the digital, plebiscitary, and immediate voting of Twitter and Facebook, of *Big Brother* and *American Idol*, these institutions have come to seem strangely cumbersome.

Today's citizens may not be as invested in the outcome of debates on public policy as they are in who gets voted out of the *Big Brother* house. They may not even want their influence on the system of government to be as immediate as their vote in the season finale of *American Idol*. But, for all of that, they have a very clear model for what it feels like to have a real, direct impact. They know that if we wanted to design a system of government that truly allowed the people to rule, it would not look much like representative democracy.

There is another, even more important reason why democracy's founding myth no longer has the same hold over our imagination: over the past decades, political elites have insulated themselves from popular views to a remarkable extent.

While the system was never set up to let the people rule, it did have important elements of popular participation. Most political decisions were made by an elected legislature. And many of these legislators had deep links with their constituents: they came from all parts of the country and had close connections with local associations, from churches to trade unions.

Legislators were also likely to be deeply imbued with an ideology that gave them a sense of purpose. Whether they were Social Democrats who hailed from poor families and saw themselves as advocates for ordinary workers, or Christian Democrats who came from religious families and saw themselves as defenders of tradition, they had a clear political mission—and often anticipated returning to the communities from which they hailed after leaving office.

Today, this is true for very few professional politicians. The legislature, once the most important political organ, has lost much of its power to courts, to bureaucrats, to central banks, and to international treaties and organizations. Meanwhile, the people who make up the legislature have in many countries become less and less similar to the people they are meant to represent: nowadays, few of them have strong ties to their local communities and even fewer have a deep commitment to a structuring ideology.

As a result, average voters now feel more alienated from poli-

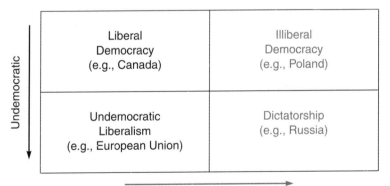

Rights without Democracy

	Liberal Democracy (e.g., Canada)	Illiberal Democracy (e.g., Poland)
Undemocratic →	Undemocratic Liberalism (e.g., European Union)	Dictatorship (e.g., Russia)

Illiberal →

tics than they ever have before. When they look at politicians, they don't recognize themselves—and when they look at the decisions taken by them, they don't see their preferences reflected in them.

There has never been a time of perfect popular participation. As the founding myth of democracy reminds us, the glass has always been half full. But now, it is in danger of going on empty.

Limits on Electoral Institutions

Over the last decades, the elected representatives of the people have lost a lot of their power.

Since the end of World War II, the complexity of the regulatory challenges facing the state has vastly increased: Technology advanced and economic processes became more intricate. Monetary policy grew to be a core tool for stabilizing the economy. Even more important, some of the most pressing political challenges now facing mankind, from climate change to growing inequality, have deeply global roots, and seemingly outstrip the ability of nation states to find an adequate response.

Each of these changes has prompted a shift of power away from national parliaments. To deal with the need for regulation in highly technical fields, bureaucratic agencies staffed with subject-matter experts began to take on a quasi-legislative role. To set monetary policy and resist political pressure to create artificial booms in election years, more and more central banks became independent. Finally, to do everything from setting rules about trade to negotiating agreements regarding climate change, an array of international treaties and organizations came into being.

This loss of power for the people's representatives is not a result of elite conspiracy. On the contrary, it has occurred gradually, and often imperceptibly, in response to real policy challenges. But the cumulative result has been a creeping erosion of democracy: as more and more areas of public policy have been taken out of popular contestation, the people's ability to influence politics has been drastically curtailed.

BUREAUCRATS AS LAWMAKERS

When Great Britain's Ministry of Administrative Affairs was found to indulge in waste of gargantuan proportions, Sir Humphrey, its most senior civil servant, was hauled in front of a Select Committee of the House of Commons. But instead of showing contrition for the fact that his department had spent a boatful of taxpayers' money on maintaining an unused roof garden, he tried to deflect the blame.

"It was thought that the sale of flowers and vegetable produce might offset the cost," he ventured.

"And did it?" a member of Parliament asked.

"No," he admitted.

"You agree the money was wasted?" she asked.

"It's not for me to comment on government policy. You must ask the minister."

"Look, Sir Humphrey. Whatever we ask the minister, he says is an administrative question for you. And whatever we ask you, you say is a policy question for the minister. How do you suggest we find out what's going on?"

"Yes, yes, yes, I do see that there's a real dilemma here, in that while it is government policy to regard policy as the responsibility of ministers and administration as the responsibility of officials, the questions of administrative policy can cause confusion between the policy of administration and the administration of policy, especially when responsibility for the administration of the policy of administration conflicts or overlaps with responsibility for the administration of policy."

"Well that's a load of meaningless drivel, isn't it?" the MP asked.

"It's not for me to comment on government policy," Sir Humphrey replied. "You must ask the minister."

Sir Humphrey and the Ministry of Administrative Affairs are, as you will have guessed, fictional. They are drawn from *Yes Minister,* a beloved 1980s BBC sitcom that portrayed the daily struggles of a feckless politician trying to get his agenda past a bureaucracy intent on frustrating his plans and serving its own interests.[13]

But while Sir Humphrey's exploits and verbal acrobatics were exaggerated for comedic effect, they contained a sizeable kernel of truth. "Its perceptive portrayal of what goes on in the corridors of power," Margaret Thatcher raved while in office, "has given me hours of pure joy."[14] David Cameron, one of Thatcher's real-life successors at 10 Downing Street, echoed the sentiment some three decades later. Studying politics at Oxford, he had once "had to write an essay on 'How true to life is Yes, Minister.' I think I wrote . . . that it wasn't true to life. I can tell you, as prime minister, it is true to life."[15]

Frustrated politicians aren't the only ones to emphasize the outsized role bureaucracy now plays in the politics of many democracies around the world. On the contrary, a broad field of academic study has found both that it is very hard for politicians to control the bureaucracy, and that the scope of decisions made by bureaucratic agencies has expanded over the past years.

On the simplest account of the state, the people elect legislators who turn the popular will into laws. Bureaucrats then apply those laws to particular cases. They play an important role, yes, but also a subordinate one. Ultimately, their task is to serve the popular will as it is expressed in legislation.

In reality, the story has never been quite so simple. In summarizing Max Weber's account of bureaucracy, for example, textbooks usually emphasize that civil servants follow "general rules" rather than settling cases "by individual commands given for each case."[16] But Weber realized that a judge or a bureaucrat is not just "an automaton into which legal documents and fees are stuffed at the top in order that it may spill forth the verdict at the bottom."[17] On the contrary, the process of implementing legislation has always allowed for discretion and creativity: even a meticulously written law leaves questions of detail unanswered, and important bureaucratic procedures unstipulated. As a result, civil servants have played an important political role ever since the rise of the modern-day bureaucracy. They were never quite as subordinate as the simplest models of politics would have us believe.[18]

And yet the recent growth in the numbers of bureaucrats and the expansion of their role has been striking. Over the course of the twentieth and early twenty-first centuries, the number of civil servants has skyrocketed and the scope of their influence has immensely expanded. As a result, the degree to which public policy is determined by the elected representatives of the people has been significantly curtailed.

The figures are striking. In Great Britain, for example, the number of national bureaucrats has gone from about 100,000 in 1930 to 400,000 in 2015. (Over the same time period, the overall population only increased by about a third.)[19]

While the increase in the size of the bureaucracy is remarkable, two qualitative changes may be even more important: Government agencies have become increasingly influential in the design of laws passed by parliaments.[20] At the same time, they have increasingly taken on the role of quasi-legislators, gaining the authority to design and implement broad rules in key areas like financial or environmental regulation. Taken together, these two developments mean that a vast share of the rules to which ordinary citizens are subject are now written, implemented, and sometimes even initiated by unelected officials.

Traditional bureaucratic bodies are charged with implementing legislation drawn up by the legislature, and they are led by a politician—often a member of Parliament in his or her own right—who has been appointed by the president or prime minister. But in a growing number of policy areas, the job of legislating has been supplanted by so-called "independent agencies" that can formulate policy on their own and are remarkably free from oversight by either the legislature or the elected head of government.[21] Once they are founded by the legislature, these boards and commissions are charged with taking "legally difficult, technically complex, and often politically sensitive decisions." Many of them are given full regulatory authority—in other words, "they can issue regulations, take administrative action to enforce their statutes and regulations, and decide cases through administrative adjudication."[22]

In the United States, these independent agencies include the Federal Communications Commission (FCC), created in 1934, which regulates radio and television networks and rules on key questions of the digital age like net neutrality;[23] the Securities Exchange Commission (SEC), also created in 1934, which is charged with protecting investors by regulating the operation of banks and other financial service providers, with maintaining fair markets, and with facilitating capital formation;[24] the Environmental Protection Agency (EPA), created in 1970, which is empowered to pass regulation for such broad objectives as maintaining clean water and protecting endangered species;[25] and the Consumer Financial Protection Bureau (CFPB), created in 2010, which regulates personal financial services like mortgages and credit cards.[26]

The range of contentious issues about which these independent agencies have ruled in the last years testifies to their importance. The FCC has long determined what words are verboten on cable television, making it largely responsible for the peculiar American custom of bleeping curse words in many television programs.[27]

Key to regulating the most important medium of the late twentieth century, the FCC is now shaping the future of the most important medium of the early twenty-first century: in 2015, it ruled to require internet providers to follow "net neutrality" rules designed to ensure equal access to a wide variety of web offerings.[28] Similarly, the EPA has been a key player in fights about environmental policy for the past fifty years, from banning the use of DDT to ensuring the quality of public drinking water.[29] Over the last years, it has also made itself central to the American policy response to climate change, deeming carbon a pollutant and proposing limits on admissible emissions from new power plants.[30] Meanwhile, in the first five years of its existence, the CFPB has proposed a rule to curtail payday lending and required financial advisors to act in the best interest of investors, eliminating some of the risky practices that led to the 2008 mortgage crisis.[31]

Far from making decisions about a few blockbuster cases, independent agencies are now responsible for the vast majority of laws, rules, and regulations. In 2007, for example, Congress enacted 138 public laws. In the same year, US federal agencies finalized 2,926 rules.[32] And it is simply not clear that voters enjoy any real form of oversight over the rules by which they are bound.[33]

The United States is not alone. Equivalents to America's independent agencies have developed in other countries as well. In Britain, for example, there were once over 900 Quasi-Autonomous Non-Governmental Organizations (QUANGOs), governmental bodies that are funded by taxpayer money yet have little or no democratic oversight.[34] While some QUANGOs, like the Environmental Agency, were performing essential tasks, the rapid increase in their number and the breadth of their tasks worried the public more and more.[35] In 2010, Parliament listened to the critics, promising to cut or merge about a third of existing QUANGOs.[36] But most QUANGOs survived the cull, and many changes turned out to be cosmetic: "A closer analysis reveals that whilst the government have reduced the number of public bodies, they have got rid of relatively few functions and have instead engaged in . . . 'bureau-shuffling.'"[37]

But perhaps the most powerful "independent agency" in the world is the European Commission. In most countries, the bureaucracy's power is somewhat limited by the presence of a strong head of government on the one side and the energy of a legislature with real backing from ordinary citizens on the other side. In the European Union, by contrast, broad policy priorities are set at a summit of the heads of government of individual member states that meets only a few times a year. The legislature, meanwhile, is selected in an electoral contest that sees abysmal turnout and is largely regarded by voters as an opportunity to protest against unpopular national governments—in part because the European Parliament's powers are, in any case, highly restricted. As a result, the European Commission, an organization of career bureaucrats, has historically been the motor of most of the EU's activities: it is the commission that initiates, writes, and implements a lot of EU law.[38]

Make no mistake: independent agencies have real accomplishments to their name. By and large, I believe that the decisions of the FCC and the SEC, of the EPA and the CFPB have made the United States a better place. The same is true of the European Commission and a variety of British QUANGOs. And yet, there is a real trade-off between respect for the popular will and the ability to solve complicated policy problems. While independent agencies accomplish crucial tasks not easily performed by other institutions, it is difficult to deny that they take important decisions out of political contestation.

CENTRAL BANKS

When I was growing up in Germany in the 1980s and 1990s, some six decades after hyperinflation had eaten away at the value of paper money and the stability of the Weimar Republic, my teachers would recount stories about those years as though they had happened just a few months before I was born.

"My father had some savings," I remember Frau Limens, my third-grade teacher, telling us. "He just wanted to keep them in the bank. But everyone was telling him he had to find a way to spend the money. It kept losing value. He needed to act as soon as possible. So, after much consideration, he decided to buy something people would always want: sugar. That way, he thought, he could sell the sugar bit by bit, buying bread and clothes for us until the whole chaos was over."

"Did it work?" one of my classmates asked. "Could you buy everything you needed?

"Well," she said, gravely, "he borrowed the neighbor's oxcart and went to purchase the sugar. It was a large amount of sugar, and it filled the whole cart. A big, white mountain. But it took him longer than he thought to drag the sugar back to our barn. And just as he was beginning to unload the su—"

"Oh, oh," my classmate said.

"Just as he was beginning to unload the sugar, it started to rain. In buckets. A few short minutes, and the whole big mountain—all of those precious savings—washed away."

"Whoa," my classmate said.

"Yes, whoa," my teacher agreed.

In one form or another, implicitly or explicitly, such stories always followed a clear arc from danger to redemption. The whole trouble, Frau Limens told our group of confused nine-year-olds, had started because "politicians were making all the decisions about money." That is why, after the war, "we made the Bundesbank independent. Nowadays, we wouldn't have that problem."

The real history of inflation and central bank independence is a little more complicated than Frau Limens had led us to believe. Faced with huge debt from World War I and a set of debtors highly determined to extract what they could from the country they had just defeated, the German government was desperate to find ways to acquire foreign currency. Presented with a lot of bad options, it chose a terrible one: printing mountains of money.[39]

But the political lessons the country drew about the resulting hyperinflation really were about as blunt as what Frau Limens taught us in the third grade. After World War II, many Germans blamed Hitler's rise to power on the destabilizing experience of hyperinflation, and the destabilizing experience of hyperinflation on political meddling with the money supply. To avoid a slide back into chaos or even fascism, they concluded, the new Bundesbank would have to be as independent as possible. This independence encompassed not only an interdiction on elected politicians interfering with its day-to-day operations or making decisions on the appointment of its governors. In stark contrast to other central banks around the world, the Bundesbank also gained the right to determine its own policy objectives, deciding on its own whether to prioritize low inflation or low unemployment.[40]

Germany's postwar economic success and the great stability of the Deutschmark soon became a core object of national pride. So when European political elites decided to embark on the process of monetary union in the course of the 1980s, one of the features on which German leaders insisted was that the European Central Bank (ECB) would have to follow the model of the Bundesbank.

That is exactly what eventually came to pass: "The ECB," according to Daniel Gros, "was the Bundesbank 2.0, but even a bit stronger in terms of its independence."[41] The whole point of its institutional design, writes Christopher Alessi, was to ensure that it would be "governed by unelected technocrats who fell outside the purview of political accountability."[42]

The influence of the Bundesbank goes even further: Over the course of the 1970s and 1980s, economists began to make more far-reaching arguments for central bank independence on the German model. Since politicians who are up for election at regular intervals have a strong incentive to create short-term booms, leading scholars like Robert Barro and Robert J. Gordon argued, dependent central banks would boost inflation in the short run without sustainably decreasing unemployment in the long run.[43] Making central banks independent would put decisions about interest rates in the hands of people who are insulated from such short-term incentives, and thereby boost long-term economic performance. And so countries from Great Britain to Japan, and from Moldova to Kenya gave their central bankers a much greater degree of independence. Over the course of the 1990s, Simone Polillo and Mauro Guillén write, 54 countries all around the world "made statutory changes towards greater independence . . . Only 24 countries without a strongly independent central bank as of 1989 did not introduce any statutory changes during the 1990s."[44]

There is another reason why the greater independence of central banks around the world matters so much: it is not only that many institutions that were under the effective control of elected legislators fifty years ago are now ruled by unelected technocrats who are free from political accountability. It is also that the importance of decisions taken by these institutions has grown over that same time period.

For most of the history of liberal democracy, central banks only had limited weapons at their disposal. For much of the nineteenth and early twentieth centuries, the value of most currencies was tied to its gold reserves. In the Bretton Woods system, which came to dominate in the wake of World War II, exchange rates were largely fixed; on the relatively rare occasions when they had to be adjusted, the decision was usually taken by elected politicians rather than unelected bureaucrats. During this period, Polillo and Guillén write, "finance ministers became the key decision-makers, while central banks . . . played a relatively limited and quiet role in economic and financial policymaking."[45]

Only since the demise of Bretton Woods in the early 1970s did central banks gain the leeway to set interest rates in keeping with their policy objectives. Long consigned to keeping a system designed by elected politicians stable, they are now the key institutions deciding, for example, whether it is more important for a country to minimize inflation or unemployment.[46] As a result, some of the most important economic decisions facing countries around the world are now taken by technocrats.

JUDICIAL REVIEW

In the 250 years since the Founding Fathers set up a republic that sought to exclude the people, in their collective capacity, from any share in the government, the hard-won introduction of universal suffrage was the second biggest institutional innovation. The biggest was entrusting nine unelected judges with the power to overrule the will of the people whenever it came into conflict with the preservation of individual rights.

This power has, historically, been used for some extraordinarily noble purposes. At times when most Americans were unwilling to grant the rights they claimed for themselves to a horrifically mistreated minority, it was the Supreme Court that stepped in. The end of segregation was brought about not by the will of the American people but rather by an institution that had the constitutional power to override it. When we think of the civil rights movement, we tend to think of the brave acts of ordinary citizens, from Rosa Parks to James Hood. And yet its history was just as much one of liberal decisions won against the resistance of electoral majorities.[47]

There can be no doubt that many of the most important advances for the rights of US citizens were handed down from a judicial bench. There can also be no doubt that nine unelected judges hold a vast amount of power—and that there is at least a reasonable case that they have become more willing to exercise that power over the course of the twentieth century.[48]

Since 1954, the Supreme Court has ended segregation in schools and universities.[49] It has ended and then reintroduced the death penalty.[50] It has legalized abortion.[51] It has limited censorship on television and radio.[52] It has decriminalized homosexuality and instituted same-sex marriage.[53] It has struck down campaign finance regulations and gun control measures.[54] It has determined whether millions of people would get health insurance[55] and whether millions of "Dreamers" needed to live in fear of being deported.[56]

That's why the American right has long railed against activist judges while the American left, which enjoyed a majority on the court for much of the postwar era, has long claimed that judges were merely doing their job. And it's also why these roles are slowly reversing now that the court is starting to lean right.[57] But though the question of whether the rule of the court has expanded over the past decades may be fraught with controversy, the best studies of the Supreme Court do suggest that its role is far larger than it was when the Constitution was written—and that it remains insulated from the will of the people in important ways.[58]

In most parts of the world, the rise of judicial review over the course of the past century is even more clear-cut than it is in America. According to my research, for example, only eight of the twenty-two countries that could be classified as democracies in 1930 had judicial review. Today, twenty-one of them do.[59]

The global rise of constitutional review is even more striking when we widen the sample to include both new democracies and autocracies. According to a study by Tom Ginsburg and Mila Versteeg, 38 percent of countries guaranteed the power of judicial review to a constitutional court in 1951; by 2011, 83 percent of them did.[60]

Even in some of the countries where the constitution does not explicitly grant the power of judicial review to the courts, they have, in effect, started to play this role. The United Kingdom is Exhibit A.

Britain has long prided itself in a system of parliamentary sovereignty that gave the Houses of Parliament plenipotentiary powers. For many centuries, the country did not entrust its judges with the power of judicial review.[61] This began to change after the United Kingdom joined the European Union in 1973.[62] UK courts could now review acts of Parliament under EU law.[63] Judicial review was further expanded after Britain incorporated the European Convention of Human Rights into domestic law.[64] The attenuation of the doctrine of parliamentary sovereignty was completed in name as well as in practice in 2005, when the highest court in the land was given an appellation that evokes its new importance. While the country's most senior judges had once been part of the House of Lords, they were now reconstituted as a separate body: the Supreme Court of the United Kingdom.[65]

A similar story could be told in other countries that had once limited the power of judicial review. In Canada, the 1982 Charter of Rights and Freedoms turned parliamentary into constitutional sovereignty.[66] In France, the powers of the Conseil d'État have gradually expanded, with its judges now making roughly 10,000 rulings every year.[67] Even in the Netherlands, where Article 120 of the Constitution makes clear that no court can review the constitutionality of parliamentary acts, the introduction of international human rights treaties has, de facto, expanded the powers of unelected judges.[68] As a result, the only holdout among the many democracies that did not let judges overrule parliaments in 1930 has now, to all intents and purposes, introduced a soft form of judicial review.

Legal theorists like Jeremy Waldron have made some forceful arguments against judicial review. The influence of the courts is meant to act as a safeguard against the tyranny of the majority. But, Waldron argues, it is far from obvious that countries that have historically eschewed a system of judicial review, like the United Kingdom, have a worse record on protecting individual rights than countries that have always had a strong form of judicial review, like the United States.[69] Similarly, courts are meant to be better at dealing with complex legal or philosophical questions, like abortion, for which ordinary people and their representatives may not be properly trained. But Waldron finds that parliamentary debates about issues like abortion have actually been carried out at a very high level in countries without judicial review—and that the resulting political compromises have helped to establish a wide social consensus on morally fraught questions that still eludes countries with judicial review.[70]

Though Waldron's points are powerful, I ultimately agree with the long list of eminent theorists, from Hans Kelsen to Ronald Dworkin, who have defended the legitimacy of judicial review. In moments of crisis, judges who are insulated from the popular will are more likely to protect vulnerable minorities and to stand up to power grabs by strongman leaders. Judicial review is a necessary safeguard.[71]

And yet, our support for judicial review should not blind us to its nature: the simple truth is that it takes many issues on which ordinary people have strong opinions out of political contestation.[72] It's perfectly reasonable to think that, say, protecting sexual and religious minorities from discrimination is so important that it justifies overriding the will of the people. But if that is the case, intellectual honesty demands that we acknowledge the nature of the institution to which we are so committed: though it often sets itself against the popular will, we might then say, judicial review is justified by the fact that it protects individual rights and the rule of law.

INTERNATIONAL TREATIES AND ORGANIZATIONS

Since the end of World War II, countries have become more and more enmeshed with each other along a variety of dimensions: political, cultural, military, and of course economic.

Back in 1960, only about a quarter of the world's GDP was bound up in foreign trade. By the turn of the millennium, over half was generated from cross-border trade—and the share has only kept on rising since. The amount of foreign direct investment has increased even more dramatically: over the course of the last two decades of the twentieth century, foreign investment tripled, from one in ten dollars to over one in three dollars.[73]

It is only natural that the greater degree of global interconnectedness has led to a much larger number of international treaties and organizations. How can nation states remain fully in control of economic policy when over half of mankind's economic activity flows across borders? And what point could there be in making environmental regulations without any process of international coordination when carbon emissions in one country can raise temperatures across the globe?

These are questions that staunch opponents of free trade, of treaties between states, and of international organizations don't take seriously enough. While they like to portray the rise of new modes of "international governance" as an elite conspiracy of corporations and technocrats, it is in fact a gradual response to underlying trends that nobody can wish away.

As valid as the reasons for the rise of international treaties and organizations are, though, it would be dishonest to pretend that they don't have an impact on the nature of domestic politics. As the range of political decisions that are precluded by international treaties or delegated to international bodies has risen, so too has the range of policy areas effectively taken out of democratic contestation.

The point of an international agreement is to coordinate the actions of different countries in order to set stable expectations and make them better able to achieve a common objective. So the loss of national control involved in becoming subject to international agreements is not a bug of the system of international agreements; it is its primary feature. This is true of treaties stipulating the emission of noxious gases as much as it is true of treaties establishing international organizations like the World Bank or the United Nations.

Free trade treaties are a strong case in point. To enter such an agreement, a state needs to abdicate (some of) its ability to make independent decisions on things like import tariffs: if it could reintroduce tariffs at any point, the free trade agreement would have failed in setting the stable expectations that account for a big part of its economic benefits.

Free trade offers big benefits to all countries that enjoy it. Even so, the inability to charge these kinds of tariffs restricts the freedom of maneuver for participating states in important ways. In the past, many developing countries managed to foster high-level industries by temporarily shielding them from competition. The United States did this for steel in the nineteenth century as surely as Japan and Taiwan did this for cars and electronics in the twentieth century.[74] Today, developing countries that are subject to the World Trade Organization, or to even more onerous regional trade agreements, are effectively barred from employing the same industrial strategy to grow their economy.[75]

This loss of control is compounded by the fact that modern-day trade deals go well beyond reducing or abolishing tariffs. Prohibitions on protecting domestic industries from foreign takeover make it more difficult for governments to slow the job loss from globalization or to cushion the social effect of these transformations. The attempt to eliminate hidden barriers to trade, including diverging regulatory and technical standards, makes it more difficult for national governments to pass new environmental protections. More ambitious agreements, like the North American Free Trade Agreement (NAFTA), also include provisions for short-term work visas, lessening a country's control over the inflow of immigrants.[76] Finally, the rise of "investor-state dispute settlements" gives corporations far-reaching powers to demand compensation for local regulations that might dampen their profits in front of international tribunals.[77]

Many of these effects are most pronounced in the European Union. To create a truly "single market," the EU has introduced far-reaching limitations on the autonomy of its member states.[78] For example, their ability to tax different forms of alcohol at differential rates is limited because of fears that, say, Belgium, which produces a lot of beer, might choose to impose a heavy tax on wine while Italy, which produces a lot of wine, might impose a heavy tax on beer.[79] Technical and environmental standards are frequently set by Brussels rather than by national capitals, putting significant powers in the hands of the European Commission.[80] And finally, the free movement of people gives European citizens far-reaching rights to access the territory of other member states[81]—but limits the ability of member states to decide who should get to live in their territory.[82]

Free trade treaties constitute only a small subset of the international agreements and organizations that now structure the international system. In fact, the United States is a party to so many agreements that the State Department has to prepare a "List of Treaties and Other International Agreements of the United States" as a stand-alone publication—one that runs to some 568 pages.[83]

Just as free trade deals have real economic benefits, so too many of these treaties help to keep the world secure or make a huge contribution in dealing with global problems like climate change. Though I—like just about every citizen—can hardly claim to have a detailed knowledge of most of these treaties, I do not doubt that they were concluded for good reason, and continue to play an important role.

But that, for our present purposes, is not the point. The case for taking so many policy decisions out of democratic contestation may be perfectly sound. But even if it is, this does not change the fact that the people no longer have a real say in all these policy areas. In other words, undemocratic liberalism may have great benefits—but that doesn't give us a good reason to blind ourselves to its nature.

Co-optation of Electoral Institutions

One reason why our system has become less democratic—why, in my terms, it has become less effective at translating popular views into public policies—is that many important topics have been taken out of political contestation over the past decades. Legislatures, so this story goes, are hamstrung in their ability to enact the will of the people due to the growing power of bureaucrats, the large role played by central banks, the rise of judicial review, and the greater importance of international treaties and organizations. But there is also another big piece of the undemocratic puzzle: Even in areas where parliaments retain real power, they do a bad job of translating the views of the people into public policy. Elected by the people to represent their views, legislators have become increasingly insulated from the popular will.

As Martin Gilens and Benjamin Page explain in a recent paper, there have long been four broad theories that sought to answer a question that is as simple as it is fundamental: "Who rules?"[84] On one theory, the views of average people are decisive. On another theory, it is the views of the economic elite. A third theory holds that it is mass-based interest groups like the American Association of Retired Persons (AARP). Finally, a fourth predicts that narrow interest groups like the National Potato Council carry the day. Gilens and Page put those theories to the test by tracking how well the policy preferences of these respective groups predicted how Congress would act on 1,779 policy issues over a span of two decades.

The results are shocking. Economic elites and narrow interest groups were very influential. Mass-based interest groups had little effect on public policy. The views of ordinary citizens had virtually no independent impact at all. "When the preferences of economic elites and the stands of organized interest groups are controlled for, the preferences of the average American appear to have only a minuscule, near-zero, statistically non-significant impact upon public policy."[85] The upshot seems inescapable. "In the United States," Gilens and Page conclude, "the majority does *not* rule."[86]

To understand why ordinary people seem to have so little influence on the legislative branch even in areas where parliaments still call the shots, we need to understand some of the roots of their dispossession. What can explain why the views of ordinary people now have "near-zero" influence on how their elected representatives act?

MONEY

Campaigning for reelection, Rupert Allason, a Conservative member of Parliament, went out to the pub in his constituency in Torbay. Although Allason had a reputation as a hard-living playboy, a penchant for Porsches, and a personal fortune reported to be in the millions, he neglected to tip the waitress. She was, local papers later reported, so furious that she decided to change her vote from the Conservatives to the Liberal Democrats—and to persuade her co-workers to do the same.[87]

Going into election night, Allason had high hopes. Five years before, he had beaten his opponent by a comfortable margin of 5,787 votes. But when the results started to come in, they showed an un-expectedly close race. In the end, after three recounts, Adrian Sanders, Allason's main rival, won by twelve votes—one of the most narrow victories in the history of British parliamentary elections.

If local press reports are to be believed, the case of the missing tip made all the difference. And if a recent study by Andrew C. Eggers and Jens Hainmueller is to be believed, Allason's stinginess did not just cost him his seat in Parliament; it may also have reduced his long-term earnings prospects.[88]

About ten years ago, Eggers and Hainmueller set out to study whether politicians stood to gain financially from being elected to Parliament. But they ran into an obvious problem: All kinds of factors—charm, skill, prior wealth, and so on—might determine both whether candidates would win and whether they would be likely to be appointed to lucrative positions outside Parliament. To control for this confounding factor, Eggers and Hainmueller focused on those "pseudo-random" cases in which elections were so close that it seemed to be a matter of sheer luck who won and who lost. The data they found were striking: "Conservative MPs," they concluded, "died almost twice as wealthy as similar Conservatives who unsuc-cessfully ran for Parliament."[89]

A big part of the reason for this worrying conclusion seems to be that candidates who had narrowly won election were more than three times as likely to serve on the board of companies listed on the London Stock Exchange than candidates who had narrowly lost election. The overall conclusion thus seems to follow naturally: "office was lucrative for Conservative politicians because it en-dowed them with political connections and knowledge that they could put to personal financial advantage."[90]

When we think about the corrosive effect of money on the politi-cal system, it is easy to focus on the most clear-cut and extreme

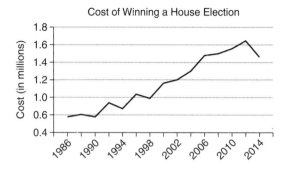

Cost of Winning a House Election

cases. We picture men carrying suitcases full of money, or perhaps a brown envelope furtively exchanged in a busy public square. In many fledgling democracies around the world, these kinds of straight-up bribes are indeed a huge problem. In countries like India or Iraq, a cash payment is required to do everything from getting a driving license to obtaining a building permit.

Even in consolidated democracies like Germany or the United States, there are cases of this kind of explicit exchange of an agreed sum of money for a particular political favor—what legal scholars call "quid pro quo" corruption. That is what Illinois governor Rod Blagojevich may have been hoping to obtain back in 2009, when Barack Obama's victory allowed him to fill the Senate seat the president-elect was about to vacate: "A fucking valuable thing," Blagojevich called it in one wiretapped phone call. "I've got this thing and it's fucking golden," he added in another call. "I'm just not giving it up for fucking nothing."[91]

Blagojevich ultimately went to prison for his shenanigans. In this, he was not alone. In the dozen years between 1990 and 2002, about 10,000 US officials were convicted for corrupt practices ranging from the blatant to the ridiculous.[92]

Even so, the role of money in the political system tends to be more subtle in consolidated democracies. Instead of extracting rents

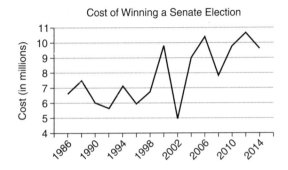

Cost of Winning a Senate Election

from the political system through explicit bribes, individuals and corporations mostly try to sway political decisions in their favor through political donations, lobbying, or the prospect of a lucrative job.

Campaign contributions are an especially large problem in countries, like the United States, in which existing limits on political spending are extremely weak. As a result, total spending on American elections has continually grown in the last decades, and now stands at unprecedented levels. In 2012, for example, "reported federal campaign spending . . . reached almost $6.3 billion," or over twice as much as the total annual GDP of an African country like Burundi.[93]

Some politicians are perfectly happy with this system: so long as they maintain friendly relations with big donors, it is easy for them to build up a big financial advantage over would-be challengers; if they tried and failed to change the rules about campaign finance, they might face the wrath of the donor class; and if they did somehow manage to change the rules, they would enter a new, uncertain world. Better just to keep things the way they are . . .

But just as many politicians feel trapped in a system they find it impossible to change. And so the political will to reform the system has, at rare moments, materialized. Back in 2002, for example, two

Senate heavyweights worried by the perennially growing influence of money in politics worked across the aisle to change how elections are fought. John McCain and Russ Feingold co-sponsored a bill to limit the pernicious influence of "soft money"—funds donated to parties to support political issues rather than specific candidates. To general surprise, it passed. For the first time in decades, it seemed as though the role of money in politics might go somewhere other than up.[94]

The legislation, widely known as McCain-Feingold, stayed on the books for about seven years. Then a conservative lobbying group by the name of Citizens United mounted a legal challenge. It had produced a documentary—in reality, little more than an extended attack ad—on Hillary Clinton. Under the new rules, it was prohibited from paying to air the documentary in the thirty days running up to a primary or the sixty days running up to a general election. This, it claimed, violated its right to free speech, as guaranteed by the First Amendment.

Finding that corporations—as well as other associations, like interest groups or trade unions—have many of the same rights as natural people, a majority of the justices on the Supreme Court agreed. The McCain-Feingold Act, Justice Kennedy wrote, violated the free speech rights of Citizens United. Corporations and political action groups would be allowed to spend as much money as they choose on supporting one candidate or attacking another. Though some limits on direct contributions to candidates remain in place, the court's decision essentially opened the floodgates to private interests.[95]

Hundreds of books and articles have been written about *Citizens United* and the corrosive effect it is (or is not) having on American democracy. But one of the important aspects of the decision that has mostly gone unnoticed is that different forms of undemocratic liberalism are reinforcing each other in this case: because the expanded role of judicial review takes important decisions out of the political process, a bench of unelected judges could overturn a law passed by the representatives of the people. The effect of this ruling, in turn, has been to make it more difficult for legislators to reflect the views of the people even in those parts of the political process where they retain real power.[96]

The evolution of lobbying has, in many ways, been even more dramatic than the growth in campaign contributions.

The Founding Fathers, Zephyr Teachout argues in *Corruption in America*, were extremely worried about the myriad ways in which people might seek to sway political decisions. Whereas European countries allowed their ambassadors to keep extravagant gifts from monarchs, which they thought a sign of respect, Congress was deeply concerned when Benjamin Franklin was presented a lavish snuff box by Louis XVI. It is perhaps understandable that the Founding Fathers regarded with some suspicion a gift encrusted with 408 diamonds, and depicting a foreign potentate "with powdered hair, and red cheeks, wearing white lace around his throat, two gold chains on his shoulders, and a blue robe with gold fleurs-de-lis."[97] But as Teachout shows, their concern extended even to forms of political activity that might look harmless to modern eyes.

In one especially striking example, an old, sick man was owed money by the federal government. Unable to retrieve it himself, he hired a lawyer to act on his behalf. When his son later refused to pay the lawyer the agreed fee, a court refused to compel him to pay his dues. Though the original purpose of the arrangement hardly seems illicit, the judges were concerned about providing a legal basis for the activities of lobbyists:

> If any of the great corporations of the country were to hire adventurers who make market of themselves in this way, to procure the passage of a general law with a view to the promo-

tion of their private interests, the moral sense of every right-minded man would instinctively denounce the employer and employed as steeped in corruption.[98]

Extreme as this case may seem, Teachout argues, it was far from idiosyncratic. For much of the history of the United States, the federal government banned many forms of lobbying. In Georgia, the state constitution was, at one time, amended to read that "lobbying is declared to be a crime."[99] In California, it was a felony.[100]

Over the course of the twentieth century, lobbying gradually lost the stench of the illicit. But even once the activity became normalized, businesses remained more reluctant to exert their influence—and the playing field remained far more equal than it is now.

As late as the 1960s, Lee Drutman shows in *The Business of America Is Lobbying,* labor unions were much more powerful and public interest groups had a much bigger voice than they do now. Major corporations did not lobby directly on their own behalf. "As every business executive knows," the future Supreme Court justice Lewis F. Powell Jr. wrote at the time, "few elements of American society today have as little influence in government as the American businessman, the corporation, or even the millions of corporate stockholders. If one doubts this, let him undertake the role of 'lobbyist' for the business point of view before Congressional committees."[101]

All of this quickly began to change in the early 1970s. Determined to fight the high costs of rising wages and complying with new legislation, a group of prominent CEOs banded together to expand their influence on Capitol Hill. At first, these activities were mostly defensive: the goal was to stop legislation that might harm their interests. But as the political influence of big corporations expanded and their profits soared, a new class of professional lobbyists managed to convince corporations that their activity "was not just about keeping the government far away—it could also be about drawing government close."[102]

Today, the attempt to influence legislation is a core part of what lobbyists do. When Drutman asked lobbyists about their goals, he found that "the top reason was 'to protect the company against changes in government policy.'" But another reason was nearly as important: the "'need to improve ability to compete by seeking favorable changes in government policy.'"[103]

It is hardly surprising, then, that lobbying expenditures in the United States have continued to increase at a rapid pace. In the first fifteen years of the twenty-first century, for example, they doubled, growing from a little under $1.6 billion to a little over $3.2 billion.[104]

The result has been not only to flush a lot more money into the system but also to distort the playing field. Unlike in the past, corporations now hold a huge advantage. "For every dollar spent on lobbying by labor unions and public-interest groups," Drutman

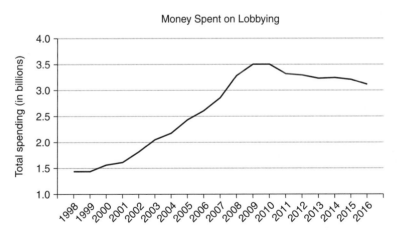

Lobbying expenditures in the United States, 1998–2016.

shows, "large corporations and their associations now spend $34. Of the 100 organizations that spend the most on lobbying, 95 consistently represent business."[105]

If anything, the explosion of the lobbying industry has been even more remarkable in Europe. In the 1970s, for example, there were fewer than one thousand registered lobbyists in Brussels. Today, more than thirty thousand are tasked with influencing EU policies.[106]

When Hillary Clinton was asked why she had attended Donald Trump's wedding back in 2005, her response was hardly convincing: "I thought it'd be fun," she said.[107]

Donald Trump offered a rather more blunt reason for inviting the Clintons: "As a contributor, I demanded that they be there—they had no choice and that's what's wrong with our country. Our country is run by and for donors, special interests and lobbyists, and that is not a good formula for our country's success."[108]

Trump's spectacular unwillingness to disclose his finances, or to take real steps to limit his many conflicts of interest, drives home what should have been obvious all along: his complaints about lobbying were insincere. And yet, his description of the basic reality of the American political system contains a large grain of truth. While it is an exaggeration to say that the country is run "by and for donors, special interests and lobbyists," the running of the country certainly requires a lot of complaisance with just those groups.

The fact that people may gain "influence over or access to elected officials" through donations or through lobbying, Justice Kennedy wrote in *Citizens United*, "does not mean that these officials are corrupt."[109] This is true. It does not constitute bribery for lobbyists to write legislation on behalf of elected representatives, and for the companies they represent to send those same representatives lavish campaign donations a few weeks later. Nor does it constitute bribery for British MPs to champion the interests of big public companies when they are in office, and to take a seat on their boards after they retire from Parliament. So long as their political survival depends on playing along with these practices, it may not even make sense to blame politicians for doing what the system requires. And yet, these accepted practices may cumulatively add up to what Lawrence Lessig has called "dependence corruption":[110] a system that "arises as a result of a gift economy based on the giving and receiving of political favors [and] operates at the level of the institution."[111]

In other words, Kennedy is right to point out that there is an important legal—and probably even moral—distinction between dependence corruption and cases of actual bribery. But from the point of view of undemocratic liberalism, they each have a rather similar effect. Thanks to the expenditure of private money, the powerful profit and public policy is redirected. Tasked with translating popular views into public policy, legislators are, to a disheartening degree, captured by special interests.

MILIEU

The people we are around day in, day out help to shape our tastes, our values and our assumptions. So one of the most insidious ways in which the influence of lobbying and campaign finance distorts the political system is, quite simply, in helping to shape the worldview of politicians who have to spend a large chunk of their time interacting with donors and lobbyists. In many cases, they don't have to compromise their ideals when the time comes to vote on a bill of concern to their major donors; because they spend so much of their lives around the representatives of special interest groups, they have, more likely than not, long ago come to share a lot of their views.[112]

While nobody has yet studied the magnitude of this effect in a systematic manner, it is reasonable to assume that it is quite large. After all, the amount of time politicians are now forced to spend on fundraising is itself considerable. Between 1986 and 2012, the average cost of a Senate race increased 62 percent; the average cost of a congressional seat increased a whopping 344 percent. So it makes sense that, according to anecdotal evidence, members of Congress now spend up to half of their working time on fundraising activities.[113]

The transformation is equally stark at the highest levels. Jimmy Carter and Ronald Reagan went to a fundraiser about once every twenty days during their first terms in office. Unlike Reagan, Barack Obama reportedly hated fundraisers. Even so, he remained captive to the exigencies of his political age—and organized a presidential fundraiser about once every five days.[114]

The imperative to raise money is one reason why politicians spend much of their time in a peer group that is very unlike the people they are supposed to represent. But this is just the tip of the iceberg. The truth is that, well before they reach office, most lawmakers have already been socialized into a cultural, educational, and financial elite that sets them apart from average Americans.

In the general US population, fewer than one in two hundred people hold a law degree. In the House of Representatives, it is over one in three. In the Senate, it is over one in two. Statistics on wealth are just as striking. The median net worth of an average American is just under $45,000.[115] The median net worth of an average member of Congress, by contrast, is over ten times as high, and that of senators higher still.[116]

To be sure, the Founding Fathers always envisaged lawmakers as an elite class. The fact that Americans choose highly educated— or financially successful—members of the community to represent them need not be a problem. But what surely is a problem is that, by just about every metric from geography to life experience, this elite is now thoroughly disconnected from the rest of the population.

A few generations ago, most members of Congress had deep roots in a particular part of the country. While they may have been local notables, they were notables with a strong sense of place. Democrats had frequently risen through the ranks of local trade unions or schoolhouses. Republicans might have been local business or community leaders. Born, raised, and frequently educated in their state, most of them expected to return to their home once they retired from Congress.

Today, by contrast, the connection average members of Congress have to their districts is, according to the limited research that has been undertaken on this question, markedly more tenuous. Fewer, it seems, were born and raised in the part of the country they represent. And even if they do hail from their district, it is no longer the center of their lives in a comparable way. Often educated at elite colleges on the East or West Coast, many of them spend their early working lives in the nation's great metropolitan centers. After stints in business, finance, the law, or on Capitol Hill, it is, in many cases, out of political ambition that they move back to their districts. And though many of them retain some kind of home in their district after leaving Congress, few make it the true center of their lives upon retirement: once they leave office, they are more likely than their predecessors to pursue lucrative opportunities in the great metropolitan centers.[117]

Many Europeans like to think that their countries do a lot better on all of these metrics than the United States. Whereas American democracy has long ago been captured by a hypercapitalist mindset and the corporations it emboldens, they like to claim, things are much better on the continent.

There is something to this claim. In most European countries, limits on campaign contributions are more stringent.[118] While lobbying has skyrocketed, political expenditures remain much lower.[119] Most importantly, European societies remain far more equal; in part as a result, the social and economic gulf between legislators and ordinary people is less stark.

And yet, the estrangement between voters and legislators is pervasive in Europe as well. While restrictions on campaign finance are real, for example, the advantage this affords to incumbents who are willing to play nice with special interests may be just as big— and even more difficult to track.

For one, the difficulty of raising money legally also makes it much more tempting for politicians to raise campaign contributions illegally. Helmut Kohl, Germany's longtime chancellor, is perhaps the most famous example: While he was leader of the Christian Democrats, the party developed a sprawling system of secret campaign donations that may well have swayed government policies on important issues like weapons exports.[120] Illegal campaign donations are an even bigger problem in France, where dozens of top politicians have been investigated for corrupt practices over the last decades.[121]

For another, the relative difficulty of raising money makes it much harder for politicians to stay in control of their own message. This increases the relative importance of their portrayal in major media outlets. In countries, from Italy to Great Britain, in which one owner controls a vast swathe of the media landscape, this essentially makes him a kingmaker. It is hardly a coincidence, for example, that the candidate backed by the *Sun,* Britain's most widely read newspaper, has gone on to win ten out of the last ten parliamentary elections.[122] Nor is it surprising that Silvio Berlusconi, who owns Italy's biggest private television network, could dominate his country's politics for two decades despite the dismal performance of his governments.

Europeans also have good reason to worry about the extent to which their political elite has become a class apart. The case is most easily made in countries like France, where it passes for news when a politician rises to the top *without* having attended the tiny École National d'Administration. But lawmakers in most other European countries have also become increasingly disconnected from the bulk of their electorate.

As recently as a generation ago, most left-wing leaders across Europe had strong roots in the trade-union movement. Even if they had not themselves been workers, their parents had been, and they were raised in a working-class milieu. Their ties with the working class were thus cultural and biographical as well as political.[123]

Similarly, most right-wing leaders had strong ties in a religious movement or an agricultural community. Even if they now lived in the big city, they likely ran in very different social circles, and remained proudly conservative in their lifestyle.

Even at a time when politics was highly consensual and policies pursued by Social Democrats and Christian Democrats resembled each other in important ways, this cultural dimension helped to structure European politics: The gulf between the mass of voters and their national representatives was comparatively small. By contrast, the gulf between the national representatives of rival political parties was comparatively large. As a result, there would have been many party leaders who felt more at ease having dinner with their constituents than with their main political rivals. Today, that is no longer the case.

All of this has a real political impact. It is natural to give more weight to legitimate interests that are salient to us than to those we have trouble imagining. And it is very easy to favor laws of which all of our friends approve over those supported by people we have never met. If legislators have done an increasingly poor job of translating the views of their constituents into public policy, the great social and cultural divide between political elites and the bulk of the electorate is a big part of the reason.

No Easy Outs

Democracy has nearly as many definitions as there are political thinkers. It is, as one philosopher put it, an essentially contested concept—one that will brook no agreed-upon definition so long as we continue to disagree about what exactly is valuable about it.[124] But one need not pull the old scoundrel's trick of reaching for a dictionary to call in doubt whether the United States is fully democratic today.

At a minimum, I suggest, any democracy should have in place a set of effective institutional mechanisms for translating popular views into public policy. In the United States, these mechanisms are now significantly impaired. The country's commitment to liberal rights remains deeply ingrained. But the form this liberalism takes is increasingly undemocratic.

America is not alone in its tendency toward undemocratic liberalism. Virtually all developed democracies now feature strong tutelary mechanisms. A lot of important issues have been taken out of political contestation by trade treaties and independent agencies. When the popular will strays beyond the bounds of the acceptable, it is constrained by technocratic institutions, from the US Supreme Court to the European Central Bank. Even in areas in which the people formally remain master of their own fate, the mechanisms for translating popular views into public policy are so attuned to the interests of social or economic elites that the people's influence over their own government is severely restricted.

Across the West, the last three decades have been marked by the growing role of courts, of bureaucratic agencies, of central banks, and of supranational institutions. At the same time, there has been a rapid growth in the influence of lobbyists, in the money spent on political campaigns, and in the gulf that separates political elites from the people they are supposed to represent. Taken together, this has effectively insulated the political system from the popular will.

Steven Levitsky and Lucan Way argue that "unfair competition" defines "competitive authoritarian" regimes where, as in Hungary, elections retain some real significance even though the government has ensured that it gets to compete on an uneven playing field.[125] Similarly, many supposed democracies now resemble competitive oligarchies: even though debates about proposed laws seemingly retain significance, an unfair policy-making process gives ruling elites a huge advantage in advancing their own interests.

The few scholars who have written about this phenomenon tend to argue that its roots are as simple as its remedies are obvious.

The origins of the people's disempowerment, they claim, lie in a power grab by political and financial elites. Large corporations and the super-rich advocated independent central banks and business-friendly trade treaties to score big windfalls. Politicians, academics, and journalists favor a technocratic mode of governance because it insulates their decisions from the popular will. And all of this selfishness is effectively cloaked by a neoliberal ideology that is propagated by think tanks and academic departments which are, themselves, funded by rich donors.

Since the roots of the current situation are straightforwardly sinister, the solutions to it are, supposedly, similarly simple: The people need to reclaim their power.

Experts claim that independent central banks are good for economic growth, and trade treaties drive down consumer prices. They insist on the need for big bureaucratic agencies and powerful international organizations because they deal with issues that are supposedly too complicated for the common man to understand. But once these institutions are exposed as complicit in a conspiracy to disinherit the people, it becomes obvious that this simply isn't true. The solution to the ills of undemocratic liberalism is to abolish tutelary institutions, to boot elites out of power, and to put the people back in charge.[126]

This basic set of intellectual instincts manifests itself in debates about a large range of issues and holds a significant amount of sway on both the far left and the far right. It fuels arguments against trade treaties as well as central banks. And it animates the language of Donald Trump as well as Jill Stein, and Stephen Bannon as well as Naomi Klein.

The problem with all this is that it caricatures the origin, the operation, and the purpose of these institutions.

It is true that political elites are overly comfortable with technocratic institutions that so happen to give them a lot of power. It is obvious that financial elites spend a lot of money and effort to mold these institutions to their own advantage. And there can be little doubt that funding streams favor some ideas over others, helping to set narrow bounds on the range of "serious" opinion.[127]

And yet, the history of most institutions that constrain the popular view is much more complicated than its detractors are willing to admit. The European Union, for example, has its origins not in a conspiracy of corporations, but rather in a reasonably idealistic attempt to rebuild the continent in the aftermath of World War II. Meanwhile, institutions from the Environmental Protection Agency to the International Atomic Energy Agency were designed to respond to genuine problems—like pollution and nuclear proliferation—that had previously been difficult to address.

The day-to-day operation of these institutions is a little more complicated than meets the eye as well. The negotiations between Greece and the troika have, for example, often been portrayed as a clash between Greek voters and international technocrats. And in important ways, they really were (which is why I myself used them as an example of undemocratic liberalism in the Introduction). But a big part of the reason why leaders like Angela Merkel were unwilling to offer Greece a better deal is that they were themselves responsive to the views of their own constituents; from this perspective, the will of the Greek people was ignored in part because it consisted in ignoring the will of other European peoples.[128]

Just as the history and the operation of technocratic institutions is rather more complicated than their critics claim, so too the solution to the problem of undemocratic liberalism is rather less clear than they posit. For while it is easy to malign imperfect institutions as useless or self-serving, they do play three important roles.

The world we now inhabit is extremely complex. To keep the economy moving and avoid major disasters, we need to regulate banks and enforce consumer safety standards, monitor hurricanes and inspect power plants. There are many different ways of structuring how these tasks are carried out. It makes sense to search for reforms that would give legislatures more power to set the necessary rules and hold the bureaucratic agencies that enforce them accountable.

But in the end, both the design and the implementation of these regulations really does require considerable technical expertise. It really is difficult to imagine that most citizens would take an active interest in them—or that elected politicians could come to master all their intricate details. And so it remains unclear how these tasks could be accomplished if we simply abolished technocratic institutions.

The challenge is even bigger when it comes to policy areas that require extensive international cooperation. To slow climate change or contain the spread of nuclear weapons, virtually all of the world's nations have to come to an agreement about what to do. At the moment, these kinds of decisions are usually made by heads of government (or the ministers they appoint). In democratic countries, these are of course elected. But the chain of delegation is extremely long, and the ability of ordinary citizens to influence international treaties highly restricted. Agreements like the Paris Treaty on Climate Change do suffer from a real democratic deficit.

And yet, it is once again difficult to see what the realistic alternative might be. A true world parliament is nowhere near in sight and would, in any case, feel incredibly remote to most citizens. Conversely, allowing each country to go its own way makes it impossible to confront a whole range of global challenges like climate change. In the end, it seems we must choose between achieving international cooperation on key issues by a troublingly undemocratic path—and not achieving it at all.

Finally, the relationship between liberalism and democracy is much more intricate than the opponents of technocratic institutions like to claim. For all of their shortcomings, countermajoritarian institutions like constitutional courts do have a proud record of protecting individual rights. So their opponents should at least take seriously the possibility that the members of ethnic and religious minorities might become more vulnerable if they were abolished. More broadly, independent institutions have historically proven very important in keeping democracy on an even keel. As the recent experiences of countries like Hungary or Turkey demonstrate, a system in which the will of the people can override judges and bureaucrats may appear more democratic in the short run; in the long run, it also makes it easier for an autocrat to extinguish democracy.

The double crisis of liberal democracy makes it tempting to go in search of easy solutions.

Observers who are most worried by the illiberal attitudes of the populists are unwilling to acknowledge that there is something democratic to the energy that drives it; some of them have even advocated insulating more and more political decisions from the popular will.[129] Conversely, observers who are most worried by the

technocratic attitudes of existing elites are unwilling to acknowledge that there may have been good reason to construct these institutions in the first place; as a result, they believe that many of them
should simply be abolished.[130]

But no such easy outs can solve the crisis of democracy. If we are
to preserve the liberal elements of the system, it won't do to constrain the influence of the populists by putting all the important
decisions in the hands of experts; instead, we need to persuade voters to defeat them at the polls. Similarly, if we are to preserve the
democratic elements of the system, it won't do to abolish institutions that help to stabilize the economy and to address some of the
world's most urgent problems; instead, we need to find ways of reforming these institutions to strike a better balance between expertise and responsiveness to the popular will.

The first big assumption of the postwar era appears to be wrong:
liberalism and democracy do not go together nearly as naturally as
most citizens—and many scholars—have assumed. As the popular
will increasingly clashes with individual rights, liberal democracy is
splitting into its component parts.

This is deeply worrying. For one, liberalism and democracy are
both nonnegotiable values. If we have to give up on either individual rights or the popular will, we are being asked to make an impossible choice. For another, it is looking increasingly doubtful that
either illiberal democracy or undemocratic liberalism will turn out
to be especially stable. A system that dispenses with individual
rights in order to worship at the altar of the popular will may ultimately turn against the people. Conversely, a system that dispenses
with the popular will in order to protect individual rights may ultimately have to resort to increasingly blatant repression to quell
dissent.

This casts doubt on the second, even more fundamental assumption of the postwar era: Democracy, so that story goes, is difficult to achieve. But once a country is both affluent and democratic, its political system is set in stone. In countries like France or the United States, democracy is "consolidated." But if liberalism and democracy do not form nearly as stable an amalgam as scholars have long believed, and if each of these values becomes even more vulnerable when the other is lost, then our political system seems to face a much greater threat than we have recognized. So are today's imperfect liberal democracies really as safe as we have long believed?

3

Democracy Is Deconsolidating

THE 1960S AND EARLY 1970S shattered many Americans' trust in the political class. The turbulence wrought by the student movement, the Vietnam War, and Watergate started to call into doubt what had long seemed an unshakable faith. When it was becoming increasingly clear that Richard Nixon would have to resign from office in disgrace, cultural critics proclaimed a severe crisis of confidence in American democracy. "The revelations of presidential duplicity and paranoia," David Runciman recently wrote about that time, "seemed to be stripping democracy bare, exposing something rotten underneath."[1]

It's hardly a coincidence that it was in this same year that Gallup first bothered to ask a question to which the answer would have seemed obvious a few years earlier: Did Americans trust the "men and women in political life . . . who either hold or are running for public office?" But the picture the poll revealed was remarkably rosy. Even in 1974, amid all that scandal, a clear majority of Americans retained confidence in people holding office.[2]

In the decades since then, by contrast, the number of Americans who trust their politicians has rapidly shrunk. Today, a clear majority of Americans say that they distrust people in public life.[3]

Interest in Politics

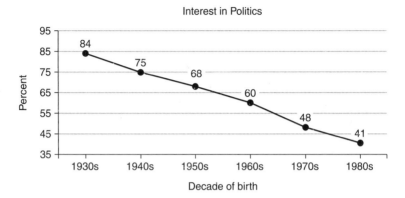

US respondents who express interest in politics, by decade of birth.

Trust in institutions is just as low. In June 2014, for example, only 30 percent of Americans reported having confidence in the Supreme Court. Twenty-nine percent expressed confidence in the presidency. Approval ratings for the legislative branch were even more dismal: in the early 1970s, over 40 percent of Americans had expressed confidence in Congress; by 2014, that figure had fallen to 7 percent.[4]

Given these stratospheric levels of dissatisfaction with the political system, it is perhaps unsurprising that many young Americans simply don't want to bother with politics. Even so, it is striking just how rapidly interest in politics has dwindled. While Americans born in the 1930s or 1940s are overwhelmingly likely to say that they take an active interest in politics, less than half of young Americans do.[5]

Similar trends are visible in many longstanding democracies across the world. In much of Europe, for example, citizens are less likely now than a few decades ago to believe that their elected representatives prioritize the interests of the general public.[6] They participate less in formal political institutions than they used to.[7] And like their American counterparts, young Europeans are much less interested in politics than their elders.[8]

This discontent is also expressing itself in unforgiving assessments of particular governments. In June 2005, the approval rating for Jacques Chirac fell to a record low. Only one in four French voters said that he was doing a good job, the lowest level the pollster TNS-Sofres had recorded since it started to look at presidential approval ratings in 1979.[9] Half a decade later, Chirac could take some comfort in the fate of his successor. Nicolas Sarkozy had come to the presidency offering the French a different leadership style and a brighter future. But as he failed to deliver on his promises, the voters' judgment was even more unsparing. By April 2011, no more than one in five voters approved of Sarkozy's job performance.[10] Another half decade later, it was Sarkozy who could take some comfort in the dismal fate of his successor. François Hollande swept to office on a wave of discontent. Then he became so disliked by so many that he didn't even seek reelection. By November 2016, only one in twenty voters approved of the job he was doing.[11] When Emmanuel Macron was elected to the presidency in May 2017, pulverizing the existing political system and enjoying tremendous popularity, everything seemed to change. But by the end

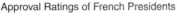

Approval Ratings of French Presidents

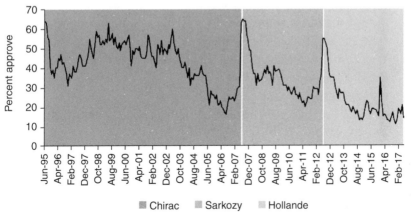

of that same summer, his popularity stood at 37 percent, the most precipitous decline of all.[12]

Across North America and Western Europe, in short, citizens trust politicians less than they used to. They are losing confidence in democratic institutions. And they take an increasingly negative view of their governments. All of this is worrying. But perhaps the most striking sign of the times is something rather less tangible: while politicians have always had to bear the public's displeasure, the intensity of the mistrust, hatred, and intimidation they now encounter on a daily basis is unprecedented. Even veteran politicians are taken aback by the vitriol they face.

After I gave a talk at a gathering of state legislators a few months ago, a senior Republican—a staunch conservative who has helped pass highly controversial reforms in his state—came up to me. Over the years, he said, he has slowly seen his constituents grow more angry and mistrustful. He has gotten used to the sour mood. And he has even started to accept that, when a rival offers a one-sentence solution to a complex policy question and he offers a three-sentence retort, most voters assume it is *he* who's pulling wool over their eyes.

But though this legislator was hardly a naive newbie, a recent encounter had left him shaken. He had, he told me, gotten into politics thanks to his sixth grade teacher, a woman who'd been his mentor since he was twelve years old, and who now knew him better than just about anybody outside his family. "Why are you lying to us?" this woman demanded when she called him on the phone a few days before we talked.

"What do you mean?" he asked.

"They said it on the radio. They said you're lying to us about this new bill."

He tried to explain that he hadn't deviated from the conservative principles they share but merely delayed a vote for tactical reasons. "You know me," he told her. "Won't you let me explain what's going on?"

But his teacher would hear none of it. "I don't know," she said. "They're saying on the radio that you are lying to us. I'm really disappointed in you."[13]

Political scientists have long been aware that trust in democratic institutions has declined; that appraisals of politicians have turned negative; and that approval ratings for office-holders and institutions have been falling. But until recently, they mostly waved these facts away.

For many years, leading scholars like Ronald Inglehart, Pippa Norris, and Russell J. Dalton tried their best to see the light amid the darkness. Perhaps, they suggested, earlier generations of citizens were simply too tame and credulous? Could the disillusion of today's voters not be interpreted as a sign of maturity rather than a portent of instability? As Lynn Vavreck argued as late as the summer of 2015, "some of the recent decline [in trust] may have less to do with how the government has disappointed people and more to do with an increasing knowledge of how the government works." While she admitted that it is "of some concern that trust in government is objectively low," she ultimately put this trend down to "a steady march away from government opaqueness—a longstanding American tradition dating to the candid submission of grievances outlined in the Declaration of Independence."[14]

One common way of making the case for optimism was to distinguish between "government legitimacy" and "regime legitimacy."[15] Government legitimacy, these scholars admitted, had declined: citizens have become much more willing to challenge their current rulers. But regime legitimacy, they insisted, had remained stable: citizens, they argue, are no more critical of the basic political system than they were in the past.

This is an appealing story. But over recent years, it has started to look less and less plausible. For one, it is difficult to imagine that ordinary people might turn against particular governments so radically—and take such a dim view of the day-to-day functioning of their institutions—without becoming more critical of the system itself. For another, the evidence that democracy is under attack just keeps piling up.

In Western Europe, parties that systematically assail core democratic norms keep rising in the polls. Across the world, from Egypt to Thailand, fledgling experiments with democracy have been crushed and existing democracies degenerated into dictatorship. For the first time in decades, Freedom House—which measures the extent of democratic government across the world—has recorded more countries taking steps away from democracy than taking steps toward it. In the words of Larry Diamond, a "democratic recession" is now underway.[16]

It is therefore high time to develop an empirical way to test the assumptions on which optimists have relied for so long. Is regime legitimacy still as high in North America and Western Europe as it once was? What would it look like if supposedly consolidated democracies were starting to deconsolidate? And at what point would we have reason to conclude that democracy is no longer the only game in town?

At least three things, I'd like to suggest, would have to be true for us to think that democracy is still the only game in town—and, by implication, that it is still as safe as most political scientists assume:

- Most citizens would have to be strongly committed to liberal democracy.
- Most citizens would have to reject authoritarian alternatives to democracy.
- Political parties and movements with real power would have to agree on the importance of basic democratic rules and norms.

Is this still the case?

There are many different ways of finding an answer to this question. Looking at opinion polls is only one of them. And yet, survey research is a very helpful tool for getting at a first answer. If the best available data showed that many citizens are critical not only of particular governments but also of democracy itself, this would lend real credence to the fear that democracy is no longer the only game in town.

So, together with my colleague Roberto Stefan Foa, I set out to examine the level of support for democratic institutions by looking at the World Values Survey, the largest cross-national sample of public attitudes on everything from politics to social issues. What we found shocked us: across North America and Western Europe, citizens really are turning away from democracy in large numbers.

Citizens Are Falling Out of Love with Democracy

One straightforward way to get a sense for how attached citizens are to their political system is to ask them how important it is to

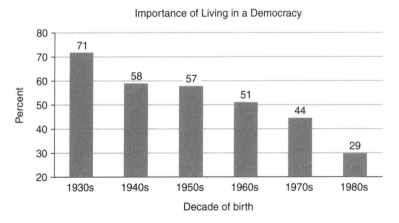

Share of US respondents who believe it is "essential" to live in a democracy, by decade of birth.

them to live in a democracy. If citizens are deeply committed to democracy, they should find it unacceptable to live in a dictatorship. Conversely, if they don't ascribe any real importance to living in a democracy, then the system's defenses look rather weak.[17]

Most older people do seem to have such a fervent attachment to democracy. Asked on a scale of one to ten how important it is to them to live in a democracy, about two-thirds of Americans born in the 1930s or 1940s give the highest response: they consider it essential. But most younger people are far less invested in their political system. Among American millennials, born since 1980, less than one-third consider it essential to live in a democracy.[18]

Outside the United States, the picture is a little more complicated. In some countries that have a recent history of authoritarian rule, young people are not significantly less invested in living in a democracy than older ones.[19] But in most longstanding democracies, especially in the English-speaking world, millennials are similarly disillusioned. Just as young people are less invested in their regime form in the United States, so too young people give less im-

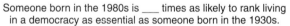

Someone born in the 1980s is ___ times as likely to rank living in a democracy as essential as someone born in the 1930s.

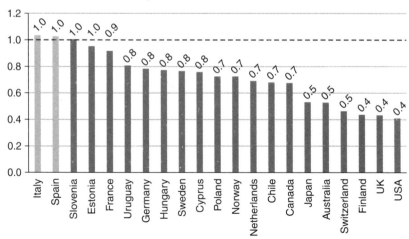

portance to living in a democracy from Sweden to Australia and from Great Britain to the Netherlands.

It is one thing for citizens to be indifferent toward living in a democracy, critics have pointed out, but quite another for them to reject democracy as a political system.[20] So would citizens go so far as to say that democracy is a "bad" or "very bad" way of running their country?

Sadly, the answer is yes.

In the United States, for example, close to one in four millennials now think that democracy is a bad way of running the country—an increase of over 100 percent compared to the oldest cohorts in the sample.

The global picture is once again similar: disappointment with democracy has also increased in Great Britain and the Netherlands, in Sweden and New Zealand. Indeed, even young people in countries that are often portrayed as especially resistant to the current crisis of liberal democracy—like Canada, Germany, and Sweden—are much more critical of democracy than their parents or grandparents.[21]

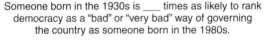

Someone born in the 1930s is ___ times as likely to rank democracy as a "bad" or "very bad" way of governing the country as someone born in the 1980s.

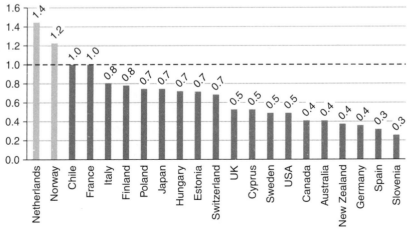

Citizens Are Increasingly Open to Authoritarian Alternatives

All in all, it is painfully clear that citizens have more critical views of democracy than they used to and that young people are especially likely to give less importance to living in a democracy. This is evidently worrying. But it may also reflect a lack of alternatives. Perhaps citizens are less sanguine about their system of government without thereby becoming more open to alternatives?

To test this hypothesis, we set out to look at explicit support for more authoritarian modes of governance. At first, we were a little skeptical how fruitful this undertaking would be. In a democracy, there is a strong taboo against saying that you favor abolishing elections or having the military take over the government. Even if many people did secretly wish for an alternative to democracy, it's not obvious that a larger number would actually be willing to look a stranger in the eye and admit to their antidemocratic sentiments.

And yet, we soon discovered, that is just what they did.

One way to assess the extent of openness to authoritarian alternatives is to ask whether respondents think that having a strong leader who doesn't have to bother with Congress or elections would be a good system of government. This isn't asking people whether they want to abolish democracy outright. And yet, it clearly captures openness to a system that would, in crucial respects, be deeply antidemocratic: a strong leader who is unencumbered by elections and doesn't need the support of the legislature would, to all intents and purposes, be a dictator by another name. So, have Americans become more open to a strongman leader?

Yes. In fact, not only are young Americans much more likely to favor a strongman leader than their elders, Americans of *all* ages are more in favor of a strongman leader now than they were twenty years ago.

In 1995, 34 percent of young Americans aged 18–24 felt that a political system with a strong leader who does not have to bother with Congress or elections was either good or very good. By 2011, 44 percent of young Americans felt the same way. The story among Americans of all age groups is similar: whereas 24 percent of all Americans endorsed a strongman leader in 1995, 32 percent do so today.

Surprised by the number of people who favored a strongman leader, we wanted to find out how many voters were willing to endorse an even more radical alternative to liberal democracy. Would a significant share of Americans be willing to say that they support an outright military dictatorship?

The good news is that the number of people who say that army rule is a good way to run America is indeed smaller than the number of people who hanker after a strongman who doesn't have to bother with Congress or elections. The bad news is that it is rising rapidly.

In 1995, about one in sixteen Americans said that they favored army rule, a markedly lower number than had been recorded in countries that actually experienced military coups. But over the past two decades, that number has increased steadily. By the time the question was last asked, in 2011, over twice as many—one in six—favored military rule. This means that the number of people who support army rule is now about as high in the United States as it is in countries with such turbulent histories of civil-military relations as Algeria (where 17 percent favored military rule in 2013) or Yemen (where 20 percent favored it).

Remarkably, support for military rule has grown even in segments of the population that once rejected it with one voice. Back in 1995, wealthy Americans were markedly less likely than poorer ones to favor military rule. Now, they are more likely to do so. The speed of this transformation becomes clear when we look at support for military rule among young, rich Americans. Twenty years

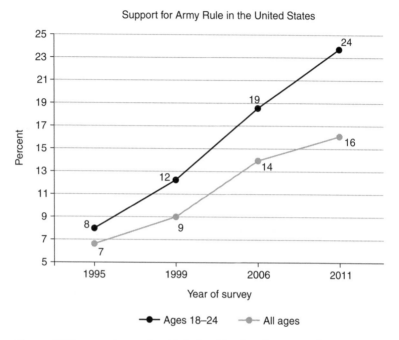

Share of US respondents who think that "having the army rule" is a "good" or "very good" political system, by age group, 1995–2011.

ago, only 6 percent of this group favored military rule. Since then, their support for military rule has increased nearly sixfold, from 6 to 35 percent.

Once again, this development is not exclusive to the United States. Looking beyond the American context, there are some countries in which support for army rule has actually fallen over the past decades. But for the most part these are nations, like Chile, with a very recent experience of military dictatorship. By contrast, in the vast majority of countries for which we have data—including long-standing democracies like Germany, Great Britain, Sweden, and especially India—the number of citizens who believe that it would be good to have the army rule increased markedly.

Support for Army Rule around the World

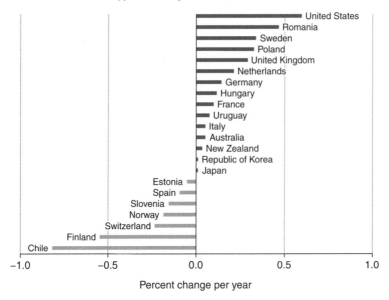

Percent change, per year, in worldwide respondents who think that "having the army rule" is a "good" or "very good" political system.

We see a similar trend in the percentage of citizens who support a strong leader who does not have to bother with parliament and elections. Once again, there are some countries, including Sweden and Switzerland, in which this number has declined. But there are many more, from Germany to the United States, in which it has significantly increased. Worryingly, more recent (and as yet unpublished) data suggest that the trend has only accelerated since. In a 2017 poll, for example, the number of German voters who supported a strongman leader had doubled from 16 percent to 33 percent; that of French voters had grown from 35 percent to 48 percent. In Britain, the finding was even more stark: while only 25 percent had supported a strongman leader in 1999, 50 percent now do.

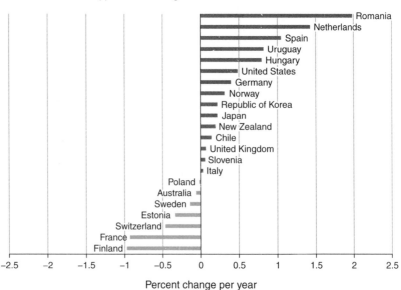

Percent change, per year, in worldwide respondents who think that "having a strong political leader who does not have to bother with parliament or elections" is "good" or "very good."

Eroding Respect for Democratic Norms

These survey results are evidently concerning. But to see whether or not democracy is still the only game in town, we have to look beyond the numbers. When democracy is stable, it is in good part because all major political actors are willing to adhere to the basic rules of the democratic game most of the time.

Some of these rules are formal: A president or prime minister allows the judiciary to investigate wrongdoing by members of his government instead of firing the prosecutor. He puts up with critical coverage in the press instead of shutting down newspapers or persecuting journalists. When he loses an election, he leaves office peacefully instead of clinging to power.

But many of these rules are informal, making it less clear-cut when they are violated. The government does not rewrite electoral rules months before an election to maximize its chance of winning. Political insurgents do not glorify authoritarian rulers of the past, threaten to lock up their opponents, or set out to violate the rights of ethnic and religious minorities. The losers of an election refrain from limiting the scope of an office to which an adversary has been elected in their last days on the job. The opposition confirms a competent judge whose ideology it dislikes rather than leaving a seat on the highest court in the land vacant, and strikes an imperfect compromise about the budget rather than letting the government shut down.

In short, politicians with a real stake in the system may think of politics as a contact sport in which all participants are hustling to gain an advantage over their adversaries. But they are also keenly aware that there need to be some limits on the pursuit of their partisan interests; that winning an important election or passing an urgent law is less important than preserving the system; and that democratic politics must never degenerate into all-out war.

"For democracies to work," Michael Ignatieff, the political theorist and former leader of the Liberal Party of Canada, wrote a few years ago, "politicians need to respect the difference between an enemy and an adversary. An adversary is someone you want to defeat. An enemy is someone you have to destroy."[22]

In the United States, and many other countries around the world, that is no longer how democratic politics works. As Ignatieff put the point, we are increasingly "seeing what happens when a politics of enemies supplants a politics of adversaries."[23] And the new crop of populists who have stormed the political stage over the last decades shoulder a lot of the blame for this.

The rise of political newcomers is as likely to be a sign of democratic health and vitality as it is of impending sickness. Political systems benefit from a thorough competition of ideas and from a regular substitution of one ruling elite for another. New parties can help in both ways: By forcing long-neglected issues onto the political agenda, they increase the representativeness of the political system. And by catapulting a new crop of politicians into office, they inject the system with fresh blood.

Even so, there is good reason to think that the recent thawing of the party system is far from benign. For many of the new parties do not just provide ideological alternatives within the democratic system—they challenge key rules and norms of the system itself.

One of the earliest populists to rise to prominence was Austria's Jörg Haider, a slick, charismatic politician from Carinthia. After winning the leadership of Austria's Freedom Party in 1986, Haider quickly took the party to the far right. His stridently anti-immigrant stance might be defended as putting a topic largely neglected by mainstream political parties onto the political agenda to the evident delight of his voters. But the degree to which he was willing to undermine core norms of liberal democracy became apparent whenever he engaged in a sly revaluation of Austria's Nazi past.

Speaking to an audience including many former SS officers, Haider claimed that "our soldiers were not criminals; at most, they were victims." Doubling down on his flirtation with the Third Reich, he saluted veterans of Adolf Hitler's murderous Waffen SS by saying that "there are still decent people of good character who also stick to their convictions despite the greatest opposition."[24]

Breaking political norms is also a specialty of Geert Wilders, the leader of the Dutch Party for Freedom (PVV). Islam, he has argued, is "a dangerous totalitarian ideology."[25] While other populists have sought to outlaw minarets or burkinis, Wilders, determined not to be outdone, has gone so far as to demand a ban on the Koran.

By comparison to Haider and Wilders, a figure like Beppe Grillo seems far more benign at first blush. Grillo first entered the political scene by railing against the—all too real—corruption of Silvio Berlusconi in hilarious, expletive-laden rants. When he founded the Five Star Movement (M5S), he promised to take power from a self-serving and geriatric "political caste," and to fight for a more modern and tolerant Italy.[26]

But once the movement gained in popularity, it quickly took on an antisystem hue. Its attacks on the corruption of individual politicians slowly morphed into a radical rejection of key aspects of the political system, including parliament itself. Anger against the political establishment was sustained by a growing willingness to engage in conspiracy theories or to tell outright lies about political opponents.[27]

The reason why populists and political newcomers are so willing to challenge basic democratic norms is in part tactical: Whenever populists break such norms, they attract the univocal condemnation of the political establishment. And this of course proves that, as advertised, the populists really do represent a clean break from the status quo. There is thus something performative about populists' tendency to break democratic norms: while their most provocative statements are often considered gaffes by political observers, their very willingness to commit such gaffes is a big part of their appeal. But their recklessness is no less dangerous for all of that: Once some members of the political system are willing to break the rules, others have a big incentive to follow suit. And that, increasingly, is what they do.

Some of the most spectacular attacks on basic democratic norms have come from political newcomers. But over the last years, the representatives of old, established parties have also become increasingly willing to undermine the basic rules of the game.

At times, this has simply been a response to the new competition from the populists. Nicolas Sarkozy, for example, had always acknowledged the existence of manmade climate change when he was president of France. But, vying for far-right voters when he was running for a second term in office in 2016, he radically changed tack: he now claimed that the "climate has been changing for four billion years . . . You need to be as arrogant as men are to believe we changed the climate."[28]

Established parties on the left have at times been guilty of violating democratic norms as well. In the United States, Democrats have long engaged in unacceptable forms of gerrymandering.[29] And during the Obama presidency, the executive continued to expand its role in some worrying ways, prosecuting a record number of journalists for handling classified information and using executive orders to bypass Congress in policy areas from the environment to immigration.[30]

Even so, most political scientists agree that the Republicans are now, by far, the best example for a concerted attack on democratic norms perpetrated by a nominally establishment party.[31]

Back in 2008, John McCain demonstrated that he understood the important distinction between treating a competitor for high office as an adversary and treating him as an enemy. When a voter at a town hall meeting said that he was scared about what would happen if Barack Obama won the election, McCain came to his adversary's defense: "I have to tell you: He is a decent person, and a person that you do not have to be scared [of] as President of the United States." Later at the same town hall, when an old lady worried aloud that Obama could not be trusted because he was an "Arab," McCain was similarly unequivocal: "No Ma'am. He's a decent family man and citizen that I just happen to have disagreements with on fundamental issues, and that's what this campaign is all about."[32]

The moral clarity that moved McCain to forego partisan advantage to affirm the legitimacy of the political opposition has, over the last years, been conspicuous by its absence. By the time Obama gave his first State of the Union address, a Republican lawmaker broke a longstanding tradition of decorum by shouting "You lie!" at the president.[33] By the time the Tea Party—led by Sarah Palin, McCain's pick for vice president—was gaining ground twelve months later, some Republican politicians were willing to echo a conspiracy theory that denied President Obama's standing as a natural-born citizen.[34]

More broadly, their total opposition to Obama made Republicans willing to abuse parliamentary rules that were meant to be reserved for exceptional circumstances, or even to engage in outright dereliction of their duties. Nowhere is this transformation more prominent than in the US Senate. Its rules and procedures were designed on the assumption that senators would, when necessary, forego their partisan advantage to make the system work. But today, senators play constitutional hardball on a daily basis. Though they respect the legal limits of their authority, they unabashedly insist on getting the most mileage out of every rule and procedure—even when it evidently subverts the spirit for which it was intended. The upshot has been a slow-moving form of institutional mayhem.

The filibuster, for example, has historically been reserved for use in rare circumstances. When Lyndon Baines Johnson was president, the minority party in the Senate used the filibuster 16 times. When Obama was president, by contrast, the minority party in the Senate used the filibuster 506 times.[35]

An even more blatant abuse of constitutional norms came in the wake of Justice Antonin Scalia's death. On March 16, 2016, Barack Obama nominated Merrick Garland, a moderate jurist who had enjoyed strong bipartisan support throughout his distinguished career, for the vacant seat on the Supreme Court.[36] But though the Constitution charges the Senate with the task of advising on the president's nominees, Senate Leader Mitch McConnell refused even to let the Judiciary Committee hold hearings on Garland's confirmation. Against all precedent, a seat on the Supreme Court remained vacant for most of 2016. And while the Senate's refusal to consider Garland's nomination was especially visible, it was part of a much wider pattern of stonewalling Obama's judicial and executive appointees.[37]

But it is in the states, away from the national limelight, that violations of basic democratic norms have been most blatant. For many decades now, partisan commissions have drawn electoral maps with the obvious purpose of giving the Republican Party an advantage at the next elections.[38] For many decades, Republican lawmakers have tried to disenfranchise minority voters by passing unnecessary ID laws or shutting down polling stations in heavily Democratic neighborhoods. In states like North Carolina, their determination to win has long exceeded their desire to hold a fair election.[39]

But even by those low standards, what happened in the wake of the 2016 gubernatorial elections in North Carolina was jaw-dropping. Roy Cooper, the Democratic candidate, won a highly contentious election by an extremely narrow margin. But instead of recognizing that this gave him a mandate to rule for the next four years, Republicans decided to rewrite his job description. North Carolina's governor used to be responsible for appointing 1,500 gubernatorial staffers; according to a law passed by the outgoing Republican legislature, he would henceforth be permitted to appoint only 425. The governor once had the power to appoint a majority of commissioners to the state's election boards; from now on, he would split the responsibility with the Republican-controlled legislature. Finally, the governor had previously been charged with appointing up to 66 trustees to the school boards of the University of North Carolina; now, he would be permitted to appoint a grand total of zero.[40]

The naked partisanship of these actions is undeniable. So is their import: Republicans in North Carolina have effectively rejected the notion that we resolve political differences by free and fair elections, and are willing to submit to the rule of our political rivals when we lose.

Donald Trump is now importing a supercharged version of constitutional hardball that has increasingly been practiced in the halls of Congress and of various state legislatures into the White House.

Over the course of his campaign, Donald Trump broke just about every basic rule of democratic politics. He promised to jail his political opponents. He refused to say that he would accept the outcome of the election. He bullied the press and threatened to expand libel laws. He invited a foreign power to sabotage his main competitor. He incited hatred against ethnic and religious minorities and promised to take unconstitutional action against them.[41]

After his election, Trump continued to disregard basic democratic norms. As president-elect, Trump made baseless claims about widespread voter fraud. He denigrated the neutrality of independent state institutions from courts to the intelligence agencies. He inquired about the status of planning permits for his building projects on official calls with foreign heads of state. He refused to create a blind trust for his private businesses. And he repeatedly complimented the dictatorial leader of a rival power.[42]

As president, Trump has doubled down on the same behavior. He has refused to resolve his substantial conflicts of interest. He has used the machinery of government to spread outright lies. He has tried to bar permanent residents from reentering the country. He has railed against "so-called judges." He has dubbed journalists "enemies of the American people." He has threatened the owners of critical media outlets with higher taxes. He has undermined attempts to investigate his links with Russia by colluding with loyalist legislators, firing the director of the FBI, and publicly threatening him with secret recordings.[43]

All in all, it is clear that the man who now occupies the highest office in the most powerful democracy in the world has a reckless disregard, and perhaps even a proud disdain, for the most basic rules of democratic politics. We are only just beginning to understand what that might mean for the stability of the system.

The Young Won't Save Us

Citizens are less committed to democracy and more open to authoritarian alternatives than they once were. Respect for democratic norms and rules has precipitously declined. No longer the only game in town, democracy is now deconsolidating.

That conclusion, I know, is hard to swallow. We like to think of the world as getting better over time, and of liberal democracy as deepening its roots with every passing year. That is perhaps why, of all my claims, the one that has elicited the most skepticism is the idea that young people have been especially critical of democracy.

For good reason, Americans and the British find it especially hard to believe that young people are most disaffected. After all, young people heavily leaned toward Hillary Clinton, the candidate of continuity, in the last US elections: among voters below the age of 30, 55 percent supported Clinton while only 37 percent supported Trump. The story of Brexit was very similar. Whereas two-thirds of pension-age Brits voted to leave the European Union, two-thirds of millennials voted for the status quo.[44]

It would nonetheless be facile to conclude that openness to radical change, much less to straightforward alternatives to democracy, is the exclusive preserve of the old—or that the crisis of liberal democracy will take care of itself as younger, more liberal cohorts replace their elders.

On the contrary, young people in a broad range of countries are actually more likely to identify as radical than older people. And their attraction to the political extremes has grown over time.

In countries like Germany, the United Kingdom, and the United States, for example, the number of young people who locate themselves on the radical left or the radical right has roughly doubled over the course of the past two decades; in Sweden, it has increased by more than threefold.

Polling data for populist parties bear out this story as well. While young people were less likely to vote for Trump or Brexit, they are much more likely to vote for antisystem parties in many countries around the world.

This is most obviously true in Southern European and Latin American countries, where the populist threat primarily comes from the left. Italy's Five Star Movement, Spain's Podemos, Greece's Syriza, and the France Insoumise movement led by Jean-Luc Mé-

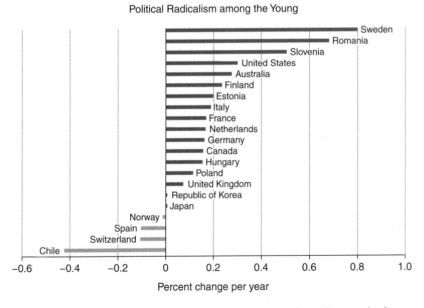

Percent change, per year, in millennials who position themselves on the far left or the far right of the political spectrum.

lenchon are all extremely popular among the young. In Italy, for example, 40 percent of voters below the age of forty supported the Five Star Movement in February 2016, compared to only 15 percent of voters over the age of sixty-five.[45]

It is not only far-left parties that profit from youth disenchantment with democracy. In many countries, the young are also more likely than the old to support far-right populists. Marine Le Pen, for example, can count young people as some of her most fervent supporters. In the second round of the 2017 presidential election, some exit polls suggested that only one in five older voters favored Marine Le Pen; among the youngest voters, nearly one in two did. (There was also some conflicting evidence, suggesting that Le Pen only outperformed her overall vote share among the young by a much smaller margin.)[46] In this, France is hardly an exception. On the contrary, polls have found similar results in countries as varied as Austria, Sweden, Greece, Finland, and Hungary.[47]

Even in Great Britain and the United States, the picture is rather less clear-cut than widely portrayed. Jeremy Corbyn, long regarded as a fringe figure, ascended to the leadership of the Labour Party and outperformed expectations in the 2017 general election in part because of his fervent support among young voters.[48] Young people are more open to populist appeals than has widely been suggested in the United States as well. Among white voters below the age of 30, for example, Donald Trump actually beat Hillary Clinton by a 48–43 margin.[49]

One possible explanation for why a lot of young people have grown disenchanted with democracy is that they have little conception of what it would mean to live in a different political system. People born in the 1930s and 1940s experienced the threat of fascism as children or were raised by people who actively fought it. They spent their formative years during the Cold War, when fears of Soviet expansionism drove the reality of communism home to them in a very real way. When they are asked whether it is important to them to live in a democracy, they have some sense of what the alternative might mean.

Millennials in countries like Great Britain or the United States, by contrast, barely experienced the Cold War and may not even know anybody who fought fascism. To them, the question of whether it is important to live in a democracy is far more abstract. Doesn't this imply that, if they were actually faced with a threat to their system, they would be sure to rally to its defense?

I'm not so sure. The very fact that young people have so little idea of what it would mean to live in a system other than their own may make them willing to engage in political experimentation. Used to seeing and criticizing the (very real) injustices and hypocrisies of the system in which they grew up, many of them have mistakenly started to take its positive aspects for granted.

It's tempting to think that the relative unpopularity of Trump among the young indicates that millennials who are openly critical of liberal democracy will come to its defense in a moment of peril— and that the crisis will subside as younger voters replace older ones. But I fear that a more pessimistic conclusion is warranted: A huge reservoir of antisystem energy still remains to be tapped. While young voters might come to the rescue of the system at the next election, it is just as likely that their opposition to the status quo might be activated in the service of some as yet obscure, insignificant, or inexistent populist movement.

The Dangerous Consequences of Deconsolidation

The evidence is highly concerning: In many countries around the world, from the United States to Great Britain, and from Sweden to Australia, democracy no longer appears to be the only game in town. A growing share of citizens either has negative views about democracy or doesn't think it's especially important. A smaller yet more rapidly growing share of citizens is open to straightforwardly authoritarian alternatives like a strongman ruler or a military dictatorship. Meanwhile, populists who have little or no attachment to basic democratic norms are gaining immense power—and one such politician has recently captured the most powerful office in the world.

But while it is clear that democracy is deconsolidating, it is as yet difficult to know what the consequences of this process are going to be. Is democratic deconsolidation a temporary process, which will soon awaken a strong immune defense—making for a turbulent decade but not much more than that? Or does democratic deconsolidation signal a real danger for the survival of political institutions that had once seemed exceptionally stable—raising the prospect that the long period of democratic stability, which has shaped the past three quarters of a century, is drawing to a close?

In theory, the way to settle these pressing questions is to look to past instances in which wealthy, consolidated democracies started to fracture. The problem is that no such examples exist. Until recently, the process of democratic consolidation really has been a one-way street. There are few examples in the historical record that give us an idea of the mayhem that might ensue when traffic suddenly starts to flow in from the other side.

But while there is no clear precedent for the situation in which we now find ourselves, a few cases do come closer than others. Countries like Poland and Venezuela, for example, were widely thought to be well on their way toward democratic consolidation until the election of populist candidates did grievous damage to their political systems. If we want to know whether we should be worried that the rise of illiberal democracy may end in dictatorship, we need to investigate whether the same process was taking place in these countries before their democracies deteriorated.

Political scientists have long portrayed Poland as the great success story of postcommunist transition toward democracy. They had strong reason for their optimism. Between 1990 and 2005, Poland's government changed hands through free and fair elections five times. The country's GDP increased sixfold, comfortably surpassing the threshold of $14,000 per capita at which democracies are supposedly stable. Other signs seemed to be encouraging as well. The country developed an unusually active set of civil society institutions. Many Poles were deeply rooted in associational life, from sports clubs to the Catholic Church. NGOs began to advocate for a wide variety of social and political issues. Excellent newspapers held successive governments to account, freely criticizing political mismanagement and investigating corruption scandals. Schools and universities flourished.[50]

By 2004, this progress secured Poland a coveted membership in the European Union. To be admitted to the EU, a country has to prove that it has developed stable institutions "guaranteeing democracy, the rule of law, [and] human rights."[51] Poland fulfilled these criteria with flying colors.

It is hardly surprising, then, that many political scientists concluded that Poland had already become "a consolidated democracy."[52] While nobody would have gone so far as to suggest that democratic institutions in Poland were as firmly rooted, or as secure, as they are in countries like Canada or the United States, liberal democracy seemed to have taken hold.

And yet, this well-founded optimism soon turned out to be premature.

The 2015 elections came at a strange moment. The Civic Platform government led by Prime Minister Donald Tusk could boast a largely positive record: It had competently steered the country through the global recession of 2008. It had improved Poland's relationships with its neighbors. It had made a success of Poland's first turn at leading the presidency of the EU. All in all, Poland was doing remarkably well.

But after nearly seven years in office, the government was starting to run out of steam. Voters were ready for a change. So when secret recordings of private conversations between leading officials showed them using crude language and engaging in suspect economic deals, the government's popularity plummeted.[53]

This gave an opening to the far-right Law and Justice Party, which had already ruled the country from 2005 to 2007 under the leadership of Jarosław Kaczynski. During its first stint in office, Law and Justice had quickly become unpopular because of a series of high-profile scandals and constant spats between members of the cabinet. Many Poles rejected the party's staunch conservatism and its divisive rhetoric. But this time, the party had seemed to moderate. Its main promises were to take back a planned increase in the retirement age, to cut taxes, and to increase childcare payments. Kaczynski, who had formally stepped down as the party's leader but continued to dominate it behind the scenes, barely appeared in public during the campaign and promised not to take a leading role in the government.[54]

In the event, the Law and Justice Party won both the presidential and the parliamentary elections, giving the party sweeping powers. Once in government, it began to subvert the basic rules of Polish democracy.

In a first step, Law and Justice undermined the neutrality of independent state institutions. To gain control of the Constitutional Tribunal, the country's highest court, the government increased the number of its judges, rushing the nomination of party loyalists through parliament overnight while stripping three previous nominees of their vote. When the Tribunal ruled that the three opposition-nominated appointees had a right to vote, parliament stripped it of much of its powers and dismissed the ruling.[55]

In a second step, Law and Justice used government funds to spread propaganda and muffle critical journalists. While past Polish governments had also tried to influence the political slant of Telewizja Polska (TVP), the state broadcaster and the dominant television network in the country, its takeover by the new team was qualitatively different. Commentators who had frequently appeared on TVP's programs for decades disappeared from television screens overnight. News programs that might at one point or another have leaned in favor of the government of the day became unremitting purveyors of naked propaganda.[56]

Not content with capturing state media, the government started to encroach on private networks and publications. Over the past years, it has stripped private companies of advertising contracts and strong-armed foreign owners into selling media corporations to domestic allies. As one Law and Justice leader boasted, the party intended to "re-Polonize" the country's media, public and private.[57]

In yet another step away from liberal democracy, the Law and Justice Party has started to attack the right to voice unpopular opinions, to protest government policy, or simply to report on such protests. Unwilling to brook criticisms of the Polish nation, the government attempted to revoke the medal a previous government had awarded to Jan Gross, a Princeton historian who has demonstrated the extent of Polish complicity in the crimes of the Holocaust, and passed a law criminalizing the use of the phrase "Polish death camps."[58] When popular protests against the government erupted in the summer of 2016, Law and Justice moved to restrict the right to assembly. And when thousands of citizens took to parliament to protest, the prime minister banned private broadcasters from the parliament building.[59]

Called upon to investigate whether liberal democracy was now in danger in Poland, the Venice Commission—an advisory body of the Council of Europe composed of senior academics and experts in constitutional law—came to an unusually undiplomatic conclusion: "Not only is the rule of law in danger, but so are democracy and human rights."[60] Guy Verhofstadt, who had been intimately involved in negotiating Poland's membership in the EU, was similarly forthright: "The measures Warsaw is taking are . . . anti-democratic and contrary to the principles of the rule of law signed by Poland upon its EU accession. It is clear that if an accession agreement was to be sought now, it would fail."[61] Jan-Werner Müller put the point even more clearly: "it is hard to avoid the feeling that Central Europe is living 1989 in reverse. In that year, peaceful revolutions in the name of liberal democracy spread from one Communist country to another. Today we witness the emergence of a new Authoritarian International."[62]

Most political scientists have been puzzled by Poland's rapid slide from liberal democracy. The country seemed to be doing so well for so long. And yet, the political system deteriorated so quickly. What could possibly explain such a rapid shift in fortunes? Or might it simply be a freak occurrence—one of those strange, unexpected twists of history that political scientists could never hope to foretell?

It would be tempting to think so. But in light of my recent work, the Polish case actually looks surprisingly straightforward. Long before democracy started to fail, Poles were already taking a remarkably dim view of democracy, evincing a striking openness to authoritarian alternatives, and voting for parties that broke with fundamental democratic norms.

- Compared to their neighbors, or indeed to the global average, Poles have long been highly critical of democracy. While, globally, only about one in ten respondents claim that democracy is a bad or very bad way of running their country, about one in six Poles have long held this view. (Among American millennials, close to one in four respondents share this bleak view.)
- Long before the current government took over, Poles had been unusually open to authoritarian alternatives. While fewer than one in ten citizens of the European Union believed that army rule was a good system of government in

the early 2010s, more than one in five Poles took this view.
(Among American millennials, the level is similarly high.)[63]

- Finally, powerful populist parties had long started to undermine key democratic norms. Law and Justice built a mass following despite (or perhaps because of) its willingness to spread conspiracy theories, to drum up fear of foreign governments, and to dismiss the parties in power as traitors to the Polish nation. In this, it was not alone. Andrzej Lepper, the late leader of Samoobrona, an agrarian party, aspired to be "a positive dictator," routinely engaged in anti-Semitic rhetoric, and issued dark warnings about clandestine plots to topple the Polish government. Meanwhile, the League of Polish Families, an ultraconservative party, warned that the EU was a communist agent, intent on subverting the country's Catholicism.[64]

In short, all the major warning signs that are now flashing red in large parts of North America and Western Europe were present in Poland long before the Law and Justice government started its concerted assault on democratic institutions. Had political scientists paid closer attention to the signs of democratic deconsolidation—signs that are now burning just as brightly in North America and Western Europe—the worrying developments in Poland need not have come as such a surprise.

The harbingers of democratic decline were there for all to see. But political scientists did not care to look.

High-minded defenders of liberal democracy believe that there is something uniquely legitimate about the political system to which they are committed.

Its democratic element, they claim, ensures citizens' equality. In a monarchy, the king is elevated above his subjects by the accident of his noble birth. In a democracy, by contrast, all citizens get one vote without regard to the color of their skin or the station of their ancestors.

Its liberal element, meanwhile, ensures citizens' freedom. In a totalitarian regime, the government can regulate the lives of its subjects in the most minute detail and punish them at whim. In a liberal polity, by contrast, the reach of the law is limited, and citizens are protected against arbitrary interference in their lives.

The peculiar genius of liberal democracy is that it is able to honor both of these values at the same time.

This account of democratic legitimacy is a little too blithe. As long as money can easily buy power, many citizens understandably feel that political equality remains an empty promise. And as long as economic necessity radically constrains the kinds of choices they can make, many citizens understandably feel that the freedom they were promised has not materialized. To live up to the most exalted claims of its adherents, liberal democracy needs to be embedded in a broader context of social and economic justice—and make citizens feel that they actually hold power. And yet, it seems to me that this rough account of what makes our political system special is more right than it is wrong: for anybody who is deeply committed to both freedom and equality, the allure of liberal democracy remains unrivaled.

But while I am convinced that liberal democracy is more legitimate than other forms of government, I am skeptical that this also explains why it has, historically, enjoyed such widespread support.

People who believe in the unique legitimacy of liberal democracy tend to assume that this legitimacy has also been the major reason for its success: By ensuring that each citizen can stand tall in the public sphere and simultaneously remain free to enjoy his private life, this story goes, only liberal democracy can fulfill some of the deepest and most universal human aspirations. That is why it has gradually conquered the world—and will, the hope goes, dominate its future.

The best available evidence, however, seems to suggest that citizens have built up loyalty to their political system because it kept the peace and swelled their pocketbooks, not because they hold a deep commitment to its most fundamental principles. Liberal democracy, this fear suggests, has only been so dominant because it has delivered such good results.

If this is true, popular attachment to liberal democracy may be rather more shallow and more brittle than its most high-minded supporters tend to think. And that would go a long way toward explaining its current woes. As liberal democracies have become less adept at delivering for citizens, they have entered a deep "performance crisis." The populist movements that are on the rise around the world are now exploiting this crisis to dismantle key elements of the system.

There is little historical precedent that can tell us how institutions in supposedly consolidated democracies fare when they stop delivering for their citizens. They may remain stable even as their economies stagnate and their power declines. To avoid nasty surprises, we must grapple with the possibility that they might not—and investigate why citizens have grown so disappointed in the performance of liberal democracy in the first place.

PART TWO

ORIGINS

IF I RECORD the temperature at which water boils in New York City, I will jot down 100° Celsius in my notebook. If I make another measurement in Boston or Miami or Seattle or San Diego, I will keep getting the same result. I could keep on going to my heart's content, and yet I would only confirm what every textbook would have told me: water boils at 100°.

But things aren't quite as simple as they appear. For if I were to repeat my experiment atop Mont Blanc, the water would boil at about 85°. And if I dragged my kettle all the way up Mount Everest, it would do so even earlier, at about 70°.[1]

In other words, the fixed association between temperature and the boiling point of water holds so long as the height at which I carry out the experiment—and, with it, the pressure of the air around me—doesn't change. If I only ever carry out my experiment in coastal cities, I won't realize that the result I get depends on conditions of which I wasn't even aware. Once the context changes, so does the link between cause and effect.

All of this is highly relevant if we wish to think seriously about what fate may be in store for democracy. Since the end of World

War II, democracies have proven incredibly stable in many parts of the world. We have fallen into the trap of assuming that they must be here to stay. But now there's good reason to fear that the world we know is just as contingent as the boiling point of water (or the farmer's desire to feed Bertrand Russell's chicken).[2]

If we want to venture an educated guess about the future of democracy, we thus have to figure out what political scientists call its "scope conditions":[3] Was the past stability of democracy brought about by conditions that are no longer in place? If so, how might the erosion of these conditions explain what has been happening over the past decades—and help us figure out how we might be able to escape the bloody fate that seemingly awaits us?

On my view, there are at least three such scope conditions:

- First, the dominance of mass media limited the distribution of extreme ideas, created a set of shared facts and values, and slowed the spread of fake news. But the rise of the internet and of social media has since weakened traditional gatekeepers, empowering once-marginal movements and politicians.
- Second, all through the history of democratic stability, most citizens enjoyed a rapid increase in their living standards, and held out high hopes for an even better future. In many places, citizens are now treading water, and fear that they will suffer much greater hardship in the future.
- And third, nearly all stable democracies were either founded as monoethnic nations or allowed one ethnic group to dominate. Now, this dominance is increasingly being challenged.

The following chapters are devoted to explaining each of these causes in detail. But while it is important to search for the big changes that might plausibly be related to the stability of democracy, we also need to avoid four common mistakes that pervade much of the recent journalistic—and scholarly—debate about the rise of populism.

Many analysts have told stories about their local context, focusing on factors that only hold in their particular countries. But since the rise of populism is a global phenomenon, we should look for causes that are common to most countries where populism has spread in the past years.

Many analysts have assumed that recent events must explain populist uprisings, invoking the Great Recession as the source of our woes. But since the rise of populism began well before 2008, we should focus our explanations on long-term trends.

Many analysts have assumed that different causes are rival to each other, debating with particular ferocity whether the political crisis we now face is explained by economic *or* cultural factors. But since economic and cultural anxieties reinforce each other, we should eschew such "mono-causal" explanations.

Finally, many analysts have assumed that the structural drivers of populist success would manifest in direct and obvious ways—so that the poor would support populists in the greatest number if economic explanations play a role, and people in areas of high immigration would support populists in the greatest number if cultural factors play a role. But since people are motivated by the fate of others as well as their own, and spend as much time reflecting on their fears about the future as they do pondering their current circumstances, we also need to consider more subtle and indirect ways in which economic anxiety and racial animus might manifest in our politics.

4

Social Media

UNTIL THE LATE MIDDLE AGES, it was prohibitively costly and cumbersome to spread information to a large number of people. To make a copy of a long text, a professional copyist or a monk would need to transcribe each word in the original manuscript. To make another copy, he would have to start all over again.

As a result, written information was only accessible to a select elite. To share a piece of writing with fifty or a hundred people was a major undertaking. To share it with thousands was the exclusive preserve of kings or senior clergymen. Technological limits on the spread of the written word thus helped to enforce political and religious orthodoxy: with the dissemination of ideas firmly in the hands of priests and potentates, it was comparatively easy to quell political dissent and religious heresy.

This helps to explain what made the invention of the printing press so momentous. When Johannes Gutenberg first found a way to create a master plate for each page that could be copied many times over at vastly lower cost and incomprehensibly greater speed, he radically changed the structural conditions of communication. Soon, "one-to-many" communication would be within the reach of a significant number of people for the first time in human history: somebody with access to the relevant technology and the requisite capital could now impart their ideas to thousands of people, all at the same time.[1]

Gutenberg's contemporaries were quick to grasp the revolutionary implications of the printing press—and many of them were full of hope for the marvels it would bring forth. The greater ease of communication would spread ideas, increase learning, and foster economic growth.

Some of these hopes were borne out. The theses of Martin Luther, for instance, were printed some 250,000 times in the span of a few years; it is difficult to imagine that Luther would have had such a transformative impact on the world if his followers had not had access to printing technology. Without a doubt, the printing press played a major role in the revival of ideas—and the rapid spread of literacy—that took place in the sixteenth and seventeenth centuries.[2]

But though the printing press is rightly celebrated as one of the most transformative inventions in the history of mankind, it has also had hundreds of thousands of victims. As new religious ideas spread across the continent, so did religious strife. And as dissenting voices gained the ability to communicate with would-be followers, so did their ability to instigate violent political revolts. In a word, the printing press spread death as well as literacy, instability, and chaos alongside emancipation.

Over the last years, a slew of writers have compared the invention of digital technology—and especially of social media—to the invention of the printing press. In Clay Shirky's words, "you used to have to own a radio tower or television tower or printing press. Now all you have to have is access to an Internet café or a public library, and you can put your thoughts out in public."[3] Heather

Brooke makes much the same point even more concisely: "Our printing press," she wrote, "is the Internet. Our coffee houses are social networks."[4]

It is easy to dismiss these grand claims out of hand. In generation after generation, so the charge goes, some leading thinkers have fallen prey to "chronocentricism," or the erroneous belief that their own moment in time is somehow central to the history of mankind.[5] Might the widespread belief that a recent invention like Twitter or Facebook represents a fundamental shift in human history not suffer from the same cognitive bias?

It's important to be on guard against chronocentrism. But it's also difficult to deny that there are some real parallels between the invention of digital technology and the invention of the printing press: like the press, the advent of the internet and of social media fundamentally transformed the structural conditions of communication.

In the five hundred years since the invention of the printing press, the cost and the speed of one-to-many communication fell significantly, even as its content and geographical reach expanded radically. By 1992, it was possible to beam the sound and the sight of an event to billions of television viewers around the world in an instant.

But in two respects, the world of CNN still resembled the world of Martin Luther: There were a limited number of centralized communicators—TV networks and radio stations, newspapers and publishing houses—and a large number of recipients. And the costs were significant enough that most citizens were unable to turn themselves into broadcasters on any significant scale; to become an opinion-shaper, you either needed to spend a lot of money or to convince the owners of the means of distribution to feature you on their platforms.

In the quarter century since 1992, both of these constraints have disappeared.

At first, the World Wide Web made it possible for most inhabitants of developed countries to broadcast their views around the globe: once they published a website at little cost, the content they had created was available to anybody with an internet-enabled device. After over five hundred years, the promise inherent in one-to-many communication had finally been democratized.

This difference in degree soon begot a difference in kind. Although websites were accessible to anyone who could connect to the internet, they still, at first, shared a few important properties with older distribution platforms. In theory, joeboggs.com was as easy to reach as nytimes.com; in practice, it was very difficult for Joe Boggs to let would-be readers around the world know about his website.

Social media attenuated this last constraint. On Facebook and Twitter, content created by any one user can rapidly be reposted by anybody with whom this user is connected. If the content the user has created is sufficiently novel or interesting, even someone with few connections can reach a very large audience in a matter of minutes.

By creating a diffuse network of users who are all in communication with each other, social media thus altered the dynamics of distribution. There is a reason why terms like "meme" or "virality" are new to our everyday vocabulary: they could only take on the importance they now have in a world in which anybody can capture the imagination of a handful of peers, who then share their work with a global audience.

One way of putting this point is to say that, thanks to the rise of social media, one-to-many communication has now transformed into "many-to-many communication."[6] And perhaps the most significant feature of many-to-many communication is that the largest players have lost much of their ability to control the spread of ideas or messages that resonate with ordinary people.

Twenty-five years ago, traditional broadcasters could stop the spread of videos that might have been of interest to millions of people—whether they be the entertaining antics of a domestic cat or the brutal beheadings perpetrated by terrorist groups—by declining to air them. Today, traditional broadcasters still can, and sometimes do, refuse to air such content. But their function as gatekeepers has mostly evaporated: sufficiently viral content is likely to spread via social networks whether or not traditional broadcasters decide to show it.[7]

All of this suggests that the invention of digital communication technology really is going to have a big political effect. But will the gatekeepers' loss of influence empower ordinary people and boost democracy—or has it already harmed democracy by giving populists the platform they need to poison our politics?

The Rise of the Techno-Optimists

Until a few years ago, most observers were highly optimistic. In one of the most subtle early analyses of what he tellingly called "Liberation Technology," for example, Larry Diamond argued that new digital tools empower "citizens to report news, expose wrongdoing, express opinions, mobilize protest, monitor elections, scrutinize government, deepen participation, and expand the horizons of freedom."[8] In Malaysia, he showed, digital tools had allowed democratic activists to publish news stories critical of the authoritarian regime. In countries from Uzbekistan to the Philippines, and from Venezuela to Nigeria, they had allowed ordinary citizens to hold their governments to account by chronicling abuses. Even in China, where the Communist Party had instituted a "Great Firewall," users were creatively circumventing the regime's heavy-handed censorship: "There is simply too much communication and networking," Diamond observed, "for the state to monitor and censor it all."[9]

Diamond's article was published in the summer of 2010. Within the year, its most optimistic predictions seemed to come true. Mass protests erupted in Tunisia, in Egypt, in Libya, and finally in Syria. In each of these countries, long-serving autocrats were ousted from power. And in each of these countries, protestors had used social media to criticize the government, to chronicle attempted crackdowns, and to coordinate the time and location of their protests. Twitter, Andrew Sullivan wrote in the *Atlantic,* had proven to be a "critical tool for organizing."[10] In twenty-first-century conflict, Nicholas Kristof echoed in the *New York Times,* "government thugs firing bullets" would increasingly come up against the resistance of "young protestors firing 'tweets.'"[11]

The positive effects of digital technology were increasingly being felt closer to home, too. As Clay Shirky argued in *Here Comes Everybody: The Power of Organizing without Organizations,* even in countries like the United States the power of many-to-many communication made it much easier for activists to coordinate.[12] In the wake of the financial crisis, this greater ease of organizing seemed to play out in myriad forms. On the right, the Tea Party was inspired by a viral rant on CNBC, and made heavy use of online tools from meetup.org to email lists. On the left, Occupy Wall Street and Black Lives Matter heavily relied on social media to assemble and coordinate a loose network of activists all over the country. On both sides of the political spectrum, a reenergized public seemed to testify to the democratizing potential of social media.[13]

The potential of social media to both deepen and spread democracy seemed beyond doubt—and its boosters began to make ever more ambitious claims about its potential. Capturing the conventional wisdom of his time in characteristically vivid form, Thomas Friedman wrote in May 2014 that the "square people" would shape global politics for the better:

As the I. T. revolution and globalization have been democratized and diffused—as we've gone from laptops for elites to smartphones for everyone, from networking for the lucky few at Davos to Facebook for all and from only the rich heard in the halls of power to everyone being able to talk back to their leaders on Twitter—a new global political force is aborning.

They are mostly young, aspiring to a higher standard of living and more liberty, seeking either reform or revolution (depending on their existing government), connected to one another either by massing in squares or through virtual squares or both, and united less by a common program and more by a shared direction they want their societies to go.[14]

The Revenge of the Techno-Pessimists

As late as 2014 or 2015, the conventional wisdom on social media was overwhelmingly positive. Since then, it has been stood on its head.

There had been warnings from the start, of course. In "Liberation Technology," Diamond was at pains to stress that the new digital tools could be put to bad as well as good uses: "Just as radio and TV could be vehicles of information pluralism and rational debate, so they could also be commandeered by totalitarian regimes for fanatical mobilization and total state control," he speculated.[15]

In the following years, skeptics from Evgeny Morozov to Cass Sunstein deepened Diamond's critique. The biggest fans of Twitter and Facebook, Morozov argued, believed that these new technologies would reshape the local context, connecting erstwhile enemies and overcoming ancient hatreds. But in truth, the inverse would come closer to the truth: different local contexts would reshape the use of tools like Facebook, making them emancipatory in some contexts and strengthening autocratic rule—and inciting racial hatred—in others.[16]

The centrifugal forces unleashed by the internet were on Sunstein's mind as well: Since social media sites allowed people to curate their own information sources, he suggested, they would give rise to "echo chambers" in which users would effectively surround themselves with others who are politically like-minded. Paradoxically, the increased ease of communication with anybody in the world might thus lead to much less communication across the most salient social and political divides.[17]

When I started teaching a class called "Democracy in the Digital Age" at Harvard University back in the spring of 2013, most students found these warnings interesting—but also a little abstruse. On the whole, they still embraced the boosterish view of social media, seeing its liberating potential as paramount.

Then came the rise of Donald Trump.

Throughout Trump's unlikely campaign, it was obvious what an important role social media was playing in his ability to bypass the traditional gatekeepers of American politics. In an earlier age, television networks would likely have refused to air his blatant lies or his tirades against immigrants, religious minorities, and political opponents. But thanks to Twitter, Donald Trump did not need the infrastructure of traditional media outlets. Instead, he could tweet messages directly to his millions of followers. Once he had done so, established broadcasters faced a stark choice: ignore the main subject of conversation and make yourself irrelevant—or discuss each Tweet at length, thereby amplifying Trump's message even as they ostensibly scrutinized it. Perhaps unsurprisingly, they chose the latter course of action.[18]

Trump's Twitter feed gave him a powerful weapon. But it was augmented by a diffuse network of lieutenants, some acting for ideological, others for primarily financial reasons. The most prominent of these was Breitbart, a news organization whose rapid rise demonstrated the extent to which mass communication had been democratized in the digital age. A few years into its existence, the site could rival longstanding media organizations in size and influence. And since it didn't feel bound by their constraints, it repeatedly published stories that were distinguished more by being inflammatory than by being truthful.[19]

Breitbart, in turn, only stood at the apex of a large number of smaller sites that spread lies and rumors with even greater abandon. Many of the stories fabricated and disseminated on portals like Vdare, InfoWars, and American Renaissance were so far-fetched or gory that it was difficult to see how anybody could believe them. "Pope Francis Shocks World, Endorses Donald Trump for President," one headline screeched.[20] "Bombshell: Hillary Clinton's Satanic Network Exposed," another proclaimed.[21]

But believed they were by a significant portion of the population. According to one poll, taken in August of 2016, 42 percent of registered voters had come to believe that Hillary Clinton was "evil."[22] In an even more striking finding recorded in North Carolina, days after Trump had referred to Clinton as "the devil," 41 percent of his supporters claimed to believe that this was literally true.[23]

If such abstruse ideas found such easy credence, it is because the new possibilities of many-to-many communication were intersecting with the rise of ever-narrower echo chambers. In some corners of the internet—which is to say, on the Facebook feeds and the Twitter timelines of a significant portion of the American population—no bad word about Hillary Clinton seemed too outlandish to be true.

Thanks in good part to the constant vilification of his opponent, Donald Trump carried off a narrow victory. In the months that followed, the conventional wisdom flipped. If social media had been portrayed as the savior a few short years before, it now had to be the angel of death. Turning breathless claims about digital technology's liberating potential into breathless prognostications of doom, social media was now declared the most dangerous foe of liberal democracy. "It's time," Farhad Manjoo of the *New York Times* wrote a few days after the election,

> to start recognizing that social networks actually are becoming the world-shattering forces that their boosters long promised they would be—and to be unnerved, rather than exhilarated, by the huge social changes they could uncork . . . In a way, we are now living through a kind of bizarro version of the utopia that some in tech once envisioned would be unleashed by social media.[24]

Closing the Gap

Manjoo has a point: The negative potential of social media is all too real. And yet, it is overly simple to say that social media is a "world-shattering force," sure to result in a terrible dystopia.

The truth about social media, I want to suggest, is not that it is necessarily good or bad for liberal democracy. Nor is it that social media inherently strengthens or undermines tolerance. On the contrary, it is that social media closes the technological gap between insiders and outsiders.

Until a few decades ago, governments and big media companies enjoyed an oligopoly over the means of mass communication. As a result, they could set the standards of acceptable political discourse. In a well-functioning democracy, this might mean declining to publish racist content, conspiracy theories, or outright lies—and thus stabilizing liberal democracy. In an autocracy, this might mean censoring any criticism of the dictator—and thus keeping liberal democracy at bay.

With the rise of social media, this technological advantage has all but evaporated. As a result, in authoritarian countries the democratic opposition now has many more tools to topple a long-entrenched dictator. But by the same token, the hucksters of hatred and the merchants of mendacity also have a much easier time undermining liberal democracies.

The mechanisms that drive this transformation are laid bare in one of the most haunting studies on the rise of digital technology: a few years ago, Jan Pierskalla and Florian Hollenbach examined what effect the introduction of cell phone technology had had on remote African regions in which communication had previously been extremely difficult.

Economists had expected the results to be positive: As information spread, people would be able to get better medical information. It would be easier to transport goods to far-flung regions that had a desperate need for them. The closer link to the metropolitan center might even improve access to education and boost literacy rates. Some of these positive effects did materialize. But as Pierskalla and Hollenbach show, so did a very negative one: in areas where cell phone coverage was introduced, levels of political violence surged.[25]

Before the introduction of cell phones, Pierskalla and Hollenbach show, government forces had held a huge technological advantage over rebel groups. Because of their access to tools like landline phones and army radios, they could solve two challenges that insurgents found nearly impossible to overcome. First, there was the problem of collective action: even government soldiers stationed far from headquarters have an incentive to shirk their job— but their commanders had the means to check in on their daily activities, giving them direct orders on a regular basis, and thereby reducing instances of free-riding. Second, there was a problem of coordination: When engaged in battle, it is crucial for soldiers to know what other troops are doing, and to be able to share the location of opposing groups in real time. By using army radios, government forces were able to do this, boosting their tactical agility.

By contrast, rebel groups lacked access to comparable tools and kept running into big problems: Foot soldiers keen to draw a salary from rebel leaders but scared to risk their lives often shirked their duties. To make things worse, when they did engage in battle, they often suffered heavy casualties because they were unable to coordinate with their comrades. As a result, most clashes between governments and rebel groups were one-sided, helping to undermine rebellions and to reduce the overall incidence of armed conflict.

The introduction of cell phones changed all of this. Rebel leaders used the new technology to give regular commands to their subordinates, and to coordinate their actions during battles. All of a sudden, rebel groups rivaled government troops in fighting spirit and tactical agility. With many conflicts more evenly matched, they went on for much longer and proved considerably more deadly.[26]

The real reason why cell phones increased the incidence of violence in remote African regions, then, is not that digital technology somehow favors extremists over moderates, or the evil over the good. Rather, it is more prosaic: in closing the gap between political insiders and political outsiders, it favored rebels over the status quo, and the forces of instability over the forces of order.

Cell phones capable of placing calls and sending texts do not equal smart phones capable of spreading messages to millions of people via Twitter or Facebook. And remote African regions with low state capacity do not equal developed democracies in which the authorities remain firmly in control. And yet, the study by Pierskalla and Hollenbach can help us understand the mechanisms that have allowed digital technology to reshape politics in democracies like the United States or France: Once upon a recent time, would-be politicians needed access to vast resources and existing organizations to overcome key coordination and collective action problems. Now, they have the tools they need to reach potential collaborators, to motivate them to become politically active, and to coordinate their actions. The political elite's technological advantage has been drastically reduced in Michigan and South Dakota as well as in Kenya and Nigeria.

From this perspective, we can make sense of both the Green Revolution in Iran and ISIS's use of social media, of both the Arab Spring and the election of Donald Trump. What many observers took to be a paradox—that social media might have such positive effects in some contexts and such negative effects in other contexts—is a result of the same underlying dynamic: in empowering outsiders, digital technology destabilizes governing elites all over the world and speeds up the pace of change. The effects are likely to stay with us for a very long time.

A dozen years after the invention of the printing press, the new technology had not yet left the city of Mainz. Only a tiny portion of the world's population had ever held a printed book in their hands. Most things were as yet unaffected by the coming revolution in communication and politics.[27]

A dozen years after the invention of Facebook, by contrast, the new technology has spread to every corner of the globe. Some two billion people actively use the platform. The resulting revolution in communications is already a crucial feature of our political reality.[28]

It is far too early to tell whether this will, with the benefit of dozens or hundreds of years of hindsight, turn out to change the world for better or for worse. But there can be little doubt that, in the short run—which is to say, for the rest of our lives—it will make for a more chaotic world.

Over recent years, it has been the populists who have exploited the new technology most effectively to undermine the basic elements of liberal democracy. Unfettered by the constraints of the old media system, they have been willing and able to say anything it takes to get elected—to lie, to obfuscate, and to incite hatred against their fellow citizens.

Perhaps their rhetoric will prove to be unstoppable. As that state legislator pointed out to me, it is difficult for a rational politician to win a debate with a three-sentence answer when his rival is offering a one-sentence answer, especially when he's able to blast his simplistic take all over Twitter and Facebook.

But just as the pro-democracy activists who used social media to topple dictators underestimated how difficult the task of consolidating their victory would turn out to be, so the ascendant populists may yet find the technological future to be more challenging than they expect. "Whoever is winning at the moment," George Orwell once wrote, "will always seem to be invincible."[29] But once populists capture the government and start to break many of their promises, they may be rudely reminded of social media's potential to empower the new outsiders against their rule.

5

Economic Stagnation

ECONOMICALLY SPEAKING, the last three hundred years are an aberration.

For most of history, there has barely been any economic growth. In the thousands of years between the foundation of Athens and the invention of the steam engine, average annual growth remained at a modest 0.1 percent. And much of that growth was due to an increase in the overall population rather than an increase in the living standards of the average household.[1]

Because growth was so slow, economic progress rarely took place at the scale of an individual lifespan. There have always been times of plenty and times of scarcity; indeed, most of our ancestors will have felt the effect of floods or droughts on their diet at some point in their lives. And of course there has always been that rare individual who, against steep odds, managed to transcend his social station, gaining access to riches he could not have imagined as a child. But for most humans at most times in history, the economy was an essentially stagnant affair: while their fortunes might have changed from season to season, they could expect to die about as rich or (far more likely) about as poor as they had been the day they were born.

Only in the eighteenth century did economic growth come to be a lived reality for a great many people.

If an economy grows at 0.1 percent for fifty years, it will (because of compounding interest) cumulatively grow by about 5.1 percent. If it grows at 1 percent every year, it will grow by 64 percent over the course of fifty years. If it grows at 2.5 percent, it will grow by 344 percent. So when the economy in countries like England started to grow by about 1 percent per year in the eighteenth century, and accelerated its growth to about 2.5 percent per year for much of the nineteenth century, this added up to cumulative rates that were an order of magnitude higher than anything previously recorded in human history.[2] For the first time, millions of people saw the capacity of the economy—the basic ability of their civilization to provide them with food and housing, and to produce clothing or even luxury goods—fundamentally transformed over the course of their lifetimes.

There was only one problem: the bulk of these gains went to the richest members of society—and the times of the most rapid growth often coincided with the times of the greatest inequality. Between 1827 and 1851, for example, the English economy grew by about 80 percent. But during that same time period, the Gini coefficient, the standard measure of income inequality, increased just as rapidly. In effect, England had, in the span of a quarter century, gone from the level of income inequality recorded in today's Iceland to the level of income inequality recorded in today's India.[3]

Then another big aberration in human history set in: a period of unprecedented economic equality.

Back in 1928, Thomas Piketty shows, the richest 1 percent could expect to capture 15–20 percent of income in European countries like France or the United Kingdom and almost 25 percent of income in the United States. By 1960, the wealth distribution had flattened considerably: In France and the United Kingdom, the richest 1 percent now captured less than 10 percent of income. In the United States, they captured no more than 12 percent. As a result, most citizens enjoyed a huge increase in their living standards over the course of their lives.[4]

These improvements were not merely abstract. Many people alive today grew up without a fridge or a car or a television. Now they have a fridge and two cars and a giant home entertainment system. The awe-inspiring growth of the economy of developed democracies, coupled with an unprecedented period of relative equality, transformed their day-to-day lives and took physical form in their homes.

That was then.

In recent decades, by contrast, economic progress in advanced economies has slowed radically.

While the US economy grew at an average pace of 4 percent per year in the first two postwar decades, it grew by only 2 percent per year over the past two decades.[5] The difference is even bigger in Western Europe: The French economy, for example, grew by an average of 5 percent in the postwar era. For the past twenty years, it recorded annual growth of only about 1.5 percent. (The story is similarly disappointing in Germany and much worse in Italy.)[6]

At the same time as overall economic growth has slumped, inequality has risen. Starting in the 1980s, inequality grew rapidly on both sides of the Atlantic. Today, most economies in North America and Western Europe are no more equal than they had been back in the 1930s.[7]

The combined effect of slowing growth and accelerating inequality has been a stagnation in living standards for huge parts of the population. The rate of growth may still look good when measured against the long sweep of human history. Measured against the peak decades of democratic stability, by contrast, it constitutes a disastrous drop.

The story is especially stark in the United States: From 1935 to 1960, the living standard of the median American household doubled. From 1960 to 1985, it doubled again. Since 1985, it has essentially been flat: the average American household is no richer now than it was thirty years ago.[8]

This transformation is painful for older people who suddenly saw their economic progress stalled in middle age. But it is even more disturbing for younger people who were raised on the promise that hard work would translate into an improvement of their economic fortunes—and who, instead, have been falling behind the milestones their parents had easily reached at a comparable age.

Indeed, the number of people with no personal experience of improving economic fortunes has, according to eye-popping research by Raj Chetty and his team, multiplied in recent years. People who are asked how well they are doing, the authors of the study explain, "frequently compare their own standard of living to that of their parents."[9] Until recently, this comparison—which they call "absolute income mobility"—was heartening. By the time they turned thirty, over nine in ten Americans born in 1940 earned more than their parents had done at the same stage of their lives. By contrast, at a similar life stage, only one in two Americans born in 1980 earns more than their parents had done.

One way of expressing this striking finding is to say that, for a rapidly growing share of the US population, the promise of rising fortunes that is part and parcel of the American dream has turned out to be a chimera: Once upon a time, very few young Americans failed to see their standard of living improve over the course of their lives. Today, half of them do.[10]

According to an extensive study undertaken by the *Guardian*, the same basic trend holds true in large parts of Western Europe as well as in North America: "Millennials," the report shows, "have

Absolute Income Mobility

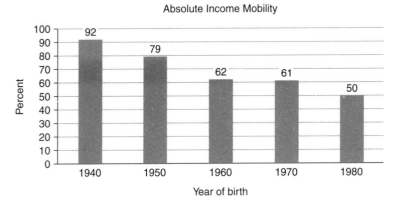

Percentage of children whose household income at age thirty is bigger than their parents' household income was when they were thirty years old, by decade of birth, for the United States.

suffered real terms losses in wages in the US, Italy, France, Spain, Germany and Canada." And while the Great Recession aggravated this trend, "in some countries this was underway even before the 2008 financial crisis."[11] A rapidly growing number of young people who cannot count on their parents to open a trust fund for them or to give them a generous down payment face the prospect of much greater financial hardship.

Much the same story emerges when we look at key noneconomic indicators for the quality of life. Take the example of life expectancy. In the postwar era, the number of years an average person could hope to live was still rapidly rising. While someone born in the United States in 1900 could expect to live until 49, for example, someone born in 1950 could expect to live until 68—a gain of nearly two decades. But as medical progress slowed, those numbers stagnated. Somebody born in 2003 can expect to live until 77, only nine years longer than members of their grandparents' generation. And as Anne Case and Angus Deaton show, the life expectancy of white Americans is now falling for the first time on record: "From

1978 to 1998, the mortality rate for US whites aged 45–54 fell by 2 percent per year on average." Since 1998, by contrast, "mortality rose by half a percent a year."[12]

The overall message thus remains much the same even if we broaden our focus beyond the narrowest forms of economic data: Since the start of the Industrial Revolution and the dawn of modern democracy, citizens enjoyed huge improvements in the conditions of their life from one generation to the next. Over the past quarter century, they have, at best, enjoyed modest gains.

What will be the impact of the resulting frustration?

Fear of the Future

The kind of rapid economic progress that was standard in the postwar era was enough to buy liberal democracy a lot of legitimacy. It's not that Americans ever loved their politicians, or thought of Washington, DC, as a unique repository of moral virtue. But so long as the system was working for them, most people were willing to believe that politicians were ultimately on their side. "I'm not sure that I trust politicians," they might have said. "But I'm twice as rich as my dad was, and my kids are probably going to be twice as rich as me. So let's give them the benefit of the doubt . . ."

Today, by contrast, that residual reason to give politicians the benefit of the doubt has evaporated. So it is little wonder that many voters are no longer willing to believe that the political establishment is on their side. "I've worked hard all my life," they might now say, "and I don't have much to show for it. My kids are probably going to have it worse. So let's throw some shit against the wall and see what sticks . . ."

This doesn't necessarily imply that there should be a straightforward correlation between a person's economic struggle and their propensity to vote for populist candidates. After all, those who grew up in a lower middle-class household and dreamed of ascending into the upper middle class might be just as frustrated by their lack of economic progress as those who were born poor and stayed poor. Similarly, comparatively wealthy citizens who feel that their economic status is very precarious—because they fear for their children's future, or because they can see a nearby neighborhood taking a turn for the worse—may be as likely to vote for populists as those who are already struggling to make ends meet. What matters, in other words, may be less economic reality than economic anxiety.

Analyzing Gallup survey data on the 2016 election comprising 125,000 American adults, Jonathan Rothwell and Pablo Diego-Rosell come to a similar conclusion. The most straightforward markers of economic well-being do not predict whether somebody voted for Trump or for Clinton. Whereas Americans who saw Trump favorably had a mean household income of nearly $82,000, for example, those who viewed him unfavorably had a household income of a little over $77,000. Similarly, Trump supporters are "less likely to be unemployed and less likely to be employed part-time" than other people in the sample.[13] In short, the popular media narrative according to which Trump primarily appealed to the poor and the lowly just doesn't hold up.

A lot of smart analysts have drawn a very straightforward conclusion from this complicated finding: economics, they claim, does not help to explain the rise of populism at all. "No, 'Economic Anxiety' Doesn't Explain Donald Trump," wrote the *New Republic*.[14] "'Economic anxieties' don't explain Donald Trump's victory," wrote MSNBC.[15] "Why I don't think it makes sense to attribute Trump's support to economic anxiety," *Vox* echoed.[16]

But when we turn our attention from the attributes of particular voters to the places in which they live and the fates they likely face, it becomes clear that economic factors do matter. For one, voters who favor Trump are much less likely to hold a college degree or to have a professional job—which implies that they have much better reason to fear that their economic fortunes might decline because of globalization and automation.[17] For another, these voters tend to

live in "communities with worse health outcomes, lower social mobility, less social capital [and a] greater reliance on social security
income"—which implies that they have much better reason to feel
that their town or region has been doing poorly.[18] In short,

> while Trump's supporters might be comparatively well off
> themselves, they come from places where their neighbors en-
> dure other forms of hardship. In their communities, white resi-
> dents are dying younger, and it is harder for young people who
> grow up poor to get ahead . . . Trump supporters might not be
> experiencing acute economic distress, but they are living in
> places that lack economic opportunity for the next generation.[19]

A number of other studies corroborate this basic finding. As Jed
Kolko demonstrates, for example, people who are engaged in highly
routinized, repetitive jobs—jobs, that is, which might more easily
be replaced by robots or shipped overseas—were much more likely
to vote for Trump.[20] A more subtle measure, like the degree to
which particular counties swung toward Trump in 2016 relative to
their support for Mitt Romney in the 2012 election, tells much the
same story. The swing toward Trump, Kolko shows, was much
stronger "where unemployment was higher, job growth was slower
and earnings were lower."

"Economic anxiety," he concludes, "is about the future, not just
the present."[21]

Ben Delsman comes to much the same conclusion by testing
whether regions in which a high percentage of jobs are subject to
automation are more susceptible to populists. His finding is stark:
twenty-one of the twenty-two states that are most prone to automation voted for Donald Trump; meanwhile, fifteen out of the fifteen states that are least prone voted for Hillary Clinton. On average, a one percentage point increase in a state's vulnerability to
automation was associated with a three point increase in Trump's
vote share.[22]

All of this suggests that the link between economic performance and political stability is rather more complicated than is often believed. It isn't necessarily the poorest members of society who turn against the political system; in part that's because they are most reliant on the benefits it provides them. Nor is it necessarily the people who have personally experienced economic calamity. Rather, it is the groups with the most to fear: those that are still living in material comfort but are deeply afraid that the future will be unkind to them.[23]

Their company may still be doing fine—but they have witnessed plenty of similar companies go bankrupt or replace a big part of their workforce. They may still be keeping up with their mortgage payments—but they have seen close-up how their neighbors were forced out of their homes when they fell behind on theirs. And their neighborhood may still be a pleasant place to live—but they are well aware that, just a mile or two down the road, slightly poorer neighborhoods have quickly deteriorated.

Since I've spent a fair bit of time speaking to supporters of populist parties in the course of my reporting, I'm far from surprised by this finding. "The economy is terrible," they would tell me. "Those politicians care more about foreigners than they do about us," they would add. "This country is going down the drain."

After hearing them out politely, I would gingerly inquire about their personal situation. "What, me?" they would ask with a smile. "Oh, I can't complain. Things are going pretty well."

Countries like the United States, Great Britain, or Italy remain incredibly affluent. Never in the history of mankind have societies been able to afford so many of their members such plenty. In a sense, the people who get to live this privilege should be counting their blessings.

But that is only one side of the coin. The other side is that these same countries can no longer offer their citizens a real sense of momentum. Though they remain affluent, their expectation of material improvement has been dashed—and they have good reason to fear that the future may bring even more bad tidings.

This raises some big, unanswered questions about our political age: What do liberal democracies need to do to extend their remarkable record of past stability? Is it enough for them to afford their citizens a decent life? Or do they need to be able to cash in on the old promise, implicitly issued in the long decades of rapidly growing plenty, that each generation will do much better than the one that came before?

Vexingly, there are no easy answers to these questions.

The history of extraordinary democratic stability still informs our political imagination, convincing us that liberal democracy must be here to stay. But throughout the period of democratic stability, two facts held true at the same time: stable democracies were very affluent, and most of their citizens enjoyed absolute income mobility. Just as Russell's chicken does not have the experience to understand the effect of weighing in at five rather than four pounds, we do not have historical precedent to help us predict the effect that affluence without growth might have on the political dynamics of liberal democracy.

6

Identity

DEMOCRACY PROMISES to let the people rule. But this immediately raises a deceptively simple question: Who, exactly, are the people?

For most of the history of democracy, the answer has been highly restrictive. It is often noted, for example, that women and slaves were never counted as full citizens in ancient Athens. But another form of exclusion—one that is more rarely discussed—may be just as revealing: immigrants and their descendants did not qualify for Athenian citizenship either.

In the first decades of Athens's existence, full membership in the polis was open only to those who "had sprung up from the earth," which is to say that they could trace their father's lineage back to the small number of people who had lived in the city at the time of its founding. Over time, as the city grew richer, the arts flourished, and more and more immigrants flocked to the Agora, the Athenian conception of the people grew even more narrow. And so it fell to Pericles, one of the most celebrated orators in the history of democracy, to propose a new citizenship law: henceforth, only those who had both an Athenian father and an Athenian mother could access the rights and duties of citizenship. Some of the most famous figures in Athenian history failed these strict criteria for citizenship, remaining "metics," or resident aliens. Neither Aristotle nor Diogenes, for example, were allowed to partake in governing the city.[1]

The Roman Republic was somewhat more generous than Athens had been. Freed slaves could become Romans. The children of mixed marriages had extensive rights. Eventually, the inhabitants of some allied states were given a form of citizenship. But even in comparatively permissive Rome, the laws of citizenship still served to create a strict hierarchy, with co-ethnics at the top and people seen as foreign at the bottom. While the inhabitants of ethnically similar territories in Latinia ascended to a nominal form of citizenship, for example, they lacked the right to vote or run for office for much of the republic's history. Meanwhile, the inhabitants of territories outside of Latinia were excluded from citizenship altogether.[2]

Only when the Roman Republic gave way to the Roman Empire—and the status of citizenship no longer carried the rights and responsibilities of self-government—did the rules of membership become more inclusive. In 212 AD, the Edict of Caracalla gave all free men, wherever in the Empire they might be residing, the same rights as Romans.[3] But by that time, those rights had lost much of their original meaning.

This points to an uncomfortable truth: It is comparatively easy for a king or an emperor to be generous in granting his subjects the equal status of citizenship; after all, in a monarchy, citizenship does not confer any actual power. It is much more difficult for a democracy or a self-governing republic to be generous in its rules for membership; after all, in a system that allows the people to rule, anybody who gains the status of citizen gets to have a say in the future of all of his compatriots. So might the fact that the Roman Empire adopted more generous rules of membership than the Roman Republic suggest that there is some kind of link between democracy and an exclusive notion of citizenship? Or, to put the question in even more stark terms, does the ideal of self-government make it more difficult for a diverse set of citizens to live alongside each other as equals?

Two thousand years of European history lend considerable support to this supposition.

The periods that are most celebrated for the peaceful co-existence of different ethnic and religious groups often took place under the watchful eyes of a powerful monarch. Both the Hapsburg Empire and the Ottoman Empire, for example, thrived in part because they drew on the industry and creativity of subjects who worshipped in a great variety of ways and spoke an even greater variety of languages.[4] By contrast, the nationalist fervor that began in the eighteenth and nineteenth centuries nearly always took the form of a hankering for ethnic purity as well as democracy.

This was most evident in nations that took on a political identity in rebellions against multiethnic empires. Czechs, Slovaks, and Hungarians, for example, felt aggrieved that they were being ruled by emperors who spoke a different language and did not take sufficient account of their local customs and concerns. The desire for collective self-rule and the desire for a collective life that would allow for their respective cultures to flourish thus went hand in hand.[5]

Though admirable in many ways, this cultural nationalism entailed an exclusionary element from the very start. In the pithy formulation of Leon Wieseltier, most European nations aspired to "a perfect union of ethnicity, territory, and state."[6] If Hungarians were to rule themselves, only true Hungarians could be allowed to participate in the nation's political life. The realization of Hungarian democracy thus necessitated that Austrians, Czechs, Slovaks, and Romanians be excluded.[7]

The same instinct also animated the liberal nationalists of Italy and Germany. The principles they embraced were, in many ways, noble: they sought to found self-governing nations that would grant citizens free speech and allow for religious dissent. But it was part and parcel of their enterprise to distinguish between those whom they considered "true" Germans or Italians (and sought to include in the states they were creating) and those whom they considered members of other nations (and sought to exclude).[8]

These exclusionary instincts only became stronger as nationalist fervor grew. By the late nineteenth century, new nations like Germany and Italy were pursuing heavy-handed policies to create a more homogeneous culture and to repress linguistic minorities.[9] In the 1920s and 1930s, as democracy struggled to gain a foothold in countries like Poland, Germany, and Spain, its internal enemies exploited anger against ethnic and religious minorities at every turn.[10] Finally, once fascists had seized power in much of Europe, their "co-ethnics" living across the border served as a ready excuse for war: the Third Reich's annexation of the Sudetenland, for example, was justified by the ill-treatment supposedly suffered by ethnic Germans living in Czechoslovakia.[11]

By the time the horrors of World War II had been unleashed and exhausted, much of the continent had been ethnically cleansed. For the first time in Europe's history, most states could boast of the perfect "union of ethnicity, territory, and state" to which they had long aspired. And it is only at this point that democracy triumphed across much of the continent.

There are many reasons why democracy in countries like Italy or Germany failed in the 1920s and 1930s and started to take firm root in the 1950s and the 1960s. But it hardly seems a coincidence that they had been reasonably heterogeneous when fascists pushed aside parliamentary institutions in the name of the people—and reasonably homogeneous by the time a large swath of the population was ready to embrace the norms and practices of liberal democracy.

Ethnic homogeneity not only contributed to the success of these new democracies; as importantly, it shaped how these democracies came to define themselves. In stark contrast to the multinational empires that had dominated European politics for the previous centuries, they were thoroughly monoethnic. To be a German or an Italian—or, for that matter, a Swede or a Dutchman—was to be descended from a particular ethnic stock.

There was, therefore, good reason all along to think that mass immigration might lead to strong tensions: throughout the history of democratic societies, citizens have always been wary of letting outsiders dilute their voice. But in contemporary Europe, which had long defined itself by its homogeneity and is now experiencing rapidly rising levels of economic anxiety, there is especially good reason to think that demographic transformation will not come easily. The question now is just how fundamental these tensions are—and whether they can be overcome.

The Rebellion against Pluralism

In historical perspective, the speed with which highly homogeneous nations have become heterogeneous since the end of World War II is remarkable. In Great Britain, for example, "the number of ethnic minority citizens [stood at] a few tens of thousands in the 1950s."[12] Today, there are over eight million.[13] The story is very similar in much of Western Europe. In Germany, the government tried to fuel its postwar economic miracle by advertising for unskilled laborers in Greece, Italy, and Turkey, welcoming the millionth "guest worker" to the country in 1964.[14] By 1968, the number of foreign citizens in the country was approaching two million. Today, about seventeen million immigrants and their descendants live in Germany.[15] In Italy, the jump is more recent, but has been just as rapid: In 2002, the country had a little over one million foreign residents. By 2011, it had a little over four million.[16]

Once mass immigration into societies that defined themselves by a shared culture and ethnicity began, the tension between theory and practice became increasingly explosive. And so it is perhaps unsurprising that political forces loudly opposed to immigration have rapidly gained support over the past decades.

Fears about immigration are now top of mind for voters across Europe. In 2016, for example, 71 percent of Danes, 67 percent of Hungarians, and 57 percent of Germans selected immigration as the most pressing political issue; in only one out of twenty-seven EU member states did voters not mention immigration as one of the top two concerns.[17] (In the United States, meanwhile, 70 percent of voters named immigration as very important to their vote in the 2016 election, up from 41 percent in 2012.)[18]

Nor can there be any doubt about the degree to which populist parties have made fears about immigration their main calling card. In Austria, the leader of the Freedom Party vowed that "Vienna must not turn into Istanbul."[19] In Germany, the AfD played on similar fears by promising "more children for German families."[20] Finally, in Denmark, the anti-immigrant sentiment of the People's Party was so blatant that their campaign slogan read, simply, "Du ved, hvad vi står for"—"You Know What We Stand For."[21]

What's more, there is a pretty tight electoral link between fears about immigration and populist success.[22] According to a host of studies, it is clear that attitudes about migration are one of the best predictors of an individual's voting intentions: negative views on immigrants and ethnic minorities are highly correlated with support for everything from Brexit to Marine Le Pen.[23]

At first sight, the United States does not seem to fit the European mold of democracies founded on a monoethnic footing. A former colony, it had thought of itself as a country of immigration since its founding. As a result, the idea that citizenship was defined by a willingness to swear allegiance to "the flag and the republic for which it stands" had been deeply ingrained from the start. Much more so than in Europe, it seems true—even obvious—to most Americans that somebody who is born in the United States is, quite simply, an American.[24]

Its history as an immigrant country better prepares the United States for the promise of multiethnic democracy. But though Americans have always been used to immigration—and actually retain a much more positive opinion of immigrants than the inhabitants of European nations—the levels of immigration they are currently experiencing are unusually high, even by the standards of their own history.[25]

In the late 1960s, only about one in twenty people living in the United States had been born abroad; today, one in seven has. The last time the share was so high, at the beginning of the twentieth century, nativist sentiment rapidly spread, leading to the adoption of highly restrictive laws on immigration.[26]

The rise of Latino and Muslim populations—prime targets of Donald Trump's ire—has been especially rapid. The foreign-born

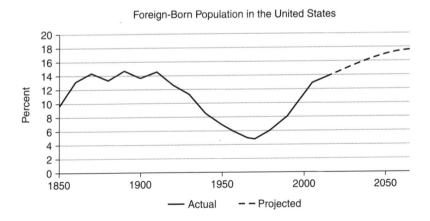

Foreign-Born Population in the United States

Latino population, for example, quadrupled between 1980 and 2008.[27] And while scholars have come to divergent conclusions about the total number of Muslims in the country, almost all agree that their numbers have also grown rapidly in the past decades, and predict that they will double again by 2050.[28]

As in Europe, far-right populists quickly exploited the rise of the foreign-born population. In the 1990s, Pat Buchanan's presidential bid was fueled by his claim that America will "become a Third World country . . . if we do not build a sea wall against the waves of immigration rolling over our shores."[29] And in 2016, Donald Trump ascended to the White House by taking the same rhetoric up another couple of notches, claiming that Mexico tended to "send" the United States "rapists and criminals."[30]

As in Europe, the rise of immigrant groups—and perhaps especially their growing cultural and political visibility—has polarized the political system along attitudes toward immigration.[31] People who believed that undocumented immigrants should be offered a chance to obtain legal status, for example, voted for Hillary Clinton by a margin of 60 percent to 34 percent. People who believed that they should be deported, by contrast, voted for Donald Trump by a margin of 84 percent to 14 percent.[32] A similarly clear pattern is apparent in broader levels of racial resentment: According to a whole slew of polls, answers to questions such as whether Barack Obama was born in the United States were highly predictive of an intention to vote for Donald Trump. According to one survey, conducted in December 2016, 82 percent of Clinton supporters but only 53 percent of Trump supporters did not believe that Obama was born in Kenya.[33]

To be sure, there really is a big difference between Europe and America: unlike their cousins across the Atlantic, Americans never indulged in the historical fantasy that all of their ancestors had once inhabited the same woods. And yet, for most of their history, the bulk of citizens who had full rights did share ethnic links in a larger sense: they were descended from Europe, and nearly all of them were Christian.

Similarly, it is true that there had always been inhabitants of the continent who are not white—including the native population, African slaves, Latin Americans along the border to Mexico, and eventually a significant number of Asian Americans. But while ethnic diversity has always been a feature of the American experience, ethnic equality has not been: for much of the country's history, many ethnic minority groups were openly repressed or even enslaved.

In other words, the history of Europe—and of most other developed democracies outside of North America—seemed to predestine democracies like Germany or Sweden for a rebellion against multiethnic democracy. The history of the United States, by contrast, seemed to predestine it for something subtly different: a rebellion against a multiethnic democracy that recognizes all individuals as truly equal.

The Geography of Resentment

So far the big picture. But just as the overall story seemed to get more murky as we started to look at detailed voting patterns in the case of the economy, so too the overall story seems to get more complicated the closer we look at the immigration story.

Here's the (apparent) rub: If a backlash against immigration—and perhaps the very idea of a multiethnic society—is so key to their appeal, then populists should be most successful among non-immigrant voters in areas with high immigration. Donald Trump should, in other words, be riding high among white voters in Chicago, Los Angeles, and New York City. Similarly, France's Marine Le Pen should be doing especially well in the less diverse parts of

Paris and Marseille. Finally, the Alternative for Germany should find its strongest support in parts of Berlin or Nordrhein-Westfalen.

But that is not happening. At all.

On the contrary, Donald Trump received 13 percent of the vote in Chicago, 17 percent of the vote in New York City, and 22 percent of the vote in Los Angeles. By contrast, he did extremely well in rural counties with few foreign-born residents: in Trinity County, California (foreign-born population: 3.4 percent), Trump received 48.6 percent of the vote; in Lewis County, New York (1.7 percent), he got 65 percent; finally, in Gallatin County, Illinois (0.3 percent), he got 72 percent.[34]

The same story holds true for most of Western Europe. In Germany, for example, the AfD celebrated its biggest success so far when, at the federal elections in September 2017, it topped all other political parties in Saxony—even though, at less than 4 percent, the state has one of the lowest foreign-born populations in the country.[35] Similarly, in the Nord-Pas-de-Calais-Picardie region of France, Marine Le Pen received 42 percent of the vote in a run-off election in December 2015, although only 5 percent of the local population is foreign-born.[36]

Countries outside North America and Western Europe further complicate the picture. After all, populists have been especially strong in Central European countries like Poland and Hungary. And yet, those countries have experienced very low levels of immigration over the past decades—and now remain far more homogeneous than their neighbors to the west.

Two equally stark trends thus seem to cut across one another. On the one hand, overall levels of immigration have rapidly risen, anti-immigrant messages are at the core of populist rhetoric, and people with higher levels of racial resentment tend to vote for populist parties in much greater numbers. On the other hand, populist parties do best in regions with few immigrants—and have found success even in some countries, like Poland or Hungary, where overall levels of immigration are very low. What can make sense of this apparent contradiction? If mass immigration is one of the major drivers for the success of the populists, why are they so much more successful in areas with relatively low immigration than they are in areas with relatively high immigration?

The idea that there's a big puzzle here rests on a deceptively simple assumption: if high levels of immigration help to explain the rise of populism, then support for populists should be especially strong among nonimmigrant voters in areas of high immigration. But it's far from clear that we should assume that. After all, there are many reasons why nonimmigrant voters in areas of high immigration might be especially tolerant.

To start off with, areas of high immigration tend to be clustered in big cities that attract a lot of young and educated residents with a taste for diversity: since people with liberal views about immigration are much more likely to move to New York City than to rural Iowa, it is not surprising that the residents of New York City have more liberal views about immigration than those of rural Iowa.[37]

What's more, a lot of studies suggest that regular contact with minority groups can decrease prejudice against them. As a long line of scholars from Gordon Allport to Thomas Pettigrew have shown, frequent contact between different ethnic groups can, under the right conditions, build trust and reduce mutual hostility. However, when highly homogeneous societies first encounter outsiders, contact can also exacerbate conflict—especially if politicians are trying to ratchet up tensions for their own purposes.[38]

This suggests that the most fundamental transition in the lives of most citizens might take place when they start having to deal with immigrants on a regular basis, not when the number of immigrants with whom they interact on a regular basis increases. People who live in areas with a high level of immigration are already used to the fact that their community is not "pure," and have built up a certain facility with people who do not share their language, culture, or ethnicity. While some of them may be dismayed when the share of the foreign-born population grows, or even become less willing to support a redistributive welfare state, such an increase does not fundamentally alter their world: whether they interact with two or four immigrants on a daily basis is ultimately a difference in degree rather than a difference in kind.[39]

But even as migration levels rose at a national level over the course of the postwar era, this description did not fit the experience of many more rural and remote areas. In a large number of communities in Western Europe, and even in North America, the level of immigration remained so low thirty or forty years ago that most of its inhabitants rarely encountered a newcomer. As a result, they had not built up the same facility in dealing with immigrants and remained more invested in a monoethnic understanding of their nation.

Today, these same areas might still record markedly lower levels of immigration than other parts of the country. But compared to their own past, they have changed radically—and passed a crucial threshold: As immigrants are starting to move to these areas in noticeable numbers, their erstwhile character is being challenged. The need to deal with people of different origin is becoming a feature of everyday life. In short, the social world of their residents has been markedly transformed even if overall levels of migration remain comparatively low.

Over the past years, a crop of new studies has given considerable support to this explanation for why the populist vote is clustered in areas like exurban Michigan rather than in Queens or downtown Los Angeles.

While researchers in the United States have long thought of big coastal cities as hot spots of immigration, it is in more remote, less densely populated counties that the most striking demographic revolution has taken place over the past decades. Back in 1980, for example, about two-thirds of all American communities were highly homogeneous, with whites making up over 90 percent of all residents. As immigration accelerated over the following three decades, a lot of these places quickly became more heterogeneous. By 2010, only about one-third of American communities were 90 percent white.[40]

A host of both academic and anecdotal evidence makes clear that this transformation instigated a lot of resentment. "We were hit like a tsunami," an elementary school principal in Arcadia, a county in Wisconsin that experienced an especially rapid demographic transformation, told a reporter. "If you'd seen the way things have changed in this town," another local resident confirmed, "you'd say, 'Something needs to be done about it.'"[41]

That something often turned out to be Donald Trump.

Many election analyses suggest that the main reason for Trump's victory was that a large number of white working-class voters who had traditionally voted for Democrats threw their support behind him.[42] So it is especially significant that a lot of these voters were located in Midwestern regions that had gone from highly homogeneous to reasonably heterogeneous over the past decades. As an analysis in the *Wall Street Journal* showed, "a distinct cluster of Midwestern states—Iowa, Indiana, Wisconsin, Illinois and Minnesota—saw among the fastest influxes of nonwhite residents of anywhere in the U.S. between 2000 and 2015. Hundreds of cities long dominated by white residents got a burst of Latino newcomers who migrated from Central America or uprooted from California and Texas." The impact this demographic shift had on voting patterns was unambiguous. In the primaries, for example, Trump won 71 percent of counties across the United States. But he won 73 percent of counties whose "diversity index" had doubled from 2000 to

2015, and 80 percent of counties whose diversity index had risen by 150 percent.[43]

Demographic Anxiety

There's another aspect to all of this: A lot of the anger at immigration is driven by fear of an imagined future rather than by displeasure with a lived reality. When immigration levels rise, it is not only the experience of day-to-day life that changes; just as importantly, the social imaginary of what the country's future might hold is transformed as well. As a result, the belief that people from the majority group will eventually be in the minority has come to play a bigger and bigger role in the political imagination of the far right both in Western Europe and in North America.[44]

In the United States, for example, Steve King, a Republican member of Congress from Iowa, recently tweeted that "demographics are our destiny. We can't restore our civilization with somebody else's babies."[45] (Not coincidentally, King represents a district that has gone through exactly the kind of demographic shift I just described, experiencing a 24 percent increase in the number of foreign-born residents between 2009 and 2015 alone.)[46] Michael Anton, now a senior foreign policy advisor in the White House, made the case for Donald Trump in even starker terms in an essay he published under a pseudonym during the run-up to the 2016 election. Worried by the "ceaseless importation of Third World foreigners," and invoking one of the planes hijacked by al-Qaida terrorists on 9/11, he argued that

> 2016 is the Flight 93 election: charge the cockpit or you die. You may die anyway. You—or the leader of your party—may make it into the cockpit and not know how to fly or land the plane. There are no guarantees. Except one: if you don't try, death is certain.[47]

These fears aren't just a matter of elite discourse; they also determine how ordinary citizens vote. According to a Pew Research Center poll taken in April 2016, in the middle of that year's primary battle, for example, about a third of Republicans thought that it would be "bad for the country" if America became majority nonwhite. Among those who shared those demographic fears, Donald Trump trounced the competition: 63 percent reported having warm feelings about him, compared to 26 percent who had cool feelings about him. Among people who did not share the same demographic fear, by contrast, Trump was seen much less positively: 46 percent reported liking him, with 40 percent disliking him.[48]

Politicians in Western Europe are just as concerned by the coming demographic transition—and just as adept at exploiting fears about it. *Germany Is Abolishing Itself,* published in 2010 and one of the bestselling books of Germany's postwar history, for example, is animated by the fear that ethnic Germans will one day cease to be a majority in their own country. (The problem is especially acute, Thilo Sarrazin, the book's author, mused, because Germans are genetically predisposed to be more intelligent than Turks.)[49] But it was a few years later, as the Syrian civil war brought millions of refugees to Western Europe, that demographic fears came to be at the center of the political discourse there.

Strikingly, the fear that native populations might cease to be in the majority is just as strong in countries where, at first glance, there appears to be little objective reason to think that this might happen anytime soon. Throughout much of Central and Eastern Europe, for example, the portion of the population that was born outside the continent is very small. And yet, fears of an impending "invasion" by ethnic and religious minorities are a prominent part of the political landscape. In Poland, Jarosław Kaczynski has repeatedly warned that immigrants could bring "parasites . . . and diseases" to the country—and stated that Muslim refugees would "threaten Poland's security."[50] Going beyond mere rhetoric, the Polish government has also passed legislation that legalizes detaining foreign nationals without court approval and shut down the Council against Racial Discrimination, Xenophobia, and Intolerance.[51] Meanwhile, in Hungary, Viktor Orbán has built a massive border fence and hired 3,000 "border hunters."[52]

The prominence of fears about migration in Estonia is even more striking. As Turkuler Isiksel points out,

> Non-European migrants in Estonia add up to 1.1% of the total population. According to one source, the total number of Africans counted in the 2011 Estonian census (which bizarrely included African-Americans) was 31. Estonia's population growth has been negative for a long time: birthrate is lower than replacement, and emigration outstrips immigration. And yet, in the May 2016 Eurobarometer survey, 73% of Estonians mentioned immigration as one of the two most important issues facing the European Union. The second, according to 46% of Estonians surveyed, was terrorism.[53]

Part of what explains this disjuncture is, quite simply, a systemic overestimation of the share of the minority—and especially the Muslim—population. This holds true in virtually all liberal democracies today. In the United States, people think that 17 percent of the population is Muslim; according to the best available estimates, it is around one percent. In France, people believe 31 percent of the population to be Muslim; the true share is 8 percent.[54]

But while these demographic fears are vastly overstated, they may, as Ivan Krastev has argued, not be as absurd as they first appear. Noting that "nations and states have the habit of disappearing in the recent history of Eastern and Central Europe," Krastev points out that the residents of Central and Eastern European countries—and indeed of rural areas in Western Europe—are keenly aware that they are rapidly losing in population; that mass immigration is frequently advocated as the only possible solution to this problem; and that migration has already transformed other parts of their continent. "In the last twenty-five years," he notes,

> around 10 percent of Bulgarians have left the country in order to live and work abroad. According to United Nations projections, Bulgaria's population is expected to shrink by 27 percent by 2050. Alarm over "ethnic disappearance" can be felt in many of the small nations of Eastern Europe. For them the arrival of migrants signals their exit from history, and the popular argument that an aging Europe needs migrants only strengthens the growing sense of existential melancholy.[55]

There is a negative way of interpreting these findings: Perhaps regions that have long been monoethnic lack the local conditions for accommodating immigration. Because they have little history of welcoming newcomers and limited facility for confronting otherness, they respond much more negatively to increases in the overall level of immigration than do the residents of areas that have a long history of immigration. In that case, there might prove to be a relatively straightforward relationship between the rise of the foreign-born population and the vote share of populist parties. As one paper suggests with the peculiar confidence of researchers who have stared at their spreadsheets for too long, "as the percentage of immigrants approaches approximately 22%, the percentage of [right-wing] populist voters exceeds 50%."[56]

But there is also a more hopeful interpretation: Perhaps the effects of the first waves of immigration into a particular area are much more negative than the effects of later waves. Once areas grow accustomed to the reality of a multiethnic society, they may find that their fears do not materialize—and that they become less anxious about a continuing process of change.

The experience of California seems to suggest that this more optimistic interpretation holds true in some places: From 1980 to 1990, the overall share of the foreign-born population rose from 15 percent to 22 percent. A great wave of anxiety washed over the state. Many native-born Californians were disoriented by the rapid pace of change, and grew furious that politicians were willing to accommodate the cultures and the languages of immigrants. The backlash soon took political form. Californians gave a big victory to a governor who staked his reelection campaign on strident anti-immigration rhetoric. Taking advantage of the state's highly democratic constitution, which allows for popular referenda on a large range of issues, they then excluded undocumented immigrants from public benefits; forbade public universities from practicing affirmative action; and banned bilingual education in schools.[57]

At the time, observers were understandably worried about the future of race relations in California. But in the 2000s and 2010s, the fever somehow broke. Most Californians grew comfortable with the fact that high levels of immigration were a part of the local experience, and that the state had become "majority minority." As a result, the state is now known as one of the most tolerant in the country. Over the past years, Californians have reversed many of the draconian laws they had passed by referendum two decades earlier with strong support from white voters. And with its political leaders openly critical of President Trump's immigration policy, the state has fast-tracked a slew of pro-immigrant bills since his election.[58]

Descending the Hierarchy

According to Abraham Maslow, humans operate according to a hierarchy of needs. At the most basic and urgent, they desire the goods that are key to their survival, including food, shelter, and safety from physical attack. When these basic needs are met, they pay increasing attention to more rarefied desires: They seek love and belonging. They aspire to be esteemed. And they search for ways in which they can achieve what Maslow called "self-actualization."[59]

Influential social scientists like Ronald Inglehart have derived a very optimistic vision from this basic conceptual framework. Back when most societies suffered from acute scarcity and violent conflict posed a constant threat, Inglehart argued in the 1970s, the main political cleavages were determined by the lower rungs of Maslow's hierarchy. The need to procure food and shelter meant that politics was largely organized along class lines, with poorer voters likely to support parties that championed the welfare state and called for redistribution, and more affluent voters likely to support parties that sought to protect their wealth. Meanwhile, the salience of fears about security meant that moral, ethnic, and national boundaries were enforced very strictly: most voters were fiercely loyal to their in-group, and adopted harsh attitudes toward "deviants," ethnic and religious minorities, and members of other nations.

But as democratic societies became more affluent and peaceful, a much greater share of human beings could start to take basic physiological and safety needs for granted—and pay increased attention to the higher rungs of Maslow's hierarchy. This, Inglehart predicted, would have a big impact on citizens' social and political attitudes. No longer worried about physical subsistence, they could focus on social issues like the environment, freedom of speech, or the fate of poor people around the world. And no longer faced with security threats, they would adopt much more tolerant attitudes toward ethnic, religious, and sexual minorities.[60]

Inglehart's insights helped to predict important political transformations, prefiguring the rise of socially liberal parties and making sense of a general rise in cultural tolerance. But just as most scholars studying liberal democracy were too quick to assume that democratic consolidation would prove to be a one-way street, so Inglehart was too quick to assume that the trend toward postmaterialist values would continue indefinitely. As a result, he did not foresee that rising immigration, coupled with a deep, sustained stagnation of living standards, might be enough to reverse the "postmaterialist turn."

When economic growth is rapid, everybody can be a winner. The rich and the poor may have competing interests. But the distributive fight is about a vast economic surplus. The question is not whether somebody might lose something; it is just how much they will gain.

When economic growth is slow, by contrast, the competition over resources becomes much more unforgiving. For the wealth of the rich to keep rising, they have to take something away from the poor. "It is zero sum," Angus Deaton, winner of the Nobel Prize in Economics, explained in a recent interview. "If you have two or three percent of growth a year, there's not a lot of goodies to be given away without goring someone's ox."[61]

The resulting transformation is psychological as well as economic. As growth has stalled, inequality has grown, and anxiety has increased, a large portion of the population has become less focused on the value of self-actualization. Instead, voters are once again turning their attention to the lower rungs of Maslow's hierarchy of needs. Worried about their sustenance, whites have grown more resentful of the immigrants and ethnic minorities that make a claim on collective resources. And threatened by the seemingly uncontrollable forces of globalization and terrorism, they are reverting to less tolerant views toward ethnic and religious minorities.

A few decades ago, Inglehart predicted that the rise of postmaterialist values would prefigure a new politics: voters seeking to actualize the self, he theorized, might vote for Green parties that worry about the environment and development aid rather than for Social Democratic parties that promise to raise their wages. In a similar vein, there is now good reason to think that the return of materialist values will have just as big an impact on our politics:

voters worried about their safety and sustenance may be much more open to the appeal of populists who offer easy economic solutions and blame outsiders for all of our problems. If populism has been so successful of late, a big part of the reason seems to be that longstanding social and economic trends have combined to bring about the rise of post-post-materialist voters.[62]

There are, I have argued, three main ways in which the politically unstable world of today is fundamentally different from the politically stable world of yesteryear: Once upon a time, liberal democracies could assure their citizens of a very rapid increase in their living standards. Now, they no longer can. Once upon a time, political elites controlled the most important means of communication, and could effectively exclude radical views from the public sphere. Now, political outsiders can spread lies and hatred with abandon. And once upon a time, the homogeneity of their citizens—or at least a steep racial hierarchy—was a big part of what held liberal democracies together. Now, citizens have to learn how to live in a much more equal and diverse democracy.

Each of these problems points the way to an urgent and daunting challenge. Meeting any of these challenges is going to be extremely difficult. Meeting all three at once may turn out to be impossible. And yet, we have to try, for the fate of liberal democracy may depend on it.

PART THREE

REMEDIES

WHEN THE "QUEEN OF ELECTIONS" ascended to the highest office in the land, a lot of her countrymen were worried that she might pose a threat to democracy in South Korea.

Park Geun-hye had always been a controversial figure. The daughter of a general who had ruled the country for a dozen years as the head of a military junta, she was fond of populist rhetoric and advocated for a tough line on law and order. For a long time, her countrymen—who had fought hard to shake military rule and establish one of the most stable democracies in Asia—mistrusted her intentions. But Park was a talented campaigner and an inspiring orator. Her promise to weaken the power of the country's major companies, known as the *chaebols*, made her highly popular. After years in the political wilderness, she proved her mettle in a string of surprise victories and slowly staged a hostile takeover of the country's biggest right-wing party.

By 2012, she had reached her goal: A landslide victory installed her in the Blue House, the country's presidential residence. Her allies enjoyed a comfortable majority in Parliament. Finally, she was in a position to transform the country.

But in the end, it wasn't Park's feared authoritarian instincts that led to a big backlash against her presidency; it was her close relationship—as close as that of her predecessors—with the country's business elites. A couple of years into her reign, accusations began to surface that the president had used the power of her office to do favors for Choi Soon-il, her friend, closest aide, and spiritual advisor. Using her access to Park, Choi had apparently extracted millions of dollars' worth of donations from the *chaebols* for charities she controlled. Choi had gotten Samsung to give her daughter, an aspiring equestrian, an expensive horse. And, worst sin of all in a country with a highly competitive educational system, Choi had used her connections to get her daughter admitted to an elite university.

When the scandal first broke, the Queen of Elections clearly intended to sit it out in the Blue House. Her allies in Parliament pledged their political support. Like many corrupt presidents before her, Park seemed likely to weather the storm.

Then the protests started. In early November 2016, about a hundred thousand people took to the streets of Seoul to ask for her resignation. By the middle of the month, about a million were calling on her to step down. By the end of the month, the crowd had swelled to form the biggest demonstration in the history of South Korea: nearly two million people gathered in Seoul Plaza to demand her impeachment.

Brazen as ever, Park refused to resign. But—confronted with her nosediving approval ratings and months of mass protests—her allies slowly inched away from her. With the support of sixty-two members of her own party, the Parliament passed a motion of impeachment. When it was upheld by the Constitutional Court, Park was finally removed from office and charged with crimes ranging from bribery to abuse of power.[1]

The successful effort to remove Park from office can serve as inspiration to defenders of liberal democracy around the world:

To stop corrupt or populist governments from entrenching their power, citizens have to uncover violations of democratic rules and norms. They have to take to the streets to show that the populists don't speak in the name of the whole people. And, no matter how righteous their disdain for the allies and flunkies of authoritarian strongmen may be, they need to do their best to peel off some members of the ruling regime.

But to stop populists from regaining power in the future and save the system in the long run, its defenders also have to do something more ambitious: they must ensure that liberal democracy once again lives up to the expectations of its citizens.

Over the past years, the Turkish government has arrested so many journalists, fired so many civil servants, and abolished so many institutional safeguards that the country is quickly turning into a straightforward dictatorship. Since taking office in 2015, the Polish government has undermined judicial independence, co-opted the state media, and colonized the bureaucracy to such an extent that the electoral playing field is increasingly skewed against the opposition. Even in the United States, where the existence of multiple veto points at both the state and the federal level has slowed the erosion of liberal institutions, the executive branch has made significant strides toward subverting the rule of law.[2]

In countries such as these, where authoritarian strongmen have already won power and are systematically starting to change the most basic rules of the game, liberal democracy faces an imminent threat to its survival. What can its would-be defenders do to stop the populists from making further power grabs?

It is rarely easy for the opposition to constrain the actions of a determined government. But when the government consists of authoritarian populists who are disdainful of traditional constraints on their power and desperate to bend the system to their will, resistance is that much harder: Like in South Korea, it involves coming out into the streets to protest dangerous laws and executive orders. It involves ringing hostile legislators to voice opposition to the causes they support. It involves plenty of meetings, complicated logistics, incessant fundraising, and any number of boring tasks that can seem strangely disconnected from the noble purpose they supposedly serve.

"Freedom," the title of a book by Francesca Polletta suggests, "is an endless meeting." The preservation of freedom, it can seem in moments of great political peril, calls for an endless series of endless meetings.[3]

But while the work of resistance is undoubtedly cumbersome, most political scientists do believe that it makes life difficult for populist governments: The painstaking work of opposition can call attention to unpopular policies; slow the progress of pending legislation; embolden judges to strike down unconstitutional laws; provide support to embattled media outlets; change the calculus for moderates within the regime; and force international governments and organizations to put pressure on a would-be dictator.[4]

Plenty of recent cases showcase such successes: In Poland, mass protests may have helped push the country's president to veto a proposed legislative reform, which would have given Kaczynski's party an even tighter grip over the judiciary.[5] In Hungary, mass protests may have helped convince Orbán to allow Central European University to keep operating even after he passed a law to shutter it.[6] And in the United States, mass protests may have helped embolden judges opposed to the administration's travel ban.[7]

The first part of the solution to the threat of populism is as straightforward as it is cumbersome, then: Even when they are faced with powerful adversaries, and even when it feels like wasted time, the defenders of liberal democracy should fight to preserve the basic rules and norms of the existing political system. Whenever a populist ruler oversteps the bounds of his rightful authority, they must pour into the streets—loudly and in large numbers.

Even when the reasons for protest proliferate, and acts of opposition come to feel dishearteningly ineffective, it's very important for the defenders of liberal democracy to resist authoritarian strongmen with courage and determination. But since anyone who seeks to constrain the populists faces a decidedly uphill struggle once the strongmen have taken office, it is even more important to beat them at the polls.

This is obviously true in countries where the populists have not yet won. In Sweden or France, in Austria or Spain, citizens retain the power to ensure that candidates with evident disdain for the rules of the democratic game do not get a chance to put their predilections into practice. It is paramount that they use it. But even in countries in which the populists are already in office, elections remain crucial. Since it usually takes years for authoritarian strongmen to consolidate their power, a lot hinges on the electoral savvy of the opposition.

Five years into the rule of Recep Erdoğan, Vladimir Putin, and Hugo Chávez, many outside observers still believed that they were strengthening democratic institutions in their countries. All three made encouraging noises about the value of political openness and the importance of breaking with an authoritarian past. And though each of them did skew the playing field in his own favor by the time he first ran for reelection, the opposition still retained a real chance of winning. It wasn't until these strongmen gained a second or even a third victory at the polls that they completed their countries' descent toward outright dictatorship.[8]

This demonstrates how high the stakes will be when authoritarian populists like Jarosław Kaczynski, Narendra Modi, and Donald

Trump first come up for reelection in the coming years. If they are soundly defeated, liberal democracy is—at least in the short run—likely to recover in Poland, India, and the United States. If they manage to win another mandate, all bets are off; given enough time and power, each of these leaders is likely to damage democracy in grave and lasting ways.

The only democratic protection from the assault of authoritarian strongmen, then, is to persuade the people to vote against them. But the most active members of the resistance are often surprisingly uninterested in helping opposition parties win. In Poland, for example, the influential Committee to Protect Democracy explicitly eschews any involvement in electoral politics. Similarly, in the United States, many members of #TheResistance are so hostile to the Democratic party that they do not see it as a priority to help the opposition win back Congress in 2018 or take the White House in 2020.

Even in circumstances where opposition parties are deeply flawed, this is the wrong approach. In the end, the only safe bulwark against the populists is to keep them far from the halls of power. Though it may be unfashionable for activists to campaign for a mainstream party, joining a political movement that has a real hope of success at the polls remains one of the best ways to stand up for democracy.

Opposition parties desperately need the infusion of energy and enthusiasm that activists could give them. But they also need a forward-looking strategy that helps them win the next election—and sets them up to implement meaningful improvements once they form the government. So what exactly does it take to beat a populist at the polls?

Electoral systems and partisan cleavages, political styles and personal values differ from country to country, and even from region to region. It would be absurd to go in search of a single winning recipe. And yet, there have now been enough cases in which defenders of democratic norms have faced authoritarian populists for us to draw a few straightforward conclusions.

The first lesson is the great importance of unity. In virtually every case in which populists have taken power or been reelected, deep divisions within the ranks of their opponents have played a large role.

In Poland, for example, the electoral system requires coalitions to gain at least 8 percent and parties at least 5 percent of the national vote to enter Parliament. This made it especially important for various leftist groupings to come to an understanding before the 2015 elections. Since they failed to do so, the United Left Coalition received 7.5 percent and the Together Party 3.6 percent of the vote. Meanwhile, a libertarian party, KORWiN, got 4.8 percent. The votes of all three were discounted. And so, despite winning only 38 percent of the vote, Kaczynski's Law and Justice Party took over half the seats in the parliament.[9]

Poland is not the only case in which the opposition has been its own worst enemy. In the past years, a divided opposition has also helped populists gain or keep power in Hungary and Turkey, in India and the United States.[10]

The second lesson is the great importance of speaking the language of ordinary people and connecting to voters' concerns. During the 2016 election campaign, a friend of mine was full of glee when she heard that Donald Trump had admitted that he "love[s] the uneducated." "Finally," she told me, "we'll have two political parties in the United States: one for people who went to college, and one for everybody else."[11] Leaving the dystopian nature of such a divide aside for a moment, I gingerly pointed out that only about a third of Americans have a four-year college degree; if "the good side" only represents people who are, by her definition, educated, it will lose every time.

In Venezuela, the opposition has long made the same mistake. "We wouldn't stop pontificating about how stupid Chavismo was," the economist Andrés Miguel Rondón has warned. "'Really, this guy? Are you nuts? You must be nuts,' we'd say. The subtext was clear: Look, idiots—he will destroy the country." According to Rondón, it took the opposition a full decade to change tack. Its fortunes started to improve only once they went "to the slums and the countryside. Not for a speech or a rally, but for a game of dominoes or to dance salsa—to show they were Venezuelans, too, that they weren't just dour scolds and could hit a baseball, could tell a joke that landed."[12]

The pitfalls of this approach are obvious: It would be easy to use the need to speak the language of ordinary people—or to tell a joke that really lands—as an excuse for emulating the divisive rhetoric of the populists. But there is a big difference between eschewing the preferred locutions of highly educated elites, on the one hand, and abandoning the core values of liberal democracy, on the other hand. As Rondón points out, the willingness to couch a principled message in relatable language "is not populism by other means. It is the only way of establishing your standing. It's deciding not to live in an echo chamber."[13]

The third lesson is the great importance of focusing on a positive message rather than obsessively recounting the failings of the populists. As Luigi Zingales, an Italian economist, warned American readers a few days after the American election, Silvio Berlusconi was so successful in Italy in part because the opposition "was so rabidly obsessed with his personality that any substantive political debate disappeared; it focused only on personal attacks, the effect of which was to increase Mr. Berlusconi's popularity."[14]

Many candidates understandably find it difficult to follow Zingales's advice. Faced with the sheer destruction that populists (threaten to) wreak, any honorable politician will be tempted to give free rein to their righteous anger. When this is done in moderation, it can serve a good purpose: a passionate disavowal of the populists can read as authentic, rally the populists' most principled enemies, and start to rebuild support for democratic norms. And yet, it is also important to remember that many voters are likely to find the promises populists make seductive, and perhaps even to believe their boasts. To rival the narrative according to which only they can fix the nation's problems, defenders of liberal democracy have to put forward realistic promises of their own.

This is related to the final, and perhaps the most important lesson: the defenders of liberal democracy will not vanquish the populists as long as they seem to be wedded to the status quo. When Donald Trump ran against Hillary Clinton in 2016, the political fronts were as clear as they could be. On one side, there was a radical candidate who wanted to bring about change: talking about "American carnage," Trump lamented "rusted out factories scattered like tombstones across the landscape of our nation . . . and the crime and the gangs and the drugs that have stolen too many lives and robbed our country of so much unrealized potential."[15] The solution, Trump made clear, was a radical shake-up. "I ask you this," he shouted at a campaign rally in Akron, Ohio, in front of a largely white audience, "to the African Americans, . . . to the Hispanics, tremendous people: What the hell do you have to lose? Give me a chance. I'll straighten it out. I'll straighten it out. What do you have to lose?"[16]

On the other side, there was a moderate candidate who gave the impression of wanting to preserve the status quo. We are, Clinton responded to Trump with characteristic blandness, "Stronger Together."[17] "America," both she and Barack Obama insisted, over and over, "is already great."[18]

My point is not that Clinton should have pandered to the populist penchant for extreme positions or simplistic solutions: though both the far left and the far right feel emboldened at the moment, most voters in both North America and Western Europe still hold moderate views on most issues. Rather, it is that Clinton needed to convince voters that she was passionate about changing the status quo: across the board, voters are deeply dissatisfied with the way things are going. According to one recent poll, for example, about half of the electorate in France, Germany, and Great Britain would like their government to move to the political center. But far more—about two in three in Germany and the United Kingdom, and about nine in ten in France—say that they prefer a politics of change to a politics of continuity.[19]

The upshot is clear: To avoid the mistake Clinton made in 2016, defenders of liberal democracy must demonstrate that they take the problems voters face seriously, and seek to effect real change. While they don't need to emulate the simplistic solutions or pander to the worst values of the populists, they urgently need to develop a bold plan for a better future.

There are deep reasons why populists have, over the past decades, celebrated such immense successes across North America, Western Europe, and beyond. Though pundits sometimes like to focus on local factors, their triumphs aren't primarily explained by the peculiarities of particular countries, or even the (lacking) political acumen of particular candidates. Rather, a number of structural transformations have weakened citizens' commitments to longstanding political norms: In many countries, the living standards of ordinary people have been stagnating. The transition from monoethnic to multiethnic democracy has proved more difficult than expected. The rise of social media has given greater power to political outsiders.

These changes have not yet transformed our societies so radically that sensible politicians are unable to win the trust of their citizens on a case-by-case basis. In the short run, charismatic candidates heeding the basic electoral lessons of the past years can still earn resounding victories.[20]

And yet, it is now clear that, in a shockingly wide range of countries, the changes of recent decades have put the populists within striking distance of the seat of power. In the long run, it will thus take something more than a well-run campaign to put liberal democracy on a secure footing. If we don't want every downturn in the business cycle or every blunder by a mainstream candidate to pose an existential threat to liberal democracy, we need to address the structural drivers of populist support.

To save democracy, we need, in other words, to unite citizens around a common conception of their nation; to give them real hope for their economic future; and to make them more resistant to the lies and the hate they encounter on social media each and every day. It is these immense challenges that will define our fight against populism, and for a better society, in the decades to come.[21]

7

Domesticating Nationalism

THERE IS NOTHING NATURAL about the idea of the nation. For most
of recorded history, humans have organized in families, tribes, cities, principalities, or religious communities. Even in the wake of the
American and the French revolutions, when the nation became a
powerful driver of history, it largely remained a project of elites. At
the height of the nationalist fervor that culminated in the country's
unification, for example, the writer Maxime du Camp looked on as
throngs of people shouted "Long Live Italy!" in the streets of Na-
ples. A moment later, some of them approached the erudite-looking
gentleman to "ask him what Italy was and what it meant."[1]

My family knows the arbitrariness of nations—and the destructive force of nationalism—more intimately than most. When my
grandfather Leon was born in a small *shtetl* close to Lviv in 1913, it
belonged to the Hapsburg Empire. Over the century since, it has
appertained to Poland, to the Soviet Union, and to Ukraine.

My grandfather's journey through the twentieth century was no
less complicated than that of his native town. He survived the Holocaust in Siberia, spent the prime decades of his life in Poland, and
finally found refuge in (of all places) Germany. Today, he lies bur-
ied in a small city in southern Sweden.[2]

It is hardly surprising, then, that I have long hoped to leave the forces of nationalism behind in the century they so cruelly shaped. When I left my native Germany to go to university in England at the turn of the millennium, I thought the way to move on from war and destruction, from ethnic hatred and religious intolerance, was to unite people around other forms of identity—or perhaps to dispense with the need for a collective form of belonging altogether.

People might define themselves as artists or as footballers, as thinkers or as doers. They could identify as residents of their cities, as citizens of Europe, or as inheritors of the earth. Most simple of all, they could just be themselves. Since the cultural differences between Germany and England, and between Italy and France, were pretty small—a mere matter of the language they spoke, or the dishes they ate—this transformation didn't seem too difficult to imagine.

My biography undoubtedly predisposed me to those utopian hopes. But my aspirations were also part of a much broader political and intellectual trend.

It is easy now to forget that the European Union was, until recently, being hailed as a model for a new form of political organization. In a rapidly globalizing world facing increasingly complex policy challenges, the comparatively small nations of Western Europe had good reason to pool their resources. And since the political leaders who dominated the conversation across the continent were largely united in their aspiration for a more integrated Europe, it was easy to believe that their voters would eventually follow suit.[3]

Countries in the periphery of the European Union, which had once been fervently nationalist, seemed keen to join the club. Meanwhile, countries in Africa, Latin America, and beyond built regional blocs of their own.[4] A slew of influential thinkers began to argue that the EU might just represent the future of world politics.[5]

The well-founded concern about Europe's hypernationalist past thus dovetailed neatly with an idealistic wish for a supranational future. Many political scientists believed that nationalism "is bound, as development advances, to outgrow its utility and become marginal or even . . . vanish altogether."[6] As the Georgian writer Ghia Nodia points out, this assumption was deeply comforting: the prediction that nationalism was bound to pass made "for a happy congruence between normative and theoretical views."[7]

After a few months of living in England, I began to recognize that the differences between British and German culture were much deeper than I had imagined. They were also more wide-ranging. Far from being confined to food or language, they extended to humor and temperament, to personal outlook and collective values.

After college, when I spent more time in Italy, and then in France, I came to the same conclusion all over again. The residents of various European countries were much more attached to their national cultures, and much more resistant to thinking of themselves primarily as Europeans, than I had wanted to believe.

If my own experiences slowly made me more skeptical of the viability of a postnational future, so too did the rapid political transformations of the past decades: Across the globe, nationalism is resurgent. Supranational ideals appear to be in retreat.

Throughout the postwar era, EU member states had given more power to Brussels, with most of their governments rarely or never consulting their own people on the decision.[8] So when citizens in a number of European countries were given an opportunity to cast their votes on the extent of European integration in the early 2000s, the degree of their opposition stunned the political class. In quick succession, the French, the Dutch, and the Irish voted against proposed moves toward further integration.[9]

Soon after, this crisis of public opinion was exacerbated by a deep crisis of European institutions. In the wake of the 2008 financial crisis, countries in southern Europe were on the brink of bankruptcy. But because they were members of the Eurozone, they could neither devalue their currency nor default on their debts. The economy shrank for the better part of a decade. Unemployment rates rose sharply.[10] It increasingly became apparent that some of the EU's most important institutions were not sustainable in their current form. To avoid a rerun of the euro crisis when the next recession hits, the continent must either dismantle the single currency or take a big, unpopular step toward further political integration.[11] Neither option seems especially palatable. Even before the British electorate voted to strike out on its own, the EU faced the deepest crisis since its founding.

If the EU attempts ambitious reforms, it might well resolve some of its problems. Prognostications of its certain doom are likely exaggerated. But the longstanding hope that regional blocs like the EU might one day eclipse the political, cultural, or emotional primacy of the nation now seems strangely anachronistic. Even on the continent that seemed most open to dreams of a postnational future, the primacy of the nation state has come roaring back.

The resurgence of nationalism has been even more pronounced outside the EU. In Central and Eastern Europe, populist governments have successfully enlisted a jealous, suspicious, xenophobic nationalism against liberal democracy. Turkey is rapidly descending into outright dictatorship under the leadership of a strongman who has fused nationalism and Islamism. Even countries like India and China—which will help to determine the future of the world order and might have been expected to experiment with postnational arrangements due to their immense size—are in the throes of a nationalist revival.[12]

Back in 2000, a little imagination was enough to dream up a postnational future. It seemed reasonable both to wish for nationalism to leave the stage of history and to believe that, obligingly, it would. In light of the past decades, this "assumption of happy congruence," as Nodia calls it, seems less and less tenable.[13] Perhaps hopes of a postnational future will return by 2036 or 2054. But as I'm writing these lines, such a future seems deeply implausible.

For better or (quite possibly) worse, nationalism seems destined to remain in the twenty-first century what it was in the nineteenth and the twentieth centuries: the most defining political force of its time.[14] A lot thus turns on the shape it is going to take. Will political entrepreneurs repress ethnic and religious minorities, fan jingoistic sentiments to quash free institutions, and rile up the people of different countries against each other? Or can the nationalism of the twenty-first century make room for ethnic and religious diversity and sustain vibrant democracies?

The Resurgence of Exclusionary Nationalism

Unlike most European nations, the United States did not have a common history, ethnicity, or religious denomination to build upon at its founding. The idea of America has always been a political one. As the most defining invocation of "We, the People" holds, the original goals of the American republic were "to form a more perfect Union, establish Justice, insure domestic Tranquility, provide for the common defense, promote the general Welfare, and secure the Blessings of Liberty to ourselves and our Posterity."[15] Anybody who obtains US citizenship and is willing to pledge support to these common goals is supposedly able to gain admission to this collective "we." It is this open understanding of membership—not the mere fact that a lot of newcomers have flocked to the United States over the years—that has made America a country of immigrants.

To be sure, these principles have always been honored as much in the breach as in the observance. Slaves and their descendants were excluded from the promise of American liberty for centuries. Catholics and Jews, Asians and Latinos, even Italians and the Irish faced acute discrimination. In practice, the universalist idealism of the

Constitution was always betrayed by a lingering attachment to a Protestant nation descended from British stock.

But just as the bitter reality of discrimination has always been a part of the American experience, so too has the erratic progress toward a more perfect union. Over decades and centuries of conflict, slavery and segregation were abolished. Prejudice against Catholics and Jews abated. The Italians and the Irish came to be seen as ordinary Americans. Latinos and Asians rapidly seemed to be following in their footsteps. Tens of millions of Americans freely cast their vote to send a black man to the White House. Though racism remained a pervasive social force, and right-wing politicians often used coded language to stoke hatred against ethnic and religious minorities, the day-to-day reality of the American nation seemed to be inching toward the realization of its high-minded conception: the day on which neither race nor creed would undermine somebody's claim to be a true American seemed considerably closer than it once had.

Then came Donald Trump.

Throughout his campaign, Trump called for a ban on Muslim immigration, implying that the adherents of one world religion ought to be excluded from membership in the nation. He launched repeated attacks on Mexican immigrants and questioned the impartiality of a judge with Mexican heritage, suggesting that some ethnicities are less American than others. Taken together, this implied a vision of American nationalism in ethnic and religious terms, one that harkened back to a time when membership in "We, the People" had, in practice, been deeply dependent on race and creed.

If Trump demonstrates how quickly an inclusive definition of the nation can revert to an exclusionary one, he also shows what a powerful tool it is for would-be authoritarians intent on attacking basic democratic norms. Since the core of the populist appeal is the claim to a "moral monopoly of representation,"[16] all opponents of populist leaders are, by definition, unpatriotic. This is the deeper significance of calling the press "enemies of the American people" or of claiming President Obama was born in Kenya. And it is, of course, also the deeper significance of the slogan "America First."[17]

To European observers of American politics, Trump's exclusionary nationalism feels strangely familiar. Many Europeans have long defined membership in the nation by descent from common ancestors. As a result, they have treated newcomers as welcome guests at best and unwelcome intruders at worst.

In the postwar decades, these attitudes limited the opportunities of immigrants, underpinning diffuse forms of discrimination and shaping the citizenship laws of many countries. At election time, conservative parties would sometimes inveigh against immigration to rile up their base. But though exclusionary nationalism rendered many residents unable to partake fully in the promise of liberal democracy, it was rarely weaponized against the system as such.

This has slowly changed over the past decades: a new brand of populists has fused a strong commitment to exclusionary nationalism with an illiberal attack on existing institutions. Like Trump, politicians from Wilders to Le Pen wield nationalism as a weapon that, they hope, might prove capable of undermining liberal democracy. On both sides of the Atlantic, nationalism and democracy now seem at odds with each other. If the advocates of an aggressive, exclusionary nationalism carry the day, the ideal of a liberal, multiethnic democracy will slowly perish. And this is just as true in Spain, Germany, or Hungary as it is in the United States.[18]

The Temptation to Abandon Nationalism

When it comes to race, the noble principles and promises of the US Constitution have been violated over and over again. For the first century of the republic's existence, African Americans were enslaved or treated as (at best) second-class citizens. For the second century, they were excluded from much of public life and suffered open discrimination. Even well into the republic's third century, they are being denied the equal protections of the law with painful frequency.

Nowadays, these realities are mostly empirical rather than legal: If African Americans face discrimination on the job market, if they are given higher prison sentences for the same crimes, or even if they are at higher risk of being shot by the police, the reason is not a difference in official legal status. Rather, it is that the neutral principles of the law are, in practice, administered in a discriminatory manner.[19]

This is why the standard conservative response to the problem of racial injustice in the United States is so unsatisfactory. People from John Roberts, the chief justice, to Tomi Lahren, the conservative commentator, like to point out how noble and neutral the country's principles are—only to use this fact to deny that there are serious racial injustices to be remedied. As Justice Roberts wrote in *Parents Involved*, a Supreme Court case on school desegregation, "the way to stop discriminating on the basis of race is to stop discriminating on the basis of race."[20]

This is disingenuous: If private actors—from real estate agents to HR managers—continue to discriminate on the basis of race, then a state that pretends that race doesn't exist can't effectively remedy the resulting injustices.[21] To add insult to injury, people of color do not, in practice, have the opportunity to be color blind. "In most social interactions," sociologist Adia Harvey Wingfield explains, "whites get to be seen as individuals. Racial minorities, by contrast, become aware from a young age that people will often judge them as members of their group, and treat them in accordance with the (usually negative) stereotypes attached to that group."[22]

The insistence that the noble principles of color blindness will fix everything is either naive or insincere. Recognizing this, parts of the left have started to claim that there is only one way to face up to racial injustice: to reject outright some of the most basic principles on which the American republic is founded.

If much of popular culture ignores or demeans ethnic and religious minorities, they claim, then insensitive portrayals of people of color, or instances of what has come to be called cultural appropriation, should be aggressively shamed. If free speech is invoked as a reason to defend a public discourse that is full of overt forms of racism and microaggressions, then this hallowed principle needs to be sacrificed to the cause of racial justice.[23] If laws that claim to be color blind can discriminate against people of color on such a consistent basis, then race and identity should be put at the heart of the legal system. And if appeals to common citizenship and the universal principles of the Constitution are so often disingenuous, then the tropes and trappings of American identity should be shunned.

There is something genuinely righteous in the anger that motivates these ideas. They stem from a real appreciation of the extent of persistent injustice and from an understandable impatience with the conservative defense of the status quo. And yet, they ultimately throw the baby out with the bathwater. Far from merely going too far or being strategically unwise—as sympathetic critics like to claim—they embrace principles that would ultimately destroy the very possibility of a truly open and multiethnic democracy.

The debate over cultural appropriation is an illustrative example. As used today, the idea of cultural appropriation holds that it is unacceptable for members of the majority group to adopt the cultural practices of ethnic and religious minorities. In the United States, for example, it is supposedly wrong for whites to wear dreadlocks or even to make sushi.[24]

It is understandable that members of groups that have suffered historical injustice and now continue to face discrimination can at times feel uncomfortable when outsiders emulate aspects of their culture. What's more, there are specific cases of cultural appropriation that really are morally reprehensible—not because members of a majority group are inspired by the culture of a minority group, per se, but because they selectively use its symbols or traditions to mock and denigrate it. A little bit of cultural sensitivity goes a long way.

And yet, the principles implied by a wholesale rejection of cultural appropriation ultimately stand in stark conflict with the ideals of a truly liberal and diverse democracy.

The most obvious charge against cultural appropriation is that it traffics in historical nonsense. Since dreadlocks were depicted as far back as Ancient Greece and Ancient Egypt, for example, a case could be made that African Americans are themselves engaging in a form of cultural appropriation when they are sporting this hairstyle.[25]

The need to resort to historical nonsense only reveals a deeper problem. As any historian knows, cultures have always been deeply malleable. Indeed, defenders of multiethnic societies have traditionally pointed to the intermingling of cultures in diverse cities from twelfth-century Baghdad, to nineteenth-century Vienna, to twenty-first century New York as one of the traits that made them so vibrant and successful.[26] But far from celebrating the way in which different cultures can take inspiration from each other, the opponents of cultural appropriation implicitly assume that cultures are pure; that they are forever owned by particular groups; and that there should be strict limits on the degree to which they influence each other. In other words, they ultimately think of the culture of particular identity groups in much the same way as right-wing xenophobes who are continually on guard against foreign influences on their national cultures.[27]

This is why a blanket acceptance of fears about cultural appropriation would be so noxious to the ideal of a society in which citizens share common experiences across racial and cultural lines:

either we accept the mutual influence of different cultures as an indispensable (and indeed desirable) element of any diverse society—or we will defend against it, erecting separate spheres for each cultural and ethnic group.

The growing rejection of the principle of free speech is similarly confused.

Once again, the basic impulse is certainly understandable. With xenophobia seemingly on the rise in both North America and Western Europe, and hate speech growing in prominence on the internet, most well-meaning people will, at some level, share the desire to mute the most incendiary voices. It is perhaps unsurprising that this instinct is especially strong in countries, like Germany, where the history of fascism is still painfully recent. And yet, as in the case of cultural appropriation, the rejection of free speech would ultimately undermine the very foundations of liberal democracy.

Some utterances really don't have any value.[28] The world would be better if they were never made, and perhaps even if they could reliably be banned. But as advocates of free speech have argued for centuries, the problem is that no authority can be trusted with the power of forbidding all noxious statements: whether out of error or self-interest, any institution with the right to censor would sooner or later start banning statements that do have real value.

The degree to which many advocates for restricting free speech are strategically short-sighted is most obvious in the American context. Much of the agitation for the notion that free speech should be subservient to social justice originates on elite college campuses or in the most progressive neighborhoods of the country's most progressive cities. So it is easy for activists to ignore what would happen if the dean of Southern Baptist University, the mayor of Hereford, Texas, or indeed the press-bashing president of the United States were to gain the right to censor utterances they dislike.[29]

But the underlying objection against attacks on free speech would, at its most fundamental level, hold even if such strategic concerns were allayed. Free societies are built on the principle that no public official gets to determine whose views about the world are right and whose views are wrong. In granting figures of authority the right to determine which utterances are so devoid of value that they can safely be banned, citizens would be compromising a key tenet of liberal democracy.[30]

Debates about free speech and cultural appropriation are often ignited by reasonably minor controversies in academia or publishing—and matter more to the writers and editors who are immersed in these communities than they do to the bulk of their readers. It is crucial to keep them in perspective. But while the importance of specific controversies is sometimes overstated, underlying questions about the kind of society which defenders of diverse democracies should be hoping to build actually remain underexplored.

To pretend that today's reality is color blind is to be politically cowardly and intellectually dishonest. As Wingfield argues, racial minorities currently do not have the privilege of being seen, or treated, as individuals.[31] But to jump to the conclusion that a more just society would be structured around group rights and obligations is to give up on rectifying this deep injustice altogether. For in such a society, the group to which one belongs would define even more—from the songs one is allowed to sing to the meals one is allowed to cook. Far from ensuring that blacks and Latinos and Asian Americans in the United States—or indeed the descendants of Turks and Syrians and Moroccans in Europe—could finally be seen as individuals, it would ensure that all members of society are forever defined by the color of their skin or the provenance of their ancestors.

The problem, in short, is not that the principles of liberal democracy—or, for that matter, the US Constitution and the German

Grundgesetz—are inherently faulty or hypocritical. It is, rather, that they have not yet been realized. And so the solution is not to jettison the universal promises of liberal democracy in favor of rights and duties rooted in particular ethnic or religious communities but rather to fight for them to be put in practice at long last.

Nobody was more conscious of this basic insight than the leaders of the civil rights movement. Far from rejecting the basic tenets of liberal democracy, they used Americans' reverence for these principles to appeal to the conscience of their contemporaries. As John Lewis, citing another civil rights leader, A. Philip Randolph, said briefly after Donald Trump got elected: "Maybe our forefathers and our foremothers all came to this great land in different ships, but we're all in the same boat now." Lewis, in short, recognizes that the best chance for bending the arc of history toward justice is to make shrewd use of the symbolism of the American republic, not to reject patriotism altogether.

The energy on today's left, by contrast, is increasingly directed toward a radical rejection of the nation and all its trappings: This is the left that delights in 4th of July op-eds entitled "The Making of a Non-patriot."[32] It is the left that chants "No Trump, No Wall, No USA at all!"[33] And it is also the left that, not content with acknowledging the copious failings of the Founding Fathers, refuses to recognize that they might be defined by anything other than their moral faults. As Shaun King put the point in an editorial that quickly went viral, Thomas Jefferson "was a monster . . . I accept that [he] played a vital role in the modern founding of what we've come to know as the United States of America, but he should not be celebrated in any way."[34]

In this respect, the American left is slowly following in the footsteps of the European left. In the United States, older generations of the left largely recognized that their country's universalist traditions made it possible to argue for a patriotism that would be more conformable with the ideal of a liberal, multiethnic society. In Europe, by contrast, the left has long recognized that the dominant conception of the nation was ethnic and religious. As a result, it has long followed the same strategy that parts of the American left are now adopting: it has abandoned democratic patriotism in favor of a radical critique of inherited institutions.[35]

The result has not been as desired. Convinced that it would be unable to redirect patriotism toward its own ends, the left has vacated the space of nationalism altogether—and allowed the right to occupy it on its own terms.

Inclusive Patriotism

Faced with parts of the right that want to exclude minorities from membership in the nation and parts of the left that emphasize the differences between citizens of different races and religions to such an extent that the bonds between them seem to dissolve, we need to forge a new language of inclusive patriotism.

This inclusive patriotism must not be blind to persisting injustices. Nor can it privilege the nation to such an extent that it either oppresses minorities within the country or promotes conflict with other countries. Instead, it should build on the tradition of multiethnic democracy to show that the ties that bind us go well beyond ethnicity and religion.

This is partially a matter of rhetoric, which makes it all the more heartening that plenty of leaders have effectively argued for this kind of patriotism over the past years. Speaking on the fiftieth anniversary of a famous civil rights protest, for example, Barack Obama emphasized the degree to which Americans of all walks of life joined forces to defeat segregation: "When the trumpet call sounded for more to join," he said, "the people came—black and white, young and old, Christian and Jew, waving the American flag and singing the same anthems full of faith and hope."[36]

In the same breath, Obama also stressed the degree to which the fight for civil rights appealed to basic values enshrined in the US Constitution. "What enormous faith these men and women had," he marveled as he stood on the same spot from which protestors had set out to march from Selma to Montgomery in March 1965.

Faith in God—but also faith in America . . . What greater expression of faith in the American experiment than this; what greater form of patriotism is there; than the belief that America is not yet finished, that we are strong enough to be self-critical, that each successive generation can look upon our imperfections and decide that it is in our power to remake this nation to more closely align with our highest ideals?

That's why Selma is not some outlier in the American experience. That's why it's not a museum or static monument to behold from a distance. It is instead the manifestation of a creed written into our founding documents:

"We the People . . . in order to form a more perfect union."

"We hold these truths to be self-evident, that all men are created equal."[37]

A few months before the 2017 presidential election, Emmanuel Macron reclaimed patriotism in an even more explicit form. Faced with rapidly growing support for the Front National and its proudly exclusionary conception of citizenship, he traveled to the highly diverse city of Marseille.[38] Speaking to a crowd of his supporters, he set out a proud conception of the French nation that puts difference at its heart:

When I look at Marseille, I see a French city, shaped by two thousand years of history, of immigration, of Europe . . . I see Armenians, Italians, Algerians, Moroccans, Tunisians. I see people from Mali, from Senegal, from the Ivory Coast. I see so many others I haven't mentioned.

But what do I see? I see the people of Marseille! What do I see? I see the people of France!

The people of France. Look at them. They are here. They are proud. Proud of being French. Take a good look at them, Ladies and Gentlemen of the *Front National:* This is what it means to be proud to be French.[39]

Rhetoric matters: Since the nation is, in the famous description of Benedict Anderson, an "imagined community," the way we talk about it has the power to affect its nature.[40] Political leaders who redescribe a nation that has a long history of being exclusionary in inclusive terms can make a real contribution to domesticating nationalism.

But rhetoric can only go so far. If a growing number of nations are turning toward an aggressive form of nationalism, there are complex political and historical reasons for this: The number of people born in other countries stands at record highs in much of North America and Western Europe. In nations that have historically been monoethnic, a large portion of the population remains unwilling to accept that immigrants or their descendants could ever turn into true compatriots. At the same time, a significant share of immigrants are struggling to adapt to the local culture, with linguistic ability and educational attainment trailing that of natives, even in the third generation.[41]

All of this calls for a response that is principled without being naive, and capable of winning popular support without being populist: To win the fight for an inclusive form of patriotism, countries will have to do much more to facilitate a real sense of community among all citizens and ease lingering fears about future migration.

The first part of this fight is to ensure that liberal principles are applied with equal vigor across the board.

Though liberal democracies claim that they treat all citizens equally, they fail to live up to this promise with disheartening frequency. In every country from Sweden to Canada, some significant form of discrimination persists. Whether that discrimination emanates from the state or from business, from private associations or from private individuals, it significantly undermines the degree to which minorities enjoy equal citizenship.

Thankfully, commonsense measures can help to reduce instances of discrimination. Many states and countries have yet to pass comprehensive bills banning employers and landlords from discriminating against minorities, for example. Changes to some longstanding conventions can also help to make a difference: European countries would, for example, do well to ban job candidates from the surprisingly widespread practice of featuring a photo on their CV. Companies, meanwhile, could mitigate unconscious biases by removing a candidate's name and race from the materials considered in the first stages of the hiring process.

Structural barriers remain an even greater obstacle to the success of racial and ethnic minorities.[42] Education is an especially stark case. In countries like Germany, a multi-tier school system effectively determines who can go on to university at the end of the fourth grade—giving children of parents who know how to maneuver the system, and are themselves well-educated, a huge advantage.[43] In countries like France, an education system that is egalitarian on its face pours huge resources into a few top schools while neglecting the disastrous performance of students in the country's most immigrant-heavy neighborhoods.[44]

In the United States, meanwhile, public schools remain remarkably segregated. Sixty years after *Brown v. Board of Education,* the landmark ruling which held that "separate but equal" schools violated the Constitution, Congress asked the Government Accountability Office to investigate how far racial integration had advanced. The results were disheartening: a depressingly large share of children still attend schools that are predominantly made up of students of their own race. In fact, the number of schools with very high concentrations of minority students had actually doubled from 2000 to 2013.[45]

Any real commitment to giving minority students the same shot at a good life has to involve a reversal of these disheartening trends. The first step to a nation in which people of different backgrounds see each other as true compatriots is to educate them together. In nearly every country, real progress toward this goal would include radical reform that is barely on the political agenda. In Germany, it would mean rethinking the three-tier school system to promote more intermingling across ethnic lines and make it much easier for immigrant children to attend university. In the United States, it would mean a renewed focus on desegregating schools.

A truly liberal integration policy would set out with renewed resolve to ensure that members of minority groups do not experience discrimination or see their prospects dimmed by structural obstacles. At the same time, it would also set itself against those who—whether out of fear that they might falsely be accused of discrimination, or due to an explicit commitment to cultural relativism—exempt minority groups from the basic rights and duties of a liberal society.

Examples are surprisingly widespread. From Sweden to the United States, a shockingly large number of girls face forced marriages or suffer from the practice of female genital mutilation.[46] In both Belgium and the United Kingdom, police investigations into serious crimes by members of minority groups have been hampered by concerns about cultural sensitivity.[47] Finally, in a growing number of cases state authorities make excuses for pernicious acts because they supposedly flow from somebody's culture of origin: in Germany, for example, a judge refused to grant a woman who had been battered by her Moroccan-origin husband an expedited divorce on the logic that "in his culture, it is not untypical for a husband to exercise corporal punishment of his wife." The woman, the judge said, should have "expected this kind of behavior" when she married him.[48]

While this kind of approach pretends to be tolerant, it actually sells minority groups short. To excuse domestic violence because it is, supposedly, a normal part of an immigrant's culture perpetuates the racism of low expectations. To look the other way as girls suffer genital mutilation is to impose the costs of the state's supposed tolerance on the most vulnerable members of minority groups. Far from being an exercise in discrimination, the state's determination to hold all of its residents to the same standard irrespective of their religion or the color of their skin is the only way to ensure that it doesn't abdicate the most essential duties it owes them.[49]

The ideal of inclusive nationalism demands that the state protect the rights of all individuals, against their own family members as well as their neighbors. If we wish to preserve liberal democracy, we cannot exempt minorities from its demands. But the same ideal provides less clear guidance on a topic that is even more emotionally charged: the nature and extent of immigration.

One thing is clear: defenders of liberal democracy must not pander to populist sentiment. To stand for their principles, they must protect immigrants from ill-treatment. And since demographic fears are intimately intertwined with economic anxiety, they should also recognize that it would ultimately be counterproductive to give in to a lot of the anti-immigrant measures proposed by populist candidates on both sides of the Atlantic: radical restrictions that severely harm the economy would, in the long run, be unlikely to weaken support for the populists.

On the other hand, defenders of liberal democracy will simply fan the flames of populism if they disregard fears about ineffective border controls or dismiss the degree of public anger about current levels of immigration. Some deviation from their preferred policies may therefore be necessary if they wish to address the deepest drivers of disenchantment with their political system.

There are no easy solutions. And yet, a principled compromise is possible: The defenders of inclusive nationalism should defend the rights of people who are already in the country and advocate for keeping the door open to close relatives of residents and highly skilled immigrants. But at the same time, they should take concerns about the rapid pace of migration seriously and acknowledge that the nation is a geographically bounded community that can only persist when it has control over its borders.[50]

In practice, this means that we must insist that all legal residents of a country be treated the same irrespective of their color or creed. We should oppose attempts, like Trump's proposed Muslim ban, to exclude people on the basis of their faith (or on the basis of other ascriptive characteristics, like race). And we should also denounce the suffering engendered by deportations of undocumented immigrants who were brought to the country as children or have been here for a long time.

But by the same token, we should acknowledge that it does not violate the principles of liberal democracy for nations to improve their ability to track and control who gets access to their territory. On the contrary, secure borders can help to win popular support for more generous immigration policies. Similarly, a streamlined process for identifying and removing immigrants who pose a security threat will help to calm, rather than to fan, ethnic tensions.

A similar compromise can be struck regarding the overall level of immigration. There are plenty of good reasons to keep welcoming a lot of newcomers to our countries. But at the same time, it is perfectly conformable with the principles of liberal democracy for nation states to honor popular preferences by lowering the overall number of immigrants. The rules regulating how many people are admitted to the country should, in short, be up to democratic contestation.

The choices we face on immigration are a lot more nuanced than the heated rhetoric on the topic tends to imply. There are plenty of ways to respect the principles of liberal democracy while allaying popular fears about immigration. Canada, for example, shows that it is possible to be very welcoming and reasonably tough-minded at the same time: by opening its doors to a large number of immigrants but making sure that most of them are highly qualified, the country has quickly become a model of tolerance.[51]

Nationalism is like a half-wild, half-domesticated animal. As long as it remains under our control, it can be of tremendous use—and genuinely enrich our lives. But it is always threatening to break free of the constraints we put on it. When it does, it can be deadly.

I remain enough of an idealist to be drawn to the vision of a world beyond nationalism—a world in which people do not need to dwell on their ethnic or cultural differences, and can define themselves by their common membership in the human race. But I am also enough of a pessimist to recognize that the nationalist beast remains very much alive.

We can, of course, ignore it or wish it away. But if we abandon it, other people are sure to step in, prodding and baiting the beast to bring out its most ferocious side. For all the well-founded misgivings about nationalism, we have little choice but to domesticate it as best we can.

8

Fixing the Economy

THERE IS A NOSTALGIC CORE to a lot of populist rhetoric. In the United States, Donald Trump famously promised to "Make America Great Again."[1] In the United Kingdom, the defining slogan of the campaign to leave the European Union was a pledge to "Take Back Control."[2]

One of the reasons why these simple slogans are so powerful is that every voter can project his or her personal form of nostalgia onto them. Some voters long for a time when their country was dominated by one ethnicity while others harken back to an age when conservative social norms reigned supreme. Some identify their country's past greatness with the imperial adventures of the nineteenth century while others fondly recall the military victories of the twentieth century. But for all the shades of meaning these simple slogans evoke, it is clear that nostalgia for an economic golden age in which people were affluent and jobs were secure is a central element of their appeal.

Much of the anxiety voters are experiencing is about hard cash. In many countries in North America and Western Europe, the standard of living of the average family hasn't improved for decades.

The young aren't doing as well as the old. Inequality is on the rise. In light of the disappointments they suffered in recent years, it is not irrational for most families to fear that the future may hold real material hardships.

Nostalgia for the economic past is not just about money, though; it's also about diminishing hope.

Most people in the United States and the United Kingdom, in Sweden and Italy are much wealthier than their grandparents were at the same age. But their grandparents had reason to be optimistic: Having grown up in poverty, they lived a life of relative affluence and expected their own children to do even better. Today, by contrast, the experience of economic stagnation has made most citizens highly apprehensive about the future. They look on with great concern as the forces of globalization are making it increasingly difficult for states to control borders or set their own economic policies. And just as their nations no longer seem able to make their own decisions, so they too feel like playthings of economic transformations that are outside their control. As jobs that had once seemed steady are shipped overseas or made redundant by technology—as storied factories shutter their doors and trade unions lose their clout—their work no longer provides them with a stable perch in society.

When people clamor to "Make America Great Again" or to "Take Back Control," they are after more than a bigger paycheck, then. Far from being motivated by sheer consumerism, they long for a sense of optimism that assures them of their place in a rapidly changing world.[3]

To stop the rise of populism, we have to allay those complex fears and envision a better tomorrow. People seek reassurance that their jobs will still command respect ten or twenty or thirty years from now. They want to know that they are sufficiently master of their own fate to be able to live out their lives in material comfort. They want to be sure that their children will get a chance to do better than them. They want their nation to be able to make its own decisions and to look after its most vulnerable citizens despite the changes wrought by globalization. Unless we can make some progress on all these fronts, nostalgia for a simpler past will reliably translate into votes for the populists who promise to recreate it.

Amid the general sense of economic gloom, it is easy to forget that the overall size of western economies has kept on growing over the past decades. Since 1986, America's GDP per capita has increased by 59 percent. The country's net worth has grown by 90 percent. Corporate profits have soared by 283 percent.[4]

But those aggregate numbers hide the distribution of gains. Only 1 percent of total wealth growth from 1986 to 2012 went to the bottom 90 percent of households. By contrast, 42 percent went to the top 0.1 percent.[5]

The most striking thing about this economic story is the degree to which American politicians conspired to accelerate, rather than to slow, the divide between the fates of the super-rich and those of ordinary citizens. Ronald Reagan slashed the top tax rate for high-income earners from 70 percent to 50 percent in 1981, and then again to 38.5 percent in 1986. George W. Bush cut the top income rate to 35 percent and the capital gains rate—which is almost exclusively paid by the wealthy—from 20 percent to 15 percent in 2003.[6]

Even as politicians changed the rules to allow the rich to keep a far greater share of their income, they hollowed out many of the provisions on which the most vulnerable members of society had long relied to stay afloat.

Reagan halved funding for rent subsidies and public housing, and kicked a million people off food stamps. Bill Clinton replaced Aid to Families with Dependent Children (a federal entitlement without lifetime limits) with Temporary Assistance for Needy Families (a program that is administered by the states and prohibits its beneficiaries from receiving assistance for more than two consecutive years, or five years over the course of a lifetime). States have, subsequently, further eroded the system of social protection by redeploying the grants they receive from the federal government: rather than providing the poor with cash aid or child care, many of them now use these grants to fill holes in their budgets.[7]

The aggregate impact of these changes has been huge: Two decades ago, 68 percent of families with children in poverty received cash assistance via welfare; today, that figure is 26 percent.[8]

The story outside the United States has not been quite as stark. In most parts of Europe, for example, tax rates for the super-rich have not come down to the same extent. But there, too, a decade of austerity has had a big impact on the degree to which people are protected against major life risks and eroded the public services they have at their disposal. Especially in the continent's south, taxes on ordinary people have been raised even as unemployment benefits have been slashed, pensions made more miserly, and state services—from public education to rural bus lines—degraded.[9]

Though the Great Recession was sparked by failures at the top of the financial industry, it has led to a rapid deepening of the economic divide between the rich and the poor, in Europe as well as in America.

The economic gloom of the past decades is often described as though it had been caused by natural forces over which politicians have no control. Technological progress and automation, so this story goes, have displaced millions of jobs.[10] The rise of competitors from China to Bangladesh has lowered wages and reduced employment for low-skilled workers.[11] Perhaps the citizens of democracies in North America and Western Europe just have to face up to the fact that the era of their unrivaled affluence is over.[12]

There is a large grain of truth to this story. It would be extremely difficult for a national government to halt technological progress or stop international trade. And even insofar as it is possible, it isn't desirable. After all, these transformations have lifted billions of people out of poverty around the world—and could, one day, provide the citizens of affluent countries with unprecedented freedom from toil and scarcity.[13]

But while the underlying trends are indeed beyond the control of national governments, the corrosive effects they have had on both the wallets and the attitudes of ordinary citizens are a result of political failure. Yes, technology is disrupting a lot of established professions—but the state could do much more to ensure that those who have been most heavily impacted by these changes get to lead a life of material dignity. And, yes, the economic predominance of Western democracies is fading fast—but the material disappointments suffered by its citizens are caused as much by an unfair distribution of the gains of globalization as they are by economic stagnation.

Some Western countries have done a much better job than others despite similar external challenges; the difference is public policy. The question, then, is not whether we can stop the economic megatrends of the last decades but rather how we can harness them in a fairer way.[14]

Taxation

One obvious way to reverse the worrying trends of the past decades is to reverse the policies that have exacerbated them. This means raising effective tax rates for the highest earners and the most profitable corporations.[15] It means restoring basic elements of the welfare state.[16] It means investing in areas—like infrastructure, research, and education—where public spending promises a positive return over the long run instead of cutting expenditure in every part of the budget.[17] And of course it means providing every citizen with decent health care.[18]

But if we are serious about making sure that all citizens share in the gains from globalization, we need to pursue an economic agenda that goes far beyond a mere restoration of the policies of yesteryear. Both the existing tax system and the existing welfare state were built at a time when (unlike today) most economic activity was constrained within the boundaries of the nation state; most people worked for the bulk of their lives; and most jobs were extremely stable. While the goals of the postwar economic order—to honor both the importance of economic equality and the generative power of the free market—remain as noble and relevant as ever, the tools that can best deliver on them have changed.

The need to find new ways to fulfill old goals is especially obvious in the case of taxation.

At 39.1 percent, the top tax rate for American corporations stood near a world record in 2012. But that same year, the effective tax rate paid by corporations was the lowest in four decades, at just 12.1 percent.[19]

One big reason for this huge differential is the thicket of absurd loopholes that were created by Congress in the full knowledge that they would channel even more money to the super-rich: to name but one example, the favorable treatment of private jets makes them extremely cheap for corporations to purchase.[20] Another big reason is that corporations have evaded the original intent of many tax laws by moving their headquarters abroad, or creating a byzantine web of legal entities that channel profits to locations where they are barely taxed. According to Oxfam, for example, the fifty largest American companies have, by perfectly legal means, shifted over $1 trillion to offshore tax havens, costing the US government about $111 billion in lost tax revenue.[21]

Rich individuals are taxed in a similarly lax manner. One reason why some billionaires pay a lower effective tax rate than their secretaries, as Warren Buffett has famously lamented, is that politicians continue to give massive handouts to them: the carried-interest deduction, for example, allows hedge fund managers to halve the tax they would ordinarily pay on the bulk of their earnings.[22] But another big reason is that rich individuals have been just as adept at evading the taxman as corporations: as the leak of the Panama Papers demonstrated, vast fortunes are channeled into offshore tax havens every year; though much of this activity is illegal, it rarely results in prosecutions.[23]

To ensure that both individuals and corporations pay their fair share of taxes, we should therefore be willing to consider what a tax system might look like if it was invented from scratch. How can nation states regain their ability to tax incomes and profits despite the massive mobility of capital in a globalized world?

The answer is in some ways simpler and more obvious than it might seem. Historically, the biggest asset of the nation state has been its territory. In fact, the very definition of a modern state has traditionally depended on its ability to enforce a particular set of rules across a particular geographic area.[24] The problem we now face stems from the fact that the economic relevance of this asset has declined over the past decades: as long as agriculture made up the bulk of the economy, most capital was unable to move across national borders. The more economic activity shifted to manufacturing, to services in general, and to the financial industry in particular, the easier it became for capital to take flight. It is little wonder that a tax regime designed in an era of captive capital is ill-suited to tackle this new reality.[25]

And yet, the powerlessness of the nation state has (to bastardize an infamous verbal bastardization) been much misoverestimated.[26] This is especially obvious in the case of personal taxation. Most people—even most super-rich people—retain a deep bond to their country. Though they might be willing to spend 183 days a year in the Bahamas in return for a much lower tax bill, very few of them would be willing to forego access to their home country altogether. This gives nation states an obvious point of leverage over their citizens: if they seek to retain access to its territory, they should have to pay taxes in the country.

The United States is the only developed country in the world that already does this. Any American citizen or permanent resident must pay taxes in the United States.[27] Other countries should follow America's lead and end the preferential treatment of citizens who move to tax havens for part of the year to evade the obligation to pay their fair share.[28] Even in the United States, the same principle could be enforced more vigorously and extended to factors beyond citizenship: for example, it might make sense to require anybody who owns residential real estate in a country to pay taxes there.[29]

While this rule would go a long way toward solving the noxious role that legal tax havens play, it would not do anything to solve the problem of illegal tax havens. But here, too, the nation state holds more trump cards than the fatalists tend to assume.

On the rare occasions in which big countries have worked together to put pressure on tax havens, they have celebrated surprising successes, as the recent series of deals between Switzerland and countries including the United Kingdom and the United States demonstrates.[30] What's more, nation states can make real inroads even in the absence of international cooperation. Governments could, for example, change the behavior of the super-rich by stepping up criminal punishments for big-time tax evaders, investing more money into fraud investigations, and becoming more willing to pay for leaked financial information that could lead to convictions: If their financial adventurism would put rich individuals in real danger of landing in prison, they would be much less likely to engage in it.[31]

The case of corporate tax is somewhat more complicated since the principle of territoriality is more difficult to apply to multinational companies with highly complex production and distribution chains. And yet, there is a lot of potential for reform on this front as well. For just as individuals are unwilling to forego access to a state's territory, so too corporations need to gain access to it to sell their products and offer their services.

Today, the amount of tax that Apple and Starbucks have to pay depends in large part on whether their nominal headquarters are based in Dublin or Düsseldorf, in Luxembourg or London, in Wilmington or Washington.[32] To remedy the corrosive impact that a few small territories with unusually low corporation taxes can have on the overall take, other states and countries should demand that companies pay tax on an appropriate share of their global tax in each territory in which they do business.[33] For while Apple may be willing to put its European headquarters in Ireland in order to cut its tax bill, it will still need to sell its iPhone in Britain—and should be obliged to pay a fair tax on the profits it makes from those sales. In that respect, the robust steps recently taken by German and French governments to ensure that tech giants pay "real tax" in these countries could be a harbinger of a much fairer future.[34]

Housing

No politician who runs for office in Norway or the United States, in Greece or Canada could get elected on the promise of raising the price of bread and butter. But when it comes to another commodity that citizens need to lead a decent life, the promise to keep its price at exorbitantly high levels does not seem especially strange: housing. In fact, though there has been significant variation from country to country, governments in democracies all around the world have explicitly tried to drive up the price of housing. Sadly, this is one of the few areas in which they have, by and large, succeeded.

Especially in the world's biggest cities, the explosion of housing prices has been staggering. In New York, for example, the average rent on an apartment in the 1960s was $200 per month, and a square foot of residential real estate cost $25 to buy. By the 2010s, average rent had grown to $3,500 and a square foot sold at $1,070. Similarly, in London, the cost of an average home has gone up from £55,000 in 1986 to £492,000 in 2014.[35]

This increase in housing prices has had a huge effect on the living standards of people in those cities, especially among the young. Tenants in London, for example, now spend a staggering 72 percent of their income on rent, making the exploding cost of housing by far and away the most important reason why their living standards have not improved in decades.[36]

The staggering cost of housing in metropolitan centers also has a pernicious impact on people who are unable to pay those exorbitant rents. As the process of gentrification advances, many people who grew up in urban areas are pushed out—and wind up being cut off from both their support networks and the economic opportunities offered by major cities.[37] Many people who have grown up in less affluent rural areas, meanwhile, remain permanently locked out of the most productive regions in the country, making it even more difficult for them to better their lot.

In short, the exorbitant cost of housing is now one of the most important reasons for the stagnation of living standards across North America and Western Europe. If defeating populism hinges in part on making citizens more optimistic about the future, a radical reorientation of housing policy is urgently needed.[38]

One important way to address the housing crisis is, quite simply, to increase the stock of available homes.

The process of obtaining permits should be made much easier, and disputes about them resolved much more quickly.[39] Towns and villages should have less power to veto developments in their jurisdiction.[40] States should do more to help in the construction of new apartments, whether directly through the addition of new units of public housing or indirectly through financial assistance to local municipalities.[41] Finally, the introduction of land value taxes —which levy the same charge on a patch of land irrespective of whether its owner lets it lie barren or decides to erect a building on it—would provide a strong incentive to build new homes.[42]

A different tax system could also improve the distribution of housing. Higher rates on second homes and vacant properties could drive up occupancy rates.[43] Existing incentives for rich people to buy bigger homes or purchase additional properties—like the mortgage-interest tax deduction in the United States or the easy availability of buy-to-let mortgages in the United Kingdom—could be abolished.[44]

None of these policies will be easy to pass: Since the equity they own in their homes is a primary source of wealth for many middle-class people, they have a strong incentive to vote for higher home prices.[45] And since a precipitous drop in housing prices can, as the world painfully learned in 2008, lead to a huge short-term shock, politicians are understandably worried about any policy that might pop a speculative bubble.[46]

But if we take housing seriously as an artificial restraint on our affluence—and thus a danger to our democracies—there are ways to compensate the losers of falling home prices, and to make potential gains more salient to the winners. (States could, for example, auction off development rights, cutting every citizen a check from the profits.)[47]

Of the many economic challenges we face in the decades to come, the exorbitant price of housing is the easiest to solve if only we are willing to do the right thing. To give up on pursuing these policies because they would be politically difficult is to aim too low.

Productivity

Over the past years, the bulk of the public conversation about the economy has focused on inequality.[48] This is welcome for many reasons: rampant inequality corrupts the political process, allows the upper middle class to hoard the best educational and professional opportunities, and weakens the social ties that bind citizens together.[49] But though containing income inequality is important in itself, the role that the rise of inequality plays in the stagnation of living standards has sometimes been overstated.

According to the 2015 Economic Report of the President, for example, the income of the median American household would be significantly higher today if inequality had not risen so dramatically: if the share of income going to the bulk of the population had not shrunk since the 1970s, the average American household would now have $9,000 more at its disposal every year. That would make a real difference. And yet, that same study also shows that there is a much more important driver of stagnating living standards: a significant slowdown in productivity. In fact, if productivity had grown at the same rate in the past decades as it did in the postwar era, the average American household would now be able to spend $30,000 more every year.[50]

Raising levels of labor productivity (the amount of output workers are able to produce in a given amount of time) should thus be a key priority for anybody who cares about the stagnation of living standards. That makes it all the more unfortunate that it is far less clear how to increase labor productivity than it is to figure out how to build lots of cheap housing. But though economists agree that there is no magic bullet, most also believe that there are some underutilized avenues—and that nearly all of these point to research and education.

Though research is one of the biggest long-term drivers of productivity, the share that governments at all levels spend on it as a total of GDP has steadily declined in many countries. In the American context, this is especially striking in individual states: infamously, for example, California now spends a lot more on its prisons than it does on its world-class universities.[51]

Things are even worse outside of the United States. Germany, for instance, prides itself on its educational system and has a much-vaunted funding stream for excellence in research. And yet, the total funding for the country's *Exzellenzinitiative* is smaller than the annual budget of Harvard University.[52]

The lack of investment by various governments is compounded by falling levels of research and development by corporations. Though it is difficult for economists to measure the exact amount businesses spend on such activities, a recent paper concludes that there was a significant "shift away from scientific research by large corporations between 1980 and 2007."[53]

So a lot could be accomplished if governments recommitted themselves to funding long-term research and provided much stronger incentives for private companies to do the same. But to keep raising the productivity levels of their citizens, they also have to radically reimagine their educational system. In the postwar era, universal literacy, a big expansion of high schools, and a rapidly growing share of university students prepared workers in advanced economies for the transition from a manufacturing to a service economy. Now, a similarly ambitious set of educational reforms is needed to prepare citizens for the world of work they will encounter in the digital age.

These changes should include a radical reimagination of the way education is organized from kindergarten to college. The invention of digital tools that can tailor instruction to the needs, aptitudes, and learning styles of individual students should radically transform the prevailing form of instruction. Instead of lecturing their students from the front of the classroom, for example, teachers should spend much more time on one-on-one coaching, on leading small-group discussions, and on facilitating collaborative work.[54]

Finally, it is clear that in a rapidly changing economy, workers must continue to update their skills long after they have left high school—or grad school. At the moment, governments mostly think of lifelong learning as something that is there for people who have lost their job. Instead, they should enable all working-age adults to take regular sabbaticals to upgrade their skills. To make this financially viable, the entire approach to funding postsecondary education should be reconsidered from scratch.[55]

In much of the recent economic debate, the need to boost productivity and the need to reduce inequality is implicitly treated as if the two goals stood in conflict with each other. Instead, it would be more helpful to think of them as complementary. After all, low productivity and high inequality tend to be mutually reinforcing: Workers who have low skills don't have much bargaining power. This, in turn, depresses their wages, and makes it more likely that their children will also fail to acquire sufficient skills to succeed.

By the same token, many of the policies designed to address inequality would also help to boost productivity. Any success in closing the huge economic and racial disparities in the quality of public schools, for example, would reduce both income inequality and the amount of talent that is being squandered. Similarly, an improvement in the bargaining power of ordinary workers would both boost the wages of the less well-off and make it easier for them to improve their skills.[56]

In the long term, educational and industrial policy alike should therefore aim to move us from a vicious to a virtuous cycle: the goal is to get to a world in which the workforce is both more skilled and has the power to negotiate for higher wages.[57]

A Modern Welfare State

A modernized tax system can raise the money states need to meet their obligations and remain in control of their spending priorities. A revamped housing system can reduce living costs and help preserve access to opportunity for all citizens. Renewed investment in productivity can contribute to rising wages and help the workers of the future compete. But to be inclusive as well as vibrant, developed economies also need to preserve one of their greatest historical achievements: their ability to protect the most vulnerable citizens against major life risks, from sickness to destitution.

This task is complicated by the fact that welfare states have largely failed to adapt to the big structural changes developed economies have undergone in the past decades. Designed in the postwar era, they were built on the assumption that most citizens were relatively young and worked a full-time job. As a result, they structured both contributions and benefits around employment. This makes them reasonably generous to people who retire after decades of working full time, and even to those who suffer a brief spell of sickness or unemployment before returning to a traditional job. But they often provide inadequate coverage to the growing ranks of "labor market outsiders," including freelancers, temporary and part-time workers, and the long-term unemployed.[58]

The link between work and the welfare state has also created bad incentives, both political and economic. Since social contributions are tied to full-time employment, the cost of labor is artificially inflated—creating disincentives for companies to hire new workers. And since key benefits are so intimately tied to full-time employment, labor market insiders seek to protect their current jobs at any cost—turning them into strong supporters of rigid labor markets even in countries, like Italy or Greece, where such rules have proven to be a major obstacle to economic growth.[59]

Costs are another major problem. Faced with a rapidly aging

population, traditional welfare states are having trouble sustaining their pension obligations, financing their health care systems, and providing adequate care for the elderly. The most common way of dealing with these financial difficulties has been to scale back the generosity of the welfare state. While few programs have been cut outright, governments have downsized retirement benefits, introduced new conditions on the receipt of unemployment benefits, and failed to provide protection against new forms of social risk. As a result, the overall level of protection has markedly fallen on both sides of the Atlantic. Whereas the welfare state once provided a social safety net that caught those who were in need, no matter the reason, it increasingly lets anybody who is judged to be improvident or irresponsible crash to the ground.[60]

In short, in their current form, welfare states hamper economic growth even though they provide a rapidly deteriorating level of benefits. To fix these deep problems, states need to find the courage to redesign welfare states in a radical way.

The most important goal of a redesigned welfare state should be to decouple social benefits from traditional employment.

This makes a lot of sense when it comes to raising the money that is needed to sustain the welfare state: While it is paramount that businesses help to bear the burden of key social provisions, it makes little sense to ask corporations that create a lot of jobs for a proportionally higher contribution than corporations who create very few jobs. The same is true of individuals: With the number of people who live off accumulated wealth rising rapidly, it makes less and less sense to place the burden of financing the welfare state predominantly on wage-earners.

At the same time, a decoupling of the welfare state and traditional employment also makes sense when it comes to protecting citizens against misfortune—or indeed empowering them to take

risks. By making health insurance and pension benefits fully portable, for example, a modern welfare state could significantly reduce
barriers to labor mobility, increasing the productivity of both firms
and individuals. In fact, recent studies have provided good evidence
that a generous welfare state that combines flexible labor markets
with portable benefits can even breed entrepreneurial spirit: Since
young Swedes are not worried about suffering destitution or losing
their health benefits if they quit their job, for example, they are actually more likely to found businesses than their American counterparts.[61]

A lot of debates about the welfare state remain stuck in bina-
ries that don't capture the real challenge we face. The key question is not whether to make welfare states more or less generous, or
even whether to make them more or less forgiving of supposedly
irresponsible behavior. Rather, it is how to create a welfare state
that protects labor market outsiders as well as insiders; encourages
businesses to hire rather than to fire; and provides citizens with the
safety net they need to take risks that are economically beneficial
for all.

Meaningful Work

"If you had asked one of my constituents who he is a few decades
ago, he would have said: 'I'm a foreman in the factory,'" a senior
politician told me recently. "But then a lot of manufacturing jobs
up and went. People took an economic hit. But they also lost a
sense of identity. If I ask them who they are nowadays, they tell me:
'I'm white. And I don't like all those immigrants coming in.'"[62]

The politician's point was as startling as it was simple: While we
are constantly talking about the economic effects of the transformations we are seeing on both sides of the Atlantic, we are only just
starting to understand how big their cultural implications will be.
When people lose high-paying, unionized jobs they do not just lose

their footing in the middle class; rather, they also stand to lose a whole set of social connections that structure their lives and give them meaning. As an "earned" identity slips out of their reach, they are likely to default to an "ascriptive" identity—making their ethnicity, their religion, and their nationality more central to their worldview.[63]

This cultural transformation helps to explain the widening disconnect between the downwardly mobile or already poor, on the one hand, and the upwardly mobile or already affluent, on the other hand. People who have, or aspire to, the kind of job that allows them to sustain an earned identity are tempted to think of their ascriptive identities as immaterial. This allows them to bridge cultural and ethnic divides, finding common ground with people who share their professional status or their personal tastes. And it also tempts them to look down on people who insist on "clinging," as they might put it, to the importance of such social markers as race or religion.[64]

Meanwhile, people who no longer derive a sense of earned identity from their jobs often harbor a growing sense of resentment: Perhaps unsurprisingly, they feel insulted by people who are leading much more comfortable lives than they are and then have the gall to sit in judgment of them. And they are also increasingly resentful toward people who are in a similar economic position, but do not come from the same racial or religious group.

Populists are highly skilled at weaponizing these forms of resentment: their rhetoric simultaneously aims to turn the growing anger at affluent people against the ruling elite and to turn the growing focus on ascriptive identity against immigrants as well as ethnic and religious minorities.

To combat the economic drivers of populism, it therefore isn't enough to make sure that the overall pie keeps on growing, or even that the bulk of citizens gets a fairly-sized slice. Rather, we should also be thinking about how to structure the world of work in such a way as to make it possible for people to derive a sense of identity and belonging from their jobs—and to remind the winners of globalization of the links they share with their less fortunate compatriots.

There is, as yet, barely any thinking on this topic, especially as it relates to the millions of new jobs that are already being created in the sharing economy. Take the example of Uber. It seems relatively clear that governments should neither forbid the service, as some countries in Europe are proposing, nor allow it to circumnavigate key protections for their workforce, as most parts of the United States have effectively done. Rather, they should steer a forward-looking middle course—celebrating the huge increase in convenience and efficiency that ride-sharing offers while passing new regulations which ensure that drivers earn a living wage.[65]

But even if policymakers get that mix right, it seems unlikely that Uber drivers will ever derive the sense of identity and meaning from their work that factory workers once did. The reason for this is neither that their jobs will necessarily be less well-paid, nor that the service they provide is somehow less important. Rather, it is that it will never be embedded in the shared culture of earlier forms of work.

Manufacturing jobs saw thousands of workers converge on the factory gates at the same time every day to commence their shifts. Traditional offices allowed for repeated social interaction in teams and at meetings, in the breakroom and at the water cooler. Even cab drivers met their peers when they picked up their cars at the garage, and spent the whole day interacting with the same dispatcher.

Uber drivers, by contrast, gain no in-built community from their work: while the app's rating system encourages a stream of pleasant one-off interactions, there is no lasting connection to other human beings. Since the old practices that embedded workers in a community, and thereby helped lend meaning to their jobs, are rapidly eroding, a new sense of pride in a very different kind of mass employment is desperately needed.

As the new digital economy is threatening to dissolve the meaning of work, so too globalization is threatening to dissolve the meaning of the nation.

The nostalgia of the populists promises people an era in which their country will go back to being great. At the core of this nostalgia stands a double desire for control: Citizens want their nation to be able to make its own decisions, unencumbered by the constraints of the global economy. And they want that powerful nation to help them take control of their lives, providing them with the resources and the opportunities to improve their lot in the face of growing insecurity.

Turning back the clock is not a realistic option: the populists delude themselves if they think that they can return us to the world as they imagine it to have been thirty or fifty or a hundred years ago. But while it would be naive to aim for a restoration of an idealized past, it is certainly possible to find real ways to respond to the growing sense of economic frustration—and to deliver on the longstanding promise of double control.

The citizens of North America and Western Europe have very good reason for wanting to feel both that their nations retain some economic room to maneuver on the international stage and that their governments will help them control their own fate. Though nation states cannot meet these expectations with the same tools they used in the postwar era, they can do so by using their resources in new and imaginative ways. Since individuals and corporations seek to access their territory, national governments can ensure that the rich continue to pay their fair share of taxes. And since governments retain control over housing and infrastructure, education and the welfare state, they can boost the productivity of their citizens and ensure a better distribution of the gains from economic growth.

Big changes in the world economy are straining the social compact that made liberal democracies so stable in the postwar era. It is unsurprising that so many citizens feel angry and disoriented—or that the resulting nostalgia is providing ample breeding ground for authoritarian populists. But if liberal democracies dare to take bold approaches to the biggest economic challenges of our time, they remain capable of providing citizens with real improvements in their standard of living. By using their resources much more proactively than they have done so far, they retain the ability to shape a future in which an openness to the world does not need to be synonymous with a loss of control.

9

Renewing Civic Faith

THE RISE of digital technology has boosted economic growth and made it easier for people to connect across borders. It has also favored the spread of hate speech and conspiracy theory.

This is because the rise of the internet and of social media has fundamentally transformed the structural conditions of communication: The longstanding promise of one-to-many communication has been democratized. The rise of many-to-many communication has made it easy for viral information to race around the world. As a result, traditional gatekeepers have lost much of their power. Ordinary people with a knack for catchy content can now reach millions on a regular basis. Politicians with a big following on social media can set the agenda even if their claims would never pass a basic fact-check. It is impossible to understand today's politics without understanding the transformative nature of the internet.

Since a big part of the reason for the rise of populism is technological, it is tempting to think that the solution must be technological too. And so it is hardly surprising that tech companies have come under increasing social and political pressure over the past years. As high hopes for the beneficial effects of Facebook and Twitter have given way to intense worries about their corrosive influence, a broad coalition of activists has demanded that tech companies change—or that governments adopt a more proactive approach to making them change.

In the United States, activists have mostly focused on getting social media platforms to make reforms on a voluntary basis. In Europe, politicians have been debating (and increasingly enacting) laws that mete out substantive fines to companies that fail to get with the program. But the nature of the fix is surprisingly similar in both cases: social media platforms, activists on both sides of the Atlantic have argued, should enforce a comprehensive ban on hate speech and fake news.[1]

The forceful demands made by advocates of regulation are matched by equally forceful rebuttals by its opponents. Tech executives have argued that effectively identifying fake news, or demarcating the boundaries of hate speech, lies beyond the power of algorithms. To stop the spread of noxious ideas, they would have to hire a small army of moderators—who would not only be expensive to maintain but also bear an uncomfortable resemblance to old-style censors.[2] This objection is especially powerful against the prospect of formal government intervention. At first governments may, for reasons that really are selfless, seek the power to censor political speech that is genuinely corrosive. But, free speech advocates rightly ask, should citizens trust that politicians wouldn't eventually abuse their far-reaching powers to shape public discourse and restrict criticism?[3]

Since a wide gulf separates the sides of this debate, it would be tempting to think that we are faced with two equally unappealing alternatives: intrusive regulation or outright censorship on the one side, inaction and fatalism on the other. But in truth, there are some pragmatic and plausible alternatives to these extremes.

The first is to emulate the model of self-regulation that has historically averted the need for more heavy-handed forms of government intrusion in the film and television industries. If social media companies begin to take the problem seriously, governments should be willing to give them a large degree of leeway.[4]

The second is to recognize that platforms like Facebook and Twitter can do a lot to stop the spread of fake news or hate speech without going all the way to outright censorship. Indeed, these platforms have already begun to curate what posts users see for commercial reasons: Facebook bumps live video to the top of its news feeds to encourage its adoption among users.[5] Twitter has recently introduced a curated section of featured tweets marked "In Case You Missed It."[6] In a similar vein, social media platforms could boost civil posts conveying reliable information, ding hateful posts spreading falsehoods—and finally refuse to accept advertising from hate groups.[7]

The third is to distinguish between harmful speech by humans and harmful speech by robots. Studies have shown that a significant percentage of the misinformation and the hate spread on platforms like Twitter comes from so-called bots. This in effect allows a few users with malicious intent to use their bot alter egos to drown out more moderate voices and distort the nature of the conversation.[8] The moral pitfalls involved in banning such bots are therefore much less serious than those involved in banning speech by real people. As Tom Malinowski, the Assistant Secretary of State for Democracy, Human Rights, and Labor in the Obama administration, told me: "When I was in office, I passionately fought to defend freedom of speech for individuals on the internet. But I don't believe that bots spreading hate should enjoy those same freedoms."[9]

Rebuilding Trust in Politics

Commonsense measures can make it a bit more difficult for the enemies of democracy to use social media platforms as a propaganda tool. But we should not be naive about how much they can accomplish. Without the kind of outright censorship that a liberal society has strong reason to reject, neither Facebook nor Twitter will ever turn into a utopia of civility and moderation. So is there anything else we can do to confront the ease with which antidemocratic ideas take root in the digital age?

To answer that question, it is worth remembering that fake news and hate speech aren't new phenomena. Before Twitter and Facebook, a significant minority of Americans believed that 9/11 was a hoax. Before the internet, a large share of people around the world believed that Stanley Kubrick staged the moon landing. Before television or radio, the Protocols of the Elders of Zion spread anti-Semitism from the cold steppes of Siberia to the hot sands of the Sinai desert.[10]

Conspiracy theories, in short, have long been a stubborn reality of politics. And yet, their role used to be far more marginal in most liberal democracies. The reasons for this go well beyond the rise of social media: the spread of conspiracy theories was contained, in part, because the government was much more transparent and most citizens had much higher trust in politicians.[11]

In a functioning liberal democracy, there are plenty of safeguards to stop politicians from conspiring with each other and to empower citizens to track what is going on. Officials are tasked not only with avoiding corruption but also with avoiding the appearance of corruption.[12] Different branches of government jealously hold each other to account. Opposition politicians have an incentive to uncover gross forms of misconduct. As a result, citizens can find rational explanations for most events. Conspiracy theories remain the preserve of cranks. Though they never quite die out, the media pays little attention to them, and most citizens dismiss them out of hand.

The degree to which conspiracy theories have come to stand at the center of politics in many countries across North America and

Western Europe over the past years thus demonstrates the degree to which liberal democracy has eroded in these countries. No country showcases this trend more clearly than the United States.

In his first forays into politics, Donald Trump rode the wave of conspiracy theory by "investigating" whether Barack Obama had forged his birth certificate. While he was campaigning for the presidency, outlandish conspiracy theories about Hillary Clinton rose to unprecedented prominence on Twitter, Facebook, and talk radio. As president, Trump has continued to use his bully pulpit to spread a series of deliberate falsehoods—from his oft-repeated claim that three million Americans voted illegally to his baseless assertions that the Obama administration had secretly wiretapped him.[13]

Even as Trump spread conspiracy theories from the White House, his opponents increasingly resorted to baseless accusations of their own. Some of the most viral articles spread by #TheResistance blithely subordinated the factual truth to a pursuit of the (supposed) political truth: websites like Addicting Info and Occupy-Democrats, and prominent Twitter accounts like that of former British member of Parliament Louise Mensch, ran made-up stories claiming that a Donald Trump sex tape was about to be released, or that hundreds of mainstream American journalists were secretly Russian agents.[14]

These wild accusations were deeply irresponsible. But some speculation was unavoidable: With Trump unwilling to divest himself from his business empire, and more and more details about his entanglements with Russia coming to light in his first months in office, even the most scrupulous observers were reduced to making educated guesses as to what might really be going on.[15]

One effective means against the spread of conspiracy theory, then, is to reestablish traditional forms of good governance. To regain the trust of the population once Trump leaves office, politicians will have to stick to the truth in their campaigns; avoid the perception of a conflict of interest; and be transparent about their dealings with lobbyists at home and government officials abroad. Politicians and journalists in countries where the norms of good governance have not yet eroded to the same degree should, meanwhile, double down on them with renewed zeal: as the American case shows, such norms can erode frighteningly quickly—and with terrible consequences.

After Trump won the 2016 elections, Barack and Michelle Obama were mocked in some quarters for having insisted throughout the campaign that "when they go low, we go high."[16] It is, of course, easy to mock a team that continues to play by the rules even when the opposing team turns up with goons in tow and clubs in their hands. But for anybody who wishes to keep playing the game, it's not clear what the alternative is: if both sides take up arms, its nature changes irrevocably.

Unlikely as it might seem at the moment, the only realistic solution to the crisis of government accountability (and, most likely, the larger crisis of democratic norms) is therefore a negotiated settlement, in which both sides agree to disarm. Like the favorite incantation of the Obamas, that may sound hopelessly naive. But as political scientists have consistently found, the survival of stable democracies has always depended on the willingness of major political figures to play by the basic rules of the game.

Given the depth of the ethical degradations wrought by Trump and his team, a return to rules that most politicians have followed for the past decades would be a big improvement. But to regain the trust of the population—which, in both North America and Western Europe, had begun to erode long before Trump took office— much more is needed.

Ordinary people have long felt that politicians don't listen to them when they make their decisions. They are skeptical for a reason: The rich and powerful really have had a worrying degree of influence over public policy for a very long time. The revolving door between lobbyists and legislators, the outsized role of private money in campaign finance, the big speaking fees for former officials, and the tight links between politics and industry really have undermined the degree to which the popular will steers public policy.[17]

Some elements of undemocratic liberalism are difficult to avoid. If we want to deal with climate change, we need international cooperation. And if we want to ensure that there are no dangerous chemicals in our food, we need to give considerable power to scientists and bureaucrats. An indiscriminate dash to return power to the people by scrapping independent agencies and abolishing international organizations would accomplish little.

But at the same time, there are plenty of ways in which the popular will is being subverted without good reason. In particular, nation states could take much more robust measures to reform the political system and curtail the influence of money on politics.

To push conspiracy theories back to the fringes, politicians need to shake up the cozy habits that have long prevailed in Washington and Brussels, in Berlin and Athens. By making it much more difficult for private money to influence public policy—and for legislators to profit from their connections after they leave office—political systems around the world can start to rebuild the trust they have lost in the past decades.[18]

In many European countries, there is strong support for some of these reforms. Voters would be happy to put tighter limits on campaign donations or even to institute much more extensive restrictions on the cushy sinecures politicians can accept after leaving office. There is also significant support for reforming the European Union: while most Europeans strongly favor preserving the EU, a large majority wants to make it more democratic.[19]

But to fix the system, European governments also need to be willing to make some less popular changes. One of the most effective ways to limit private influence on politics would, for example, be to increase the capacity of parliaments: if they were given sufficient staff to do their own research and draft their own legislation, they would not need to rely on lobbyists for information.[20] Another effective way would be to raise the salaries of politicians so that they are less susceptible to outside incentives.[21]

Since a series of recent Supreme Court cases has held that strict restrictions on campaign contributions violate the First Amendment, it is going to be more difficult to fix the system in the United States. The justices urgently need to recognize that the current system threatens the working of American democracy—and rethink the protection of political speech for big corporations. But until this piece of the puzzle falls into place, there are other reforms that do not face the same obstacles: As in Europe, legislators should make it easier for members to retain talented staffers by improving the woefully inadequate funding of Congress. They should pass a more robust set of bribery statutes to make sure that pernicious practices that fall just short of quid-pro-quo corruption can at last be prosecuted. And they should finally desist from blatantly antidemocratic practices like gerrymandering and voter suppression.

In the postwar decades, a lot of the same lies and calumnies that now proliferate on social media were already in circulation. Many citizens were already worried that their public officials might be corrupt. But back then, the threat of fascism was a part of living memory. The threat of communism remained a live reality. Civics was an integral part of the educational system, from nurseries all across the country up to the faculty lounges of the nation's leading universities. As a result, most citizens had a better understanding of the practices and a deeper commitment to the principles of liberal democracy—making them far less likely to give credence to conspiracy theories based on lies or disinformation.

This points to another important measure we can take: Unable

to restrict the supply of attacks on the basic principles of liberal
democracy through outright censorship, we have all the more reason to lessen the demand for them. While we cannot recreate the
threat of communism or fascism, we can remember that civics education is an essential bulwark against authoritarian temptations.
And so the best way to defend liberal democracy remains what it
has always been: to take seriously the task of turning children into
citizens.

Raising Citizens

Ever since philosophers began to think about the concept of self-
rule, they have put particular emphasis on civic education. From
Plato to Cicero, and from Machiavelli to Rousseau, all of them
were obsessed with the question of how to instill political virtue in
the youth.

It is hardly surprising, then, that the small band of patriots who
dared establish a new republic at a time when self-government had
all but vanished from the earth also thought very hard about how
to convey their values to the generations that would come after
them. What, George Washington asked in his Eighth Annual Address, could be more important than to pass civic values down to
"the future guardians of the liberties of the country?" Giving the
orthodox answer, he argued that "the education of our youth in the
science of government" should be a "primary object" of America's
nurseries, schools, and universities.[22]

"A people who mean to be their own Governors," James Madison echoed a few years later, "must arm themselves with the power
which knowledge gives." His fears about what would happen to
America if it neglected this crucial task sound oddly apposite today: "a popular government, without popular information, or the
means of acquiring it, is but a prologue to a farce or a tragedy; or,
perhaps both."[23]

For the first centuries of the republic's existence, this emphasis on civic education shaped the country. Parents sought to raise to-morrow's citizens, competing with each other to see whose four-year-old could name more presidents. Schools across the country devoted ample time to teaching students "How a Bill Becomes a Law."[24] So-called "great books programs" sought to give liberal arts students a deeper appreciation of the intellectual tradition on which the American republic is founded.[25] An acute sense of civic duty animated organizations as varied as the YMCA ("Democracy must be learned by each generation")[26] and the model school founded by Horace Mann ("A republican form of government, without intelligence in the people, must be, on a vast scale, what a mad-house, without superintendent or keepers, would be on a small one.")[27] The Supreme Court virtually elevated the importance of civics to the status of a constitutional principle: "public education," the justices held in *Bethel School District No. 403 v. Fraser,* "must prepare pupils for citizenship in the Republic."[28]

Civic education in all its forms stood at the core of the American project. Then, amid an era of unprecedented peace and prosperity, the idea that support for self-government had to be won anew with every passing generation started to fade. Today, it is all but extinct.

When I arrived at Harvard University to pursue a PhD in political science, I was prepared to immerse myself in history and in theory, in intricate questions about how the world is and how it should be. What I was not prepared for was the extent to which graduate school would discourage me from using my training in these abstract questions for more concrete public or pedagogical ends. As I and most of my classmates realized within a few weeks of arriving on campus, America's leading universities now measure the achievement of their graduate students in terms of their ability to publish in leading academic journals—to the virtual exclusion of everything else.

In this narrow view of the world, writing about politics for a wider audience is, at best, a distraction. Teaching undergraduates is a chore that should be carried out conscientiously, yes, but also as speedily as possible. The only life goal graduate students can talk about without risking their reputation is to land an academic job at a leading research university.

The narrow training of America's faculty members, and the perverse incentives they face from the moment they enter their PhD programs until the day they retire, helps to explain the increasingly perfunctory nature of undergraduate education. At many of the country's best colleges, students and faculty have made a tacit pact of nonaggression: as long as students don't take up too much of their time, professors will make it easy for the bulk of their charges to get a degree without thinking too hard. And so many college students have about the same attitude to their classes as their instructors have to teaching them: they accept the duty to produce essays, or to work through problem sets, as an inevitable part of what it takes to get ahead in the world—and try to get it out of the way as quickly and painlessly as possible.[29]

The pedagogical failings of elite colleges might not matter so much if they didn't stand at the apex of a similar set of failures faced by students from the moment they set foot in a public school. Just as college education has become increasingly utilitarian, so too the purpose of public education has dangerously narrowed: over the past decades, the number of hours an average high school student spends on civic education has declined precipitously.[30]

The result: generations of Americans who are dangerously ill-informed about politics. In a 2009 survey that asked participants about simple facts like the century in which the American Revolution took place, 89 percent of respondents expressed confidence that they had passed the test; only 17 percent had. In another, more recent study, students at fifty-five highly ranked colleges were asked basic civics questions. Only 50 percent could answer questions about the term lengths of Senators and Congressmen; 80 percent would have earned a D or an F on a high school civics exam.[31]

Once upon a time, a lot of American parents had their children memorize the capitals of all fifty states. "The capital of Vermont?" they would ask their four-year-old. "Montpelier," she would proudly respond. There are lots of reasons to doubt the value of such rituals. Anybody who can read and write can quickly google these facts. Professional success in tomorrow's economy will depend on acquiring skills that machines have not yet mastered, not in regurgitating facts that are already known. And since rote learning is hardly the best way to impart political values, it was always naive to think that an adorable display of civic trivia might somehow turn today's toddlers into tomorrow's courageous defenders of democracy.

And yet, it is telling that such rituals have fallen by the wayside over the past decades. Just as schools have begun to neglect the task of instilling public spirit in their students, so too many parents have seemingly become less interested in imparting a sense of civic duty to their children.[32]

It would be unfair to claim that the American educational system is altogether lacking in political zeal. After all, nearly every college campus still harbors a few heroic fiefdoms that pursue an intensely ideological mission. Especially in the humanities and the more politicized fields of the social sciences, many professors hope to effect a real change of attitude in their students. But far from seeking to preserve the most valuable aspects of our political system, their overriding objective is, all too often, to help students recognize its manifold injustices and hypocrisies.

This basic reflex takes different form in different disciplines. In many English departments, it is to deconstruct the values of the Enlightenment, all the better to expose them as racist, or colonialist, or heteronormative. In many History departments, it is to give the lie to stories of political progress, demonstrating the degree to which liberal democracies have always produced immense injustice. In many Sociology departments, it is to shine a light on the deepest pockets of poverty and disadvantage in the country, showcasing the manifold ways in which today's America remains discriminatory.

Each of these approaches points to some important insights. And yet, their combined effect is to leave many students feeling that a disdain for our inherited political institutions is a hallmark of intellectual sophistication. As one unusually bright and inquisitive English major explained to me, she felt deeply conflicted: On the one hand, she knew that democracy was a creation of the Enlightenment, and could only work when shored up by a widespread acceptance of Enlightenment values. On the other hand, she knew that the Enlightenment had been very cruel, and that its values were deeply misguided. Did this imply that she should afford greater appreciation to the Enlightenment than she had been taught, or that she should jettison the unthinking commitment to democracy on which she had been raised?

I readily agreed that the conflict she identified is real: she is absolutely right that we have to choose either to believe in both democracy and the Enlightenment or to believe in neither democracy nor the Enlightenment. My hope, of course, was that she would ultimately recognize how much there is of value in the intellectual tradition that gave rise to liberal democracy. But as the term went on, I got the impression that she had bitten the other bullet—and decided to rethink her belief in democracy instead of her hostility to the Enlightenment.

The kind of attitude my student has imbibed at Harvard now has a degree of pedagogical influence that is vastly out of proportion to its prominence in the country's faculty lounges, in part because it has deeply shaped the pedagogical mission of graduate schools of education across America. These schools have, in turn, acquired a much greater role in shaping the nation's educators now that graduate degrees in pedagogy have become an all-but-necessary qualification for senior jobs in the field. As a result, schools of education now play a big role in shaping the political values students of all ages are taught at schools across America.[33]

In many places, the result has been to turn civics into an anticivic enterprise. Having imbibed sociological accounts about the pervasive injustices that define modern society and learned to deconstruct the "problematic" values of the Enlightenment, teachers and principals have become much less likely to teach civics in a way that encourages their students to become proud defenders of liberal democracy.[34]

Many conservative thinkers have suggested a simple remedy to these complex ills. As David Brooks put the point in a recent column, the history of western civilization should be taught in a "confidently progressive" manner: "There were certain great figures, like Socrates, Erasmus, Montesquieu and Rousseau, who helped fitfully propel the nations to higher reaches of the humanistic ideal."[35]

Brooks is right to emphasize the importance of civic education. But he is wrong to suggest that the future of civics should consist in quite so hagiographic an account of the past. For all of its flaws, there is, after all, an important kernel of truth to the critiques that parts of the academic left level against liberal democracy. Even though they aspired to universality, many Enlightenment thinkers wound up excluding large groups from moral consideration. Even though they have huge accomplishments to their name, many of the "great men" of history committed horrifying misdeeds. And even though the ideal of liberal democracy is very much worth defending, its current practice continues to tolerate some shameful injustices.

Both the history of the Enlightenment and the reality of liberal democracy are complex. Any attempt to present them in uncritical terms is bound to run counter to the basic Enlightenment value of veracity, and to undermine the basic democratic principle of striving toward political equality. It is the recognition of these facts—as well as understandable anger at the blithe dismissal of them on large parts of the right—that make it so tempting for the bulk of today's journalists and academics to settle into a pose of pure and persistent critique.

But an exclusive focus on today's injustices is no more intellectually honest than an unthinking exhortation of the greatness of western civilization. To be true to its own ideals, civic education thus needs to feature both the real injustices and the great achievements of liberal democracy—and strive to make students as determined to rectify the former as they are to defend the latter.

One integral part of this education should be an account of the reasons why the principles of liberal democracy retain a special appeal. Teachers and professors should spend much more time pointing out that ideological alternatives to liberal democracy, from fascism to communism, and from autocracy to theocracy, remain as repellent today as they have been in the past. And they should also be much more clear about the fact that the right response to hypocrisy is not to dismiss appealing principles that are often invoked insincerely—but rather to work even harder for them to be put into practice at long last.

Over the past decades, our habits of mind were shaped by the favorable circumstances in which we lived.

The forward march of history seemed assured. Opportunities were many and enemies were few. And so the age-old belief that political liberty needs to be defended anew by each generation came to seem increasingly arcane. Though we never quite disavowed it, it ceased to guide us to any significant degree.

How quickly the winds of change have turned: Donald Trump

is sitting in the White House. Authoritarian populists are on the rise across much of Western Europe. The rapid erosion of political liberty in Poland and Hungary shows that, even in the twenty-first century, the process of democratic consolidation remains a two-way street. The arc of history, it seems, need not bend toward democracy after all.

If the future is not foreordained, the mission the Founding Fathers gave to anybody who occupies the high office of citizen is more timely than ever: We all have a solemn duty to uphold and promote democratic institutions. A key part of this duty is to persuade those around us—and to prepare those who will come after us—to do the same.

Humans are astoundingly versatile. Our grandparents would have found it inconceivable that civic education would atrophy to the degree it has. Conversely, it now seems inconceivable that we might rebuild a country in which writers aim to spread the values of liberal democracy; civics stands at the core of the curriculum; teachers at all levels spare no effort to impart a deep understanding of the Constitution and its intellectual moorings to their students; and most citizens recognize that, if they want it to survive, they need to do ideological battle for their political system at every opportunity.

But one thing is clear: Social media has only had such a corrosive effect on liberal democracy because the moral foundations of our political system are far more brittle than we realized. And so anybody who seeks to make a contribution to revitalizing liberal democracy must help to rebuild it on a more stable ideological footing.

CONCLUSION

Fighting for Our Convictions

WHEN A POLITICAL SYSTEM persists for decades or centuries, it is easy for those who have never known anything else to assume that it is immutable. History, it seems to them, has finally come to a halt. Stability will reign forevermore.

But while the chronicles of humanity contain plenty of regimes that enjoyed remarkable longevity, all of them have one thing in common: eventually, they failed. Athenian democracy lasted for about two centuries. Romans ruled themselves for nearly five hundred years. The Republic of Venice remained serene for over a millennium. Anybody who predicted the demise of these polities in their later years could easily have been mocked. Why, they might have been asked by their contemporaries, should a system that has survived for hundreds of years collapse in the next fifty? And yet, there did come a moment in which Athenian democracy, self-government in Rome, and even the Republic of Venice left the stage of history.[1]

We would do well to take this lesson to heart.

The seven decades since the end of World War II have afforded the peoples of North America and Western Europe unprecedented peace and prosperity. Unlike most of our ancestors, many of us have never had to brave war or revolution, starvation or civic strife. The idea that democracy might suddenly give way—that the dawn of a new era might bring death or hunger instead of tolerance and affluence—goes against every hour and every day of our lived experience.

But history is full of people who could not imagine that the peace and stability to which they had grown accustomed over the course of their brief lives might somehow end. It is full of pagan priests and French aristocrats, of Russian peasants and German Jews. If we do not want to end like them, we need to be more vigilant—and start to fight for our most fervently held values.

For the better part of a century, liberal democracy has been the dominant political system in much of the world. That era may now be drawing to a close.

Over the past decades, countries across North America and Western Europe have become less democratic. Our political system promises to let the people rule. But in practice, it ignores the popular will with disheartening frequency. Unnoticed by most political scientists, a system of rights without democracy has taken hold.

More recently, political newcomers have found great success by promising to return power to the people. But where they have managed to form a government, they have made their societies a lot less liberal—and quickly begun to ignore the people's true preferences. In Hungary and the Philippines, in Poland and the United States, individual rights and the rule of law are now under concerted attack from populist strongmen. The most serious competitor to the system of rights without democracy has turned out to be a system of democracy without rights.

Will the current crisis end in a dramatic swing from undemocratic liberalism to illiberal democracy, followed by a gradual descent into outright dictatorship? Or can the defenders of liberal democracy manage to weather the populist onslaught—and renew a political system that has, for all its shortcomings, fostered unprecedented peace and prosperity?

It's tempting to assume that the populists who are now in the ascendant in so many parts of the world will fail to deliver on their promises and quickly fall from grace.

There have certainly been cases in which strongman leaders have been booted from power after brief and disastrous terms in office. The first Law and Justice Party government in Poland, for example, lost its parliamentary majority when a key ally defected in 2007, and was soundly defeated in subsequent elections. In South Korea, meanwhile, millions of citizens took to the streets to protest a corrupt president with authoritarian predilections in the fall of 2016; Park Geun-hye was eventually impeached and is now an inmate at the Seoul Correctional Facility.[2]

A one-time victory for a populist strongman need not mean that the bell has irrevocably tolled for liberal democracy. When its defenders make common cause against the populists, use mass protests to resist their power grabs, and boot them from office at the first opportunity, they have a decent chance of saving the system.

But for every story of populist demise, there are two or three of populist triumph. In many countries around the world, authoritarian strongmen who were widely expected to fail or flail have consolidated their hold on power and made it impossible for the opposition to oust them in free and fair elections.

In Turkey and Venezuela, for example, populist governments delivered real economic improvements during their first terms in office and won reelection by handsome margins. But before long, their short-sighted policies began to backfire, and their repression of the opposition grew increasingly heavy-handed. By the time their popularity declined, these populists had effectively dismantled independent checks on their power. The defenders of liberal democracy were, despite their best efforts, unable to stop their countries from slouching toward dictatorship.[3]

This creates a scary precedent for the countries that have only just elected strongmen to the highest office in the land. In India, Poland, and the Philippines, authoritarian populists have taken power over the course of the past decade. It is as yet difficult to foretell just how far their assault on liberal democracy will go, or how effective the growing resistance to them will prove. But what is beyond doubt is that they have set out on the same path as their ideological comrades in countries that can no longer be considered democracies.[4]

The first three steps taken by Narendra Modi in India or Jarosław Kaczynski in Poland bear a striking resemblance to the first three steps taken, for instance, by Recep Erdoğan in Turkey. Does that mean that they will ultimately take steps five and eight and ten as well?

We won't know for sure for another few years. There is every possibility that these countries will manage to reverse course. But the path of least resistance now seems to descend into the same abyss.

———

India is the most populous democracy in the world. Poland has long been hailed as the most successful case of postcommunist transition. If authoritarian strongmen manage to consolidate their rule in either country, it would be a big blow for the hope that freedom and self-government might eventually take root around the world. But it is less clear what a slide toward dictatorship in one of these countries would imply for the fate that awaits liberal democracy in its traditional heartlands.

In most parts of North America and Western Europe, democracy has been around for much longer than it has in countries like Hungary or Turkey, Poland or India. The region's political culture is more deeply ingrained. Its institutions are more entrenched. Its citizens are more affluent and educated. So how can we know whether the rise of authoritarian populists will prove as disastrous here as it did there?

No clear precedent can help us answer this question. Never before have the citizens of supposedly consolidated democracies been so critical of their political system. Never before have they been so open to authoritarian alternatives. And never before have they voted for populist strongmen who openly disdain the basic rules and norms of liberal democracy in such great numbers. But though it is far too early to come to a confident projection, much less a definite conclusion, the last months have provided us with a crucial test case: the election of Donald J. Trump.

Worried that a demagogue may one day capture the presidency, the Founding Fathers entrusted the legislature and the judiciary with the tools they need to stand up to an errant executive: The Supreme Court can rule that an order given by the president violates the Constitution. And if he breaks the law or ignores the courts, Congress can impeach him.

But these institutions are ultimately composed of nothing more than flesh-and-blood politicians and bureaucrats. If, out of complicity or cowardice, they do not use the tools with which the Founding Fathers have entrusted them, the letter of the law will quickly turn out to be of little consequence. So what, in practice, would it take for Congress and the courts to stand up to the president?

Not long ago, most political scientists predicted that a man with the views and the character of Donald Trump could never be elected president of the United States. Even once he was elected, they kept insisting that there were some red lines a president can never cross without incurring instant rebellion. If a president demanded a pledge of personal loyalty from the director of the Federal Bureau of Investigation or if his closest advisors collaborated with a hostile power, if he repeatedly refused to condemn white supremacists or called for his adversary to be put in jail, the blowback would be swift and it would be mighty.

The reality, it turns out, is rather more equivocal.

In his first months in office, Trump crossed each of these supposed red lines.[5] But as soon as we looked back at them through the rearview mirror, they started to appear orange, or yellow, or green.

As I am writing this conclusion, most congressional Republicans have not yet denounced Trump's repeated assaults on American democracy. He retains the fervent support of a substantial minority of voters, including a large majority of self-identified Republicans. As he himself likes to boast, it is not clear what he would have to do for this to change.[6]

Things could easily get worse. In the coming months and years, Trump could disregard a court order or fire even more officials investigating his alleged misdeeds. He could shutter a newspaper or refuse to accept the result of an election.

If Congress and the courts act with courage and resolve in such circumstances, they have every chance of containing his authoritarian instincts. But the Constitution cannot defend itself. Until Trump's allies and accomplices prove willing to put country above party, the imminent danger to the American Republic will not be banished.

So far the pessimistic scenario. Without a doubt, plenty of signs suggest that liberal democracies might prove more susceptible to populist takeover than scholars have long believed. But there are also some good reasons to be optimistic about America's ability to renew its democracy after Trump leaves office.

Since the inauguration, millions of Americans have voiced their opposition to his most egregious actions and policies. Grassroots opposition groups have been very effective at demonstrating that the president does not speak in the name of all Americans. If his opponents are able to retain some of their energy in the years to come, they will pose a formidable obstacle to any major power grab.

Independent institutions have not opposed Trump nearly as swiftly or as strongly as political scientists might have predicted a few years ago. And yet, they too are finally starting to take important steps in the right direction. Robert Mueller's appointment as Special Counsel has helped preserve the independence of the country's law enforcement agencies. Even congressional Republicans are gradually becoming more willing to take on the president.[7]

Public opinion is starting to shift as well. The polls are not nearly as disastrous for Trump as his opponents like to believe or the cherry-picked surveys they spread on social media would suggest. But Trump's popularity really did decline during his first nine months in office, leaving him with less support than any of his predecessors enjoyed at a comparable stage of their tenure.[8]

It remains completely unclear what the rest of Trump's presidency might bring. But at this point, it does seem likely that the coming years will be a minefield for his administration. So, by the time you're reading this, his popularity may have fallen to new lows. Congressional Republicans may finally have found the courage of their convictions. Some of his closest advisors may have been indicted. It is not beyond the realm of possibility that he himself might be facing impeachment hearings—or has already resigned. And even if nothing quite so drastic should come to pass, he is probably more likely to lose than to win his bid for reelection.[9]

It's tempting to take the optimistic scenario one step further, then: If Trump winds up flaming out, his brief presidency might help to inoculate the United States against illiberal democracy. After years in which citizens took an increasingly dim view of their political system, the prospect of the country's imminent descent into authoritarianism has already reawakened some citizens' attachment to the Constitution. If Trump should leave office in disgrace, his demise could forge a new spirit of unity. Determined never to repeat the ghastly experience of his presidency, Americans might rally around the flag and embark on a phase of civic renewal. And by fighting off the current infection, they might just build up the necessary antibodies to remain immune against new bouts of the populist disease for decades to come.

Both the straightforwardly pessimistic and the straightforwardly optimistic scenarios ultimately seem implausible.

Trump will likely find it hard to recover from the turmoil he has created during his first year in office. With his approval ratings continuing to fall and his legislative agenda stalled in Congress, with a major investigation into his campaign proceeding apace and Republican legislators gradually growing more willing to distance themselves from the president, he probably lacks the support to concentrate power in his own hands.

But optimists should recall that Trump could inflict immense damage on American institutions (or provoke an unnecessary war) even if he continues to be relatively isolated and reasonably unpopular. At some point over the coming years, he may well provoke a constitutional crisis. Even if the president should ultimately be forced to back down from any power grab, the damage to America's constitutional norms would likely be enormous. The acute danger he poses to the rules of the democratic game is far from over.

Similarly, it is certainly within the realm of imagination that a failure of the Trump presidency could somehow unite Americans around a renewed commitment to liberal democracy. But it is probably more likely to deepen the country's poisonous partisan divide. A significant minority of Americans who now regard Trump as a hero would then see him as a martyr, growing even more angry at the political establishment. And even some of the erstwhile supporters who do turn on him might conclude that they need to put their trust into an even more radical and uncompromising tribune if they are to drain the swamp.

Like populist insurgents around the world, Trump is as much a symptom of the current crisis as he is its cause. He could only have conquered the White House in the first place because so many citizens have grown deeply disenchanted with democracy. In turn, so many citizens could only have grown so deeply disenchanted with democracy because of longstanding social and economic trends.

So when Donald Trump leaves office, he may well be succeeded by a surprisingly conventional figure. For a few election cycles, the reins of government may once again rest with a capable politician who respects the basic norms of liberal democracy. But unless politicians from both sides of the aisle come together to address the trends that are driving citizens' disenchantment with the status quo, a new crop of populists is likely to arise. And when the next would-be authoritarian enters the White House fifteen or thirty years from now, I fear that America may turn out to be even more vulnerable to his appeal. If the current erosion of democratic norms continues apace, and the deep partisan divide continues to fester, the American immune system will have become even more compromised at that point. The virus of authoritarianism could then ravage the body politic without meeting much resistance.

The Trump presidency will, most likely, be no more than the opening salvo to a much more protracted fight—one that will last well beyond his retirement and extend well beyond the United States.

And so the historical example that most haunts me when I think about the likely future of France or Spain, of Sweden or the United States is neither Hungary nor Turkey; it is the Roman Republic.

By the second century BC, rapid social change and longstanding economic conflicts had fused into a toxic brew of anger and resentment. Promising to fix the woes of poor Romans by redistributing land, Tiberius Gracchus was elected Tribune of the Plebs in 133 BC. Old patrician elites were horrified and tried to stop his most radical reforms. When he attempted to override their veto, and the ensuing constitutional crisis showed no sign of abating, the conflict turned violent. In a chaotic scene fueled by mutual apprehension, Tiberius and three hundred of his followers were clubbed to death. It was the first outbreak of large-scale civic strife in the history of the Roman Republic.

In the wake of Tiberius's assassination, relative calm returned to Rome. But a decade later, his brother, Gaius Gracchus, succeeded him as Tribune. Trying to institute even more radical reforms, and provoking an even deeper constitutional crisis, he too was killed by his political opponents. This time, 3,000 of his followers were put to death.[10]

Over the next decades, much the same pattern played out over and over again. The tumultuous rule of a proud people's tribune led to violent clashes with obstinate patricians. Normality was restored for a little while. Passions subsided. Peace returned. But the republic's underlying problems had not been solved, and the anger they occasioned was only waiting in the wings.

As a result, the brand of politics propagated by the Gracchi and perpetuated by their opponents shaped the Roman Republic long after they themselves had left the scene. Every dozen or so years, a new follower was able to capture power. Each time, the norms and rules of the Roman Republic were a little less capable of containing the assault.

There was no one breaking point, no clear moment at which contemporaries realized that their political institutions had become obsolete. And yet, over the course of a tumultuous century, the Roman Republic slowly withered. As the old norms of restraint crumbled, violence spiraled out of control. By the time ordinary Romans recognized that they had lost the freedom to rule themselves, the republic had long been lost.[11]

———

At the height of his cruel reign, Nero set about humiliating his rivals and killing his relatives. He murdered his mother and his stepbrother. He executed a long succession of senior statesmen. Then he turned his attention to an influential senator from a storied Roman family. Florus, he commanded, was to dance at his games, making a fool of himself in front of a jeering crowd.

Florus did not know what to do. If he obeyed the command, he would legitimate Nero's rule and bring shame upon his family. If he refused, Nero would likely have him killed. Desperate for advice, he turned to Agrippinus, a famous Stoic philosopher.

The Stoics were known for arguing that people with the right philosophical training could always triumph over their circumstances. Nobody, their logic went, can sway your mind. As long as you learn to be indifferent to everything outside of that—giving up your attachment to material things and even to other people—your well-being is under your own control. A true philosopher, they concluded, can be happy even when he is being tortured on the rack.

So in turning to Agrippinus, Florus was hardly making a neutral choice. Given what he would have known about Stoic philosophy, he must have expected the advice to be unequivocal: "Stand up to the tyrant. Don't worry about what happens once you've done the right thing."

But that is not what Agrippinus told Florus. Instead, he said that his choice no longer made a difference: "Go take part in the games!"

Florus was flummoxed. "So why don't you take part in them yourself?" he asked.

"Because I haven't even considered the possibility," Agrippinus explained. "Anybody who stoops to think about this kind of thing is already on the way to losing his character. Is life preferable to death? It is. Is pleasure preferable to pain? Of course it is. 'If I don't take part in the tragic spectacle,' you tell me, 'he'll cut off my head!' Go, then, and take part in the games. But I will not."[12]

I've been thinking about the Stoics a lot in the past months. There is something off-puttingly austere about their worldview. As they recognized, the only way to gain complete control over your fate is to become indifferent to everything around you. If you love another person, you cannot be happy if terrible things are happening to him or her. If you like your fellow citizens, you cannot be content if they are suffering economic hardship or facing racial discrimination. And if you care about values like freedom or equality, you cannot be serene when the fate of liberal democracy hangs in the balance.

For all these reasons, I do not consider myself a Stoic. Far from being indifferent about things outside of my control, I value them so much that I am willing—even keen—to entwine their well-being with my own. To be content as everything around me is falling apart does not seem to me to be the life of an enlightened philosopher but rather that of a cynic or a sociopath.

And yet, there is a deep font of wisdom in the teachings of the Stoics. For they rightly recognize that I am never going to do the right thing if I calculate what the likely outcome of my actions is going to be at each and every turn. When I am faced with real danger, my incentives are always going to point me in the direction of inaction or acquiescence:

"I should probably say something. But what difference will it make?"

"I should probably call them out on this. But how will I feed my family if I lose my job?"

"I should probably stand up to the government. But what will I do if its loyalists come after me?"

Agrippinus, then, was completely right on one important point: If I wait for imminent danger to figure out what risks I am willing to take, I am likely to lose myself in the one moment that truly counts. Since I hope to do the right thing when courage will most be needed—and most difficult to come by—I am therefore trying to heed his advice. Long before I actually face a dangerous decision, I am building up the resolve to do the right thing.

One of the great privileges of living in a stable democracy is that we don't usually have to confront these kinds of questions.

Until very recently, most of us lived in ordinary times. The stakes of politics have always been high. But it rarely took great courage to stand up for what we hold dear. Doing the right thing did not require huge sacrifices. If we lost an important battle, we knew that there would be another chance to win the war.

Now, by contrast, we are entering extraordinary times. The stakes of politics have become existential. In the years to come, it may take more and more courage to stand up for what we hold dear. If we are to do the right thing at the decisive hour, we need to be willing to make a real sacrifice. For if we lose the next few battles to the populists, the war may be over much too soon.

Thankfully, there is a lot that those of us who want liberal democracy to survive the dawning age of populism can do: We can take to the streets to stand up to the populists. We can remind our fellow citizens of the virtues of both freedom and self-government. We can push established parties to embrace an ambitious program capable of renewing liberal democracy's promise of a better future for all. And if we do win—as I very much hope we shall—we can muster the grace and the determination to bring our adversaries back to the democratic fold.

It is, as yet, impossible to predict what the ultimate fate of our political system will be. Perhaps the rise of the populists will turn out to be a short-lived phase, remembered with some mix of bafflement and curiosity a hundred years from now. Or perhaps it will turn out to be an epochal change, heralding a world order in which individual rights are violated at every turn and true self-government vanishes from the face of the earth. Nobody can promise us a happy end. But those of us who truly care about our values and our institutions are determined to fight for our convictions without regard for the consequences. Though the fruits of our labor may remain uncertain, we will do what we can to save liberal democracy.

Notes

Introduction

1. Margaret Talev and Sahil Kapur, "Trump Vows Election-Day Suspense without Seeking Voters He Needs to Win," Bloomberg, 20 October, 2016, https://www.bloomberg.com/news/articles/2016-10-20/trump-vows-election-day-suspense-without-seeking-voters-he-needs-to-win; Associated Press, "Trump to Clinton: 'You'd Be in Jail'" *New York Times* website, video, October 10, 2016, https://www.nytimes.com/video/us/politics/100000004701741/trump-to-clinton-youd-be-in-jail.html; Yochi Dreazen, "Trump's Love for Brutal Leaders Like the Philippines' Rodrigo Duterte, Explained," *Vox*, May 1, 2017, https://www.vox.com/world/2017/5/1/15502610/trump-philippines-rodrigo-duterte-obama-putin-erdogan-dictators.
2. Francis Fukuyama, "The End of History?" *National Interest,* no. 16 (Summer 1989): 3–18, quotation on p. 4; Francis Fukuyama, *The End of History and the Last Man* (New York: Free Press, 1992).
3. For a variety of early responses to Fukuyama, see for example essays by Harvey Mansfield, E. O. Wilson, Gertrude Himmelfarb, Robin Fox, Robert J. Samuelson, and Joseph S. Nye, "Responses to Fukuyama," *National Interest,* no. 56 (Summer 1989): 34–44.
4. Adam Przeworski, Limongi Neto, and Fernando Papaterra, "Modernization: Theories and Facts," *World Politics* 49, no. 2 (1997): 155–183, 165. (The figure given by Przeworski, Neto, and Papaterra is $6,055 in 1985 PPP USD. Adjusting for an average inflation rate of 2.62 percent, this makes about $13.503 USD in 2016.)

5. Przeworski, Limongi, and Papaterra, "Modernization," 170–171.
6. See Andreas Schedler, "What Is Democratic Consolidation?" *Journal of Democracy* 9, no. 2 (1989): 91–107; Larry Jay Diamond, "Toward Democratic Consolidation," *Journal of Democracy* 5, no. 3 (1994): 4–17; and Scott Mainwaring, "Transitions to Democracy and Democratic Consolidation: Theoretical and Comparative Issues," Working Paper no. 130, The Helen Kellogg Institute for International Studies, University of Notre Dame, November 1989.
7. Juan Linz and Alfred Stepan, "Toward Consolidated Democracies," *Journal of Democracy* 7, no. 2 (1996): 14–33.
8. Roberto Stefan Foa and Yascha Mounk, "The Democratic Disconnect," *Journal of Democracy* 27, no. 3 (2016): 5–17; Roberto Stefan Foa and Yascha Mounk, "The Signs of Deconsolidation," *Journal of Democracy* 28, no. 1 (2017): 5–15.
9. Foa and Mounk, "Democratic Disconnect."
10. See for example "Trump Attacks China in Twitter Outburst," BBC News, December 5, 2016, http://www.bbc.co.uk/news/world-asia -china-38167022; Katie Reilly, "Here Are All the Times Donald Trump Insulted Mexico," *Time,* August 31, 2016, http://time.com/4473972 /donald-trump-mexico-meeting-insult/; Adam Liptak and Peter Baker, "Trump Promotes Original 'Travel Ban,' Eroding His Legal Case," *New York Times,* June 5, 2017, https://www.nytimes.com/2017/06/05/us /politics/trump-travel-ban.html.
11. On Poland, see Joanna Fomina and Jacek Kucharczyk, "Populism and Protest in Poland," *Journal of Democracy* 27, no. 4 (2016): 58–68; Jacques Rupnik, "Surging Illiberalism in the East," *Journal of Democracy* 27, no. 4 (2016): 77–87; as well as Bojan Bugaric and Tom Ginsburg, "The Assault on Postcommunist Courts," *Journal of Democracy* 27, no. 3 (2016): 69–82. On Turkey, see Berk Esen and Sebnem Gumuscu, "Turkey: How the Coup Failed," *Journal of Democracy* 28, no. 1 (2017): 59–73; Dexter Filkins, "Erdogan's March to Dictatorship in Turkey," *New Yorker,* March 31, 2016; and Soner Cagaptay, *The New Sultan: Erdogan and the Crisis of Modern Turkey* (London: I. B. Tauris, 2017).
12. Andrew Bennett, "Case Study Methods: Design, Use, and Comparative Advantages," in *Models, Numbers, and Cases: Methods for Studying International Relations,* ed. Detlef F. Sprinz and Yael Wolinsky-Nahmias (Ann Arbor: University of Michigan Press, 2004), 29.
13. As György Lengyel and Gabriella Ilonszki put the point in 2010, "most local and foreign political observers had, for many years, regarded Hungary as the foremost example of a smooth transition from state socialism to democracy, the most consolidated democracy in East Central Eu-

rope." György Lengyel and Gabriella Ilonszki, "Hungary: Between Consolidated and Simulated Democracy," in *Democratic Elitism: New Theoretical and Comparative Perspectives,* ed. Heinrich Best and John Higley (Leiden: Brill, 2010), 150. See also Attila Ágh, "Early Democratic Consolidation in Hungary and the Europeanisation of the Hungarian Polity," in *Prospects for Democratic Consolidation in East-Central Europe,* ed. Geoffrey Pridham and Attila Ágh (Manchester: Manchester University Press, 2001), 167; and Miklós Sükösd, "Democratic Transformation and the Mass Media in Hungary: From Stalinism to Democratic Consolidation," in *Democracy and the Media: A Comparative Perspective,* ed. Richard Gunther and Anthony Mughan, 122–164 (Cambridge: Cambridge University Press, 2000).

14. Marton Dunai and Krisztina Than, "Hungary's Fidesz Wins Historic Two-Thirds Mandate," Reuters, April 25, 2010. See also Attila Ágh, "Early Consolidation and Performance Crisis: The Majoritarian-consensus Democracy Debate in Hungary," *West European Politics* 24, no. 3 (2001): 89–112.

15. See János Kornai, "Hungary's U-turn: Retreating from Democracy," *Journal of Democracy* 26, no. 3 (2015): 34–48; and Miklós Bánkuti, Gábor Halmai, and Kim Lane Scheppele, "Disabling the Constitution," *Journal of Democracy* 23, no. 3 (2012): 138–146. Jan Puhl, "A Whiff of Corruption in Orbán's Hungary," *Spiegel Online,* January 17, 2017; Keno Verseck, "Amendment Alarms Opposition: Orbán Cements His Power with New Voting Law," *Spiegel Online,* October 30, 2012; Lili Bayer, "Hungarian Law Targets Soros, Foreign-Backed NGOs," Politico, March 9, 2017. Andrew MacDowall, "US-Linked Top University Fears New Rules Will Force It Out of Hungary," *Guardian,* March 29, 2017.

16. Csaba Toth, "Full Text of Viktor Orbán's Speech at Băile Tuşnad (Tusnádfürdő) of 26 July 2014," *Budapest Beacon,* July 29, 2014, http://budapestbeacon.com/public-policy/full-text-of-viktor-orbans-speech-at-baile-tusnad-tusnadfurdo-of-26-july-2014/10592.

17. "In the Final Hour, a Plea for Economic Sanity and Humanity," Letter to the Editor, signed by Joseph Stiglitz, Thomas Piketty, Massimo D'Alema, et al., *Financial Times,* June 4, 2015. "Europe Will Benefit from Greece Being Given a Fresh Start," Letter to the Editor, signed by Joseph Stiglitz et al., *Financial Times,* January 22, 2015. See also J. Gordon et al., "Greece: Ex-Post Evaluation of Exceptional Access under the 2010 Stand-By Arrangement," IMF Country Report no. 13/156, International Monetary Fund, Washington, DC, June 2013, https://www.imf.org/external/pubs/ft/scr/2013/cr13156.pdf.

18. Lucy Rodgers and Nassos Stylianou, "How Bad Are Things for the People of Greece?" BBC News, July 16, 2015.

19. Liz Alderman, "Tsipras Declares Creditors' Debt Proposal for Greece 'Absurd,'" *New York Times,* June 5, 2015. See also "In the Final Hours" letter from Stiglitz et al., and Gordon, IMF Country Report, "Greece: Ex-Post Evaluation."

20. Helen Nianias, "Alexis Tsipras of Syriza Is Far from Greek Orthodox: The Communist 'Harry Potter' Who Could Implode the Eurozone," *Independent,* January 21, 2015; C. J. Polychroniou, "Syriza's Lies and Empty Promises," *Al Jazeera,* July 6, 2015; Andreas Rinke, "Tsipras Has Caused a Disaster, Says German Conservative Lawmaker," Reuters, July 5, 2015; "Bumbling toward Disaster: Greece's Leaders Look a Poor Match to the Challenges Facing the Country," *Economist,* March 19, 2015.

21. Renee Maltezou and Lefteris Papadimas, "Greeks Defy Europe with Overwhelming Referendum 'No,'" Reuters, July 5, 2015.

22. Peter Spiegel, "A Comparison of Greece's Reform List and Creditors' Proposals," *Financial Times,* July 10, 2015.

23. Suzanne Daley and Liz Alderman, "Premier of Greece, Alexis Tsipras, Accepts Creditors' Austerity Deal," *New York Times,* July 13, 2015.

24. However, as described at the end of Chapter 2, the reality was a little more complicated than suggested in this brief summary. A big part of the reason why other European leaders were reluctant to cut Greece a better deal is that they were mindful of their citizens' strong opposition to a more generous bailout package. In imposing their will on the Greek people, they were, in other words, largely following the will of their own people.

25. See T. C. W. Blanning, "Frederick the Great and Enlightened Absolutism," in *Enlightened Absolutism: Reform and Reformers in Late Eighteenth Century Europe,* ed. H. M. Scott (London: Macmillan, 1990); Jonathan I. Israel, "Libertas Philosophandi in the Eighteenth Century: Radical Enlightenment versus Moderate Enlightenment (1750–1776)," in *Freedom of Speech,* ed. Elizabeth Powers (Lewisburg, PA: Bucknell University Press, 2011).

26. The classic essay on the strict limits on individual freedom in the ancient world remains Benjamin Constant, "The Liberty of the Ancients Compared with That of the Moderns," in *Political Writings,* ed. Biancamaria Fontana, 309–328 (New York: Cambridge University Press, 1988).

27. Bertrand Russell, *The Problems of Philosophy* (Oxford: Oxford University Press, 1912), 63.

28. US Department of Labor, Bureau of Labor Statistics, "100 Years of U.S. Consumer Spending: Data for the Nation, New York City, and Boston," Report 991, May 2006, (Washington, DC: BLS, 2006); https://www.bls

.gov/opub/uscs/report991.pdf; US Census Bureau, "Income and Poverty in the United States: 2015," Table A-1: Households by Total Money Income, Race, and Hispanic Origin of Householder: 1967 to 2015, https://www.census.gov/data/tables/2016/demo/income-poverty/p60-256.html (accessed July 12, 2017).

29. For a detailed account of the economic causes of populism, see Chapter 5.
30. For a detailed account of the cultural causes of populism, see Chapter 6.
31. For a detailed account of the technological causes of populism, see Chapter 4.
32. For a detailed account of how to combat the economic causes of populism, see Chapter 8.
33. For a detailed account of how to build an inclusive patriotism, see Chapter 7.
34. For a detailed account of how to respond to the rise of social media and reinvigorate civic education, see Chapter 9.
35. Yascha Mounk, *The Age of Responsibility: Luck, Choice, and the Welfare State* (Cambridge, MA: Harvard University Press, 2017).

Part One. The Crisis of Liberal Democracy

1. Tony Judt, *The Memory Chalet* (London: Penguin, 2010).
2. This particular formulation is taken from Steven Levitsky and Lucan Way, *Competitive Authoritarianism* (New York: Cambridge University Press, 2010), 5–6.
3. This problem, which stems from an overemphasis on the *mechanism* of elections, rather than the *outcome* of popular rule which that mechanism is supposed to ensure, also holds for even more minimalist definitions. Joseph Schumpeter, for example, defined a democracy as any political system in which the most powerful political offices are filled "through a competitive struggle for the people's vote." Joseph Alois Schumpeter, *Capitalism, Socialism, and Democracy* (1942; London: Routledge, 2004), 269.
4. Democracy, on this (and indeed any sensible) account, is a scale. A set of binding institutions is democratic *to the extent* that it actually serves to translate popular views into public policy. Also note that, though I do not explicitly mention the requirement of "free and fair" elections in this definition, it is implied in it: any system that effectively translates popular views into public policy to a significant extent must realistically feature reasonably free and fair elections.

1. Democracy without Rights

1. Anthony Oberschall, "Opportunities and Framing in the Eastern European Revolts of 1989," in *Comparative Perspectives on Social Movements: Political Opportunities, Mobilizing Structures, and Cultural Framings,* ed. Doug McAdam, John D. McCarthy, and Mayer N. Zald (New York: Cambridge University Press, 1996), p. 93; Andreas Hadjar, "Non-violent Political Protest in East Germany in the 1980s: Protestant Church, Opposition Groups and the People," *German Politics* 12, no. 3 (2003): 107–128; Andrew Curry, "'We Are the People': A Peaceful Revolution in Leipzig," *Spiegel Online,* October 9, 2009.

2. H. Vorländer, M. Herold, and S. Schäller, *PEGIDA: Entwicklung, Zusammensetzung und Deutung einer Empörungsbewegung* (Wiesbaden: Springer-Verlag, 2015); J. M. Dostal, "The Pegida Movement and German Political Culture: Is Right-Wing Populism Here to Stay?" *Political Quarterly* 86, no. 4 (2015): 523–531; Naomi Conrad, "Leipzig, a City Divided by Anti-Islamist Group PEGIDA," *Deutsche Welle,* January 11, 2016.

3. Personal communication.

4. Personal communication.

5. For a more detailed account of my reporting on the refugee crisis, see Yascha Mounk, "Echt Deutsch: How the Refugee Crisis Is Changing a Nation's Identity," *Harper's,* April 2017.

6. On the definition of populism, and the important role played by its claim to speak for the people, see Cas Mudde, "The Populist Zeitgeist," *Government and Opposition* 39, no. 4 (2004): 541–563; Cas Mudde, *Populist Radical Right Parties in Europe* (Cambridge: Cambridge University Press, 2007); Jan-Werner Müller, *What Is Populism?* (Philadelphia: University of Pennsylvania Press, 2016), John B. Judis, *The Populist Explosion: How the Great Recession Transformed American and European Politics* (New York: Columbia Global Reports, 2016); as well as Yascha Mounk, "Pitchfork Politics: The Populist Threat to Liberal Democracy," *Foreign Affairs* 93 (2014): 27–36; and Yascha Mounk, "European Disunion: What the Rise of Populist Movements Means for Democracy," *New Republic* 248, no. 8–9 (2017): 58–63.

7. Seymour Martin Lipset and Stein Rokkan, "Cleavage Structures, Party Systems, and Voter Alignments: An Introduction," in *Party Systems and Voter Alignments: Cross-National Perspectives* (New York: Free Press, 1967), 1–64.

8. Peter Mair, *Party System Change: Approaches and Interpretations* (Oxford: Oxford University Press, 1997).

9. J. E. Lane and P. Pennings, eds., *Comparing Party System Change* (London: Routledge, 2003); and R. J. Dalton and M. P. Wattenberg, eds., *Parties without Partisans: Political Change in Advanced Industrial Democracies* (Oxford: Oxford University Press, 2002).

10. On Silvio Berlusconi's rise and rule, see Alexander Stille, *The Sack of Rome: Media + Money + Celebrity = Power = Silvio Berlusconi* (New York: Penguin, 2006). On the collapse of the postwar party system, see L. Morlino, "Crisis of Parties and Change of Party System in Italy," *Party Politics* 2, no. 1 (1996): 5–30; and L. Bardi, "Anti-party Sentiment and Party System Change in Italy," *European Journal of Political Research* 29, no. 3 (1996): 345–363.

11. Tsipras's Syriza took 26.3 percent of the vote and was able to form a government with the help of a right-wing populist party, Independent Greeks (ANEL). See Yascha Mounk, "The Trouble with Europe's Grand Coalitions," *New Yorker*, December 27, 2014, http://www.newyorker.com/news/news-desk/trouble-europes-grand-coalitions. See also Yannis Stavrakakis and Giorgos Katsambekis, "Left-wing Populism in the European Periphery: The Case of SYRIZA," *Journal of Political Ideologies* 19, no. 2 (2014): 119–142; and Paris Aslanidis and Cristóbal Rovira Kaltwasser, "Dealing with Populists in Government: The SYRIZA-ANEL Coalition in Greece," *Democratization* 23, no. 6 (2016): 1077–1091.

12. Sam Jones, "Spanish Election: Conservatives Win but Fall Short of Majority—As It Happened," *Guardian*, December 20, 2015; Giles Tremlett, "The Podemos Revolution: How a Small Group of Radical Academics Changed European Politics," *Guardian*, March 31, 2015.

13. Jacopo Barigazzi, "Beppe Grillo's 5Star Movement Hits Record High: Poll," Politico, March 21, 2017. For the latest polling in Italy, see https://en.wikipedia.org/wiki/Opinion_polling_for_the_next_Italian_general_election, accessed October 1, 2017. On the nature of the Five Star Movement, see Gianluca Passarelli and Dario Tuorto, "The Five Star Movement: Purely a Matter of Protest? The Rise of a New Party between Political Discontent and Reasoned Voting," *Party Politics* (2016).

14. Jon Sharman, "Anti-immigrant Party Takes First Place in Sweden, Poll Shows: Its Support Is at Nearly Double the Level during 2014 General Election," *Independent*, March 25, 2017. On the nature of the Sweden Democrats and the reasons for their rise, see Jens Rydgren and Sara van der Meiden, "Sweden, Now a Country Like All the Others? The Radical Right and the End of Swedish Exceptionalism," Working Paper 25, Department of Sociology, Stockholm University, June 2016.

15. Gregor Aisch, Matthew Bloch, K. K. Rebecca Lai, and Benoît Morenne, "How France Voted," *New York Times*, May 7, 2017. On the changing

nature of the Front National under Marine Le Pen's leadership, see Daniel Stockemer and Mauro Barisione. "The 'New' Discourse of the Front National under Marine Le Pen: A Slight Change with a Big Impact," *European Journal of Communication* 32, no. 2 (2017): 100–115; and Francesca Scrinzi, "A 'New' National Front? Gender, Religion, Secularism and the French Populist Radical Right," in *Gender and Far Right Politics in Europe*, ed. M. Köttig, R. Bitzan, and A. Petö, pp. 127–140 (Cham, Switzerland: Springer International Publishing, 2017).

16. For a different index that shows even more significant growth in antiestablishment voting over the past fifty years than the figure shown here, see Pippa Norris and Ronald Inglehart, "Trump, Brexit, and the Rise of Populism: Economic Have-Nots and Cultural Backlash," HKS Working Paper No. RWP16–026, Harvard Kennedy School, July 29, 2016, figure 4, available at https://papers.ssrn.com/sol3/papers.cfm?abstract_id=2818659.

17. Astra Taylor, "The Anti-democratic Urge," *New Republic*, August 18, 2016, https://newrepublic.com/article/135757/anti-democratic-urge.

18. Frank Furedi, "Populism: A Defence," Spiked Review, November 2016, http://www.spiked-online.com/spiked-review/article/populism-a-defence/19042#.WN8JlaOZP-Y.

19. Ivan Krastev, blurb on back cover of Müller, *What Is Populism?*

20. The economist Max Roser has done excellent work to show significant global improvements across a broad variety of metrics. See Max Roser, "The Short History of Global Living Conditions and Why It Matters That We Know It," Our World in Data website, https://ourworldindata.org/a-history-of-global-living-conditions-in-5-charts/. See also Christopher Fariss, "Respect for Human Rights Has Improved over Time: Modeling the Changing Standard of Accountability," *American Political Science Review* 108, no. 2 (2013): 297–318.

21. See Thomas Piketty and Gabriel Zucman, "Capital Is Back: Wealth-Income Ratios in Rich Countries 1700–2010," *Quarterly Journal of Economics* 129, no. 3 (2014): 1255–1310; Emmanuel Saez and Gabriel Zucman, "Wealth Inequality in the United States since 1913: Evidence from Capitalized Income Tax Data," *Quarterly Journal of Economics* 131, no. 2 (2016): 519–578; Branko Milanovic, *Global Inequality: A New Approach for the Age of Globalization* (Cambridge, MA: Harvard University Press, 2016); and Lawrence H. Summers, "US Economic Prospects: Secular Stagnation, Hysteresis, and the Zero Lower Bound," *Business Economics* 49, no. 2 (2014): 65–73.

22. Eliana Dockterman, "NYC Mayor to Skip Hillary Clinton Launch Event," *Time*, June 10, 2015, http://time.com/3916983/bill-de-blasio-hillary-clinton-campaign-launch-nyc/.

23. Kevin Williamson, "What Does Hillary Want?" *National Review,* July 21, 2016, http://www.nationalreview.com/article/438170/hillary-clinton -what-does-she-want.

24. See Hillary Clinton, "Hillary's Vision for America," The Office of Hillary Rodham Clinton website, https://www.hillaryclinton.com/issues/.

25. On Trump University, see Steve Eder, "Donald Trump Agrees to Pay $25 Million in Trump University Settlement," *New York Times,* November, 18, 2016; on unpaid workers, see Harper Neidig, "Report: Trump Has Refused to Pay Hundreds of Workers," *Hill,* June 9, 2016; also Alexandra Berzon, "Donald Trump's Business Plan Left a Trail of Unpaid Bills," *Wall Street Journal,* June 9, 2016.

26. On the border wall, see Donald Kerwin and Robert Warren, "The 2,000 Mile Wall in Search of a Purpose: Since 2007 Visa Overstays Have Outnumbered Undocumented Border Crossers by a Half Million," Center for Migration Studies, 2017, http://cmsny.org/publications/jmhs-visa -overstays-border-wall/; on lost jobs, see Federica Cocco, "Most US Manufacturing Jobs Lost to Technology, Not Trade," *Financial Times,* December 2, 2016.

27. Mounk, "Pitchfork Politics."

28. Carlos de la Torre, *Populist Seduction in Latin America,* 2nd ed. (Athens: Ohio University Press, 2010).

29. Tim Hains, "Trump: Hillary Clinton Can Be Understood with One Simple Phrase—'Follow the Money,'" Real Clear Politics, September 28, 2016, https://www.realclearpolitics.com/video/2016/09/28/trump_ hillary_clinton_can_be_understood_with_one_simple_phrase_--_follow _the_money.html.

30. James Traub, "The Party That Wants to Make Poland Great Again," *New York Times,* November 2, 2016, https://www.nytimes. com/2016/11/06/magazine/the-party-that-wants-to-make-poland-great -again.html.

31. "French Far-Right's Marine Le Pen Lauds Greek Vote as Win over 'EU Oligarchy,'" Reuters, July 5, 2015, http://www.reuters.com/article/euroz one-greece-france-lepen-idUSL8N0ZL0TX20150705.

32. Alastair Smart, "Beppe Grillo Interview," *Telegraph,* March 4, 2011, http://www.telegraph.co.uk/culture/comedy/8362260/Beppe-Grillo -interview.html.

33. Luis Giménez San Miguel and Pablo Iglesias, "Mañana Sequirá Goberanando la Casta," *Público,* May 26, 2014 [my translation], http://www .publico.es/actualidad/pablo-iglesias-manana-seguira-gobernando.html. Carolina Bescansa, their former chief political analyst, has made a similar point: "We didn't set up Podemos to become like the PSOE or PP— historical parties for our children and grandchildren to join as heirs of

the founders." James Badcock, "Spain's Anti-Corruption Parties Shake Up Old Politics," *BBC*, March 14, 2015, http://www.bbc.com/news /world-europe-31852713.

34. Avi Asher-Schapiro, "Donald Trump Said Goldman Sachs Had 'Total Control' over Hillary Clinton—Then Stacked His Team with Goldman Insiders," *International Business Times,* November 16, 2016, http:// www.ibtimes.com/political-capital/donald-trump-said-goldman-sachs -had-total-control-over-hillary-clinton-then.

35. Sam Koppelman, "A Timeline of Donald Trump's Birther Conspiracy Theory about President Obama," Hillaryclinton.com, October 25, 2016, https://www.hillaryclinton.com/feed/a-timeline-of-donald-trumps-presi dent-obama-birther-conspiracy-theory/.

36. Nick Corasaniti, "Donald Trump Calls Obama 'Founder of ISIS' and Says It Honors Him," *New York Times,* August 10, 2016, https://www .nytimes.com/2016/08/11/us/politics/trump-rally.html; Del Quentin Wilber, "Call to 'Lock Her Up' Puts Trump in a Bind over His Threat to Prosecute Hillary Clinton," *Los Angeles Times,* November 11, 2016.

37. Aditya Chakrabortty, "For Years Britain Shunned Narendra Modi. So Why Roll Out the Red Carpet Now?" *Guardian,* November 10, 2015, https://www.theguardian.com/commentisfree/2015/nov/10/britain -shunned-narendra-modi-india-hindu-extremist-lynch-mobs.

38. Ercan Gurses and Orhan Coskun, "Erdogan Risks Losing Turkish Swing Voters with Harsh Referendum Rhetoric," *Star,* February 17, 2017, http://www.thestar.com.my/news/world/2017/02/17/erdogan-risks-losing -turkish-swing-voters-with-harsh-referendum-rhetoric/; and Roy Gut-man, "As a Constitutional Referendum Looms, Some in Turkey Say Er-dogan Is Steering the Country toward Autocracy," *Los Angeles Times,* February 12, 2017, http://www.latimes.com/world/middleeast/la-fg -turkey-referendum-20170212-story.html.

39. See Jared Malsin, "Turkey Rounds Up Erdogan's Political Opponents as Crackdown Widens," *Time,* November 4, 2016; Rod Nordland, "Tur-key's Free Press Withers as Erdogan Jails 120 Journalists," *New York Times,* November 17, 2016; Jordan Bhatt, "Erdogan Accused of Geno-cide against Kurds by Swedish MPs," *International Business Times,* July 11, 2017; Alon Ben-Meir, "The Kurds under Erdogan's Tyrannical Gov-ernance," *Huffington Post,* July 5, 2017; Aykan Erdemir and Merve Ta-hiroglu, "Erdogan's Further Consolidation of Power Would Cement Tur-key's Demise," *Huffington Post,* January 26, 2017; Kara Fox, with Dilay Yalcin, "'They Turn Their Backs': In Turkey, Violent Homophobia Fes-ters in Erdogan's Shadow," CNN, June 23, 2017.

40. Mary Riddell, "Exclusive Interview with France's Youngest and Most Controversial MP: Marion Maréchal-Le Pen on Brexit, the Nice Attack,

Gay Marriage and Her Aunt Marine," *Telegraph,* July 23, 2016, http://www.telegraph.co.uk/women/politics/exclusive-interview-with-frances-youngest-and-most-controversial/.

41. David Smith, "Trump's Republican Convention Speech: What He Said and What He Meant," *Guardian,* July 22, 2016, https://www.theguardian.com/us-news/ng-interactive/2016/jul/22/donald-trump-republican-convention-speech-transcript-annotated.

42. Ibid.

43. Ibid.

44. Hofer and Erdoğan are quoted in Jan-Werner Müller, "Trump, Erdoğan, Farage: The Attractions of Populism for Politicians, the Dangers for Democracy," *Guardian,* September 2, 2016, https://www.theguardian.com/books/2016/sep/02/trump-erdogan-farage-the-attractions-of-populism-for-politicians-the-dangers-for-democracy. See also Marine Le Pen, "Remettre la France en Ordre," Marine Presidente website, https://www.marine2017.fr/au-nom-du-peuple/.

45. Jan-Werner Müller, "Capitalism in One Family," *London Review of Books* 38, no. 23 (2016): 10–14.

46. Lucy Maulsby, *Fascism, Architecture, and the Claiming of Modern Milan, 1922–1943* (Toronto: University of Toronto Press, 2014), 136. On Mussolini, see Richard Collier, *Duce! A Biography of Benito Mussolini* (New York: Viking, 1971). On Robespierre, see Patrice L. R. Higonnet, *Goodness beyond Virtue: Jacobins during the French Revolution* (Cambridge, MA: Harvard University Press, 1998).

47. Mark Leibovich, "Palin Visits a 'Pro-America' Kind of Town," *New York Times,* October 17, 2008, https://thecaucus.blogs.nytimes.com/2008/10/17/palin-visits-a-pro-america-kind-of-town/.

48. Glenn Beck, *The Real America: Messages from the Heart and Heartland* (New York: Pocket Books, 2003).

49. Jan-Werner Müller, "Donald Trump's Use of the Term 'the People' Is a Warning Sign," *Guardian,* January 24, 2017, https://www.theguardian.com/commentisfree/2017/jan/24/donald-trumps-warning-sign-populism-authoritarianism-inauguration.

50. Robert Reich, "Donald Trump's Plan to Neuter the White House Press Corps Could Neuter Our Democracy," *Salon,* January 16, 2017, http://www.salon.com/2017/01/16/robert-reich-donald-trumps-plan-to-neuter-the-white-house-press-corps-could-neuter-our-democracy_partner/.

51. John Cassidy, "Trump's Attack on the Press Shows Why Protests Are Necessary," *New Yorker,* January 22, 2017, http://www.newyorker.com/news/john-cassidy/trumps-attack-on-the-press-shows-why-protests-are-necessary.

52. Michael Grynbaum, "Trump Calls the News Media the 'Enemy of the

American People,'" *New York Times,* February 17, 2017, https://www
.nytimes.com/2017/02/17/business/trump-calls-the-news-media-the
-enemy-of-the-people.html.

53. Sonam Sheth, "One of Trump's Most Vocal Supporters Left CNN to
Make a Pro-Trump News Video That's Been Compared to State TV,"
Business Insider, August 6, 2017, http://www.businessinsider.com
/kayleigh-mcenany-left-cnn-to-host-pro-trump-news-videos-2017-8.

54. See Anne Applebaum, "It's Now Clear: The Most Dangerous Threats to
the West Are Not External," *Washington Post,* July 16, 2017; and "Poland: Draft Law Threatens Supreme Court," Human Rights Watch website, July 20, 2017, https://www.hrw.org/news/2017/07/20/poland-draft
-law-threatens-supreme-court.

55. Niki Kitsantonis, "In Greece, a Fierce Battle over TV Licenses," *New
York Times,* August 29, 2016, https://www.nytimes.com/2016/08/30
/world/europe/greece-cracks-down-on-triangle-of-corruption-in-tv.html;
Kerin Hope, "Minister's Court Win Intensifies Fears for Rule of Law in
Greece," *Financial Times,* August 8, 2017, https://www.ft.com/content
/b1e23838-779a-11e7-90c0-90a9d1bc9691. Note that the *Athens Review of Books* went into bankruptcy because of an unprecedented award
of damages by a court reflecting the will of the government, not because
it was closed by direct government order.

56. Tom Mueller, "What Beppe Grillo Wants," *New Yorker,* March 6, 2013,
http://www.newyorker.com/news/news-desk/what-beppe-grillo-wants.

57. In countries without a deep democratic culture, established political parties also try to fill key posts with party members to reward their loyalists
or ensure more positive coverage on state TV. But only populists "undertake such colonization openly and with the support of their core claim to
moral representation of the people" (Müller, *What Is Populism?,* 45).
They alone, in other words, undertake these actions with the aim of si-
lencing the opposition altogether.

58. Simon Kennedy, "Pro-Brexit Press Rages at 'Enemies of the People' on
Court," *Bloomberg,* November 4, 2016, https://www.bloomberg.com
/news/articles/2016-11-04/pro-brexit-press-rages-at-enemies-of-the
-people-on-court.

59. Peter Exinger, "Streit ums Minarett," *Blick,* February 11, 2006; Thomi
De Rocchi, "Minarette stören den Blick auf die Alpen," *Blick,* July 18,
2008; René Steege Ter, "Zwitsers ruziën over verbod op minaretten,"
Het Parool, November 26, 2009; Janine Gloor, "Turm des Schweigens:
'An den Anblick des Minaretts hat man sich gewöhnt,'" *Solothurnerzei-
tung,* January 8, 2017; Simone Bretscher, "(K)eins aufs Dach?" Lizenti-
atsarbeit, Historisches Seminar, Universität Basel, November 5, 2008,
76–91, http://www.bmk-online.ch/files/Eins-aufs-Dach.pdf; Lorenz
Langer, "Panacea or Pathetic Fallacy? The Swiss Ban on Minarets,"

Vanderbilt Journal of Transnational Law 43, no. 4 (2010): 865–870; David Miller, "Majorities and Minarets: Religious Freedom and Public Space," Working Paper Series in Politics, Nuffield College, University of Oxford, 8–10; https://www.nuffield.ox.ac.uk/Politics/Papers/2013/WP -2013-03.pdf; Swiss Federal Supreme Court, Ruling 1P. 26 / 2007, July 4, 2007, http://www.polyreg.ch/bgeunpub/Jahr_2007/Entscheide_1P_ 2007/1P. 26__2007.html.

60. Exinger, "Streit ums Minarett."
61. Nick Cumming-Bruce and Steven Erlanger, "Swiss Ban Building of Minarets on Mosques," *New York Times,* November 29, 2009, http://www .nytimes.com/2009/11/30/world/europe/30swiss.html.
62. "Federal Constitution of the Swiss Confederation," The Portal of the Swiss Government, 2016, Articles 15 and 72, https://www.admin.ch/opc /en/classified-compilation/19995395/201601010000/101.pdf.
63. See "The Swiss Ban Minarets, ctd.," *Atlantic,* November 30, 2009, https://www.theatlantic.com/daily-dish/archive/2009/11/the-swiss-ban -minarets-ctd/193550/; Ian Traynor, "Swiss Ban on Minarets Draws Widespread Condemnation," *Guardian,* November 30, 2009, https:// www.theguardian.com/world/2009/nov/30/switzerland-ban-minarets -reaction-islam; and Charlemagne, "The Swiss Minaret Ban," *Economist,* November 30, 2009, http://www.economist.com/blogs/charlemagne /2009/11/_normal_0_false_false_6.
64. See Benjamin Shingler, "Ban on New Places of Worship Upheld in Montreal's Outremont Borough," CBC News, November 20, 2016, http:// www.cbc.ca/news/canada/montreal/outremont-places-of-worship-ban -hasidic-1.3859620.
65. "Alternative for Germany Slams Church over Refugees," *The Local,* February 18, 2016, https://www.thelocal.de/20160218/alternative-for -germany-slams-dishonest-church-over-refugees.
66. Charlotte Beale, "German Police Should Shoot Refugees, Says Leader of AfD Party Frauke Petry," *Independent,* January 31, 2016.
67. Some aspects of my description of Petry's rally, as well as of the PEGIDA march described earlier in the chapter, are informed by Mounk, "Echt Deutsch."
68. Author's reporting.
69. "Preliminary Election Program PVV 2017–2021," Geert Wilders Weblog, August 26, 2016, https://www.geertwilders.nl/94-english/2007 -preliminary-election-program-pvv-2017-2021.
70. Angelique Chrisafis, "Jean-Marie Le Pen Fined Again for Dismissing Holocaust as 'Detail,'" *Guardian,* April 6, 2016, https://www.theguardian .com/world/2016/apr/06/jean-marie-le-pen-fined-again-dismissing -holocaust-detail.
71. "NPD Leader Charged with Inciting Race Hate," *Spiegel,* August 24,

2007, http://www.spiegel.de/international/germany/after-nominating
-rudolf-hess-for-nobel-peace-prize-npd-leader-charged-with-inciting
-race-hate-a-501910.html.

72. "French National Front Expels Founder Jean-Marie Le Pen," BBC, August 20, 2015, http://www.bbc.com/news/world-europe-34009901.

73. Björn Höcke, "Gemutszustand eines total besiegten Volkes," *Der Tagesspiegel,* January 1, 2015, http://www.tagesspiegel.de/politik/hoecke-rede
-im-wortlaut-gemuetszustand-eines-total-besiegten-volkes/19273518.
html (my translation); AfD Berlin: "Weil wir für #EUCH sind, sind sie gegen uns," tweet, August 21, 2016, https://twitter.com/afdberlin/status
/767225661920542720?lang=en; "Bundesvorstand beantragt Parteiausschluss von Höcke," *Zeit Online,* March 31, 2017, http://www.zeit.de
/politik/deutschland/2017-03/afd-bundesvorstand-bjoern-hoecke
-parteiausschlussverfahren.

74. Gergely Szakacs, "U.S. Vote Marks End of 'Liberal Non-democracy': Hungary PM," Reuters, November 10, 2016, http://www.reuters.com
/article/us-usa-election-hungary-orban-idUSKBN13510D.

75. Jan-Werner Müller, "The Problem with 'Illiberal Democracy,'" *Social Europe,* January 27, 2016, https://www.socialeurope.eu/2016/01/the
-problem-with-illiberal-democracy/.

2. Rights without Democracy

1. Christian Graf von Krockow, *Warnung vor Preußen* (Berlin: Severin und Siedler, 1982), 99.

2. Barrington Moore, *Social Origins of Dictatorship and Democracy: Lord and Peasant in the Making of the Modern World* (Boston: Beacon Press, 1993); Robert Alan Dahl, *Polyarchy: Participation and Opposition* (New Haven: Yale University Press, 1973); Charles Tilly, *Popular Contention in Great Britain, 1758–1834* (1995; New York: Routledge, 2015); Daniel Ziblatt, *Conservative Parties and the Birth of Democracy* (Cambridge: Cambridge University Press, 2017), 24–171.

3. James Madison, "The Federalist No. 10," in Alexander Hamilton, James Madison, and John Jay, *The Federalist Papers,* ed. Ian Shapiro (1787; New Haven: Yale University Press, 2009), 51.

4. Ibid.

5. Ibid., 322.

6. Garry Wills, *Lincoln at Gettysburg: The Words that Remade America* (New York: Simon & Schuster, 1992), 145; Abraham Lincoln, *The Gettysburg Address* (London: Penguin, Great Ideas, 2009); George P. Fletcher, *Our Secret Constitution: How Lincoln Redefined American Democracy* (New York: Oxford University Press, 2003), 53.

7. The Constitution, Amendments 11–27, Archives.gov, accessed April 1, 2017, Amendment XV; https://www.archives.gov/founding-docs /amendments-11-27#toc-amendment-xv; Michael Perman, *Struggle for Mastery: Disfranchisement in the South, 1888–1908* (Chapel Hill: University of North Carolina Press, 2001); Jerrold M. Packard, *American Nightmare: The History of Jim Crow* (New York: St. Martin's Press, 2002).

8. The Constitution, Amendment XVII.

9. The Constitution, Amendment XIX.

10. Benjamin Constant, "The Liberty of the Ancients Compared with That of the Moderns," in *Political Writings,* ed. Biancamaria Fontana (New York: Cambridge University Press, 1988), 309–328.

11. John Adams, "A Defence of the Constitution," in *The Political Writings of John Adams,* ed. George Carey (Washington, DC: Regnery Publishing, 2000), 27.

12. *The Bible: Authorized King James Version,* ed. Robert Carroll and Stephen Pricket (New York: Oxford University Press, 2008); Luke 5:37.

13. You can watch the exchange in all of its televised glory here: *Yes Minister. A Question of Loyalty.* Television. Created by Antony Jay and Jonathan Lynn (1981; BBC); https://www.youtube.com/watch?v= dIto5mwDLxo.

14. "Speech (and sketch) for BBC1 *Yes, Prime Minister,*" Margaret Thatcher Foundation, January 20, 1984; http://www.margaretthatcher.org /document/105519.

15. Shaun Ley, "Yes, Prime Minister: Still True to Life after 30 Years?" BBC, January 9, 2016; http://www.bbc.com/news/uk-politics-35264042.

16. See "Max Weber on Bureaucracy," New Learning website, supplement to Mary Kalantzis and Bill Cope, *New Learning,* 2nd ed. (Cambridge: Cambridge University Press, 2012), http://newlearningonline.com/new -learning/chapter-9/max-weber-on-bureaucracy.

17. Max Weber, *Economy and Society: An Outline of Interpretative Sociology,* trans. E. Fischoff, 3 vols. (New York: Bedminster Press, 1968), 3:979.

18. For the most insightful and wide-ranging treatment of the multiple roles played by bureaucrats, and the normative creativity this requires, see Bernardo Zacka, *When the State Meets the Street: Public Service and Moral Agency* (Cambridge, MA: Harvard University Press, 2017).

19. "Workforce," Institute for Government, London, 2017; https://www .instituteforgovernment.org.uk/publication/whitehall-monitor-2017 /workforce. The share of civil servants among all workers is even higher in other European countries, with Denmark (32 percent), France (24 percent), Finland (23 percent), Poland (22 percent), the Netherlands (21 percent), and Greece (21 percent) leading the European list. Statista, "An-

teil der Staatsbediensteten an der Gesamtzahl der Beschäftigten in aus-
gewählten Ländern weltweit," https://de.statista.com/statistik/daten
/studie/218347/umfrage/anteil-der-staatsbediensteten-in-ausgewaehlten
-laendern/. The case is a little more complicated in the United States,
where a strong political imperative to limit the number of federal employees has led to a considerable fall in the ratio between the overall
population and the number of official civil servants. However, these
headline figures cloak the rapid increase in bureaucrats at the state and
local level, as well as in the number of people working for nonprofit or
private organizations that perform quasi-governmental functions. See
John J. DiIulio, *Bring Back the Bureaucrats: Why More Federal Workers
Will Lead to Better (and Smaller!) Government* (West Conshohocken,
PA: Templeton Foundation Press, 2014). See also a similar phenomenon
in France: Philippe Bezes and Gilles Jeannot, "The Development and
Current Features of the French Civil Service System," in Frits van der
Meer, ed., *Civil Service Systems in Western Europe*, 185–215 (Chelten-
ham: Edward Elgar, 2011), 272, https://hal-enpc.archives-ouvertes.fr
/hal-01257027/document.

20. In the case of Great Britain, for example, Edward Page has found that
politicians tend to shape the broad outlines of major reforms. Edward
Page, "The Civil Servant as Legislator: Law Making in British Administration," *Public Administration* 81 no. 4 (2003): 651–679. But the ultimate nature of acts of Parliament is powerfully shaped by the bureaucrats who have a huge amount of discretion in writing the legislation. In
such varied areas as criminal or labor law, they were thus able to take a
vague political impulse in their favored direction. Edward Page, *Policy
without Politicians: Bureaucratic Influence in Comparative Perspective*
(Oxford: Oxford University Press, 2012). Especially in "everyday policy
making," the influence of the bureaucracy thus comes to be more pervasive than many citizens realize. Edward Page, *Governing by Numbers:
Delegated Legislation and Everyday Policy Making* (Oxford: Hart Publishing, 2001). But it can go beyond that as well: in a surprising number
of cases, the actual impetus for new legislation came from unelected civil
servants rather than politicians or the general public. Page, "The Civil
Servant as Legislator."

21. Cornelius M. Kerwin and Scott R. Furlong, *Rulemaking: How Government Agencies Write Law and Make Policy* (Washington, DC: CQ Press,
1994).

22. Marshall J. Breger and Gary J. Edles, "Established by Practice: The Theory and Operation of Independent Federal Agencies," *Administrative
Law Review* 52, no. 4 (2000): 1111–1294, 1112.

23. Communications Act of 1934. Pub. L. 73–416. 48 Stat. 1064, June 19,

1934, Government Publishing Office, https://www.gpo.gov/fdsys/pkg /USCODE-2009-title47/html/USCODE-2009-title47-chap5.htm.

24. Securities Exchange Act of 1934, Pub. L. 73–291. 48 Stat. 881, June 6, 1934, Government Publishing Office; https://www.gpo.gov/fdsys /granule/USCODE-2011-title15/USCODE-2011-title15-chap2B-sec78a.

25. Reorganization Plans Nos. 3 and 4 of 1970, Message from the President of the United States to the House of Representatives, Environmental Protection Agency, https://archive.epa.gov/ocir/leglibrary/pdf/created.pdf, accessed April 2, 2017.

26. Dodd-Frank Wall Street Reform and Consumer Protection Act, Pub. L. 111–203. 124 Stat. 1376, July 21, 2010, Government Publishing Office, https://www.gpo.gov/fdsys/granule/STATUTE-124/STATUTE-124 -Pg1376/content-detail.html.

27. "Obscene, Indecent, and Profane Broadcasts," Federal Communications Commission, 2016, https://www.fcc.gov/consumers/guides/obscene -indecent-and-profane-broadcasts.

28. "Open Internet," Federal Communications Commission, 2016, https:// www.fcc.gov/general/open-internet.

29. "DDT—A Brief History and Status," Environmental Protection Agency, https://www.epa.gov/ingredients-used-pesticide-products/ddt-brief -history-and-status; "EPA History: Clean Water Act," Environmental Protection Agency, https://www.epa.gov/history/epa-history-clean-water -act; both accessed April 2, 2017.

30. "Carbon Pollution Standards for New, Modified and Reconstructed Power Plants," Environmental Protection Agency, https://www.epa.gov /cleanpowerplan/carbon-pollution-standards-new-modified-and- reconstructed-power-plants, accessed April 2, 2017.

31. Yuka Hayashi and Anna Prior, "US Unveils Retirement-Savings Revamp, with a Few Concessions to Industry," *Wall Street Journal,* April 6, 2016, https://www.wsj.com/articles/u-s-unveils-retirement-savings-revamp-but -with-a-few-concessions-to-industry-1459936802. On the rule regarding payday lending, which has not yet been adopted, see Yuka Hayashi, Rachel Witkowski, and Gabriel T. Rubin, "Dueling Payday-Lending Campaigns Deluge CFPB with Comments," *Wall Street Journal,* October 10, 2016, https://www.wsj.com/articles/dueling-payday-lending-campaigns -deluge-cfpb-with-comments-1476131725. For a general assessment of the CFPB, see Ian Salisbury, "The CFPB Turns 5 Today. Here's What It's Done (and What It Hasn't)," *Time,* July 21, 2016, http://time.com /money/4412754/cfpb-5-year-anniversary-accomplishments/.

32. Jonathan Turley, "The Rise of the Fourth Branch of Government," *Washington Post,* May 24, 2013.

33. As the Supreme Court decided all the way back in 1935, when indepen-

dent agencies were still in their infancy, they would be "independent of executive authority, except in its selections, and free to exercise its judgment without the leave or hindrance of any other official or any department of the government." *Humphrey's Executor v. United States,* 295 US 602 (1935). Over the years, the Supreme Court has only added to the prerogatives of independent agencies. *Chevron USA v. Natural Resources Defense Council, Inc.* 467 US 837 (1984) ruled that they are entitled to heavy deference in their interpretations of the laws. *Arlington v. FCC* (2013) gave each agency deference in determining their own jurisdictions. *City of Arlington, TX v. FCC,* 569 US (2013).

34. Polly Curtis, "Government Scraps 192 Quangos," *Guardian,* October 14, 2010, https://www.theguardian.com/politics/2010/oct/14/government -to-reveal-which-quangos-will-be-scrapped.

35. For an early investigation of QUANGOs, see for example Brian W. Hogwood, "The Growth of Quangos: Evidence and Explanations," *Parliamentary Affairs* 48, no. 2 (1995): 207–225.

36. Curtis, "Government Scraps 192 Quangos"; "Quango List Shows 192 to Be Axed," BBC News, October 14, 2010; http://www.bbc.com/news /uk-politics-11538534.

37. Kate Dommett, "Finally Recognising the Value of Quangos? The Coalition Government and a Move beyond the 'Bonfire of the Quangos,'" *Democratic Audit UK,* January 14, 2015, http://www.democraticaudit. com/2015/01/14/finally-recognising-the-value-of-quangos-the-coalition -government-and-a-move-beyond-the-bonfire-of-the-quangos/.

38. On the role of the European Commission, see Miriam Hartlapp, Julia Metz, and Christian Rauh, *Which Policy for Europe? Power and Conflict inside the European Commission* (Oxford: Oxford University Press, 2014). Also note that the EU has increasingly developed a network of independent agencies that resemble British QUANGOs and American institutions like the EPA, including such varied bodies as the European Environment Agency, the European Agency for Safety and Health at Work, the European Food Safety Agency, and the European Banking Authority. See Arndt Wonka and Berthold Rittberger, "Credibility, Complexity and Uncertainty: Explaining the Institutional Independence of 29 EU Agencies," *West European Politics* 33, no. 4 (2010): 730–752.

39. See Theo Balderston, *Economics and Politics in the Weimar Republic* (Cambridge: Cambridge University Press, 2002).

40. "The Road to Central Bank Independence," Deutsche Bank, October 29, 2013, https://www.bundesbank.de/Redaktion/EN/Topics/2013/2013_10 _29_bank_independence.html.

41. Quoted in Christopher Alessi, "Germany's Central Bank and the Euro-

zone," *Council on Foreign Relations*, February 7, 2013, http://www.cfr
.org/world/germanys-central-bank-eurozone/p29934. On the role of
hyperinflation in German historical memory, see Toni Pierenkemper,
"Die Angst der Deutschen vor der Inflation oder: Kann man aus der Geschichte lernen?" *Jahrbuch für Wirtschaftsgeschichte/Economic History
Yearbook* 39, no. 1 (1998): 59–84; and Alexander Ebner, "The Intellectual Foundations of the Social Market Economy: Theory, Policy, and
Implications for European Integration," *Journal of Economic Studies* 33,
no. 3 (2006): 206–223.

42. Alessi, "Germany's Central Bank." However, as Wade Jacoby points out,
while the Bundesbank was set up with the primary goal of focusing on
price stability, the treaty that set up the European Central Bank also en-
visioned that it would pursue many other goals, including "social peace"
(personal communication).

43. The technical reason for this is rather more complicated, and includes
the market's anticipation of likely future inflation. See R. J. Barro and
D. B. Gordon, "Rules, Discretion and Reputation in a Model of Monetary Policy," *Journal of Monetary Economics* 12, no. 1 (1983): 101–
121.

44. Simone Polillo and Mauro Guillén, "Globalization Pressures and the
State: The Worldwide Spread of Central Bank Independence," *American
Journal of Sociology* 110, no. 6 (2005): 1764–1802, 1770.

45. Ibid., 1767.

46. In the years following the financial crisis in 2008, central banks have
started to take an even more important political role. Back in the 1990s
and early 2000s, the Federal Reserve, the Bank of England, and the European Central Bank had simply ridden the business cycle's low inflation
and impressive growth. Their failure to predict that massive deregulation
would destabilize the financial sector helped to bring about one of the
most catastrophic economic downturns in modern history. But rather
than losing their power in the aftermath of the financial crisis, many central banks actually grew more powerful—and less accountable. While
the American government was paralyzed by extreme partisanship in
Congress and the European government struggled to reconcile the diverging interests of northern and southern European countries, central
banks spent trillions on assets to boost economies across the globe and
moved to shore up regulations on the banks and markets they had let
roam free in the years prior. As a result, central banks have played a
more active and controversial role since 2008 than they had before.

47. See Jack Greenberg, *Crusaders in the Courts: How a Dedicated Band of
Lawyers Fought for the Civil Rights Revolution* (New York: Basic
Books, 1995); Michael J. Klarman, *From Jim Crow to Civil Rights: The*

Supreme Court and the Struggle for Racial Equality (Oxford: Oxford University Press, 2004); and Risa L. Goluboff, "The Thirteenth Amendment and the Lost Origins of Civil Rights," *Duke Law Journal* 50, no. 6 (2000): 1609–1685.

48. See Thomas M. Keck, *The Most Activist Supreme Court in History: The Road to Modern Judicial Conservatism* (Chicago: University of Chicago Press, 2010); Richard A. Posner, "The Rise and Fall of Judicial Self-restraint," *California Law Review* 100, no. 3 (2012): 519–556; Jack M. Balkin and Sanford Levinson, "Understanding the Constitutional Revolution," *Virginia Law Review* 87, no. 6 (2001): 1045–1109. One of the striking things about this moment is that prominent scholars on each side accuse the other side of engaging in unprecedented forms of judicial activism. See Cass Sunstein, "Tilting the Scales Rightward," *New York Times,* April 26, 2001. But see also the critique of the idea of judicial activism in Kermit Roosevelt, *The Myth of Judicial Activism: Making Sense of Supreme Court Decisions* (New Haven: Yale University Press, 2006).

49. *Brown v. Board of Education of Topeka,* 349 US 294 (1955).

50. *Furman v. Georgia,* 408 US 238 (1972) ruled that the death penalty was unconstitutional. *Gregg v. Georgia,* 428 US 153 (1976) reversed this decision.

51. *Roe v. Wade,* 410 US 113 (1973).

52. *FCC v. Pacifica Foundation,* 438 US 726 (1978).

53. *Lawrence v. Texas,* 539 US 558 (2003) legalized homosexual sex. *Obergefell v. Hodges,* 576 US (2015) legalized same-sex marriage.

54. For examples, see *Buckley v. Valeo,* 424 US 1 (1976); and *Citizens United v. FEC,* 558 US (2010).

55. In *King v. Burwell,* 576 US (2015), the Supreme Court upheld key provisions of the Affordable Care Act.

56. In *United States v. Texas* 579 US __ (2016), the Supreme Court left in place an appeals court ruling blocking the Deferred Action for Parents of Americans and Lawful Permanent Residents (DAPA) program that would have prevented millions of undocumented immigrants from being deported. *United State v. Texas,* 507 US 529 (1993).

57. See Jonathan Chait, "Conservative Judicial Activists Run Amok," *New York Magazine,* March 28, 2012; Adam Cohen, "Psst . . . Justice Scalia, You Know, You're an Activist Judge, Too," *New York Times,* April 19, 2005, http://www.nytimes.com/2005/04/19/opinion/psst-justice-scalia-you-know-youre-an-activist-judge-too.html; Seth Rosenthal, "The Jury Snub," *Slate,* December 18, 2006, http://www.slate.com/articles/news_and_politics/jurisprudence/2006/12/the_jury_snub.html; William P. Marshall, "Conservatism and the Seven Sins of Judicial Activism," *Uni-*

versity of Colorado Law Review 73 (2002): 1217–1401; and Geoffrey R. Stone, "*Citizens United* and Conservative Judicial Activism," *University of Illinois Law Review* 2012, no. 2 (2012): 485–500.

58. Measuring whether or not all of this constitutes an expansion of the court's role in American life is difficult. It won't do simply to count up the number of times the Supreme Court struck down acts of Congress, overturned state law, or threw out rules made by regulatory agencies, for example. After all, it matters greatly how important a particular piece of legislation was—and that question necessarily involves value judgments about which reasonable people can disagree. For more on this subtle question, see A. E. Dick Howard, "The Supreme Court Then and Now," History Now, The Gilder Lehrman Institute of American History, 2017, https://www.gilderlehrman.org/history-by-era/government-and-civics /essays/supreme-court-then-and-now; Larry D. Kramer, "Judicial Supremacy and the End of Judicial Restraint," *California Law Review* 100, no. 3 (2012): 621–634; and Christopher Wolfe, *The Rise of Modern Judicial Review: From Constitutional Interpretation to Judge-Made Law* (Lanham, MD: Rowman and Littlefield, 1994).

59. Based on the 2014 Polity IV dataset, twenty-two countries scored well enough on the DEMOC indicator to qualify in 1930 as a democracy for present purposes: Australia, Austria, Belgium, Canada, Costa Rica, Denmark, Finland, France, Germany, Greece, Ireland, Italy, Japan, Luxembourg, Netherlands, New Zealand, Norway, Sweden, Switzerland, South Africa, the United Kingdom, and the United States. Of these countries, only Austria, Denmark, Luxembourg, New Zealand, Norway, Sweden, Switzerland, and the United States had judicial review at the time. Today, all countries except for the Netherlands formally have judicial review; the Netherlands, though counted as not having judicial review for the purposes of this figure, effectively have a soft form of judicial review as well. Special thanks to Daniel Kenny for research assistance on this point.

60. Tom Ginsburg and Mila Versteeg, "Why Do Countries Adopt Constitutional Review?" *Journal of Law, Economics, and Organization* 30, no. 3 (2014): 587–622, 587. According to an earlier study, 158 out of 191 constitutional systems in the world "explicitly empowered one or more judicial bodies to . . . protect its constitutional provisions and principles against infringements, notably by Parliament." Maartje De Visser, *Constitutional Review in Europe: A Comparative Analysis* (Oxford: Hart Publishing, 2014), 53.

61. The House of Lords served as the court of last resort on particular cases, and at times clarified how particular laws should be interpreted. But what it could not do was to rule an act of Parliament unconstitutional.

On the broader British stance to judicial review, see Jeremy Waldron, "The Core of the Case against Judicial Review," *Yale Law Journal* 115, no. 6 (2006): 1346–1406.

62. At the time Britain joined, the European Union was still known as the European Community.

63. See Karen J. Alter, *Establishing the Supremacy of European Law: The Making of an International Rule of Law in Europe* (Oxford: Oxford University Press, 2001); and Mark Elliott, *The Constitutional Foundations of Judicial Review* (Oxford: Hart Publishing, 2001).

64. UK courts were now empowered to check all UK legislation for compliance with European human rights law, and to overrule it if necessary. See A. Kavanagh, *Constitutional Review under the UK Human Rights Act* (Cambridge: Cambridge University Press, 2009); A. Z. Drzemczewski, *European Human Rights Convention in Domestic Law: A Comparative Study* (New York: Oxford University Press, 1985); and B. A. Simmons, *Mobilizing for Human Rights: International Law in Domestic Politics* (Cambridge: Cambridge University Press, 2009); "Human Rights Act 1998," Legislation.gov.uk, http://www.legislation.gov.uk/ukpga /1998/42/crossheading/introduction, accessed April 2, 2017.

65. "Constitutional Reform Act 2005," Legislation.gov.uk, http://www .legislation.gov.uk/ukpga/2005/4/contents, accessed April 2, 2017.

66. "Canadian Charter of Rights and Freedoms," Parliament of Canada, http://www.lop.parl.gc.ca/About/Parliament/Education/ourcountryour parliament/html_booklet/canadian-charter-rights-and-freedoms-e.html, accessed April 2, 2017. See also J. B. Kelly, *Governing with the Charter: Legislative and Judicial Activism and Framers' Intent* (Vancouver: University of British Columbia Press, 2014); D. R. Songer and S. W. Johnson, "Judicial Decision Making in the Supreme Court of Canada: Updating the Personal Attribute Model," *Canadian Journal of Political Science / Revue canadienne de science politique* 40, no. 4 (2007): 911–934.

67. "Judging," Conseil D'Etat, http://english.conseil-etat.fr/Judging, accessed April 2, 2017. See also F. Fabbrini, "Kelsen in Paris: France's Constitutional Reform and the Introduction of A Posteriori Constitutional Review of Legislation," *German Law Journal* 9, no. 10 (2008): 1297–1312.

68. "The Constitution of the Kingdom of the Netherlands," Rechtspraak.nl (2002), https://www.rechtspraak.nl/SiteCollectionDocuments /Constitution-NL.pdf; M. Adams and G. van der Schyff, "Constitutional Review by the Judiciary in the Netherlands," *Zeitschrift für ausländisches öffentliches Recht und Völkerrecht* 66 (2006): 399–413.

69. Waldron, "Core of the Case." See also J. Waldron, "Judicial Review and the Conditions of Democracy," *Journal of Political Philosophy* 6, no. 4 (1998): 335–355.

70. Waldron, "Judicial Review," 339.

71. See Hans Kelsen, "La garantie juridictionelle de la constitution (La justice constitutionelle)," *Revue de Droit Publique et de la Science Politique en France et a L'Etranger* 35 (1928): 197–259; Hans Kelsen, *General Theory of Law and State,* trans. Anders Wedberg (Cambridge, MA: Harvard University Press, 1945); Ronald Dworkin, *Law's Empire* (Cambridge, MA: Harvard University Press, 1988); Ronald Dworkin, *Taking Rights Seriously* (Cambridge, MA: Harvard University Press, 1978). See also Daniel F. Kelemen, "Judicialisation, Democracy and European Integration," *Representation* 49, no. 3 (2013): 295–308; and Aharon Barak, *The Judge in a Democracy* (Princeton: Princeton University Press, 2006).

72. To be sure, to say that judicial review takes decisions out of political contestation does not mean that jurists themselves are free from political considerations. On the contrary, the highly politicized nature of judicial decisions, especially in the United States, is one of the strongest arguments against it. As Ezra Klein has argued, "[t]he people who serve as judges on the Supreme Court have been vetted by political parties, have often worked for political parties, frequently have loyalties to people in political parties who helped their career, and spend much of their time in Washington, where they sort into social groups they find congenial. They are, in other words, more, not less, political than most Americans." Ezra Klein, "Of Course the Supreme Court Is Political," *Washington Post,* June 21, 2012. See also the extensive academic literature on the topic, including Jeffrey A. Segal and Albert D. Cover, "Ideological Values and the Votes of U.S. Supreme Court Justices," *American Political Science Review* 83, no. 2 (2014): 557–565; and William Mishler and Reginald S. Sheehan, "The Supreme Court as a Countermajoritarian Institution? The Impact of Public Opinion on Supreme Court Decisions," *American Political Science Review* 87, no. 1 (2013): 87–101.

73. Both the figure about cross-border trade and the figure about foreign direct investment are drawn from Shujiro Urata, "Globalization and the Growth in Free Trade Agreements," *Asia-Pacific Review* 9, no. 1 (2002): 20–32.

74. On US steel, see Douglas Irwin, "Historical Aspects of U.S. Trade Policy," NBER Reporter: Research Summary, National Bureau of Economic Research, Summer 2006, http://www.nber.org/reporter/summer06/irwin .html. On cars and electronics, see Robert Feenstra, "How Costly Is Protectionism?" *Journal of Economic Perspectives* 6, no. 3 (1992): 159–

178; and Ashoka Moda, "Institutions and Dynamic Comparative Advantage: The Electronics Industry in South Korea and Taiwan," *Cambridge Journal of Economics* 14 (1990): 291–314, 296.

75. On this tension, see Dani Rodrik, "Can Integration into the World Economy Substitute for a Development Strategy?" in *World Bank ABCDE-Europe Conference Proceedings*, 2000; Kenneth C. Shadlen, "Exchanging Development for Market Access? Deep Integration and Industrial Policy under Multilateral and Regional-Bilateral Trade Agreements," *Review of International Political Economy* 12, no. 5 (2005): 750–775; and Bijit Bora, Peter J. Lloyd, and Mari Pangestu, "Industrial Policy and the WTO," *World Economy* 23, no. 4 (2000): 543–559.

76. North American Free Trade Agreement, NAFTA, 2014, https://www.nafta-sec-alena.org/Home/Texts-of-the-Agreement/North-American-Free-Trade-Agreement?mvid=2.

77. See Cory Adkins and David Singh Grewal, "Democracy and Legitimacy in Investor-State Relations," *Yale Law Journal Forum* 65 (2016); as well as James Surowiecki, "Trade-Agreement Troubles," *New Yorker*, June 22, 2015, http://www.newyorker.com/magazine/2015/06/22/trade-agreement-troubles.

78. See Kenneth A. Armstrong and Simon Bulmer, *The Governance of the Single European Market* (Manchester: Manchester University Press, 1998); Gerda Falkner, *Complying with Europe: EU Harmonisation and Soft Law in the Member States* (Cambridge: Cambridge University Press, 2005); and Frans Vanistendael, "The ECJ at the Crossroads: Balancing Tax Sovereignty against the Imperatives of the Single Market," *European Taxation* 46, no. 9 (2006): 413–420.

79. Dermot Cahill, Vincent Power, and Niamh Connery, *European Law* (New York: Oxford University Press, 2011), 65–66.

80. See Burkard Eberlein and Edgar Grande, "Beyond Delegation: Transnational Regulatory Regimes and the EU Regulatory State," *Journal of European Public Policy* 12, no. 1 (2005): 89–112; and Olivier Borraz, "Governing Standards: The Rise of Standardization Processes in France and in the EU," *Governance* 20, no. 1 (2007): 57–84.

81. This feature is not as exclusive to the European Union as it might seem. In fact, the new regulations on government procurement, investment, and services that are part and parcel of most free-trade agreements often limit the sovereignty of subnational governments, including individual states in the United States. In many cases, subnational governments are forced to amend existing measures related to economic development policies, including laws preventing jobs from moving offshore, "buy local" policies, and environmental regulations related to recycling and renewable energy.

82. The rise of international treaties and organizations has not only shifted power away from the nation state; within nation states, it has shifted power from the legislature to bodies that are subject to less democratic accountability, like the courts and the bureaucracy.

This transformation starts with the bodies that are negotiating trade treaties and international agreements in the first place. As the complexity of such agreements has increased, and the number of their signatories has multiplied, it has become more and more difficult to come to an agreement while giving parliaments a real voice in the process. As a result, authority over negotiations has slowly shifted from the legislative to the executive branch, with the role of legislators confined to giving their grudging assent to treaties that are largely set in stone by the time they get to vote on them.

In many countries, this transformation has taken place in practice without being explicitly acknowledged. In the United States, it has actually been codified in law. According to the Constitution, international treaties can be negotiated by the president but need to gain the assent of two-thirds of senators in order to become effective—a burdensome requirement that has frustrated the ambitions of many presidents. (In the wake of World War I, for example, Woodrow Wilson failed to win the votes he needed for the United States to join the organization he had master-minded, the League of Nations, the predecessor to the United Nations.) To facilitate the passage of free-trade agreements, the Trade Act of 1974 thus established "fast-track authority," which allows the House and the Senate to pass free-trade agreements negotiated by the president with a simple majority.

Although such arrangements technically augment the power of a democratically elected president or prime minister, they actually hand a lot of power to the bureaucratic agencies in charge of negotiating trade agreements. This is especially true where, as in the United States, such agencies serve a single purpose: since negotiating free trade deals is the primary task of the Office of the US Trade Representative, it is hardly surprising that its employees try to initiate more and more of them.

On fast-track authority, see Trade Act of 1974, Pub. L. 93–618. 88 Stat. 1978–2. January 3, 1975; Government Publishing Office Communications Act of 1934, Pub. L. 73–416. 48 Stat. 1064, June 19, 1934; Government Publishing Office, https://www.gpo.gov/fdsys/pkg/USCODE -2009-title47/html/USCODE-2009-title47-chap5.htm. In addition, note that fast-track authority rescinded Congress's power to amend or filibuster free-trade agreements. Fast-track authority was in effect from 1975– 1994, then renewed from 2002 to 2007, and then renewed again in 2015. Carolyn Smith, "Fast-Track Negotiating Authority for Trade

Agreements and Trade Promotion Authority: Chronology of Major Votes," Congressional Research Services, December 18, 2001, https://digital.library.unt.edu/ark:/67531/metacrs2031/m1/1/high_res_d/RS21004_2001Dec18.pdf; "'Fast Track' Trade Legislation," *Wall Street Journal,* April 28, 2015, http://blogs.wsj.com/briefly/2015/04/28/fast-track-trade-legislation-at-a-glance/; Paul Lewis, "Barack Obama Given 'Fast-Track' Authority over Trade Deal Negotiations," *Guardian,* June 24, 2015, https://www.theguardian.com/us-news/2015/jun/24/barack-obama-fast-track-trade-deal-tpp-senate.

On the League of Nations, see Stephen Wertheim, "The League That Wasn't: American Designs for a Legalist-Sanctionist League of Nations and the Intellectual Origins of International Organization, 1914–1920," *Journal of the Society for Historians of American Foreign Relations: Diplomatic History,* 35, no. 5 (2011): 797–836, 802, 832; Martyn Housden, *The League of Nations and the Organization of Peace* (New York: Routledge, 2014), xvii.

83. Treaties in Force, US Department of State, https://www.state.gov/documents/organization/267489.pdf, accessed April 2, 2017.

84. Martin Gilens and Benjamin Page, "Testing Theories of American Politics: Elites, Interest Groups, and Average Citizens," *Perspectives on Politics* 12, no. 3 (2014): 564–581.

85. Ibid., 575. For an earlier study with a similar finding, see Frank R. Baumgartner, Jeffrey M. Berry, Marie Hojnacki, David C. Kimball, and Beth L. Leech, *Lobbying and Policy Change: Who Wins, Who Loses, and Why* (Chicago: University of Chicago Press, 2009).

86. Gilens and Page, "Testing Theories," 576. To be sure, the basic fear that, despite appearances, a small elite determines the most important decisions in a democracy is of much longer standing. See, for example, C. Wright Mills, *The Power Elite* (New York: Oxford University Press, 1956).

87. Kevin Dixon, "Torquay's Past MPs: Rupert Allason—Always Tip the Waiter!" *We Are South Devon,* May 6, 2015; http://wearesouthdevon.com/torquays-past-mps-rupert-allason-always-tip-waiter/. As is inevitable with these kinds of anecdotes, there is of course no conclusive evidence that the waitress really did have such a strong impact on her co-workers, or that these votes really were enough to swing the election.

88. Andrew Eggers and Jens Hainmueller, "MPs for Sale? Returns to Office in Postwar British Politics," *American Political Science Review,* 103, no. 4 (2009): 513–533.

89. Ibid., 514. I should add that Eggers and Hainmuller did not specifically study the financial effects of winning or losing *re*election to Parliament. So it is possible that Allason's loss simply increased the number of years

in which, unbound by restrictions on wage-earning activities while in office, he could capitalize on his political connections.

90. Ibid., 514. For the figure on ex-MPs serving on company boards, see ibid., 528.

91. Suzanne Goldenberg, "Want to Be Senator? Governor Tried to Auction Obama's Old Seat, Says FBI," *Guardian,* December 9, 2008. https://www.theguardian.com/world/2008/dec/10/illinois-governor-rod-blagojevich-bribes.

92. Peter Leeson and Russell Sobel, "Weathering Corruption," *Journal of Law and Economics* 51, no. 4 (2008): 667–681.

93. On the United States, see Daniel Tokaji and Renata Strause, *The New Soft Money* (Columbus: Ohio State University Michael E. Moritz College of Law, 2014), 32. On Burundi, see "The World Bank in Burundi," The World Bank, http://www.worldbank.org/en/country/burundi, accessed 2016.

94. Bipartisan Campaign Reform Act, Pub. L. 107–155. 116 Stat. 81 *thru* Stat. 116, Nov. 6 2002, Government Publishing Office, https://www.gpo.gov/fdsys/pkg/PLAW-107publ155/html/PLAW-107publ155.htm. Note, however, that critics argued that the effect of the McCain-Feingold reform would be very limited: major donors, they predicted, would simply redirect their money into different kinds of legal entities.

95. *Citizens United v. FEC,* 558 US (2010). Technically, *Citizens United* only established this principle for nonprofit corporations, but it was quickly applied to for-profit organizations as well as entities like labor unions in subsequent decisions like *Speechnow.org v. FEC,* 599 F.3d 686 (D.C. Cir. 2010). See Lyle Denniston, "Widening Impact of Citizens United," Scotusblog, March 26, 2010, http://www.scotusblog.com/2010/03/widening-impact-of-citizens-united/.

96. For two strong takes on the corrosive influence of campaign contributions on American politics, see Heather K. Gerken, "The Real Problem with Citizens United: Campaign Finance, Dark Money, and Shadow Parties," *Marquette Law Review* 97, no. 4 (2014): 903–923; and Jane Mayer, *Dark Money: The Hidden History of the Billionaires behind the Rise of the Radical Right* (New York: Doubleday, 2016). More broadly, there are good reasons to fear that any increase in the number of veto points in a political system makes it easier for lobbyists to wield influence. On this point, see Ian Shapiro, *Politics against Domination* (Cambridge, MA: Harvard University Press, 2016).

97. Zephyr Teachout, *Corruption in America: From Benjamin Franklin's Snuff Box to Citizens United* (Cambridge, MA: Harvard University Press, 2014), quotation on 1.

98. Zephyr Teachout, "The Forgotten Law of Lobbying," *Election Law*

Journal 13, no. 1 (2014): 4–26, 22. However, critics have argued that Teachout may be exaggerating the extent to which lobbying was viewed negatively in the nineteenth century, and that corruption is not the most helpful lens for effecting meaningful reform. See the exchange between Lee Drutman and Zephyr Teachout at Lee Drutman, "Bring Back Corruption!" review of Teachout, Corruption in America, *Democracy,* no. 35, 2015, http://democracyjournal.org/magazine/35/bring-back-corruption/?page=all; and Zephyr Teachout, "Quid Pro Con," response to Drutman, *Democracy,* no. 36, 2015, http://democracyjournal .org/magazine/36/quid-pro-con/.

99. William Luneburg and Thomas Susman, *The Lobbying Manual: A Complete Guide to Federal Law Governing Lawyers and Lobbyists* (Chicago: ABA Section of Administrative Law and Regulatory Practice, 2005).

100. "Lobbying as a Felony," *Sacramento Daily Union,* November 6, 1879, https://cdnc.ucr.edu/cgi-bin/cdnc?a=d&d=SDU18791106.2.8.

101. Lee Drutman, *Business of America Is Lobbying* (New York: Oxford University Press, 2015), 57. See also the insightful passages at 49–56, 71, 79, and 218.

102. Lee Drutman, "How Corporate Lobbyists Conquered American Democracy," *Atlantic,* April 20, 2015, https://www.theatlantic.com/business /archive/2015/04/how-corporate-lobbyists-conquered-american -democracy/390822/.

103. Ibid.

104. Lobbying Database, Center for Responsive Politics, https://www .opensecrets.org/lobby/, accessed March 31, 2017.

105. Drutman, "How Corporate Lobbyists Conquered American Democracy." De Figueiredo likewise comes to the conclusion that business groups are responsible for the lion's share of lobbying expenditures: more than 84 percent of total interest group lobbying expenditures at the US federal level and 86 percent of total lobbying expenditures at the state level. See J. M. de Figueiredo, "The Timing, Intensity, and Composition of Interest Group Lobbying: An Analysis of Structural Policy Windows in the States," NBER Working Paper 10588, National Bureau of Economic Research, June 2004.

106. Ian Traynor, "30,000 Lobbyists and Counting: Is Brussels under Corporate Sway?" *Guardian,* May 8, 2014.

107. Jesse Byrnes, "Hillary 'Thought It'd Be Fun' to Attend Trump's Wedding," *Hill,* August 10, 2015, http://thehill.com/blogs/ballot-box /presidential-races/250773-hillary-thought-itd-be-fun-to-attend-trumps -wedding.

108. Michael Kruse, "Hillary and Donald's Wild Palm Beach Weekend," *Politico,* July 28, 2015, http://www.politico.com/magazine/story/2015/07 /hillary-and-donald-trump-were-once-friends-wedding-120610.

109. *Citizens United v. FEC,* 558 US 310 (2010).
110. Lawrence Lessig, *Republic, Lost* (New York: Hachette Book Group, 2011), 107–124.
111. This apt summary of Lessig's thought is by Yasmin Dawood. See Yasmin Dawood, "Campaign Finance and American Democracy," *Annual Review of Political Science* 18 (2015): 329–348, 336.
112. The huge influence of peer groups on individual behavior has been documented in a wide variety of settings in fields including medicine, psychology, and politics. See for example Solomon E. Asch, "Opinions and Social Pressure," *Scientific American* 193, no. 5 (1955): 31; Solomon E. Asch, "Effects of Group Pressure upon the Modification and Distortion of Judgments," in *Groups, Leadership, and Men: Research in Human Relations,* ed. H. Guetzkow, 177–190 (Pittsburgh: Carnegie Press, 1951); Susan T. Ennett and Karl E. Bauman, "The Contribution of Influence and Selection to Adolescent Peer Group Homogeneity: The Case of Adolescent Cigarette Smoking," *Journal of Personality and Social Psychology* 67, no. 4 (1994): 653–663; and Cass R. Sunstein, David Schkade, Lisa M. Ellman, and Andres Sawicki, *Are Judges Political? An Empirical Analysis of the Federal Judiciary* (Washington, DC: Brookings Institution Press, 2007); Herbert Hyman, *Political Socialization* (New York: Free Press, 1959).
113. Ezra Klein, "The Most Depressing Graphic for Members of Congress," *Washington Post,* January 14, 2013, https://www.washingtonpost.com /news/wonk/wp/2013/01/14/the-most-depressing-graphic-for-members -of-congress/?utm_term=.420bbfa0a5f6; and Tim Roemer, "Why Do Congressmen Spend Only Half Their Time Serving Us?" *Newsweek,* July 29, 2015; http://www.newsweek.com/why-do-congressmen-spend-only -half-their-time-serving-us-357995.
114. Brendan Doherty, *The Rise of the President's Permanent Campaign* (Lawrence: University Press of Kansas, 2012), 16–17.
115. Credit Suisse, "Global Wealth Databook" (2013), 101, https://publications.credit-suisse.com/tasks/render/file/?fileID=1949208D-E59A-F2D9 -6D0361266E44A2F8.
116. Russ Choma, "Millionaires' Club: For First Time, Most Lawmakers Are Worth $1 Million-Plus," Opensecrets.org, January 9, 2014.
117. The educational record alone is astounding: at least thirty-six members of the 111th Congress went to Stanford, Harvard, or Yale universities for their undergraduate degrees. (Many more received graduate degrees from one of these institutions.) See Michael Morella, "The Top Ten Colleges for Members of Congress," *US News and World Report,* August 10, 2010, https://www.usnews.com/news/slideshows/the-top-10-colleges-for -members-of-congress. Similarly, a full fifth of the senators in the 114th Congress went to one of four universities: Harvard, Yale, Stanford, or

Dartmouth, for their undergraduate degrees. See Aaron Blake, "Where the Senate Went to College—In One Map," *Washington Post,* January 30, 2015, https://www.washingtonpost.com/news/the-fix/wp/2015/01/30 /where-the-senate-went-to-college-in-one-map/?utm_term=. c88fa8c67482. For full biographical information on current and past members of Congress and senators, see Biographical Directory of the United States Congress, http://bioguide.congress.gov/biosearch/biosearch .asp. The academic literature on this subject is surprisingly thin. But for an earlier study, see N. Polsby, "The Social Composition of Congress," in *The US Congress and the German Bundestag: Comparisons of Democratic Processes,* ed. Uwe Thayson, Roger H. Davidson, and Robert Gerald Livingston (Boulder, CO: Westview Press, 1990).

118. Arthur B. Gunlicks, ed., *Campaign and Party Finance in North America and Western Europe* (Boulder, CO: Westview Press, 1993). For a comparison with Canada, see Daniel P. Tokaji, "The Obliteration of Equality in American Campaign Finance Law: A Trans-Border Comparison," Ohio State Public Law Working Paper no. 140, http://dx.doi.org/10 .2139/ssrn.1746868.

119. Nick Thompson, "International Campaign Finance: How Do Countries Compare?" CNN, March 5, 2012, http://www.cnn.com/2012/01/24 /world/global-campaign-finance/.

120. Clay Clemens, "A Legacy Reassessed: Helmut Kohl and the German Party Finance Affair," *German Politics* 9, no. 2 (2000): 25–50; Erwin K. Scheuch and Ute Scheuch, *Die Spendenkrise–Parteien außer Kontrolle* (Rowohlt Verlag GmbH, 2017).

121. John R. Heilbrunn, "Oil and Water? Elite Politicians and Corruption in France," *Comparative Politics* 37, no. 3 (2005): 277–296; Jocelyn A. J. Evans, "Political Corruption in France," in *Corruption in Contemporary Politics,* ed. Martin J. Bull and James L. Newell, 79–92 (Basingstoke, UK: Palgrave Macmillan, 2003). See also Aurelien Breeden, "Francois Fillon, French Presidential Candidate, Is Charged with Embezzlement," *New York Times,* March 14, 2017; Rory Mulholland, "Nicolas Sarkozy Charged with Corruption," *Daily Telegraph,* July 2, 2014; Jennifer Thompson, "Chirac Found Guilty of Corruption," *Financial Times,* December 15, 2011; and Ullrich Fichtner: "A Crisis of Democracy Rocks the Fifth Republic," *Spiegel Online,* April 8, 2013.

122. The last time the *Sun* backed a losing candidate was in February 1974, when Harold Wilson gained fourteen more seats than Edward Heath despite losing the popular vote by a narrow margin. James Thomas, *Popular Newspapers, the Labour Party and British Politics* (London: Routledge, 2005), 73. While Theresa May, the candidate backed by the *Sun* in 2017, did not win an outright majority, she was able to stay in government thanks to a coalition with the Democratic Unionist Party.

123. This is probably a very large—and commonly overlooked—explanation for how the uneasy coalition between factory workers and school teachers, and between coal miners and artists, on which Social Democrats have always relied to gain majorities, could hold together for so long.

124. W. B. Gallie, "Essentially Contested Concepts," *Proceedings of the Aristotelian Society* 56 (1955–56): 167–198.

125. Steven Levitsky and Lucan Way, *Competitive Authoritarianism: Hybrid Regimes after the Cold War* (New York: Cambridge University Press, 2010), 12.

126. Some of the best empirical and normative accounts of what I would call undemocratic liberalism include Colin Crouch, *Post-democracy* (Cambridge: Polity, 2004); and Colin Crouch, *Coping with Post-democracy,* Fabian Pamphlets (London: Fabian Society, 2000); Christopher Bickerton and Carlo Invernizzi Accetti, "Populism and Technocracy: Opposites or Complements?" *Critical Review of International Social and Political Philosophy* 20, no. 2 (2017): 186–206; Christopher Bickerton, "Europe's Neo-Madisonians: Rethinking the Legitimacy of Limited Power in a Multi-level Polity," *Political Studies* 59, no. 3 (2011): 659–673.

127. See Daniel W. Drezner, *The Ideas Industry: How Pessimists, Partisans, and Plutocrats Are Transforming the Marketplace of Ideas* (New York: Oxford University Press, 2017).

128. See "Mehrheit der Deutschen gegen neue Griechen-Milliarden," *Spiegel Online,* February 2, 2012.

129. See Fareed Zakaria, *The Future of Freedom* (New York: Norton, 2007); and Parag Khanna, *Technocracy in America* (Parag Khanna, self-published, 2017).

130. See Richard Tuck, "The Left Case for Brexit," *Dissent,* June 6, 2016, https://www.dissentmagazine.org/online_articles/left-case-brexit; and Tuck, "Brexit: A Prize in Reach for the Left," *Policy Exchange,* July 17, 2017, https://policyexchange.org.uk/pxevents/brexit-a-prize-in-reach-for-the-left/.

3. Democracy Is Deconsolidating

1. David Runciman, *The Confidence Trap: A History of Democracy in Crisis from World War I to the Present* (Princeton: Princeton University Press, 2015), 210.

2. Jeffrey M. Jones, "American's Trust in Political Leaders, Public, at New Low," Gallup, September 21, 2016, http://www.gallup.com/poll/195716/americans-trust-political-leaders-public-new-lows.aspx.

3. Ibid.

4. "Confidence in Institutions," Gallup poll, 2017, http://www.gallup.com

/poll/1597/confidence-institutions.aspx. Note that it has moderately increased since then, to 12 percent in 2017. However, this may well reflect a bump at the beginning of a new presidency, and could decline rapidly in the years to come.

5. See Roberto Foa and Yascha Mounk, "Are Americans Losing Faith in Democracy?" *Vox*, December 18, 2015, https://www.vox.com/polyarchy/2015/12/18/9360663/is-democracy-in-trouble.

6. In 1972, for example, many more German citizens believed that members of Parliament primarily advocate for the interests of the population than believed that they prioritize other interests. By 2014, this trend had reversed, with the number of people ascribing good motives to politicians down significantly. Germans don't just trust politicians less than they used to; they also take a much dimmer view of their abilities. In 1972, close to two-thirds of respondents in West Germany believed that it took great skill to become a member of Parliament, with less than a quarter believing that it did not. By 2014, sentiments had reversed: over half of respondents now believe that it doesn't take special skill to become a politician, with less than a quarter believing that politicians have some special talent. See Thomas Petersen, "Anfag vom Ende der Politikverdrossenheit?" *Frankfurter Allgemeinen Zeitung* 66, no. 19 (March 5, 2014).

7. Across longstanding democracies in Western Europe, voter turnout has decreased significantly in recent decades. And membership in political parties has sunk even more rapidly. In France, for example, there were over 1.7 million party members in 1978; by 2009, there were many fewer than a million. Ingrid Van Biezen, Peter Mair, and Thomas Poguntke, "Going, Going, . . . Gone? The Decline of Party Membership in Contemporary Europe," *European Journal of Political Research* 51, no. 1 (2012): 24–56, 44.

8. Roberto Stefan Foa and Yascha Mounk, "The Danger of Deconsolidation: The Democratic Disconnect," *Journal of Democracy* 27, no. 3 (2016): 10–12.

9. Jon Henley, "Chirac's Popularity Hits New Low as Public Loses Faith in Politicians," *Guardian*, June 7, 2005, https://www.theguardian.com/world/2005/jun/08/france.jonhenley.

10. "Support for Sarkozy Hits Record Low," *France 24*, April 19, 2011.

11. "Into the Abyss," *Economist*, November 5, 2016.

12. Jeremy Berke, "Emmanuel Macron's Approval Rating Is Taking a Massive Nosedive," *Business Insider*, August 22, 2017, http://www.businessinsider.com/emmanuel-macron-poll-approval-rating-trump-2017-8.

13. Personal communication.

14. Lynn Vavreck, "The Long Decline of Trust in Government, and Why That Can Be Patriotic," *New York Times,* July 3, 2015, https://www.nytimes.com/2015/07/04/upshot/the-long-decline-of-trust-in-government-and-why-that-can-be-patriotic.html.

15. David Easton, "A Re-assessment of the Concept of Political Support," *British Journal of Political Science 5,* no. 4 (1975): 435–457.

16. Larry Diamond, "Facing Up to the Democratic Recession," *Journal of Democracy* 26, no. 1 (2015): 141–155. See also Freedom House, *Freedom in the World 2016: The Annual Survey of Political Rights and Civil Liberties* (Rowman & Littlefield, 2016); and Freedom House, *Freedom in the World 2017: Populists and Autocrats: The Dual Threat to Global Democracy* (Rowman & Littlefield, 2017).

17. Indeed, it might then be enough for a demagogue to claim that they will accomplish something that *is* important to these citizens—a symbolic victory against an external enemy, perhaps, or simply a slightly bigger paycheck—for them to abandon key aspects of democracy.

18. This does not mean that most millennials are actively opposed to democracy. As some critics have pointed out, the average score has not changed drastically. Erik Voeten, "That Viral Graph about Millennials' Declining Support for Democracy? It's Very Misleading," *Washington Post,* December 5, 2016. A substantial minority still considers it crucial to live in a democracy. And most of the rest think of it as perfectly fine—something that is desirable, even if it is not especially important. But the contrast to older generations is still striking. If we include people who consider it reasonably important to live in a democracy in the sample (a scale of 8–10), about nine out of ten older Americans think it important to live in a democracy but fewer than six out of ten younger Americans do. The rapid rise in the number of people who are neutral about democracy (a scale of 4–7) is even more striking. While only about one in ten older Americans fit this description, nearly four out of ten younger Americans are neutral about democracy. See Yascha Mounk and Roberto Foa: "Yes, People Really Are Turning Away from Democracy," *Washington Post,* December 8, 2016.

19. One good example is Nigeria, where 22 percent of millennials ranked democracy as very important (10), while 15 percent of people over 65 did. About the same percentage of millennials and people over the age of 65 gave relatively low (1–5) importance to democracy, however.

20. Amanda Taub, "How Stable Are Democracies? 'Warning Signs Are Flashing Red,'" *New York Times,* November 29, 2016.

21. These findings are so disconcerting that it's tempting to find a way to discount them.

    Aren't young people always more critical of their political system than older people? Not really. While we do not yet have time series data that would allow us to test whether young people today are less likely to say that it is important to them to live in a democracy than their parents or grandparents did at a similar age, we do have such data for negative views on democracy. What it shows is unambiguous: in both Europe and the United States, 16–24 year olds are much more critical of democracy today than people of the same age were two decades ago.

And isn't it reassuring that a clear majority of young people still think that democracy is a good system of government? Not at all. It's true that the 23 percent of American millennials who openly claim that democracy is a bad or very bad way of running their country remain in a minority. But in international perspective, this is actually an extremely high number. The highest average recorded for any one country is just a little higher: in Russia, about 26 percent of respondents hold a similarly bleak view of democracy. By contrast, across the globe, only about one in ten respondents share such a negative view of democracy—and this includes many countries that are stable dictatorships or have seen frequent military coups in the past.

22. Michael Ignatieff, "Enemies vs. Adversaries," *New York Times,* October 16, 2013, http://www.nytimes.com/2013/10/17/opinion/enemies-vs -adversaries.html?mcubz=3. See also Ignatieff's gracious and insightful rumination on political failure in Michael Ignatieff, *Fire and Ashes* (Cambridge, MA: Harvard University Press, 2013).

23. Ignatieff, "Enemies vs. Adversaries."

24. "Jörg Haider: Key Quotes," BBC News, February 2, 2000, http://news .bbc.co.uk/2/hi/europe/628282.stm.

25. "Wilders Warns Australia of 'Dangerous' Islam," *Al Jazeera,* February 20, 2013, http://www.aljazeera.com/news/asia-pacific/2013/02 /2013220145950228630.html.

26. Gavin Jones, "Insight: Beppe Grillo—Italian Clown or Political Mastermind?" Reuters, March 7, 2013, http://www.reuters.com/article/us-italy -vote-grillo-insight-idUSBRE92608G20130307.

27. The party now relies on funds that come from fake news inspired by Russian disinformation—and so it is hardly surprising that, to give but one example, a recent video from a party-controlled news source claimed that Turkey and the United States are secretly conspiring to stop Russia from fighting ISIS. See Alberto Nardelli and Craig Silverman, "Italy's Most Popular Political Party Is Leading Europe in Fake News and Kremlin Propaganda," Buzzfeed, November 29, 2016, https://www.buzzfeed .com/albertonardelli/italys-most-popular-political-party-is-leading-europe -in-fak?utm_term=.is5qZZWjgy#.ekqA77x1jD. The party has also inched away from its left-wing roots, with key politicians voicing ever

more vociferous anti-immigrant slogans in recent months. See Stefano Pitrelli and Michael Birnbaum, "Anti-immigrant, Anti-Euro Populists Gain Ground in Italy as Prime Minister Resigns," *Washington Post,* December 5, 2016, https://www.washingtonpost.com/world/as-italys-leader-exits-a-door-opens-for-anti-elite-populists/2016/12/05/9eb4a5d6-ba83-11e6-ae79-bec72d34f8c9_story.html.

28. Hortense Goulard, "Nicolas Sarkozy Says Climate Change Not Caused by Man," Politico, September 14, 2016, http://www.politico.eu/article/nicolas-sarkozy-says-climate-change-not-caused-by-man-cop-21/.

29. See David Lublin, *The Paradox of Representation: Racial Gerrymandering and Minority Interests in Congress* (Princeton: Princeton University Press, 1999). Note also the interesting passages on Barack Obama's attempt to gerrymander his district in the Illinois House of Representatives in Ryan Lizza, "The Obama Memos," *New Yorker,* January 30, 2012.

30. Richard Moberly, "Whistleblowers and the Obama Presidency: The National Security Dilemma," *Employee Rights and Employment Policy Journal* 16, no. 1 (2012): 51–141; Binyamin Appelbaum and Michael D. Shear, "Once Skeptical of Executive Power, Obama Has Come to Embrace It," *New York Times,* August 13, 2016, https://www.nytimes.com/2016/08/14/us/politics/obama-era-legacy-regulation.html?_r=0.

31. Thomas E. Mann and Norman J. Ornstein, *It's Even Worse than It Looks: How the American Constitutional System Collided with the New Politics of Extremism* (New York: Basic Books, 2016).

32. Associated Press, "McCain Counters Obama 'Arab' Question," YouTube, October 11, 2008, https://www.youtube.com/watch?v=jrnRU3ocIH4.

33. Carl Hulse, "In Lawmaker's Outburst, a Rare Breach of Protocol," *New York Times,* September 9, 2009.

34. Sarah Palin, Newt Gingrich, David Vitter, and Mike Huckabee are among the Republican politicians who spread the birther conspiracy either explicitly or gave it implicit support. Glenn Kessler, "More 'Birther' Nonsense from Donald Trump and Sarah Palin," *Washington Post,* April 12, 2011; Brian Montopoli, "New Gingrich Pandering to Birthers, White House Suggests," CBS News website, September 13, 2010; Nia-Malika Henderson, "Gingrich Says Birther Claims Not Racist, Are Caused by Obama's 'Radical' Views," *Washington Post,* May 29, 2012; Andy Barr, "Vitter Backs Birther Suits," Politico, July 13, 2010; Michael D. Shear, "Huckabee Questions Obama Birth Certificate," *New York Times* website, March 1, 2011. For a robust critique of his own party's willingness to pander to so-called "birthers," see Jeff Flake, *Conscience of a Conservative: A Rejection of Destructive Politics and a Return to Principle* (New York: Random House, 2017), 31–33.

35. Since it is difficult to give a precise definition to what constitutes a "fili-buster," I am using the number of motions for cloture that occur in any given session of Congress here. The 88–90th US senates under Lyndon B. Johnson had 16 votes to invoke cloture, whereas the 111–114th US senates under Obama had 506 votes to invoke cloture. See Molly Reynolds, Curtlyn Kramer, Nick Zeppos, Emma Taem, Tanner Lockhead, Michael Malbin, Brendan Glavin, Thomas E. Mann, Norman J. Ornstein, Raffaela Wakeman, Andrew Rugg, and the Campaign Finance Institute, "Vital Statistics on Congress," Report, Brookings Institution, September 7, 2017, https://www.brookings.edu/multi-chapter-report/vital-statistics -on-congress/.

36. Garland was confirmed for the DC Circuit Court by a Republican-controlled Senate in 1996, winning the vote 76–23. The American Bar Association called him "unanimously well-qualified." Melanie Garunay, "The American Bar Association Gives Its Highest Rating to Chief Judge Garland," The White House, June 21, 2016.

37. Patrick Caldwell, "Senate Republicans Are Breaking Records for Judicial Obstruction," *Mother Jones,* May 6, 2016.

38. Richard L. Hasen, "Race or Party? How Courts Should Think about Republican Efforts to Make It Harder to Vote in North Carolina and Elsewhere," *Harvard Law Review Forum* 127 (2014); Anthony J. McGann, Charles Anthony Smith, Michael Latner, and Alex Keena, *Gerrymandering in America: The House of Representatives, the Supreme Court, and the Future of Popular Sovereignty* (New York: Cambridge University Press, 2016); Tim Dickinson, "How Republicans Rig the Game," *Rolling Stone,* November 11, 2013, http://www.rollingstone.com/politics /news/how-republicans-rig-the-game-20131111. While Democrats have long played this game as well, they have been less guilty of the same sin in the past years, in part because their weakness in state houses across the country has given them little opportunity to engage in similar shenanigans.

39. William Wan, "How Republicans in North Carolina Created a 'Monster' Voter ID Law," *Chicago Tribune,* September 2, 2016, http://www .chicagotribune.com/news/nationworld/politics/ct-north-carolina-voter -id-law-20160902-story.html.

40. Alison Thoet, "What North Carolina's Power-Stripping Laws Mean for New Gov. Roy Cooper," PBS Newshour, January 3, 2017, http://www .pbs.org/newshour/updates/north-carolinas-power-stripping-laws-mean -new-gov-roy-cooper/. Since then, there has been a complicated legal back-and-forth about the legality of this move. See Mitch Smith, "North Carolina Judges Suspend Limit on Governor's Powers," *New York Times,* February 8, 2017, https://www.nytimes.com/2017/02/08/us

/politics/north-carolina-judges-suspend-limit-on-governors-powers.
html?_r=0; Jason Zengerle, "Is North Carolina the Future of American
Politics?" *New York Times,* June 20, 2017, https://www.nytimes.
com/2017/06/20/magazine/is-north-carolina-the-future-of-american
-politics.html; Mark Joseph Stern, "North Carolina Republicans Are
Trying to Strip the Governor of His Power to Challenge Laws," *Slate,*
June 21, 2017, http://www.slate.com/blogs/the_slatest/2017/06/21
/north_carolina_republicans_budget_prevents_governor_from_suing
.html; Colin Campbell, "Cooper Vetoes Budget—And Hints at Another
Lawsuit, as Senate Overrides," *News & Observer,* June 27, 2017, http://
www.newsobserver.com/news/politics-government/state-politics
/article158409209.html.

41. Dan Roberts, Ben Jacobs, and Sabrina Siddiqi, "Donald Trump Threat-
ens to Jail Hillary Clinton in Second Presidential Debate," *Guardian,*
October 10, 2016; Demetri Sevastoplou and Barney Jopson, "Trump Re-
fuses to Say If He Will Accept Election Result in Final Debate," *Financial
Times,* October 20, 2016; Sydney Ember, "Can Libel Laws Be Changed
Under Trump?" *New York Times,* November 13, 2016; and Madeline
Conway, "In Twitter Attack on New York Times, Trump Floats Changing Libel Laws," Politico, March 30, 2017; Simon Saradzhyan, Natasha
Yefimova-Trilling, and Ted Siefer, "How Trump Invited Putin to Hack
the Election. Every Last Utterance," *Newsweek,* July 16, 2017; Anthony
D. Romero, "Donald Trump: A One-Man Constitutional Crisis," Me-
dium, July 13, 2016, https://medium.com/acluelection2016/donald
-trump-a-one-man-constitutional-crisis-9f7345e9d376.

42. Justin Levitt, "A Comprehensive Investigation of Voter Impersonations
Finds 31 Credible Incidents Out of One Billion Ballots Cast," *Washington Post* Wonkblog, August 6, 2014, https://www.washingtonpost.com
/news/wonk/wp/2014/08/06/a-comprehensive-investigation-of-voter-im
personation-finds-31-credible-incidents-out-of-one-billion-ballots
-cast/?utm_term=.9935eee8566d; and Maggie Koerth-Baker, "The Tan-
gled Story behind Trump's False Claims of Voter Fraud," FiveThirtyEight
website, May 11, 2017, https://fivethirtyeight.com/features/trump-non-
citizen-voters/; Fred Barbash, "Appeals Court Judges Rebuke Trump
for 'Personal Attacks' on Judiciary, 'Intimidation,'" *Washington Post,*
March 16, 2017; Michael C. Bender, "After Setback on Sanctuary Cities
Order, Trump Attacks 'Messy' Federal Court System," *Wall Street Journal,* April 26, 2017; Louis Nelson, "Trump Likens Intel Community to
Russia in Renewed Barrage Against Agencies," Politico, February 15,
2017; Peter Schroeder, "Report: Trump Pressed Argentina's President
about Stalled Building Project," *Hill,* November 21, 2016; Susanne
Craig and Eric Lipton, "Trust Records Show Trump Is Still Closely Tied

to His Empire," *New York Times,* February 3, 2017; and Jeremy Nevook, "Trump's Interests vs. America's, Dubai Edition," *Atlantic,* August 9, 2017, https://www.theatlantic.com/business/archive/2017/08/donald-trump-conflicts-of-interests/508382/; Domenico Montanaro, "6 Strongmen Trump Has Praised—and the Conflicts It Presents," NPR website, May 2, 2017, http://www.npr.org/2017/05/02/526520042/6-strongmen-trumps-praised-and-the-conflicts-it-presents.

43. "Trump Wiretapping Claim: Did Obama Bug His Successor?" BBC News website, March 20, 2017, http://www.bbc.co.uk/news/world-us-canada-39172635; Amy B. Wang, "Trump Lashes Out at 'So-Called Judge' Who Temporarily Blocks Travel Ban," *Washington Post,* February 4, 2017; CNN Staff, "Timeline of Donald Trump Jr.'s Meeting Revelations," CNN website, August 4 2017, http://edition.cnn.com/2017/08/01/politics/timeline-donald-trump-jr-/index.html; Donald J. Trump, Twitter post, February 17, 2017, 5:48 PM, https://twitter.com/realdonaldtrump/status/832708293516632065?lang=env; Donald J. Trump, Twitter post, June 28, 2017, 9:06 AM, https://twitter.com/realDonaldTrump/status/880049704620494848; Matthew Rosenberg, Maggie Haberman, and Adam Goldman, "2 White House Officials Helped Give Nunes Intelligence Reports," *New York Times,* March 30, 2017, https://www.nytimes.com/2017/03/30/us/politics/devin-nunes-intelligence-reports.html?_r=0; Michael D. Shear and Matt Apuzzo, "FBI Director James Comey Is Fired by Trump," *New York Times,* May 9, 2017, https://www.nytimes.com/2017/05/09/us/politics/james-comey-fired-fbi.html; Donald J. Trump, Twitter post, May 12, 2017, 8:26 AM, https://twitter.com/realDonaldTrump/status/863007411132649473.

44. Alec Tyson and Shiva Maniam, "Behind Trump's Victory: Divisions by Race, Gender, Education," Pew Research Center, November 9, 2016, http://www.pewresearch.org/fact-tank/2016/11/09/behind-trumps-victory-divisions-by-race-gender-education/; "EU Referendum: The Result in Maps and Charts," BBC News, June 2016, http://www.bbc.com/news/uk-politics-36616028.

45. "M5S secondo partito nei sondaggi: ma tra i giovani e la prima scelta," *L'Espresso,* February 3, 2016, http://espresso.repubblica.it/palazzo/2016/02/03/news/m5s-secondo-partito-nei-sondaggi-ma-tra-i-giovani-e-la-prima-scelta-1.248910. See also Tristan Quinault-Maupoli, "Les jeunes plébiscitent Le Pen et Mélenchon, les cadres votent Macron," *Le Figaro,* April 24, 2017; Víctor Ruiz De Almirón López, "Podemos se impone entre los jóvenes y ya muestra más fidelidad que el PSOE," ABC España, May 5, 2016; and Emilia Landaluce, "¿A quién votan los jóvenes?" *El Mundo,* April 25, 2016.

46. See Ben Kentish, "Nearly Half of Young French Voters Backed Marine
Le Pen, Projections Suggest," *Independent,* May 7, 2017; Emily Schul-
theis, "Marine Le Pen's Real Victory," *Atlantic,* May 7, 2017, https://
www.theatlantic.com/international/archive/2017/05/le-pen-national
-front-macron-france-election/525759/; and Anne Muxel, "Les jeunes
qui votent pour la première fois préfèrent Marine Le Pen," Slate.fr,
March 24, 2017, http://www.slate.fr/story/141710/jeunes-presidentielle.
See also the strong support for Le Pen in earlier regional elections: Claire
Sergent and Katy Lee, "Marine Le Pen's Youth Brigade," *Foreign Policy,*
October 7, 2016; and Joseph Bamat, "Mélenchon and Le Pen Win Over
Youth in French Vote," *France 24,* April 24, 2017, http://www.france24
.com/en/20170424-france-presidential-election-youth-vote-melenchon
-le-pen; and Schultheis, "Marine Le Pen's Real Victory." But compare
Jonathan Bouchet-Petersen and Laurent Troude, "Qui sont les 21,4 %
d'électeurs de Marine Le Pen," *Liberation,* April 24, 2017, https://oeil
surlefront.liberation.fr/les-idees/2017/04/24/qui-sont-les-214-d-electeurs
-de-marine-le-pen_1565123.
47. See Carla Bleiker, "Young People Vote Far-Right in Europe," *Deutsche
Welle,* December 14, 2015, http://www.dw.com/en/young-people-vote
-far-right-in-europe/a-18917193; Benjamin Reuter, "'Right-Wing Hip-
sters' Increasingly Powerful in Austria," WorldPost, May 20, 2016,
http://www.huffingtonpost.com/entry/right-wing-hipsters-increasingly
-powerful-in-austria_us_573e0e07e4b0646cbeec7a07; "Populism in Europe: Sweden," *Demos,* February 23, 2012, https://www.demos.co.uk
/project/populism-in-europe-sweden/; Alexandros Sakellariou, "Golden
Dawn and Its Appeal to Greek Youth," Friedrich Ebert Stiftung, July
2015, http://library.fes.de/pdf-files/bueros/athen/11501.pdf; Veronika
Czina, "The Rise of Extremism among the Youth of Europe: The Case of
Hungary's Jobbik Party," Project for Democratic Union, November 29,
2013, http://www.democraticunion.eu/2013/11/popularity-extremism
-among-youth-europe-case-hungarys-jobbik-party/; and Hillary Pilking-
ton, "Are Young People Receptive to Populist and Radical Right Political Agendas?" MYPLACE Policy Forum, November 20, 2014, http://
www.fp7-myplace.eu/documents/policy-forum/Policy%20Forum,%20
Session%202%20presentation%20v.8.pdf.
48. Matthew Smith, "Theresa May Is Britain's Most Popular Politician,"
YouGov, August 15, 2016, https://www.theguardian.com/politics/2017
/jun/10/jeremy-corbyn-youth-surge-votes-digital-activists. (Note, however, that later evidence suggests that the boost in youth turnout at the
2017 elections may have been significantly overstated in initial exit
polls.)
49. Emma Fidel, "White People Voted to Elect Donald Trump," Vice News,

November 9, 2016, https://news.vice.com/story/white-people-voted-to
-elect-donald-trump. It's also worth noting that, while Clinton did win
the overall youth vote quite decisively thanks to her huge advantage
among young black and Latino voters, her overall margin of victory was
lower than that enjoyed by Barack Obama in 2012. See Emily Rich-
mond, Mikhail Zinshteyn, and Natalie Gross, "Dissecting the Youth
Vote," *Atlantic,* November 11, 2016, https://www.theatlantic.com
/education/archive/2016/11/dissecting-the-youth-vote/507416/.

50. On Polish elections, see Frances Millard, *Democratic Elections in Poland, 1991–2007* (London: Routledge, 2010); on Poland's GDP, see "Poland GDP," *Trading Economics,* 2017, http://www.tradingeconomics
.com/poland/gdp; on Poland's active civil society, see Grzegorz Ekiert
and Jan Kubik, "Civil Society in Poland," paper presented at the international conference The Logic of Civil Society in New Democracies: East
Asia and East Europe, Taipei, Taiwan, June 5–7, 2009; Grzegorz Ekiert
and Roberto Foa, "Civil Society Weakness in Post-Communist Europe:
A Preliminary Assessment," *Carlo Alberto Notebooks* 198 (2011); and
Grzegorz Ekiert and Jan Kubik, *Rebellious Civil Society: Popular Protest
and Democratic Consolidation in Poland, 1989–1993* (Ann Arbor: University of Michigan Press, 2001). Finally, on the Polish press and higher
education, see Frances Millard, "Democratization and the Media in Po-
land 1989–97," *Democratization* 5, no. 2 (1998): 85–105; J. Reichel and
A. Rudnicka, "Collaboration of NGOs and Business in Poland," *Social
Enterprise Journal* 5, no. 2 (2009): 126–140; and Marek Kwiek, "From
System Expansion to System Contraction: Access to Higher Education in
Poland," *Comparative Education Review* 57, no. 3 (2013): 553–576.

51. "Briefing No 20: Democracy and Respect for Human Rights in the En-
largement Process of the European Union," *European Parliament,* April
1, 1998, http://www.europarl.europa.eu/enlargement/briefings/20a2_en
.htm.

52. Daniel Treisman, a leading scholar in the field, for example, called Poland a "consolidated democracy" as late as the summer of 2014. Daniel
Treisman, "Lessons from 25 Years of Post-Communism: The Importance
of Reform, Democracy, and Geography," *Washington Post* Monkey
Cage, June 10, 2014, https://www.washingtonpost.com/news/monkey
-cage/wp/2014/06/10/lessons-from-25-years-of-post-communism-the
-importance-of-reform-democracy-and-geography/?utm_term=
.b4026c436666. See also Radosław Markowski, "Party System Institu-
tionalization in New Democracies: Poland—A Trend-Setter with No Followers," in *Party Development and Democratic Change in Post-communist Europe,* ed. Paul G. Lewis, 55–77 (Portland, OR: Frank Cass,
2001).

53. Rick Lyman, "Secret Tapes of Politicians Cause a Stir in Poland," *New*

York Times, June 16, 2014, https://www.nytimes.com/2014/06/17/world/europe/secret-tapes-of-politicians-cause-a-stir-in-poland.html.

54. "Polish PM Sacks Coalition Partner Ahead of Early Elections," *Deutsche Welle,* August 13, 2007; "Program Prawa i Sprawidliwosci 2014," http://pis.org.pl/document/archive/download/128. See also David Ost, "Regime Change in Poland, Carried Out from Within," *Nation,* January 8, 2016, https://www.thenation.com/article/regime-change-in-poland-carried-out-from-within/; Gerhard Gnauck, "The Most Powerful Man in Poland," *Deutsche Welle,* October 25, 2016.

55. See Guy Verhofstadt, "Is Poland a Failing Democracy?" Politico, January 13, 2016, http://www.politico.eu/article/poland-democracy-failing-pis-law-and-justice-media-rule-of-law/; Neil Ascherson, "The Assault on Democracy in Poland Is Dangerous for the Poles and All Europe," *Guardian,* January 17, 2016, https://www.theguardian.com/commentis free/2016/jan/17/poland-rightwing-government-eu-russia-democracy-under-threat; and The Editorial Board, "Poland's Constitutional Crisis," *New York Times,* March 18, 2016, https://www.nytimes.com/2016/03/18/opinion/polands-constitutional-crisis.html?_r=0.

56. Annabelle Chapman, "Pluralism Under Attack: The Assault on Press Freedom in Poland," Freedom House Report, June 2017, https://freedomhouse.org/sites/default/files/FH_Poland_Report_Final_2017.pdf. See also Alison Smale and Joanna Brendt, "Poland's Conservative Government Puts Curbs on State TV News," *New York Times,* July 3, 2016, https://www.nytimes.com/2016/07/04/world/europe/polands-conservative-government-puts-curbs-on-state-tv-news.html.

57. Henry Foy and Zosia Wasik, "Poland: An Inconvenient Truth," *Financial Times,* May 1, 2016, https://www.ft.com/content/4344ca44-0b94-11e6-9cd4-2be898308be3. See also Chapman, "Pluralism Under Attack."

58. On Jan Gross, see Alex Duval Smith, "Polish Move to Strip Holocaust Expert of Award Sparks Protests," *Guardian,* February 13, 2016, https://www.theguardian.com/world/2016/feb/14/academics-defend-historian-over-polish-jew-killings-claims; on law criminalizing language, see "Poland Approves Bill Outlawing Phrase 'Polish Death Camps,'" *Guardian,* August 16, 2016, https://www.theguardian.com/world/2016/aug/16/poland-approves-bill-outlawing-phrase-polish-death-camps.

59. "If this bill enters into law," the Helsinki Foundation for Human Rights said in a statement, "it will significantly limit the possibility of organizing counter-demonstrations and spontaneous rallies." Marcin Goettig, "Polish Ombudsman, Rights Activists Rap Freedom of Assembly Bill," Reuters, November 30, 2016. In part because of such international protests, the Polish president ended up rejecting this bill. See also Chapman, "Pluralism Under Attack."

60. European Commission for Democracy through Law (Venice Commission), "Draft Opinion on Amendments to the Act of 25 June 2015 on the Constitutional Tribunal of Poland," February 26, 2016, http://static .presspublica.pl/red/rp/pdf/kraj/komisjawenecka.pdf. See also Jan Cienski and Maia De La Baume, "Poland's 'Rule of Law in Danger,'" Politico, March 1, 2016, http://www.politico.eu/article/poland-kaczynski -szydlo-tribunal-constitution-crisis/.

61. Verhofstadt, "Is Poland a Failing Democracy?"

62. Jan-Werner Müller, "The Problem with Poland," *New York Review of Books,* February 11, 2016, http://www.nybooks.com/daily/2016/02/11 /kaczynski-eu-problem-with-poland/.

63. Technically, at 23.7 percent, the support among American millennials was a little higher than the support among the general population in Poland. All the above figures are drawn from the World Values Survey.

64. On Andrzej Lepper, see Natalja Reiter, "Ich, Der Diktator," *Zeit,* June 17, 2004, http://www.zeit.de/2004/26/Polen/komplettansicht; Vanessa Gerra, "Andrzej Lepper, at 57; Populist Polish Politician," *Boston Globe,* August 6, 2011, http://archive.boston.com/bostonglobe/obitu aries/articles/2011/08/06/andrzej_lepper_at_57_populist_polish _politician/; Clare McManus-Czubińska, William L. Miller, Radosław Markowski, and Jacek Wasilewski, "The New Polish 'Right'?" *Journal of Communist Studies and Transition Politics* 19, no. 2 (2003): 1–23. On the League of Polish Families, see "Poland's Right-wingers: On the Rise," *Economist,* December 12, 2002, http://www.economist.com/ node/1494297.

Part Two. Origins

1. For a useful tool that allows you to calculate the boiling point of water at different altitudes, see http://www.csgnetwork.com/h2oboilcalc.html.

2. Bertrand Russell, *Problems of Philosophy* (Oxford: Oxford University Press, 1912), 63. See also Introduction.

3. On scope conditions, see Jeffrey W. Lucas, "Theory-testing, Generalization, and the Problem of External Validity," *Sociological Theory* 21, no. 3 (2003): 236–253; and Martha Foschi, "On Scope Conditions," *Small Group Research* 28, no. 4 (1997): 535–555.

4. Social Media

1. The definitive treatment of the rise of the printing press, and its effects, remains Elizabeth L. Eisenstein, *The Printing Press as an Agent of*

Change (Cambridge: Cambridge University Press, 1980). On "one-to-many communication," see also Lucien Febvre and Henri-Jean Martin, *The Coming of the Book: The Impact of Printing 1450–1800* (New York: Verso, 1976) and Clay Shirky, *Here Comes Everybody: The Power of Organizing without Organizations* (New York: Penguin, 2008).

2. Further to Eisenstein as well as to Febvre and Martin, see Jeremiah E. Dittmar, "Information Technology and Economic Change: The Impact of the Printing Press," *Quarterly Journal of Economics* 126, no. 3 (2011): 1133–1172.

3. Andrew Keen, "Can the Internet Save the Book?" *Salon,* July 9, 2010, http://www.salon.com/2010/07/09/clay_shirky/.

4. Helen Waters, "Entering the Second Age of Enlightenment: Heather Brooke at TEDGlobal 2012," TEDblog, June 28, 2012, http://blog.ted.com/entering-the-second-age-of-enlightenment-heather-brooke-at-tedglobal-2012/.

5. See Jib Fowles, "On Chronocentrism," *Futures* 6, no. 1 (1974): 65–68.

6. Shirky, *Here Comes Everybody,* 87. For an incredibly prescient description of many-to-many communication, see also Chandler Harrison Stevens, "Many-to-Many Communication," Sloan Working Paper no. 1225–81, Center for Information Systems Research, Sloan School of Management, M.I.T., 1981, https://dspace.mit.edu/bitstream/handle/1721.1/48404/manytomanycommun00stev.pdf.

7. See Bruce A. Williams and Michael X. Delli Carpini, "Unchained Reaction: The Collapse of Media Gatekeeping and the Clinton-Lewinsky Scandal," *Journalism* 1, no. 1 (2000): 61–85; Philip Seib and Dana M. Janbek, *Global Terrorism and New Media: The Post-Al Qaeda Generation* (New York: Routledge, 2011); Manuela Caiani and Linda Parenti, *European and American Extreme Right Groups and the Internet* (Surrey, UK: Ashgate, 2013; Routledge, 2016).

8. Larry Diamond, "Liberation Technology," *Journal of Democracy* 21, no. 3 (2010), reprinted in Larry Diamond and Marc F. Plattner, ed., *Liberation Technology: Social Media and the Struggle for Democracy* (Baltimore: Johns Hopkins University Press, 2012), 70.

9. Ibid., 74.

10. Quoted in Evgeny Morozov, *Net Delusion* (New York: PublicAffairs, 2011), 1. Sullivan was actually ahead of the curve, talking about the failed Green Revolution in Iran. See Andrew Sullivan, "The Revolution Will Be Twittered," *Atlantic,* June 13, 2009, https://www.theatlantic.com/daily-dish/archive/2009/06/the-revolution-will-be-twittered/200478/.

11. Quoted in Morozov, *Net Delusion,* 2.

12. Shirky, *Here Comes Everybody.*

13. On the Tea Party, see Vanessa Williamson, Theda Skocpol, and John Coggin, "The Tea Party and the Remaking of Republican Conserva-

tism," *Perspectives on Politics* 9, no. 1 (2011): 25–43, 28. On Occupy Wall Street and Black Lives Matter, see Monica Anderson and Paul Hitlin, "Social Media Conversations about Race," Pew Research Center, August 15, 2016, http://assets.pewresearch.org/wp-content/uploads/sites/14/2016/08/PI_2016.08.15_Race-and-Social-Media_FINAL.pdf; Bijan Stephen, "Social Media Helps Black Lives Matter Fight the Power," Wired, November 2015, https://www.wired.com/2015/10/how-black-lives-matter-uses-social-media-to-fight-the-power/; Michael D. Conover, Emilio Ferrara, Filippo Menczer, and Alessandro Flammini, "The Digital Evolution of Occupy Wall Street," *PLoS ONE* 8, no. 5 (2013); and Munmun De Choudhury, Shagun Jhaver, Benjamin Sugar, and Ingmar Weber, "Social Media Participation in an Activist Movement for Racial Equality," paper presented at the Tenth International AAAI Conference on Web and Social Media, Cologne, May 2016.

14. Thomas L. Friedman, "The Square People, Part 1," *New York Times,* May 13, 2014, https://www.nytimes.com/2014/05/14/opinion/friedman-the-square-people-part-1.html.

15. Diamond, "Liberation Technology," 71.

16. See for example Morozov, *Net Delusion;* and Evgeny Morozov, "Whither Internet Control?" in *Liberation Technology,* ed. Diamond and Plattner.

17. See Cass R. Sunstein, *Republic.com 2.0.* (Princeton: Princeton University Press, 2009); Elanor Colleoni, Alessandro Rozza, and Adam Arvidsson, "Echo Chamber or Public Sphere? Predicting Political Orientation and Measuring Political Homophily in Twitter Using Big Data," *Journal of Communication* 64, no. 2 (2014): 317–332; and Walter Quattrociocchi, Antonio Scala, and Cass R. Sunstein, "Echo Chambers on Facebook," June 13, 2016, https://ssrn.com/abstract=2795110.

18. See Hunt Allcott and Matthew Gentzkow, "Social Media and Fake News in the 2016 Election," *Journal of Economic Perspectives* 31, no. 2 (2017): 211–236. Compare Jonathan Mahler, "CNN Had a Problem. Donald Trump Solved It," *New York Times,* April 4, 2017, https://www.nytimes.com/2017/04/04/magazine/cnn-had-a-problem-donald-trump-solved-it.html?_r=0.

19. See Wil S. Hylton, "Down the Breitbart Hole," *New York Times Magazine,* August 16, 2017, https://www.nytimes.com/2017/08/16/magazine/breitbart-alt-right-steve-bannon.html; Michael M. Grynbaum and John Herrman, "Breitbart Rises from Outlier to Potent Voice in Campaign," *New York Times,* August 26, 2016, https://www.nytimes.com/2016/08/27/business/media/breitbart-news-presidential-race.html; David van Drehle, "Is Steve Bannon the Second Most Powerful Man in the World?" *Time Magazine,* February 2, 2017.

20. "Pope Francis Shocks World, Endorses Donald Trump for President, Releases Statement," Newsbreakshere, September 27, 2016, https://news breakshere.com/pope-francis-shocks-world-endorses-donald-trump -president-releases-statement.

21. "Bombshell: Hillary Clinton's Satanic Network Exposed," InfoWars, November 4, 2016, https://www.infowars.com/bombshell-hillary-clintons -satanic-network-exposed/.

22. James Barrett, "Poll: Who's More 'Evil,' Hillary or Trump?" Daily Wire, August 29, 2016, http://www.dailywire.com/news/8720/poll-whos-more -evil-hillary-or-trump-james-barrett.

23. Rafi Schwartz, "41% of Trump Supporters in North Carolina Think That Hillary Clinton Is Literally the Devil," Fusion, August 9, 2016, http://fusion.net/story/334920/hillary-clinton-devil-poll/.

24. Farhad Manjoo, "Social Media's Globe-Shaking Power," *New York Times*, November 16, 2016, https://www.nytimes.com/2016/11/17 /technology/social-medias-globe-shaking-power.html.

25. Jan H. Pierskalla and Florian M. Hollenbach, "Technology and Collective Action: The Effect of Cell Phone Coverage on Political Violence in Africa," *American Political Science Review* 107, no. 2 (2013): 207–224. On economists' expectations of positive effects, see Jenny C. Aker and Isaac M. Mbiti, "Mobile Phones and Economic Development in Africa," *Journal of Economic Perspectives* 24, no. 3 (2010): 207–232; Jenny C. Aker, "Information from Markets Near and Far: Mobile Phones and Agricultural Markets in Niger," *American Economic Journal: Applied Economics* 2, no. 3 (2010): 46–59; Jenny C. Aker, Christopher Ksoll, and Travis J. Lybbert, "Can Mobile Phones Improve Learning? Evidence from a Field Experiment in Niger," *American Economic Journal: Applied Economics* 4, no. 4 (2012): 94–120; Reuben Abraham, "Mobile Phones and Economic Development: Evidence from the Fishing Industry in India," *Information Technologies and International Development* 4, no. 1 (2007): 5–17.

26. Pierskalla and Hollenbach, "Technology and Collective Action," 220–221. See also Jacob N. Shapiro and Nils B. Weidmann, "Is the Phone Mightier than the Sword? Cellphones and Insurgent Violence in Iraq," *International Organization* 69, no. 2 (2015): 247–274.

27. On the initially slow diffusion of the printing press, see Dittmar, "Information Technology and Economic Change."

28. Josh Constine, "Facebook Now Has 2 Billion Monthly Users . . . and Responsibility," Techcrunch, June 27, 2017, https://techcrunch.com /2017/06/27/facebook-2-billion-users/.

29. George Orwell, "Second Thoughts on James Burnham," *Polemic* 3 (May 1946).

5. Economic Stagnation

1. See Thomas Piketty, *Capital in the Twenty-First Century* (Cambridge, MA: Belknap Press of Harvard University Press, 2014), 72–112.

2. S. N. Broadberry and Bas van Leeuwen, "British Economic Growth and the Business Cycle, 1700–1870: Annual Estimates," Working Paper, Department of Economics, University of Warwick, Coventry, UK, February 2011, CAGE Online Working Paper Series, vol. 2010 (20), http://www2 .warwick.ac.uk/fac/soc/economics/events/seminars-schedule/conferences /venice3/programme/british_economic_growth_and_the_business_cycle _1700-1850.pdf.

3. According to Jeffrey Williamson, the Gini coefficient for male earners rose from .293 to .358 between 1827 and 1851. By comparison, the Gini coefficient of today's Iceland is .280 while that of today's India is .352. See Jeffrey G. Williamson, "Earnings Inequality in Nineteenth-Century Britain," *Journal of Economic History* 40, no. 3 (1980): 457–475, 467; as well as the World Factbook, 2017: Distribution of Family Income— Gini Index, Central Intelligence Agency, https://www.cia.gov/library /publications/the-world-factbook/rankorder/2172rank.html.

4. Facundo Alvaredo, Anthony B. Atkinson, Thomas Piketty, and Emmanuel Saez, "The Top 1 Percent in International and Historical Perspective," *Journal of Economic Perspectives* 27, no. 3 (2013): 3–20, https:// eml.berkeley.edu/~saez/alvaredo-atkinson-piketty-saezJEP13top1percent .pdf.

5. Kimberly Amadeo, "U.S. GDP by Year Compared to Recessions and Events," The Balance, April 4, 2017, https://www.thebalance.com/us -gdp-by-year-3305543. See also Juan Antolin-Diaz, Thomas Drechsel, and Ivan Petrella, "Tracking the Slowdown in Long-run GDP Growth," *Review of Economics and Statistics* 99, no. 2 (2017): 343–356; and Robert J. Gordon, *The Demise of U.S. Economic Growth: Restatement, Rebuttal, and Reflections,* NBER Working Paper No. 19895, National Bureau of Economic Research, February 2014, http://www.nber.org /papers/w19895.

6. For France, see Pierre Sicsic and Charles Wyplosz, "France: 1945–92," in *Economic Growth in Europe since 1945,* ed. Nicholas Crafts and Gianni Toniolo, 210–239 (Cambridge: Cambridge University Press, 1996); and "France GDP Growth Rate by Year," Multpl, http://www.multpl .com/france-gdp-growth-rate/table/by-year, accessed April 5, 2017. For Germany, see Jurgen Weber, *Germany, 1945–1990: A Parallel History* (Budapest: Central European University Press, 2004), 37–60; and "Germany GDP Growth Rate by Year," Multpl, http://www.multpl.com

/germany-gdp-growth-rate/table/by-year, accessed April 5, 2017. For Italy, see Vera Zamagni, *The Economic History of Italy 1860–1990* (Oxford: Oxford University Press, 1993); and "Italy GDP Growth Rate by Year," Multpl, http://www.multpl.com/italy-gdp-growth-rate/table/by -year, accessed April 5, 2017.

7. Different measures of equality paint a slightly divergent picture of just how strong the increase in inequality has been. In this case, I have been referring to the Gini coefficient for earned income. See, for example, Anthony B. Atkinson, J. Hasell, Salvatore Morelli, and M. Roser, Chartbook of Economic Inequality, 2017, http://www.chartbookofeconomi cinequality.com/inequality-by-country/usa/. But similar findings also hold true about other ways of measuring income inequality, or indeed about wealth inequality. See for example Piketty, *Capital*.

8. See note 28 in the Introduction.

9. Raj Chetty, David Grusky, Maximilian Hell, Nathaniel Hendren, Robert Manduca, and Jimmy Narang, "The Fading American Dream: Trends in Absolute Income Mobility since 1940," *Science* 356, no. 6336 (2017): 398–406. See also John H. Goldthorpe, *Social Mobility and Class Structure in Modern Britain* (Oxford: Oxford University Press, 1987); and compare the more qualitative Arlie Hochschild, *Strangers in Their Own Land: Anger and Mourning on the American Right* (New York: New Press, 2016).

10. David Leonhardt, "The American Dream, Quantified at Last," *New York Times*, December 8, 2016, https://www.nytimes.com/2016/12/08 /opinion/the-american-dream-quantified-at-last.html?_r=0. On the political importance of economic expectations, see also Justin Gest, *The New Minority: White Working Class Politics in an Age of Immigration and Inequality* (Oxford: Oxford University Press, 2016).

11. "It is," the report notes, probably "the first time in industrialised history, save for periods of war or natural disaster, that the incomes of young adults have fallen so far when compared with the rest of society." Caelainn Barr and Shiv Malik, "Revealed: The 30-Year Economic Betrayal Dragging Down Generation Y's Income," *Guardian*, March 7, 2016, https://www.theguardian.com/world/2016/mar/07/revealed-30-year -economic-betrayal-dragging-down-generation-y-income.

    Some economists believe that reality is not as bad as these statistics suggest. Aggregate data on income, they claim, cannot adequately capture technological advances. Take computers and smartphones: a generation ago, even the most avid music lovers or movie buffs had a limited collection of LPs and could not rewatch their favorite movies unless they happened to pass on TV. Today, they have nearly all of the world's music and many of the world's movies available for streaming at the touch of a button. Is the economic data understating the progress the last years have brought if it cannot incorporate the vast difference in the quality of their consumer experience? I'm sure it is. But, wonderful as Spotify and Netflix may be, it is doubtful that they can compensate for economic stagnation in areas like food or housing. And (as I briefly mention below) noneconomic data about life expectancy, happiness, and a range of other indicators do not show a vastly more positive picture. See Chad Syverson, *Challenges to Mismeasurement Explanations for the U.S. Productivity Slowdown*, NBER Working Paper No. 21974, National Bureau of Economic Research, February 2016, http://www.nber.org/papers /w21974; and David M. Byrne, John G. Fernald, and Marshall B. Reinsdorf, "Does the United States Have a Productivity Slowdown or a Measurement Problem?" *Brookings Papers on Economic Activity* 2016, no. 1 (2016): 109–182.

12. Anne Case and Angus Deaton, "Rising Morbidity and Mortality in Midlife among White Non-Hispanic Americans in the 21st Century," *Proceedings of the National Academy of Sciences of the United States of America* 112, no. 49 (2015): 15078–15083. On life expectancy, see Elizabeth Arias, "United States Life Tables, 2003," *National Vital Statistics Reports* 54, no. 14 (2006): 1–40, https://www.cdc.gov/nchs/data/nvsr /nvsr54/nvsr54_14.pdf.

13. Jonathan T. Rothwell and Pablo Diego-Rosell, "Explaining Nationalist Political Views: The Case of Donald Trump," draft working paper, November 2, 2016, https://papers.ssrn.com/sol3/papers.cfm?abstract_id= 2822059. More broadly, voting along class lines has markedly declined over the last decades, both in North America and Western Europe. Perhaps as a result of these developments, the salience of economic issues also declined markedly. Whereas the manifestos of major European parties used to prioritize economic issues, most of them now accord noneconomic issues much more space. And though populists are often thought to succeed because of economic frustrations, their rhetoric mostly focuses on social and cultural issues. It is perhaps unsurprising, then, that even some obscure cultural markers are better at predicting votes for populist candidates and positions than economic ones. In the British case, as Eric Kaufmann has pointed out, support for Brexit is better predicted by support for the death penalty—which was not in any way part of the political debate in the run-up to the referendum—than by income or class. See Eric Kaufmann, "It's NOT the Economy, Stupid: Brexit as a Story of Personal Values," London School of Economics, British Politics and Policy blog, July 7, 2016, http://blogs.lse.ac.uk/politicsandpolicy /personal-values-brexit-vote/.

More broadly, Ronald Inglehart and Pippa Norris show that straightforward measures of social deprivation do not predict support for populist parties, which was stronger among the comparatively affluent petit bourgeoisie than it was among the working class. By contrast, the cultural factors they tested—including "anti-immigrant attitudes, mistrust of global and national governance, support for authoritarian values, and left-right ideological self-placement"—all were strongly predictive of support for populist parties. Ronald Inglehart and Pippa Norris, "Trump, Brexit, and the Rise of Populism: Economic Have-Nots and Cultural Backlash," HKS Working Paper no. RWP16–026, Harvard Kennedy School, July 29, 2016, p. 4, https://ssrn.com/abstract=2818659.

14. Bryce Covert, "No, 'Economic Anxiety' Doesn't Explain Donald Trump," *New Republic,* November 18, 2016, https://newrepublic.com /article/138849/no-economic-anxiety-doesnt-explain-donald-trump.

15. Steve Benen, "'Economic Anxieties' Don't Explain Donald Trump's Victory," MSNBC, December 28, 2016, http://www.msnbc.com/rachel -maddow-show/economic-anxieties-dont-explain-donald-trumps-victory.

16. Matthew Yglesias, "Why I Don't Think It Makes Sense to Attribute Trump's Support to Economic Anxiety," *Vox,* August 15, 2016, http:// www.vox.com/2016/8/15/12462760/trump-resentment-economic -anxiety.

17. Rothwell and Diego-Rosell, "Explaining Nationalist Political Views," 11.

18. Ibid., 1.

19. Max Ehrenfreund and Jeff Guo, "A Massive New Study Debunks a Widespread Theory for Donald Trump's Success," *Washington Post,* August 12, 2016, https://www.washingtonpost.com/news/wonk/wp/2016 /08/12/a-massive-new-study-debunks-a-widespread-theory-for-donald -trumps-success/?utm_term=.0dde2f2e2004.

20. As Jed Kolko shows, in counties with relatively few routine jobs, Clinton was ahead by over 30 percent. By contrast, in counties with a lot of routine jobs, Trump was ahead by just as much. Jed Kolko, "Trump Was Stronger Where the Economy Is Weaker," FiveThirtyEight, November 10, 2016, https://fivethirtyeight.com/features/trump-was-stronger-where -the-economy-is-weaker/.

21. Ibid.

22. Ben Delsman, "Automation and Populist Vote Share," forthcoming. On the economic causes of populism, see also Martin Eiermann, "The Geography of German Populism: Reflections on the 2017 Bundestag Elections," forthcoming; Dani Rodrik, "Populism and the Economics of Globalization," NBER Working Paper No. 23559, National Bureau of Economic Research, June 2017, http://www.nber.org/papers/w23559; Noam Gidron and Peter A. Hall, "Populism as a Problem of Social Inte-

gration," draft working paper, https://scholar.harvard.edu/hall/publica
tions/populism-problem-social-integration; and Chase Foster and Jeffry
Frieden, "Crisis of Trust: Socio-Economic Determinants of Europeans'
Confidence in Government," *European Union Politics* (2017).
23. There is plenty of precedent for this, of course. In interwar Europe, for
example, the "petit bourgeoisie" was often most hostile to democracy
and played a key role in the rise of fascism. See, for example, Richard F.
Hamilton, *Who Voted for Hitler?* (Princeton: Princeton University Press,
2014), 9–36. But compare, in the same book, 37–63.

6. Identity

1. Ironically, Pericles came to regret the rule change he himself had initi-
ated: After marrying Aspasia of Miletus he had to seek yet another
change of the law so that his own son could count as an Athenian citi-
zen. On the status of Aristotle and Diogenes, see Ben Akrigg, "Metics in
Athens," in *Communities and Networks in the Ancient Greek World,* ed.
Claire Taylor and Kostas Vlassopoulos (Oxford: Oxford University
Press: 2015), 155–157; on metics more broadly, see David Whitehead,
The Ideology of the Athenian Metic (Cambridge: Cambridge Philological
Society, 1977). For a broader treatment of Athenian citizenship laws, see
Philip Brook Manville, *The Origins of Citizenship in Ancient Athens*
(Princeton: Princeton University Press, 2014).
2. The classic treatment of Roman laws and practices of citizenship remains
Adrian Nicholas Sherwin-White, *The Roman Citizenship* (New York:
Oxford University Press, 1980).
3. Peter Garnsey, "Roman Citizenship and Roman Law in the Late Empire," in *Approaching Late Antiquity: The Transformation from Early
to Late Empire,* ed. Simon Swain and Mark J. Edwards (New York: Oxford University Press, 2004).
4. On the Ottoman Empire, see Halil Inalcik, *The Ottoman Empire: The
Classical Age, 1300–1600,* translated by Norman Itzkowitz and Colin
Imber (New York: Praeger, 1973); Stanford J. Shaw, *The Jews of the Ottoman Empire and the Turkish Republic* (Basingstoke: Macmillan,
1991); and Will Kymlicka, "Two Models of Pluralism and Tolerance,"
Analyse & Kritik 14, no. 1 (1992): 33–56. On the Hapsburg Empire, see
Carlile Aylmer Macartney, *The Habsburg Empire: 1790–1918* (London:
Weidenfeld and Nicolson, 1968); as well as the early classic by Robert A.
Kann, *The Multinational Empire: Nationalism and National Reform in
the Habsburg Monarchy, 1848–1918,* vol. 1: *Empire and Nationalities*
(New York: Columbia University Press, 1950).

5. See John W. Mason, *The Dissolution of the Austro-Hungarian Empire, 1867–1918,* 2nd ed. (New York: Longman, 1997); and Tibor Iván Berend, *History Derailed: Central and Eastern Europe in the Long Nineteenth Century* (Berkeley: University of California Press, 2003).
6. Personal communication.
7. See Roger D. Petersen, *Understanding Ethnic Violence: Fear, Hatred, and Resentment in Twentieth-Century Eastern Europe* (Cambridge: Cambridge University Press, 2002); Eagle Glassheim, *Noble Nationalists: The Transformation of the Bohemian Aristocracy* (Cambridge, MA: Harvard University Press, 2005); T. Mills Kelly, *Without Remorse: Czech National Socialism in Late-Habsburg Austria* (Boulder, CO: East European Monographs, 2006); as well as the varied essays in Pieter M. Judson and Marsha L. Rozenblit, eds., *Constructing Nationalities in East Central Europe* (New York: Berghahn Books, 2004).
8. For a general critique of the exclusionary aspects of self-determination movements, see Amitai Etzioni, "The Evils of Self-Determination," *Foreign Policy* 89 (1992): 21–35; but compare the more balanced account of the advantages and disadvantages of different kinds of state formation for minorities in Michael Walzer, "States and Minorities," in *Minorities: Community and Identity,* ed. C. Fried, 219–227 (Berlin: Springer, 1983).
9. On the *Kulturkampf,* see Michael B. Gross, "Kulturkampf and Unification: German Liberalism and the War against the Jesuits," *Central European History* 30, no. 4 (1997): 545–566; and Ronald J. Ross, "Enforcing the Kulturkampf in the Bismarckian State and the Limits of Coercion in Imperial Germany," *Journal of Modern History* 56, no. 3 (1984): 456–482. On Italy, Suzanne Stewart-Steinberg, *The Pinocchio Effect: On Making Italians, 1860–1920* (Chicago: University of Chicago Press, 2007). Compare also the classic study in this genre, on France: Eugen Weber, *Peasants into Frenchmen: The Modernization of Rural France, 1870–1914* (Stanford: Stanford University Press, 1976).
10. See Francis Ludwig Carsten, *The Rise of Fascism* (Berkeley: University of California Press, 1982); Sheri Berman, "Civil Society and the Collapse of the Weimar Republic," *World Politics* 49, no. 3 (1997): 401–429; and the classic treatment of the question in William L. Shirer, *The Rise and Fall of the Third Reich: A History of Nazi Germany* (1960; New York: Random House, 1991).
11. See Ronald M. Smelser, *The Sudeten Problem, 1933–1938: Volkstumspolitik and the Formulation of Nazi Foreign Policy* (Middletown, CT: Wesleyan University Press, 1975). For an interesting recent analysis of the effect of irredentism in the postwar world, see David S. Siroky and Christopher W. Hale, "Inside Irredentism: A Global Empirical Analysis," *American Journal of Political Science* 61, no. 1 (2017): 117–128.

12. Anthony Browne, "The Last Days of a White World," *Guardian*, September 3, 2000, https://www.theguardian.com/uk/2000/sep/03/race.world.

13. "Ethnicity and Religion Statistics," Institute of Race Relations, 2017, http://www.irr.org.uk/research/statistics/ethnicity-and-religion/.

14. Wolfgang Seifert, "Geschichte der Zuwanderung nach Deutschland nach 1950," Bundeszentrale fur politische Bildung, May 31, 2012, http://www.bpb.de/politik/grundfragen/deutsche-verhaeltnisse-eine-sozialkunde/138012/geschichte-der-zuwanderung-nach-deutschland-nach-1950?p=all.

15. "Area and Population—Foreign Population," Federal Statistical Office and the Statistical Offices of the Lander, August 26, 2016, http://www.statistik-portal.de/Statistik-Portal/en/en_jb01_jahrtab2.asp; "Germany," Focus Migration, http://focus-migration.hwwi.de/Germany.1509.0.html?&L=1; "Die soziale Situation in Deutschland," Bundeszentrale fur politische Bildung, January 11, 2016, http://www.bpb.de/wissen/NY3SWU,0,0,Bev%F6lkerung_mit_Migrationshintergrund_I.html.

16. "Reconstruction of the Resident Population by Age, Sex and Citizenship in Common," National Institute of Statistics, 2011, http://www.istat.it/it/archivio/99464.

17. "Standard Eurobarometer 85: Public Opinion in the European Union," European Commission, Directorate-General for Communication, 2016, 6, https://ec.europa.eu/COMMFrontOffice/publicopinion/index.cfm/ResultDoc/download/DocumentKy/75902.

18. "Top Voting Issues in 2016 Election," Pew Research Center, July 7, 2016, http://www.people-press.org/2016/07/07/4-top-voting-issues-in-2016-election/.

19. "'Wien darf nicht Istanbul werden', schimpft Wiener FPÖ-Chef," *Der Standard*, March 4, 2005, http://derstandard.at/1966831/Wien-darf-nicht-Istanbul-werden-schimpft-Wiener-FPOe-Chef.

20. Alexandra Sims, "Alternative for Germany: The Anti-immigration Party Even Scarier than Donald Trump," *Independent*, March 14, 2016, http://www.independent.co.uk/news/world/europe/alternative-for-germany-the-anti-immigration-party-even-scarier-than-donald-trump-a6930536.html.

21. Michael Strange, "Why the Danish People's Party Will Do Better Sitting on the Sidelines," *Guardian*, June 19, 2015, https://www.theguardian.com/commentisfree/2015/jun/19/danish-peoples-party-denmark-government.

22. Political scientists have found that a new influx of migrants into specific parts of Austria, Germany, Denmark, and Sweden increased the vote share of populists in those regions. Boris Podobnik, Marko Jusup, Dejan

Kovac, and H. E. Stanley, "Predicting the Rise of EU Right-Wing Populism in Response to Unbalanced Immigration," *Complexity* (2017), 2; Christopher J. Anderson, "Economics, Politics, and Foreigners: Populist Party Support in Denmark and Norway," *Electoral Studies* 15, no. 4 (1996): 497–511; Matt Golder, "Explaining Variation in the Electoral Success of Extreme Right Parties in Western Europe," *Comparative Political Studies* 36, no. 4 (2003): 432–466; Daniel Oesch, "Explaining Workers' Support for Right-wing Populist Parties in Western Europe: Evidence from Austria, Belgium, France, Norway, and Switzerland," *International Political Science Review* 29, no. 3 (2008): 349–373; K. Arzheimer and E. Carter, "Political Opportunity Structures and Right-wing Extremist Party Success," *European Journal of Political Research* 45, no. 3 (2006): 419–443.

23. Brian F. Schaffner, Matthew MacWilliams, and Tatishe Nteta, "Explaining White Polarization in the 2016 Vote for President: The Sobering Role of Racism and Sexism," Working Paper, 2016, http://people.umass.edu /schaffne/schaffner_et_al_IDC_conference.pdf; Daniel Cox, Rachel Lienesch, and Robert P. Jones, "Beyond Economics: Fears of Cultural Displacement Pushed the White Working Class to Trump," PRRI, Washington, DC, September 5, 2017, https://www.prri.org/research/white-working-class-attitudes-economy-trade-immigration-election-donald -trump/; Ronald Inglehart and Pippa Norris, "Trump, Brexit, and the Rise of Populism: Economic Have-nots and Cultural Backlash," HKS Working Paper no. RWP16–026, Harvard Kennedy School, July 29, 2016; Eric Kaufmann, "It's NOT the Economy, Stupid: Brexit as a Story of Personal Values," London School of Economics, British Politics and Policy blog, July 7, 2016, http://blogs.lse.ac.uk/politicsandpolicy/personal -values-brexit-vote/.

24. Lynn Vavreck, "The Great Political Divide over American Identity," *New York Times*, August 2, 2017, https://www.newyorktimes.com/2017 /08/02/upshot/the-great-political-divide-over-american-identity.html.

25. On Americans' relatively positive view of immigrants, see Eduardo Porter, "For Immigrants, America Is Still More Welcoming than Europe," *New York Times*, December 8, 2015, https://www.nytimes.com/2015/12 /09/business/international/for-immigrants-america-is-still-more-welcom ing-than-europe.html.

26. See Mae M. Ngai, "The Architecture of Race in American Immigration Law: A Reexamination of the Immigration Act of 1924," *Journal of American History* 86, no. 1 (1999): 67–92; and Edward Prince Hutchinson, *Legislative History of American Immigration Policy 1798–1965* (Philadelphia: University of Pennsylvania Press, 1981).

27. Renee Stepler and Anna Brown, "Statistical Portrait of Hispanics in the United States," Pew Research Center, April 19, 2016, http://www.pew hispanic.org/2016/04/19/statistical-portrait-of-hispanics-in-the-united -states-key-charts/#hispanic-pop.

28. "A Demographic Portrait of Muslim Americans," Pew Research Center, August 30, 2011, http://www.people-press.org/2011/08/30/section-1-a -demographic-portrait-of-muslim-americans/#number-of-muslims-in-the -u-s; Besheer Mohamed, "A New Estimate of the U.S. Muslim Population," Pew Research Center, January 6, 2016, http://www.pewresearch .org/fact-tank/2016/01/06/a-new-estimate-of-the-u-s-muslim-population/.

29. See Philip A. Klinkner and Rogers M. Smith, *The Unsteady March: The Rise and Decline of Racial Equality in America* (Chicago: University of Chicago Press, 1999), 339.

30. Michelle Ye Hee Lee, "Donald Trump's False Comments Connecting Mexican Immigrants and Crime," *Washington Post,* July 8, 2015.

31. For an excellent summary of the literature, see Zack Beauchamp, "White Riot: How Racism and Immigration Gave Us Trump, Brexit, and a Whole New Kind of Politics," *Vox,* January 20, 2017, http://www.vox .com/2016/9/19/12933072/far-right-white-riot-trump-brexit.

32. Jon Huang, Samuel Jacoby, Michael Strickland, and K. K. Rebecca Lai, "Election 2016: Exit Polls," *New York Times,* November 8, 2016, https://www.nytimes.com/interactive/2016/11/08/us/politics/election -exit-polls.html?_r=0.

33. Catherine Rampell, "Americans—Especially But Not Exclusively Trump Voters—Believe Crazy, Wrong Things," *Washington Post,* December 28, 2016, https://www.washingtonpost.com/news/rampage/wp/2016/12/28 /americans-especially-but-not-exclusively-trump-voters-believe-crazy -wrong-things/?utm_term=.f8514ecce52c.

34. Percent foreign born comes from 2009–2013 American Community Survey Five Year estimates. http://www.indexmundi.com/facts/united-states /quick-facts/illinois/foreign-born-population-percent#chart.

35. "Area and Population—Foreign Population," Federal Statistical Office and Statistical Offices of the Lander, August 26, 2016, http://www .statistik-portal.de/Statistik-Portal/en/en_jb01_jahrtab2.asp; Frankfurter Rundschau, "AfD ist in Sachsen stärkste Kraft," September 25, 2017, http://www.fr.de/politik/bundestagswahl/der-wahlabend-afd-ist-in-sachsen -staerkste-kraft-a-1356919. Similarly, the AfD has had its strongest result in state elections so far in Saxony-Anhalt, another state where the percentage of foreign-born residents lies below 4 percent. See also Ben Knight, "Euroskeptic AfD Cements Place in German Politics, for Now," *Deutsche Welle,* September 15, 2014, http://www.dw.com/en/euroskeptic -afd-cements-place-in-german-politics-for-now/a-17921496. Compare

also Emily Hruban, "BIBrief: A Temporary Alternative for Germany? A Look at AfD's Rise," Bertelsmann Foundation, March 17, 2016, http://www.bfna.org/publication/bbrief-a-temporary-alternative-for-germany-a-look-at-afd%E2%80%99s-rise; and "German State Elections: Success for Right-Wing Afd, Losses for Merkel's CDU," *Deutsche Welle,* March 13, 2016, http://www.dw.com/en/german-state-elections-success-for-right-wing-afd-losses-for-merkels-cdu/a-19113604.

36. Ingrid Melander and Michel Rose, "French Far-Right Fails to Win Any Regions in Upset for Le Pen," Reuters, December 13, 2015.

37. On a more obvious level, areas of high immigration also, by definition, contain a high number of minority voters—who are much less likely to vote for populist candidates whose appeal is based in large part on scapegoating them.

38. Ryan D. Enos, "Causal Effect of Intergroup Contact on Exclusionary Attitudes," *Proceedings of the National Academy of Sciences of the United States of America* 111, no. 10 (2014): 3699–3704, https://static1.square space.com/static/521abb79e4b0ee5879077f61/t/58d6a6d62994ca-9ba72a184e/1490462427818/EnosTrains.pdf. For an excellent overview of contact theory, see Thomas F. Pettigrew, "Intergroup Contact Theory," *Annual Review of Psychology* 49, no. 1 (1998): 65–85. On Gordon Allport, see also Thomas F. Pettigrew and Linda R. Tropp, "Allport's Intergroup Contact Hypothesis: Its History and Influence," in *On the Nature of Prejudice: Fifty Years after Allport,* ed. John F. Dovidio, Peter Glick, and Laurie A. Rudman, 262–277 (Malden, MA: Blackwell, 2005).

39. Robert D. Putnam, "E Pluribus Unum: Diversity and Community in the Twenty-First Century: The 2006 Johan Skytte Prize Lecture," *Scandinavian Political Studies* 30, no. 2 (2007): 137–174.

40. Barrett A. Lee, John Iceland, and Gregory Sharp, "Racial and Ethnic Diversity Goes Local: Charting Change in American Communities over Three Decades," Working Paper, Project 2010, Russell Sage Foundation Report, September 2012, 11, https://s4.ad.brown.edu/Projects/Diversity/Data/Report/report08292012.pdf.

41. Janet Adamy and Paul Overberg, "Places Most Unsettled by Rapid Demographic Change Are Drawn to Trump," *Wall Street Journal,* November 1, 2016, https://www.msn.com/en-us/news/politics/places-most-unsettled-by-rapid-demographic-change-are-drawn-to-trump/ar-AAjHg76.

42. Nate Cohn, "Why Trump Won: Working-Class Whites," *New York Times,* November 9, 2016, https://www.nytimes.com/2016/11/10/upshot/why-trump-won-working-class-whites.html.

43. Adamy and Overberg, "Places Most Unsettled."

44. On top of the evidence for this from opinion polls of actual voters, presented below, there is also very suggestive evidence of the important role of demographic fears drawn from survey experiments. See, for example, the fascinating finding that American voters with a high degree of racial identification became much more likely to support Donald Trump if primed to think that whites would become a minority in the future: Brenda Major, Alison Blodorn, and Gregory Major Blascovich, "The Threat of Increasing Diversity: Why Many White Americans Support Trump in the 2016 Presidential Election," *Group Processes and Intergroup Relations* (October 2016).

45. Steve King (@SteveKingIA). "Wilders understands that culture and demographics are our destiny. We can't restore our civilization with somebody else's babies," March 12, 2017, 2:40 PM tweet, https://twitter.com/SteveKingIA/status/840980755236999169.

46. Steve King is the congressman for the 4th Congressional District in the northwestern corner of Iowa, which is made up of thirty-nine counties. According to the data released by the American Community Survey through the US Census Bureau, in 2009, 4.1 percent of the population in these counties was foreign born, a proportion which increased to 5.1 percent in 2015. I defined "foreign born" as a US citizen born in Puerto Rico or other US Island Areas, a US citizen born abroad to American parents, a US citizen by naturalization, or someone who is not a US citizen (anyone not born in the United States).

47. Publius Decius Mus, "The Flight 93 Election," Claremont Review of Books digital, Claremont Institute, September 5, 2016, http://www.claremont.org/crb/basicpage/the-flight-93-election/. See also Rosie Gray, "The Populist Nationalist on Trump's National Security Council," *Atlantic,* March 24, 2017, https://www.theatlantic.com/politics/archive/2017/03/does-trumps-resident-intellectual-speak-for-his-boss/520683/.

48. Bradley Jones and Jocelyn Kiley, "More 'Warmth' for Trump among GOP Voters Concerned by Immigrants, Diversity," Pew Research Center, June 2, 2016, http://www.pewresearch.org/fact-tank/2016/06/02/more-warmth-for-trump-among-gop-voters-concerned-by-immigrants-diversity/.

49. Thilo Sarrazin, *Deutschland schafft sich ab: Wie wir unser Land aufs Spiel setzen* (Munich: Deutsche Verlags-Anstalt, 2010). See also Kim Bode et al., "Why Sarrazin's Integration Demagoguery Has Many Followers," Part 4: "The Genetic Argument," *Der Spiegel,* September 6, 2010, http://www.spiegel.de/international/germany/the-man-who-divided-germany-why-sarrazin-s-integration-demagoguery-has-many-followers-a-715876-4.html.

50. Zosia Wasik and Henry Foy, "Immigrants Pay for Poland's Fiery Rheto-

ric: Politicians Accused as Islamophobia Sparks Rise in Hate Crimes," *Financial Times,* September 15, 2016, https://www.ft.com/content /9c59ba54-6ad5-11e6-a0b1-d87a9fea034f.

51. Ibid.

52. Yigal Schliefer, "Hungary at the Turning Point," *Slate,* October 3, 2014, http://www.slate.com/articles/news_and_politics/moment/2014/10/viktor _orban_s_authoritarian_rule_the_hungarian_prime_minister_is _destroying.html.

53. Turkuler Isiksel, "Square Peg, Round Hole: Why the EU Can't Respond to Identity Politics," forthcoming.

54. "Perils of Perception: A 40-Country Study," Ipsos, 2016; https://www .ipsos.com/sites/default/files/2016-12/Perils-of-perception-2016.pdf.

55. Ivan Krastev, "The End of the German Moment?" The German Marshall Fund of the United States, September 21, 2016, http://www.gmfus.org /blog/2016/09/21/end-german-moment.

56. Podobnik et al., "Predicting the Rise."

57. "Decennial Censuses and the American Community Survey," US Census Bureau. Cited in "Immigrants in California," Public Policy Institute of California, http://www.ppic.org/publication/immigrants-in-california/, accessed April 1, 2017; Emily Cadei, "The California Roots of Trump-ism," *Newsweek,* July 5, 2016, http://www.newsweek.com/2016/07/15 /proposition-187-anti-immigration-donald-trump-477543.html; "Propo-sition 187: Text of Proposed Law," KPBS, http://www.kpbs.org/docu ments/2014/oct/24/proposition-187-text-proposed-law/; "Proposition 209: Text of Proposed Law," Voter Information Guides, http://vigarchive .sos.ca.gov/1996/general/pamphlet/209text.htm; "Proposition 227-Full Text of the Proposed Law," Voter Information Guides, http://vigarchive .sos.ca.gov/1998/primary/propositions/227text.htm. In a related move, motivated in large part by fears about criminal immigrants, Californians also instituted a "three strikes rule" that required draconian prison terms for repeat offenders, even if their offenses were relatively minor. "Cali-fornia's Three Strikes Sentencing Law," California Courts: The Judicial Branch of California, http://www.courts.ca.gov/20142.htm; "A Primer: Three Strikes—the Impact after More Than a Decade," Legislative Ana-lyst's Office, October 2005, http://www.lao.ca.gov/2005/3_strikes/3 _strikes_102005.htm.

58. These measures included moves that would restrict law enforcement from gathering information related to residents' immigration status and to fund legal aid to support people in deportation proceedings. Kate Murphy, "Defiant California Legislature Fast-Tracks 'Sanctuary State' Bills," *Mercury News,* January 30, 2017, http://www.mercurynews.com /2017/01/30/a-defiant-california-legislature-fast-tracks-sanctuary-state

-bills/. On reversals of earlier legislation, see Patrick McGreevy, "Gov. Brown Signs Bill Repealing Unenforceable Parts of Prop. 187," *Los Angeles Times,* September 15, 2014, http://www.latimes.com/local /politics/la-me-pol-brown-bills-20140916-story.html; and Jazmine Ulloa, "California Will Bring Back Bilingual Education as Proposition 58 Cruises to Victory," *Los Angeles Times,* November 8, 2016.

59. See Abraham H. Maslow, "A Theory of Human Motivation," *Psychological Review* 50, no. 4 (1943): 370–396; and Abraham H. Maslow, *The Farther Reaches of Human Nature* (New York: Viking, 1971).

60. See Ronald Inglehart, *Culture Shift in Advanced Industrial Society* (Princeton: Princeton University Press, 1990); Paul R. Abramson and Ronald Inglehart, "Generational Replacement and the Future of Postmaterialist Values," *Journal of Politics* 49, no. 1 (1987): 231–241; and Ronald Inglehart, "Public Support for Environmental Protection: Objective Problems and Subjective Values in 43 Societies," *PS: Political Science and Politics* 28, no. 1 (1995): 57–72.

61. Quoted in: Annie Lowrey, "Is It Better to Be Poor in Bangladesh or the Mississippi Delta?" *Atlantic,* March 8, 2017, https://www.theatlantic .com/business/archive/2017/03/angus-deaton-qa/518880/.

62. On the question of what I call post-post-materialism, see the interesting recent exchange between Robert Brym and Ronald Inglehart: Robert Brym, "After Postmaterialism: An Essay on China, Russia and the United States," *Canadian Journal of Sociology* 41, no. 2 (2016): 195–211; and Ronald Inglehart, "After Postmaterialism: An Essay on China, Russia and the United States: A Comment," *Canadian Journal of Sociology* 41, no. 2 (2016): 213–222.

Part Three. Remedies

1. On Park Geun-hye, her authoritarian tendencies, the corruption scandal involving Choi Soon-il, and the protests that led to her ouster, see Dave Hazzan, "Is South Korea Regressing into a Dictatorship?" *Foreign Policy* website, July 14, 2016, http://foreignpolicy.com/2016/07/14/is-south -korea-regressing-into-a-dictatorship-park-geun-hye/; Ock-Hyum Ju, "Freedom of Assembly on Trial in South Korea," *Korean Herald,* July 1, 2016, http://www.koreaherald.com/view.php?ud=20160630001122; Jennifer Williams, "The Bizarre Political Scandal That Just Led to the Impeachment of South Korea's President," *Vox,* March 9, 2017, https:// www.vox.com/world/2016/11/30/13775920/south-korea-president-park -geun-hye-impeached; Justin McCurry, "Former South Korean President Park Geun-hye on Trial for Corruption," *Guardian,* May 23, 2017. For an insightful framework for authoritarian successor parties more

broadly, see James Loxton, "Authoritarian Successor Parties," *Journal of Democracy* 26, no. 3 (2015): 157–170.

2. On Turkey, see Soner Cagaptay and Oya Rose Aktas, "How Erdoganism Is Killing Turkish Democracy," *Foreign Affairs,* July 7, 2017; and Yusuf Sarfati, "How Turkey's Slide to Authoritarianism Defies Modernization Theory," *Turkish Studies* 18, no. 3 (2017): 395–415. On Poland, see Daniel R. Kelemen, "Europe's Other Democratic Deficit: National Authoritarianism in Europe's Democratic Union," *Government and Opposition* 52, no. 2 (2017): 211–238; and Daniel R. Kelemen, "The Assault on Poland's Judiciary," *Foreign Affairs,* July 26, 2017. On the United States, see Brian Klaas, "The Five Ways President Trump Has Already Damaged Democracy at Home and Abroad," *Washington Post,* April 28, 2017; and Yascha Mounk, "Trump Is Destroying Our Democracy," *New York Times,* August 1, 2017.

3. Francesca Polletta, *Freedom Is an Endless Meeting: Democracy in American Social Movements* (Chicago: University of Chicago Press, 2002). See also Michael Walzer's classic essay on the degree to which the work of political engagement can be in conflict with the liberatory goals of left-wing politics. Michael Walzer, "A Day in the Life of a Socialist Citizen," *Dissent* 15, no. 3 (1968): 243–247.

4. There is not yet sufficient research on the specific question of the efficacy of particular forms of protest in response to populist governments. For some recent evidence on the political effectiveness of different forms of protest in general, see, for example, Emma F. Thomas and Winnifred R. Louis, "When Will Collective Action Be Effective? Violent and Non-violent Protests Differentially Influence Perceptions of Legitimacy and Efficacy among Sympathizers," *Personality and Social Psychology Bulletin* 40, no. 2 (2014): 263–276; Andreas Madestam, Daniel Shoag, Stan Veuger, and David Yanagizawa-Drott, "Do Political Protests Matter? Evidence from the Tea Party Movement," *Quarterly Journal of Economics* 128 (2013): 1633–1685; Grzegorz Ekiert and Jan Kubik, *Rebellious Civil Society: Popular Protest and Democratic Consolidation in Poland, 1989–1993* (Ann Arbor: University of Michigan Press, 1999); Taras Kuzio, "Civil Society, Youth and Social Mobilization in Democratic Revolutions," *Communist and Post-Communist Studies* 39 (2006): 365–386. For a countervailing view, see Peter L. Lorentzen, "Regularizing Rioting: Permitting Public Protest in an Authoritarian Regime," *Quarterly Journal of Political Science* 8 (2013): 127–158.

5. See Anne Applebaum, "Poles Fought the Nationalist Government with Mass Protests—and Won," *Washington Post,* July 24, 2017, https:// www.washingtonpost.com/news/global-opinions/wp/2017/07/24/how -street-demonstrators-scored-a-victory-against-polands -government/?utm_term=.51c4821e1d0c.

6. See Nick Thorpe, "Hungary CEU: Protesters Rally to Save University," BBC News, April 3, 2017, http://www.bbc.co.uk/news/world-europe -39479398; and "CEU to Remain in Budapest for 2017–2018 Academic Year, Hopes for Long-Term Solution," Central European University, May 30, 2017, https://www.ceu.edu/article/2017-05-30/ceu-remain -budapest-2017-2018-academic-year-hopes-long-term-solution.

7. The exact degree to which public opposition to Donald Trump has helped independent institutions to flex their muscles will not be known for years to come. But there are good theoretical and practical reasons to believe that it played a significant role. Political scientists, for example, have long understood that the opinions of even the highest US courts are influenced by public opinion in deep ways. See, for example, William Mishler and Reginald S. Sheehan, "The Supreme Court as a Countermajoritarian Institution? The Impact of Public Opinion on Supreme Court Decisions," *American Political Science Review* 87, no. 1 (1993): 87–101. Meanwhile, it is reasonable to suspect that Rod Rosenstein was in part influenced by the devastating reaction by many of his peers to his apparent complicity in the firing of James Comey. See Benjamin Wittes, "Et Tu Rod? Why the Deputy Attorney General Must Resign," *Lawfare,* May 12, 2017, https://www.lawfareblog.com/et-tu-rod-why-deputy-attorney -general-must-resign.

8. Although Russia's democracy has always been imperfect at best, it was still considered "partially free" by Freedom House in 2004, months after the first time Vladimir Putin stood for reelection (Freedom House, "Russia," in *Freedom in the World 2004,* https://freedomhouse.org/report /freedom-world/2004/russia). By 2008, by contrast, when new elections were significantly less fair than previous ones had been, the country was considered "not free" by Freedom House (Freedom House, "Russia," in *Freedom in the World 2008;* https://freedomhouse.org/report/freedom -world/2008/russia). For a similar example for Turkey, see Steven A. Cook, "How Erdogan Made Turkey Authoritarian Again," *Atlantic,* July 21, 2016, https://www.theatlantic.com/international/archive/2016 /07/how-erdogan-made-turkey-authoritarian-again/492374/; and for Venezuela, compare Freedom House, "Venezuela," in *Freedom in the World 2003,* https://freedomhouse.org/report/freedom-world/2003 /venezuela to Freedom House, "Venezuela," in *Freedom in the World 2017,* https://freedomhouse.org/report/freedom-world/2017/venezuela.

9. See "Election Resources on the Internet: Elections to the Polish Sejm— Results Lookup," http://electionresources.org/pl/sejm.php?election= 2015, and "Polish Parliamentary Election, 2015," Wikipedia, https:// en.wikipedia.org/wiki/Polish_parliamentary_election,_2015.

10. On India, see Milan Vaishnav, "Modi's Victory and the BJP's Future," *Foreign Affairs,* March 15, 2017, http://carnegieendowment.org

/2017/03/15/modi-s-victory-and-bjp-s-future-pub-68281; Anita Katyal, "The Opposition Is Divided on How It Should Unite Against the BJP Ahead of the 2019 General Elections," Scroll.in, https://scroll.in /article/834312/the-opposition-is-divided-on-how-it-should-unite-against -the-bjp-ahead-of-the-2019-general-elections/. On Turkey, see "Turkish General Election, 2007," Wikipedia, https://en.wikipedia.org/wiki /Turkish_general_election,_2007. On the United States, see Christopher J. Devine and Kyle C. Kopko, "5 Things You Need to Know about How Third-Party Candidates Did in 2016," *Washington Post,* November 15, 2016, https://www.washingtonpost.com/news/monkey-cage/wp/2016/11 /15/5-things-you-need-to-know-about-how-third-party-candidates-did-in -2016/?utm_term=.a37910397372.

11. Private communication.

12. Andrés Miguel Rondón, "In Venezuela, We Couldn't Stop Chávez. Don't Make the Same Mistakes We Did," *Washington Post,* January 27, 2017, https://www.washingtonpost.com/posteverything/wp/2017/01/27/in -venezuela-we-couldnt-stop-chavez-dont-make-the-same-mistakes-we -did/?utm_term=.58b6866907f8.

13. Ibid.

14. Luigi Zingales, "The Right Way to Resist Trump," *New York Times,* November 18, 2016, https://www.nytimes.com/2016/11/18/opinion/the -right-way-to-resist-trump.html?_r=0.

15. Aaron Blake, "Trump's Full Inauguration Speech Transcript, Anno-tated," *Washington Post,* January 20, 2017, https://www.washingtonpost .com/news/the-fix/wp/2017/01/20/donald-trumps-full-inauguration -speech-transcript-annotated/?utm_term=.7e71667cfff7.

16. Jenna Johnson, "Donald Trump to African American and Hispanic Vot-ers: 'What Do You Have to Lose?'" *Washington Post,* August 22, 2016, https://www.washingtonpost.com/news/post-politics/wp/2016/08/22 /donald-trump-to-african-american-and-hispanic-voters-what-do-you -have-to-lose/?utm_term=.0faa24c31da9.

17. Hillary Clinton and Tim Kaine, *Stronger Together: A Blueprint for America's Future* (New York: Simon & Schuster, 2016).

18. Hillary Clinton (@Hillary Clinton), "'America is already great. America is already strong & I promise you, our strength, our greatness, does not depend on Donald Trump.'—@POTUS." Twitter, July 27, 2016, 8:18 PM, https://twitter.com/hillaryclinton/status/758501814945869824 ?lang=en.

19. Monica Hersher and Yascha Mounk, "The Centre in the United King-dom, France and Germany," Tony Blair Institute for Global Change, June 2017, http://institute.global/sites/default/files/field_article_attached _file/IGC_Centre%20Polling_14.07.17.pdf.

20. The most obvious example here is Emmanuel Macron's victory against

Marine Le Pen in the 2017 French presidential elections. See Tracy Mc-
Nicoll, "Macron Beats Le Pen to Win French Presidency, Toughest Tasks
to Come," *France24*, May 8, 2017, http://www.france24.com/
en/20170507-frances-macron-beats-le-pen-win-presidency-toughest
-tasks-come; and Yascha Mounk, "It's Far Too Early to Declare Victory
over Populism," *Slate*, May 8, 2017, http://www.slate.com/articles/news
_and_politics/the_good_fight/2017/05/four_reasons_not_to_be_cheered
_by_emmanuel_macron_s_defeat_of_marine_le.html.

21. Even the best books on politics and public policy tend to have the same
flaw: The bulk of the book consists of a subtle, in-depth analysis of
deeply worrying trends. Then, the conclusion suggests glib, hurried suggestions for what to do about them. This is no coincidence: It's much
easier to diagnose problems than to solve them. A deep understanding of
a problem does not necessarily point the way toward a sensible solution.
And even when a proposed solution looks to be right on the merits, it is
often obvious that it would never be adopted. All these problems apply
to my topic as much as they would to most others. And that is why I
want to offer the reader a simple deal before I launch into my own account of the potential remedies to democracy's crisis: Finding solutions
to the deep challenges I've outlined in the book is incredibly hard. I have
taken the task seriously, and identified some promising ways of approaching the problem. I genuinely think—and fervently hope—that
thinking about the challenge in the way I outline here, and even adopting
some of the concrete policies I mention, would maximize our chances of
rejuvenating our democracies, and keeping authoritarian populists in
check. But I will not pretend that these suggestions are magic bullets.
Nor can I promise that adopting them would ultimately be enough to
save liberal democracy. They may well turn out not to be enough; but if
we are serious about saving liberal democracy, they are the best we can
do.

7. Domesticating Nationalism

1. See Yascha Mounk, "*The Pursuit of Italy* by David Gilmour," book review, Bookforum, October 7, 2011, http://www.bookforum.com/review
/8442; and David Gilmour, *The Pursuit of Italy: A History of a Land, Its
Regions, and Their Peoples* (New York: Farrar, Straus and Giroux,
2011).

2. Yascha Mounk, *Stranger in My Own Country: A Jewish Family in Modern Germany* (New York: Farrar, Straus and Giroux, 2014).

3. On the need to rethink sovereignty to meet global policy challenges, see
for example the treatment of the "globalization paradox" in Anne-Marie

Slaughter, *A New World Order* (Princeton: Princeton University Press, 2004). See also Kanishka Jayasuriya, "Globalization, Law, and the Transformation of Sovereignty: The Emergence of Global Regulatory Governance," *Indiana Journal of Global Legal Studies* 6 (1999): 425–455; and a defense of nation-state sovereignty in Jean L. Cohen, *Globalization and Sovereignty: Rethinking Legality, Legitimacy, and Constitutionalism* (Cambridge: Cambridge University Press, 2012). For an example of a hope that a European public sphere would follow the creation of a European polity, see Jürgen Habermas, *Zur Verfassung Europas: Ein Essay* (Frankfurt: Suhrkamp Verlag, 2011); or the earlier Jürgen Habermas, "Why Europe Needs a Constitution," in *Developing a Constitution for Europe,* ed. Erik Oddvar Eriksen, John Erik Fossum, and Agustín José Menéndez, 17–33 (New York: Routledge, 2004).

4. Fraser Cameron, "The European Union as a Model for Regional Integration," Council on Foreign Relations, September 24, 2010, https://www.cfr.org/report/european-union-model-regional-integration.

5. See Mark Leonard, *Why Europe Will Run the 21st Century* (New York: Public Affairs, 2005). Compare also Andrew Moravcsik, *The Choice for Europe: Social Purpose and State Power from Messina to Maastricht* (Ithaca, NY: Cornell University Press, 1998); and Robert O. Keohane, "Ironies of Sovereignty: The European Union and the United States," *Journal of Common Market Studies* 40, no. 4 (2002): 743–765.

6. Ghia Nodia, "The End of the Postnational Illusion," *Journal of Democracy* 28, no. 2 (2017): 5–19, 9.

7. Ibid.

8. "Referendums Related to the European Union," Wikipedia, accessed September 9, 2017, https://en.wikipedia.org/wiki/Referendums_related_to_the_European_Union.

9. In 2005, French and Dutch voters rejected a proposed European Constitution. To preserve the bulk of the reform, European heads of government modestly modified its text and hastily relabeled it as the Lisbon Treaty. The French and the Dutch were not given another opportunity to express their opinions. But the Irish were—and duly voted against it, too. Only when their government asked them to vote again, and Irish voters dutifully complied, could the Lisbon Treaty come into effect. Ibid.

10. See the first graph in "Spain's Reforms Point the Way for Southern Europe," *Economist,* June 15, 2017, https://www.economist.com/news/europe/21723446-having-tackled-its-problems-earlier-italy-or-greece-spain-now-seeing-results-spains. For unemployment rates, see "Unemployment by Sex and Age—Annual Average," Eurostat, http://appsso.eurostat.ec.europa.eu/nui/show.do?dataset=une_rt_a&lang=en, accessed September 9, 2017.

11. See Markus K. Brunnermeier, Harold James, and Jean-Pierre Landau,

The Euro and the Battle of Ideas (Princeton: Princeton University Press, 2016); and Joseph E. Stiglitz, *The Euro: How a Common Currency Threatens the Future of Europe* (New York: Norton, 2016); see also Thomas Meaney and Yascha Mounk, "What Was Democracy?" *Nation*, May 13, 2014, https://www.thenation.com/article/what-was-democracy/.

12. See Basharat Peer, *A Question of Order: India, Turkey, and the Return of the Strongmen* (New York: Columbia Global Reports, 2017). On China, see the nuanced discussion in Alastair Iain Johnston, "Is Chinese Nationalism Rising? Evidence from Beijing," *International Security* 41, no. 3 (2016): 7–43.

13. Nodia, "The End of the Postnational Illusion."

14. Michael Lind, "In Defense of Liberal Nationalism," *Foreign Affairs*, May–June, 1994, 87.

15. US Constitution. See https://www.law.cornell.edu/constitution/preamble.

16. Jan-Werner Müller, "Capitalism in One Family," *London Review of Books* 38, no. 23 (2016): 10–14.

17. See Krishnadev Calamur, "A Short History of 'America First,'" *Atlantic*, January 21, 2017, https://www.theatlantic.com/politics/archive/2017/01/trump-america-first/514037/; and Jonah Goldberg, "What Trump Means When He Says, 'America First,'" *National Review*, January 25, 2017, http://www.nationalreview.com/article/444211/donald-trump-america-first-slogan-stands-nationalist-identity.

18. A nationalism that is based on ethnic and religious belonging, and casts all opponents of a populist leader as unpatriotic, is also likely to stir up international tensions. The problem here is not so much that nationalist leaders of Trump's ilk are determined to pursue their nations' self-interest. (After all, most democratically elected leaders believe that their primary responsibility is to their own people.) Rather, it is their assumption that another nation has to lose for their nation to win. This is encapsulated in Trump's insistence that his knowledge of the art of the deal will get America ahead. It is the subtext for his promise to stand up for the interests of Pittsburgh rather than those of Paris (as though climate change were not a threat to Paris and Pittsburgh alike). And it is also the foundation of his belief that trade deals have "enriched foreign industry at the expense of American industry." See Alan Murray, "Trump's Zero-Sum Economic Vision," *Forbes*, January 23, 2017, http://fortune.com/2017/01/23/trump-protectionism-inaugural-address-zero-sum/.

19. For an influential study on job market discrimination against African Americans, see Marianne Bertrand and Sendhil Mullainathan, "Are Emily and Greg More Employable than Lakisha and Jamal? A Field Experiment on Labor Market Discrimination," *American Economic Review* 94 (2004): 991–1013. For bias in the criminal justice system, see Alberto

Alesina and Eliana La Ferrara, "A Test of Racial Bias in Capital Sentencing," *American Economic Review* 104 (2014): 3397–3433; as well as Lawrence D. Bobo and Victor Thompson, "Unfair by Design: The War on Drugs, Race, and the Legitimacy of the Criminal Justice System," *Social Research* 73 (2006): 445–472. For risk of being shot by law enforcement, see Alison V. Hall, Erika V. Hall, and Jamie L. Perry, "Black and Blue: Exploring Racial Bias and Law Enforcement in the Killings of Unarmed Black Male Civilians," *American Psychologist* 71, no. 3 (2016): 175–186.

20. *Parents Involved in Community Schools v. Seattle School Dist. No. 1 (Nos. 05–908 and 05–915)* 2007, https://www.law.cornell.edu/supct /html/05-908.ZS.html.

21. As Eduardo Bonilla-Silva puts a related (but more controversial) point, "If race disappears as a category of official division, as it has in most of the world, this will facilitate the emergence of a plural racial order where the groups exist in practice but are not officially recognized—and anyone trying to address racial division is likely to be chided for racializing the population." Eduardo Bonilla-Silva, *Racism without Racists: Color-Blind Racism and the Persistence of Racial Inequality in America*, 5th ed. (2003; Lanham, MD: Rowman and Littlefield, 2018), 189.

22. Adia Harvey Wingfield, "Color-Blindness Is Counterproductive," *Atlantic*, September 13, 2015, https://www.theatlantic.com/politics/archive /2015/09/color-blindness-is-counterproductive/405037/.

23. For a highly viral explainer of the ills of cultural appropriation, see Maisha Z. Johnson, "What's Wrong with Cultural Appropriation? These 9 Answers Reveal Its Harm," Everyday Feminism, June 14, 2015, http:// everydayfeminism.com/2015/06/cultural-appropriation-wrong/. On microaggressions see Miguel Ceja and Tara Yosso, "Critical Race Theory, Racial Microaggressions and Campus Racial Climate: The Experiences of African American College Students," *Journal of Negro Education* 69 (2000): 60–73; Daniel Solórzano, "Critical Race Theory, Race, and Gender Microaggressions, and the Experience of Chicana and Chicano Scholars," *International Journal of Qualitative Studies in Education* 11 (1998): 121–136; and Kevin L. Nadal, *That's So Gay! Microaggressions and the Lesbian, Gay, Bisexual, and Transgender Community* (Washington, DC: American Psychological Association, 2013). Finally, on free speech, see Ulrich Baer, "What 'Snowflakes' Get Right about Free Speech," *New York Times,* April 24, 2017, https://www.nytimes.com /2017/04/24/opinion/what-liberal-snowflakes-get-right-about-free -speech.html.

24. Emanuella Grinberg, "Dear White People with Dreadlocks: Some Things to Consider," CNN, April 1, 2016, http://edition.cnn.com/2016/03/31

/living/white-dreadlocks-cultural-appropriation-feat/index.html; Clover Linh Tran, "CDS Appropriates Asian Dishes, Students Say," *Oberlin Review,* November 6, 2015, https://oberlinreview.org/9055/news/cds -appropriates-asian-dishes-students-say/.

25. Princess Gabbara, "The History of Dreadlocks," *Ebony,* October 18, 2016, http://www.ebony.com/style/history-dreadlocks#axzz4qX8wRTJe.

26. On Baghdad, see Jim Al-Khalili, "When Baghdad Was Centre of the Scientific World," *Guardian,* September 25, 2010, https://www.theguardian .com/books/2010/sep/26/baghdad-centre-of-scientific-world; on Vienna, see Carl E. Schorske, *Fin-de-Siècle Vienna: Politics and Culture* (New York: Knopf, 1980); and on New York, see E. B. White, *Here Is New York* (New York: Harper & Row, 1949).

27. Writing in the darkest days of World War I, for example, the Austrian comedian Karl Kraus depicted members of a "voluntary commission" who tried to eradicate all uses of French, English, or Italian words in the streets of Vienna. Karl Kraus, *The Last Days of Mankind: A Tragedy in Five Acts,* trans. Patrick Edward Healy (1918; Netherlands: November Editions, 2016), act 3, scene 8.

28. In philosophical terms, even forms of hate speech do, of course, have "truth value," which is to say that they express a recognizable proposition that isn't semantic gibberish. But they probably don't have value in the sense of advancing a point of view it is important for others to hear (let alone imparting some supposed insight about the world).

29. As Kenan Malik put this point, the key question is "who does the policing? Every society has its gatekeepers, whose role is to protect certain institutions, maintain the privileges of particular groups and cordon off some beliefs from challenge. Such gatekeepers protect not the marginalized but the powerful." Kenan Malik, "Cultural Appropriation and Secular Blasphemy," Pandemonium, July 9, 2017, https://kenanmalik .wordpress.com/2017/07/09/cultural-appropriation-and-secular -blasphemy/.

30. For a deeper exploration of this line of argument, see Thomas Scanlon, "A Theory of Freedom of Expression," *Philosophy and Public Affairs* 1 (1972): 204–226.

31. Wingfield, "Color Blindness Is Counter-Productive."

32. Alex Rosenberg, "The Making of a Non-patriot," *New York Times,* July 3, 2017, https://www.nytimes.com/2017/07/03/opinion/the-making-of-a -non-patriot.html. The op-ed was published online the day before Independence Day, but was clearly timed to coincide with it.

33. DisastaCaPiTaLisM, "Antifa Chanting 'No Trump, No Wall, No USA At All,'" Youtube, September 5, 2017, https://www.youtube.com/watch?v= IV440PbnIPI.

34. Shaun King, "KING: Thomas Jefferson Was a Horrible Man Who Owned 600 Human Beings, Raped Them, and Literally Worked Them to Death," *New York Daily News,* July 3, 2017, http://www.nydailynews .com/news/national/king-thomas-jefferson-evil-rapist-owned-600-slaves -article-1.3308931.

35. See Hans Kundnani, *Utopia or Auschwitz: Germany's 1968 Generation and the Holocaust* (Oxford: Oxford University Press, 2009); and Simon Erlanger, "'The Anti-Germans'—The Pro-Israel German Left," *Jewish Political Studies Review* 21 (2009): 95–106.

36. See Maya Rhodan, "Transcript: Read Full Text of President Barack Obama's Speech in Selma," *Time,* March 7, 2015, http://time.com /3736357/barack-obama-selma-speech-transcript/.

37. Ibid.

38. Alastair Jamieson and Chloe Hubbard, "Far-Right Marine Le Pen Leads French Polls but Still Seen Losing Runoff," NBC News, February 23, 2017, http://www.nbcnews.com/news/world/far-right-marine-le-pen -leads-french-election-polls-still-n724536.

39. Emmanuel Macron, "Quand je regarde Marseille je vois . . . les Algéri-ens, les Marocains, les Tunisiens . . . E. Macron," speech posted on You-tube, April 3, 2017, https://www.youtube.com/watch?v=Yxmbctib964.

40. Benedict Anderson, *Imagined Communities* (London: Verso, 1983).

41. For a good summary of the skeptical view of European migration, see Christopher Caldwell, *Reflections on the Revolution in Europe: Immi-gration, Islam, and the West* (New York: Anchor, 2009).

42. On structural injustice, see Iris Marion Young, "Structural Injustice and the Politics of Difference," in *Intersectionality and Beyond: Law, Power and the Politics of Location,* ed. Emily Grabham et al. (2008), 273.

43. Studies have suggested that this system doubly disadvantages minority students: For one, their teachers are less likely to recommend that they be admitted to more prestigious schools even if they perform at the same level. For another, talented students from disadvantaged backgrounds usually take longer than four years of formal schooling to catch up with classmates from more educated families. See the overview in Heike Solga and Rosine Dombrowski, "Soziale Ungleichheiten in schulischer und außerschulischer Bildung: Stand der Forschung und Forschungsbedarf," Working Paper, Bildung und Qualifizierung, no. 171, 2009, https://www .econstor.eu/handle/10419/116633. But consider also the more skeptical view in Cornelia Kirsten, "Ethnische Diskriminierung im deutschen Schulsystem? Theoretische Überlegungen und empirische Ergebnisse," WZB Discussion Paper, no. SP IV 2006–601, https://www.econstor.eu /handle/10419/49765.

44. See Marie Duru-Bellat, "Social Inequality in French Education: Extent

and Complexity of the Issues," *International Studies in Educational Inequality, Theory and Policy* (2007): 337–356; as well as Michel Euriat and Claude Thélot, "Le recrutement social de l'élite scolaire en France: évolution des inégalités de 1950 à 1990," *Revue française de sociologie* (1995): 403–438; and Christian Baudelot and Roger Establet, *L'élitisme républicain: l'école française à l'épreuve des comparaisons internationales* (Paris: Seuil, 2009).

45. "K-12 Education: Better Use of Information Could Help Agencies Identify Disparities and Address Racial Discrimination," US Government Accountability Office, April 2016, http://www.gao.gov/assets/680/676744 .pdf. This finding was confirmed by a recent study by the Civil Rights Project at UCLA, which similarly showed that "hyper-segregated schools, in which 90% or more of students are minorities, grew since 1988 from 5.7% to 18.4%." Gary Orfield, Jongyeon Ee, Erica Frankenberg, and Genevieve Siegel-Hawley, "*Brown* at 62: School Segregation by Race, Poverty and State," The Civil Rights Project, UCLA, May 16, 2016, https://civilrightsproject.ucla.edu/research/k-12-education /integration-and-diversity/brown-at-62-school-segregation-by-race -poverty-and-state/. See also Greg Toppo, "GAO Study: Segregation Worsening in U.S. Schools," *USA Today*, May 17, 2016, https://www .usatoday.com/story/news/2016/05/17/gao-study-segregation-worsening -us-schools/84508438/.

46. See Qanta Ahmed, "And Now, Female Genital Mutilation Comes to America," *Daily Beast*, April 18, 2017, http://www.thedailybeast.com/ and-now-female-genital-mutilation-comes-to-america; "Female Genital Mutilation Exposed in Swedish Class," The Local, June 20, 2014, https://www.thelocal.se/20140620/swedish-school-class-genitally -mutilated; and Alexandra Topping, "FGM Specialist Calls for Gynaecological Checks for All Girls in Sweden," *Guardian*, June 27, 2014, https://www.theguardian.com/society/2014/jun/27/female-genital -mutilation-fgm-specialist-sweden-gynaecological-checks-children.

47. See Helen Pidd, "West Yorkshire Police and Agencies 'Failed to Protect' Groomed Girl," *Guardian*, December 6, 2016; "Oxford Grooming: 'No Hiding' from Authorities' Failures," BBC News, March 2, 2015, http:// www.bbc.co.uk/news/uk-england-oxfordshire-31696276; and David A. Graham, "How Belgium Tried and Failed to Stop Jihadist Attacks," *Atlantic*, March 22, 2016.

48. "Gewalt-Rechtfertigung mit Koran—Richterin abgezogen," *Spiegel Online*, March 21, 2007, http://www.spiegel.de/politik/deutschland/justiz -skandal-gewalt-rechtfertigung-mit-koran-richterin-abgezogen-a -472966.html.

49. See Will Kymlicka, *Multicultural Citizenship: A Liberal Theory of Mi-*

nority Rights (Oxford: Clarendon Press, 1995), ch. 3. Compare Mounk, *Stranger in My Own Country,* ch. 10.

50. On this point, see Michael Walzer, *Spheres of Justice: A Defense of Pluralism and Equality* (New York: Basic Books, 1983), ch. 1; and David Miller, "The Ethical Significance of Nationality," *Ethics* 98 (1988): 647–662.

51. See Jeffrey G. Reitz, "The Distinctiveness of Canadian Immigration Experience," *Patterns of Prejudice* 46, no. 5 (2012): 518–538; and Garnett Picot and Arthur Sweetman, "Making It in Canada: Immigration Outcomes and Policies," *IRPP Study* 29 (2012): 1–5.

8. Fixing the Economy

1. Karen Tumulty, "How Donald Trump Came Up with 'Make America Great Again,'" *Washington Post,* January 18, 2017, https://www.washingtonpost.com/politics/how-donald-trump-came-up-with-make-america-great-again/2017/01/17/fb6acf5e-dbf7-11e6-ad42-f3375f271c9c_story.html?utm_term=.064c24103851.

2. Officially, the slogan was "Taking Back Control," though most politicians invoking the slogan did not use the gerundive form. See "Boris Johnson: UK 'Should Take Back Control,'" BBC News, http://www.bbc.com/news/av/uk-35739955/boris-johnson-uk-should-take-back-control; and Joseph Todd, "Why Take Back Control Is the Perfect Left-Wing Slogan," *New Statesman,* March 13, 2017, http://www.newstatesman.com/politics/staggers/2017/03/why-take-back-control-perfect-left-wing-slogan.

3. This is one of the reasons that minorities are, in most countries, much less tempted by populist politicians on both the far right and the far left. Although they, too, are struggling financially, they have seen real improvements in the past decades and remain much more hopeful about the future. See Mark Hugo Lopez, Rich Morin, and Jens Manuel Krogstad, "Latinos Increasingly Confident in Personal Finances, See Better Economic Times Ahead," Pew Research Center, http://www.pewhispanic.org/2016/06/08/latinos-increasingly-confident-in-personal-finances-see-better-economic-times-ahead/; and Jamelle Bouie, "Who Is Most Excited about America's Future? Minorities," *Daily Beast,* February 3, 2014, http://www.thedailybeast.com/who-is-most-excited-about-americas-future-minorities.

4. On GDP per capita, see US Bureau of Economic Analysis, "Real Gross Domestic Product per Capita (A939RX0Q048SBEA)," retrieved from FRED, Federal Reserve Bank of St. Louis, https://fred.stlouisfed.org

/series/A939RX0Q048SBEA. On net worth, see Board of Governors of the Federal Reserve System (US), "Households and Nonprofit Organizations; Net Worth, Level (TNWBSHNO)," retrieved from FRED, Federal Reserve Bank of St. Louis, adjusted for inflation, https://fred.stlouisfed .org/series/TNWBSHNO. Finally, for per capita corporate profits, see US Bureau of Economic Analysis, Corporate Profits After Tax (without IVA and CCAdj) [CP], retrieved from FRED, Federal Reserve Bank of St. Louis, adjusted for inflation, https://fred.stlouisfed.org/series/CP.

5. See Online Appendix (Table B3) in Emmanuel Saez and Gabriel Zucman, "Wealth Inequality in the United States since 1913: Evidence from Capitalized Income Tax Data," *Quarterly Journal of Economics* 131, no. 2 (2016): 519–578. As a result, the bottom 90 percent of households have seen their share of total wealth fall from 36 percent to 23 percent. Many believe this wealth was transferred to the top 5 percent or even the top 1 percent, but that's not quite right. Rather, the 13 percentage point decrease in the share of wealth held by the bottom 90 percent is equivalent to the 13 point increase in the percentage of wealth held by the top 0.1 percent. See Online Appendix (Table B1) in Saez and Zucman, "Wealth Inequality in the United States."

6. See "Tax Rate Schedules," Instructions for 1987 Form 1040, Internal Revenue Service, US Department of the Treasury, p. 47, and "Federal Capital Gains Tax Rates, 1988–2011," Tax Foundation, https://files .taxfoundation.org/legacy/docs/fed_capgains_taxrates-20100830.pdf.

7. On Reagan, see Peter Dreier, "Reagan's Real Legacy," *Nation,* June 29, 2015. On the Personal Responsibility and Work Opportunity Reconciliation Act, see Yascha Mounk, *The Age of Responsibility* (Cambridge, MA: Harvard University Press, 2017), ch. 2; and Carly Renee Knight, "A Voice without a Vote: The Case of Surrogate Representation and Social Welfare for Legal Noncitizens since 1996," forthcoming.

8. Eduardo Porter, "The Republican Party's Strategy to Ignore Poverty," *New York Times,* October 27, 2015. One of the few bright spots in this dark tale was the health reform passed by Barack Obama. For the first time in its history, the United States took seriously one of the most basic moral obligations of any affluent society: to provide medical coverage to (most of) its citizens. But while the eventual shape of the American health care system will remain uncertain for a long time to come, key elements of it are now being stripped away: if legislators turn the present administration's goals into law, millions of Americans will lose their insurance in the coming years.

9. See Marina Karanikolos et al., "Financial Crisis, Austerity, and Health in Europe," *Lancet* 381, no. 9874 (2013): 1323–1331; Emmanuele Pavolini, Margarita León, Ana M. Guillén, and Ugo Ascoli, "From Austerity

to Permanent Strain? The EU and Welfare State Reform in Italy and Spain," *Comparative European Politics* 13 (2015): 56–76; Mark Blyth, *Austerity: The History of a Dangerous Idea* (Oxford: Oxford University Press, 2013), especially ch. 3; and Matt Pickles, "Greek Tragedy for Education Opportunities," BBC News, September 30, 2015, http://www.bbc .co.uk/news/business-34384671.

10. See Horst Feldmann, "Technological Unemployment in Industrial Countries," *Journal of Evolutionary Economics* 23 (2013): 1099–1126. But consider also more skeptical voices, like James E. Bessen, "How Computer Automation Affects Occupations: Technology, Jobs, and Skills," Law and Economics Research Paper no. 15–49, Boston University School of Law, October 3, 2016, https://papers.ssrn.com/sol3/papers .cfm?abstract_id=2690435. For a consideration of a swath of potential policy responses, see Yvonne A. Stevens and Gary E. Marchant, "Policy Solutions to Technological Unemployment," in *Surviving the Machine Age,* ed. Kevin LaGrandeur and James J. Hughes (Cham, Switzerland: Palgrave MacMillan, 2017).

11. See Justin R. Pierce and Peter K. Schott, "The Surprisingly Swift Decline of US Manufacturing Employment," *American Economic Review* 106, no. 7 (2016): 1632–1662; Thomas Kemeny, David Rigby, and Abigail Cooke, "Cheap Imports and the Loss of US Manufacturing Jobs," *World Economy* 38, no. 10 (2015): 1555–1573; and William J. Carrington and Bruce Fallick, "Why Do Earnings Fall with Job Displacement?" Federal Reserve Bank of Cleveland Working Paper no. 14–05, June 19, 2014, https://papers.ssrn.com/sol3/papers.cfm?abstract_id=2456813.

12. See Lawrence H. Summer, "U.S. Economic Prospects: Secular Stagnation, Hysteresis, and the Zero Lower Bound," *Business Economics* 49 (2014): 65–73; and Tyler Cowen, *The Great Stagnation: How America Ate All the Low-Hanging Fruit of Modern History, Got Sick, and Will (Eventually) Feel Better* (New York: Dutton, 2011). For a nuanced discussion of the prospects of a convergence between countries like China, on the one hand, and North America as well as Western Europe, on the other, read Dani Rodrik, "The Future of Economic Convergence," Jackson Hole Symposium of the Federal Reserve Bank of Kansas City, 2011, http://drodrik.scholar.harvard.edu/files/dani-rodrik/files/future-economic -convergence.pdf?m=1435006479.

13. The hope that machines might one day do the labor traditionally required of humans, freeing humans for more high-minded pursuits, is of course very old. See Karl Marx, "German Ideology," in Karl Marx, *Early Political Writings,* ed. Joseph J. O'Malley (Cambridge: Cambridge University Press, 1994), 132; and Herbert Marcuse, *An Essay on Liberation* (Boston: Beacon Press, 1969), especially p. 6. For a more recent take

in a somewhat similar vein, see Rutger Bregman, *Utopia for Realists: The Case for a Universal Basic Income, Open Borders, and a 15-hour Workweek* (New York: Little, Brown and Company, 2017).

14. As the 2018 World Inequality Report chronicles, there is a lot of variation in the degree to which different countries have allowed their citizens to share in the growth of the local economy. This, its authors conclude, suggests "the importance of institutional and policy frameworks" in determining outcomes from affluence to inequality. Facundo Alvaredo, Lucas Chancel, Thomas Piketty, Emmanuel Saez, and Gabriel Zucman, eds., *The World Inequality Report* (Cambridge, MA: Belknap Press of Harvard University Press, 2018).

15. For a recent defense of the economic benefits of higher taxation, see Peter Diamond and Emmanuel Saez, "The Case for a Progressive Tax: From Basic Research to Policy Recommendation," *Journal of Economic Perspectives* 25, no. 4 (2011): 165–190. For a counterintuitive argument about the *popularity* of such taxation, see Vanessa S. Williamson, *Read My Lips: Why Americans Are Proud to Pay Taxes* (Princeton: Princeton University Press, 2017).

16. See Alberto Alesina and Dani Rodrik, "Distributive Politics and Economic Growth," *Quarterly Journal of Economics* 109 (1994): 465–490; Mounk, *Age of Responsibility*; Blyth, *Austerity*, especially chs. 6 and 7. Interestingly, there is also growing support for the welfare state from libertarians of various stripes. See Matt Zwolinski, "Libertarianism and the Welfare State," in *The Routledge Handbook of Libertarianism*, ed. Jason Brennan, Bas van der Vossen, and David Schmidtz (New York: Routledge, 2017); and Matt Zwolinski, "Libertarianism and the Welfare State," Bleeding Heart Libertarians, March 7, 2016, http://bleeding-heartlibertarians.com/2016/03/libertarianism-and-the-welfare-state/.

17. See Alicia H. Munnell, "Policy Watch: Infrastructure Investment and Economic Growth," *Journal of Economic Perspectives* 6, no. 4 (1992): 189–198; Gilles St. Paul and Thierry Verdier, "Education, Democracy, and Growth," *Journal of Development Economics* 42 (1993): 399–407; and P. Aghion, L. Boustan, C. Hoxby, and J. Vandenbussche, "The Causal Impact of Education on Economic Growth: Evidence from U.S.," unpublished manuscript, March 2009, https://scholar.harvard.edu/files/aghion/files/causal_impact_of_education.pdf.

18. For a good overview of some of the economic costs of not offering universal health care, see David Sterret, Ashley Bender, and David Palmer, "A Business Case for Universal Healthcare: Improving Economic Growth and Reducing Unemployment by Providing Access for All," *Health Law and Policy Brief* 8, no. 2 (2014): 41–55, http://digital

commons.wcl.american.edu/cgi/viewcontent.cgi?article=1132&context
=hlp.

19. Damian Paletta, "With Tax Break, Corporate Rate Is Lowest in Decades," *Wall Street Journal,* February 3, 2012, https://www.wsj.com
/articles/SB10001424052970204662204577199492233215330.

20. Tim Fernholz, "Why Buying a Corporate Jet Pays for Itself," Quartz,
April 8, 2014, https://qz.com/196369/why-buying-a-corporate-jet-pays
-for-itself/.

21. "Broken at the Top: How America's Dysfunctional Tax System Costs Billions in Corporate Tax Dodging," Oxfam America, April 14, 2016,
https://www.oxfamamerica.org/static/media/files/Broken_at_the_Top
_4.14.2016.pdf. See also Gabriel Zucman, *The Missing Wealth of Na-
tions: The Scourge of Tax Havens* (Chicago: University of Chicago Press,
2015); and Scott D. Dyreng and Bradley P. Lindsey, "Using Financial Accounting Data to Examine the Effect of Foreign Operations Located in
Tax Havens and Other Countries on U.S. Multinational Firms' Tax
Rates," *Journal of Accounting Research* 47 (2009): 1283–1316.

22. Michael S. Knoll, "The Taxation of Private Equity Carried Interests: Es-
timating the Revenue Effects of Taxing Profit Interests as Ordinary Income," *William and Mary Law Review* 50, no. 1 (2008): 115–161. On
the "Buffett Rule," see Warren E. Buffett, "Stop Coddling the Super-
Rich," *New York Times,* August 14, 2011, http://www.nytimes.com
/2011/08/15/opinion/stop-coddling-the-super-rich.html; and Chris Isa-
dore, "Buffett Says He's Still Paying Lower Tax Rate than His Secretary," CNN Money, March 4, 2013, http://money.cnn.com/2013/03/04
/news/economy/buffett-secretary-taxes/index.html.

23. For information on tax havens, see Luke Harding, "What Are the Panama Papers? A Guide to History's Biggest Data Leak," *Guardian,* April
5, 2016, https://www.theguardian.com/news/2016/apr/03/what-you
-need-to-know-about-the-panama-papers; and Jane G. Gravelle, "Tax
Havens: International Tax Avoidance and Evasion," *National Tax Journal* 62, no. 4 (2009): 727–753. For the growing tax evasion problem, see
Chuck Marr and Cecily Murray, "IRS Funding Cuts Compromise Taxpayer Service and Weaken Enforcement," Center on Budget and Policy
Priorities, April 4, 2016, https://www.cbpp.org/research/federal-tax/irs
-funding-cuts-compromise-taxpayer-service-and-weaken-enforcement;
and Emily Horton, "'Egregious' Employment Tax Evasion Grows as IRS
Enforcement Funding Shrinks," Center on Budget Policy and Priorities,
April 27, 2017, https://www.cbpp.org/blog/egregious-employment-tax
-evasion-grows-as-irs-enforcement-funding-shrinks for the American
case. See also Nikolaos Artavanis, Adair Morse, and Margarita Tsou-

tsoura, "Measuring Income Tax Evasion Using Bank Credit: Evidence from Greece," *Quarterly Journal of Economics* 131 (2016): 739–798.

24. James A. Caporaso, "Changes in the Westphalian Order: Territory, Public Authority, and Sovereignty," *International Studies Review* 2 (2000): 1–28; and Stuart Elden, "Contingent Sovereignty, Territorial Integrity and the Sanctity of Borders," *SAIS Review of International Affairs* 26 (2006): 11–24. See also Richard Tuck, *The Rights of War and Peace: Political Thought and the International Order from Grotius to Kant* (Oxford: Oxford University Press, 1999).

25. The British politician Vincent Cable wrote an interesting—and still very relevant—overview article on the ways in which globalization weakens the traditional powers of the state while opening new avenues for state intervention in the mid-1990s: Vincent Cable, "The Diminished Nation-State: A Study in the Loss of Economic Power," *Daedalus* 124, no. 2 (1995): 23–53.

26. See Merriam Webster, "Words Unfit for the Office," https://www.merriam -webster.com/words-at-play/us-presidents-say-the-darndest-things/mis underestimate, accessed September 14, 2017.

27. Internal Revenue Service, "U.S. Citizens and Resident Aliens Abroad," https://www.irs.gov/individuals/international-taxpayers/u-s-citizens-and -resident-aliens-abroad, accessed September 14, 2017; and John D. McKinnon, "Tax History: Why U.S. Pursues Citizens Overseas," *Wall Street Journal*, May 18, 2012, https://blogs.wsj.com/washwire/2012/05 /18/tax-history-why-u-s-pursues-citizens-overseas/.

28. See also Yascha Mounk, "Steuerpflicht für alle!" *Die Zeit*, July 25, 2012, http://www.zeit.de/wirtschaft/2012-07/steuerpflicht. To be sure, countries should also maintain or adopt sensible rules regarding double taxation. In many cases, it makes sense for individuals to pay tax in the place of their residence rather than in the place of their citizenship. This is why the United States allows people to deduct the taxes they pay abroad from the taxes they would have to pay if they lived in America. The point, in other words, is not so much to ensure that an American citizen will forever fill the coffers of Uncle Sam but rather that American citizens will fulfill their fiscal obligation in some country, whether it is at home or abroad.

29. There has been a lot of discussion of these proposals in both Toronto and Vancouver, where foreign investment has recently driven a huge housing boom. See Josh Gordon, "The Ethical Case for Taxing Foreign Home Buyers," *Globe and Mail*, April 12, 2017, https://www.theglobe andmail.com/report-on-business/rob-commentary/the-ethical-case-for -taxing-foreign-home-buyers/article34690709/.

30. See "Swiss Finished?" *Economist*, September 7, 2013, https://www

.economist.com/news/finance-and-economics/21585009-america-arm
-twists-bulk-switzerlands-banks-painful-deal-swiss; Ryan J. Reilly,
"Swiss Banks Deal Near in Tax Haven Crackdown, Justice Department
Says," *Huffington Post*, August 29, 2013, http://www.huffingtonpost
.com/2013/08/28/swiss-banks-deal_n_3832052.html; and Polly Curtis,
"Treasury Strikes Tax Evasion Deal with Switzerland to Recoup Unpaid
Cash," *Guardian*, August 24, 2011, https://www.theguardian.com
/business/2011/aug/24/switzerland-does-tax-deal-with-treasury.

31. See for example Michael J. Graetz, Jennifer F. Reinganum, and Louis L.
Wilde, "The Tax Compliance Game: Toward an Interactive Theory of
Law Enforcement," *Journal of Law, Economics, & Organization* 2, no.
1 (1986): 1–32.

32. See Eoin Burke-Kennedy, "Ireland Branded One of World's Worst Tax
Havens," *Irish Times*, December 12, 2016, https://www.irishtimes.com
/business/economy/ireland-branded-one-of-world-s-worst-tax-havens
-1.2901822; and Leslie Wayne, "How Delaware Thrives as a Corporate
Tax Haven," *New York Times*, June 30, 2012, http://www.nytimes.com
/2012/07/01/business/how-delaware-thrives-as-a-corporate-tax-haven
.html.

33. For one way that this might work, see Zucman, *The Missing Wealth of
Nations*. For an alternative solution to the same underlying problem, see
Reuven Avi-Yonah, "The Shame of Tax Havens," *American Prospect,*
December 1, 2015, http://prospect.org/article/shame-tax-havens.

34. Francois de Beaupuy, Caroline Connan, and Geraldine Amiel, "France
and Germany Plan Tax Crackdown on U.S. Tech Giants," *Bloomberg,*
August 7, 2017, https://www.bloomberg.com/news/articles/2017-08-07
/france-and-germany-plan-crackdown-on-tax-loopholes-used-by-apple.
See also Jim Brunsden and Mehreen Khan, "France Drives EU Tax Blitz
on Revenues of US Tech Giants," *Financial Times*, September 9, 2017,
https://www.ft.com/content/371733e8-94ae-11e7-bdfa-eda243196c2c.
One advantage of all of these proposals is that they would not require
massive international cooperation to get off the ground. This is not true
of most ideas suggested in this space. Intriguing proposals like the international financial transaction tax, advocated by Thomas Piketty among
many others, for example, might do some good if dozens of countries
managed to agree on it all at the same time. But since such cooperation is
simply unlikely to happen anytime soon, the immediate effect of concen-
trating on such policies is to achieve nothing at all.

35. In current dollars, this means that the average New York rental price has
roughly doubled, from about $1,500 in the mid-1960s to about $3,000
today, while the average purchase price of a square foot has increased
more than fivefold, from a little under $200 to well over $1,000. Simi-

larly, the purchase price of an average London home has increased from just under $200,000 in 1986 to over $600,000 in current dollars. See Jonathan Miller, "Tracking New York Rents and Asking Prices over a Century," Curbed, June 2, 2015, https://ny.curbed.com/2015/6/2 /9954250/tracking-new-york-rents-and-asking-prices-over-a-century; "The Rise and Rise of London House Prices," ITV, July 15, 2014, http:// www.itv.com/news/london/2014-07-15/the-rise-and-rise-of-london -house-prices-1986-to-2014/.

36. "English Housing Survey: Headline Report 2013–14," UK Department for Communities and Local Government, https://www.gov.uk/govern ment/uploads/system/uploads/attachment_data/file/469213/English _Housing_Survey_Headline_Report_2013-14.pdf.

37. In fact, even residents of rural towns that happen to be especially attractive are increasingly pushed out of their communities. See Olivia Rudgard, "One in Ten British Adults Now a Second-Home Owner," *Telegraph,* August 18, 2017, http://www.telegraph.co.uk/news/2017/08/18 /one-ten-british-adults-now-second-home-owner/.

38. David Adler, "Why Housing Matters," unpublished manuscript.

39. In the United Kingdom, where the housing crisis is especially acute, there have recently been some moves toward speeding up the planning process. See "Fast Track Applications to Speed Up Planning Process and Boost Housebuilding," Gov.uk, February 18, 2016, https://www.gov.uk /government/news/fast-track-applications-to-speed-up-planning-process -and-boost-housebuilding; and Patrick Wintour and Rowena Mason, "Osborne's Proposals to Relax Planning System a 'Retreat from Localism,'" *Guardian,* July 10, 2015, https://www.theguardian.com/society /2015/jul/10/osbornes-proposals-relax-planning-system-retreat-localism.

40. See "Whitehall to Overrule Councils That Fail to Deliver Housebuilding Plans," Public Sector Executive, October 12, 2015, http://www.public sectorexecutive.com/News/whitehall-to-overrule-councils-that-fail-to -deliver-housebuilding-plans/120953.

41. Nicola Harley, "Theresa May Unveils Plan to Build New Council Houses," *Telegraph,* May 13, 2017, http://www.telegraph.co.uk /news/2017/05/13/theresa-may-unveils-plan-build-new-council-houses/; see also "Forward, Together: Our Plan for a Stronger Britain and a Prosperous Future: The Conservative and Unionist Party, Manifesto 2017," Conservatives.com, 2017, 70–72, https://www.conservatives.com /manifesto.

42. A good overview of the land value tax is provided in "Why Land Value Taxes Are So Popular, Yet So Rare," *Economist,* November 10, 2014, https://www.economist.com/blogs/economist-explains/2014/11/economist -explains-0. Interestingly, the tax has strong supporters on both the left

and the right. See Andy Hull, "In Land Revenue: The Case for a Land Value Tax in the UK," *Labour List*, May 8, 2013, https://labourlist.org /2013/05/in-land-revenue-the-case-for-a-land-value-tax-in-the-uk/; and Daran Sarma, "The Case for a Land Value Tax," Institute of Economic Affairs, February 15, 2016, https://iea.org.uk/blog/the-case-for-a-land -value-tax-0.

43. A number of cities and countries, from Paris and New York to Italy, have been moving toward taxing second homes more heavily. See Megan McArdle, "Own a Second Home in New York? Prepare for a Higher Tax Bill," *Atlantic*, February 11, 2011, https://www.theatlantic.com/business /archive/2011/02/own-a-second-home-in-new-york-prepare-for-a-higher -tax-bill/71144/; Feargus O'Sullivan, "Paris Sets Its Sights on Owners of Second Homes," Citylab, June 15, 2016, https://www.citylab.com/equity /2016/06/paris-wants-to-raise-second-homes-taxes-five-times/487124/; Gisella Ruccia, "Imu, Renzi: 'Via tassa su prima casa anche per i ricchi perché impossibile riforma del Catasto,'" Il Fatto Quotidiano, September 15, 2015, http://www.ilfattoquotidiano.it/2015/09/15/imu-renzi-via -tassa-su-prima-casa-anche-per-i-ricchi-perche-impossibile-riforma-del -catasto/414080/. For an example of an empty tax penalty, see "Council Tax: Changes Affecting Second Homes and Empty Properties," Gov.uk: Borough of Poole, http://www.poole.gov.uk/benefits-and-council-tax /council-tax/council-tax-changes-affecting-second-homes-and-empty -properties/, accessed September 14, 2017.

44. The benefits of the home mortgage interest deduction—introduced in its current form in 1986—are ten times greater for a household earning more than $250,000 than for a household earning between $40,000 and $75,000. See James Poterba and Todd Sinai, "Tax Expenditures for Owner-Occupied Housing: Deductions for Property Taxes and Mortgage Interest and the Exclusion of Imputed Rental Income," paper given at the American Economic Association Annual Meeting, New Orleans, LA, January 5, 2008, http://real.wharton.upenn.edu/~sinai/papers/Poterba -Sinai-2008-ASSA-final.pdf, accessed September 14, 2017.

45. This is especially pronounced in the United States and Great Britain. See Karen Rowlingson, "Wealth Inequality: Key Facts," University of Birmingham Policy Commission on the Distribution of Wealth, December 2012, 14, http://www.birmingham.ac.uk/Documents/research/Social Sciences/Key-Facts-Background-Paper-BPCIV.pdf; and Michael Neal, "Homeownership Remains a Key Component of Household Wealth," National Association of Home Builders, September 3, 2013, http:// nahbclassic.org/generic.aspx?genericContentID=215073.

46. The most accessible description of the role of the housing bubble in creating the Great Recession remains Michael Lewis, *The Big Short: Inside*

the Doomsday Machine (New York: W. W. Norton, 2010). See also Atif Mian and Amir Sufi, *House of Debt: How They (and You) Caused the Great Recession, and How We Can Prevent It from Happening Again* (Chicago: University of Chicago Press, 2014).

47. This suggestion is inspired by similar proposals in relation to carbon taxation. See, for example, Robert O. Keohane, "The Global Politics of Climate Change: Challenge for Political Science," *PS: Political Science & Politics* 48, no. 1 (2015): 19–26.

48. There have been many reasons for this, from the Great Recession to Occupy Wall Street. But the book that has catalyzed most of this discussion has undoubtedly been Thomas Piketty, *Capital in the Twenty-First Century* (Cambridge, MA: Belknap Press of Harvard University Press, 2014).

49. On the role of lobbying in politics, see Jane Mayer, *Dark Money: The Hidden History of the Billionaires behind the Rise of the Radical Right* (New York: Doubleday, 2016); and Lee Drutman, *The Business of America Is Lobbying: How Corporations Became More Politicized and Politicians Became More Corporate* (New York: Oxford University Press, 2015). For a recent argument that the problem of opportunity hoarding extends beyond the top one percent to large swathes of the upper middle class, see Richard V. Reeves, *Dream Hoarders: How the American Upper Middle Class Is Leaving Everyone Else in the Dust, Why That Is a Problem, and What to Do about It* (Washington, DC: Brookings Institution Press, 2017). On weakening social ties, see Robert D. Putnam, *Bowling Alone: The Collapse and Revival of American Community* (New York: Touchstone, 2001).

50. The White House, *Economic Report of the President*, February 2015, p. 33, https://obamawhitehouse.archives.gov/sites/default/files/docs/cea_2015_erp.pdf.

51. See University World News, "Cuts in Spending for Research Worldwide May Threaten Innovation," *Chronicle of Higher Education*, December 14, 2016, http://www.chronicle.com/article/Cuts-in-Spending-for-Research/238693; and "Universities Report Four Years of Declining Federal Funding," National Science Foundation, November 17, 2016, https://www.nsf.gov/news/news_summ.jsp?cntn_id=190299. On California, see "State Spending on Corrections and Education," University of California, https://www.universityofcalifornia.edu/infocenter/california-expenditures-corrections-and-public-education, accessed September 14, 2017. California is far from alone in this: ten other American states also spend more on prisons than on education. See Katie Lobosco, "11 States Spend More on Prisons than on Higher Education," CNN Money, October 1, 2015, http://money.cnn.com/2015/10/01/pf/college/higher-education-prison-state-spending/index.html.

52. Yascha Mounk, "Hallo, hörst du mich?" *Die Zeit*, November 2, 2016,

http://www.zeit.de/2016/44/universitaeten-deutschland-besuch-studenten
-professoren-hoersaal.

53. Digital technology is not about to make human teachers obsolete, then; for the foreseeable future, the presence of highly trained teachers will remain just as important as it has been in the past. But it does require them to learn new skills and focus on the areas in which they retain a real advantage over digital tools. See Ashish Arora, Sharon Belenzon, and Andrea Patacconi, "Killing the Golden Goose? The Decline of Science in Corporate R&D," NBER Working Paper no. 20902, National Bureau of Economic Research, January 2015, http://www.nber.org/papers/w20902.

54. Mary Webb and Margaret Cox, "A Review of Pedagogy Related to Information and Communications Technology," *Technology, Pedagogy, and Education* 13 (2004): 235–286. For the complicated interaction between technological capacity and teachers' pedagogical convictions, see Peggy A. Ertmer, "Teacher Pedagogical Beliefs: The Final Frontier in Our Quest for Technology Integration?" *Educational Technology Research and Development* 53 (2005): 25–39; and Peggy A. Ertmer and Anne T. Ottenbreit-Leftwich, "Teacher Technology Change," *Journal of Research on Technology in Education* 42 (2010): 255–284.

55. One promising approach would be to allow adults to take courses and to draw student loans for a given number of semesters after they have concluded their education, repaying the costs with a percentage of their future earnings. See this helpful Special Report by the *Economist:* Andrew Palmer, "Lifelong Learning Is Becoming an Economic Imperative," *Economist,* January 12, 2017, https://www.economist.com/news/special
-report/21714169-technological-change-demands-stronger-and-more
-continuous-connections-between-education. There isn't enough work done on the financing of lifelong learning. For a somewhat out-of-date overview, see Gerald Burke, "Financing Lifelong Learning for All: An International Perspective," Working Paper no. 46, Acer Centre for the Economics of Education and Training, Monash University, November 2002, http://www.monash.edu.au/education/non-cms/centres/ceet/docs/working papers/wp46nov02burke.pdf.

56. The classic statement of this point remains Gøsta Esping-Andersen's point on "decommodification." See Gøsta Esping-Andersen, *The Three Worlds of Welfare Capitalism* (Princeton: Princeton University Press, 1990).

57. The problem, of course, is that the declining numbers of union membership have also led to the rapidly declining bargaining power of unions. For an insightful treatment of this problem, see Anthony B. Atkinson, *Inequality: What Can Be Done?* (Cambridge, MA: Harvard University Press, 2015), 128–132.

58. See the excellent series of essays on "dualization" in Patrick Emmeneg-

ger, ed., *The Age of Dualization: The Changing Face of Inequality in Deindustrializing Societies* (Oxford: Oxford University Press, 2012), as well as the classic Gøsta Esping-Andersen, "Welfare States without Work: The Impasse of Labour Shedding and Familialism in Continental European Social Policy," in *Welfare States in Transition: National Adaptations in Global Economies,* ed. Gøsta Esping-Andersen, 66–87 (London: Sage, 1996).

59. On disincentives for employers, see Karsten Grabow, "Lohn- und Lohnnebenkosten," in Grabow, *Die westeuropäische Sozialdemokratie in der Regierung,* 123–141 (Wiesbaden: Deutscher Universitäts-Verlag, 2005). On labor market insiders, see Assar Lindbeck and Dennis J. Snower, "Insiders versus Outsiders," *Journal of Economic Perspectives* 15, no. 1 (2001): 165–188; Samuel Bentolila, Juan J. Dolado, and Juan F. Jimeno, "Reforming an Insider-Outsider Labor Market: The Spanish Experience," *IZA Journal of European Labor Studies* 1, no. 1 (2012): 1–19, 4; as well as Silja Häusermann and Hanna Schwander, "Varieties of Dualization? Labor Market Segmentation and Insider-Outsider Divides across Regimes," in *The Age of Dualization: The Changing Face of Inequality in Deindustrializing Societies,* ed. Patrick Emmenegger et al., 27–51 (New York: Oxford University Press, 2012).

60. On the United States, see Jacob S. Hacker, "Privatizing Risk without Privatizing the Welfare State: The Hidden Politics of Social Policy Retrenchment in the United States," *American Political Science Review* 98 (2004): 243–260. On Europe, see Mounk, *Age of Responsibility,* ch. 2.

61. In per capita terms, Sweden has four times as many start-ups as the United States. See Flavio Calvino, Chiara Criscuolo, and Carlo Menon, "Cross-country Evidence on Start-Up Dynamics," OECD Science, Technology and Industry Working Papers, 2015/06 (Paris: OECD Publishing, 2015). On a good journalistic exploration of the reasons for Sweden's success, see Alana Semuels, "Why Does Sweden Have So Many Start-Ups?" *Atlantic,* September 28, 2017, https://www.theatlantic.com/business/archive/2017/09/sweden-startups/541413/. For evidence that large welfare states generally decrease the number of start-ups, see Ruta Aidis, Saul Estrin, and Tomasz Marek Mickiewicz, "Size Matters: Entrepreneurial Entry and Government," *Small Business Economics* 39, no. 1 (2012): 119–139.

62. Private communication.

63. For an interesting study on the complicated interaction between the effect of a growing minority population and perceived threats to social status, see Maureen A. Craig and Jennifer A. Richeson, "More Diverse Yet Less Tolerant? How the Increasingly Diverse Racial Landscape Affects White Americans' Racial Attitudes," *Personality and Social Psy-*

chology Bulletin 40 (2014): 750–761. See also Binyamin Appelbaum, "The Vanishing Male Worker: How America Fell Behind," *New York Times,* December 12, 2014, https://www.nytimes.com/2014/12/12 /upshot/unemployment-the-vanishing-male-worker-how-america-fell -behind.html.

64. As Barack Obama infamously put the point on the campaign trail in 2008, "it's not surprising then that they get bitter, they cling to guns or religion or antipathy to people who aren't like them or anti-immigrant sentiment or anti-trade sentiment as a way to explain their frustrations." Quoted in Mayhill Fowler, "Obama: No Surprise That Hard-Pressed Pennsylvanians Turn Bitter," *Huffington Post,* November 17, 2008, http://www.huffingtonpost.com/mayhill-fowler/obama-no-surprise-that -ha_b_96188.html.

65. For a good overview, see Valerio De Stefano, "The Rise of the 'Just-in-Time Workforce': On-Demand Work, Crowdwork, and Labor Protection in the 'Gig-Economy,'" *Comparative Labor Law and Policy Journal* 37, no. 3 (2016): 471–503. Note that even robust political approaches to the regulation of the gig economy, like a recent speech by Senator Elizabeth Warren that was widely portrayed as hostile to Uber and Lyft, seek to regulate rather than to fight these new industries. Elizabeth Warren, "Strengthening the Basic Bargain for Workers in the Modern Economy," Remarks, New American Annual Conference, May 19, 2016, https:// www.warren.senate.gov/files/documents/2016-5-19_Warren_New _America_Remarks.pdf.

9. Renewing Civic Faith

1. On Germany, see Heidi Tworek, "How Germany Is Tackling Hate Speech," *Foreign Affairs,* May 16, 2017, https://www.foreignaffairs.com /articles/germany/2017-05-16/how-germany-tackling-hate-speech; and Bundesrat, "Entwurf eines Gesetzes zur Verbesserung der Rechtsdurchsetzung in sozialen Netzwerken (Netzwerkdurchsetzungsgesetz-NetzDG)" (Köln: Bundesanzeiger Verlag, 2017), http://www.bundesrat .de/SharedDocs/drucksachen/2017/0301-0400/315-17.pdf?__ blob=publicationFile&v=2. On the United States, see Zeynep Tufekci, "Zuckerberg's Preposterous Defense of Facebook," *New York Times,* September 29, 2017, https://www.nytimes.com/2017/09/29/opinion/mark -zuckerberg-facebook.html?mcubz=3; Zeynep Tufekci, "Facebook's Ad Scandal Isn't a 'Fail,' It's a Feature," *New York Times,* September 23, 2017, https://www.nytimes.com/2017/09/23/opinion/sunday/facebook -ad-scandal.html; and Zeynep Tufekci, "Mark Zuckerberg Is in Denial,"

New York Times, November 15, 2016, https://www.nytimes.com/2016 /11/15/opinion/mark-zuckerberg-is-in-denial.html.

2. Jefferson Chase, "Facebook Slams Proposed German 'Anti-hate Speech' Social Media Law," *Deutsche Welle,* May 29, 2017, http://www.dw.com /en/facebook-slams-proposed-german-anti-hate-speech-social-media -law/a-39021094.

3. See American Civil Liberties Union, "Internet Speech," https://www.aclu .org/issues/free-speech/internet-speech, accessed September 14, 2017; Mike Butcher, "Unless Online Giants Stop the Abuse of Free Speech, Democracy and Innovation Is Threatened," TechCrunch, March 20, 2017, https://techcrunch.com/2017/03/20/online-giants-must-bolster-democracy -against-its-abuse-or-watch-innovation-die/; "Declaration on Freedom of Expression," http://deklaration-fuer-meinungsfreiheit.de/en/, accessed September 14, 2017; and Global Network Initiative, "Proposed German Legislation Threatens Free Expression around the World," http://global networkinitiative.org/news/proposed-german-legislation-threatens-free -expression-around-world, accessed April 19, 2017. For a more specific objection about the way Facebook currently tries to censor some content, see Julia Angwin and Hannes Grassegger, "Facebook's Secret Censorship Rules Protect White Men from Hate Speech but Not Black Children," ProPublica, June 28, 2017, https://www.propublica.org/article /facebook-hate-speech-censorship-internal-documents-algorithms; and Jeff Rosen, "Who Decides? Civility v. Hate Speech on the Internet," *Insights on Law and Society* 13, no. 2 (2013), https://www.americanbar. org/publications/insights_on_law_andsociety/13/winter_2013/who _decides_civilityvhatespeechontheinternet.html.

4. Though much remains to be done, the major social networks have started to take their responsibilities more seriously in this regard. See Todd Spangler, "Mark Zuckerberg: Facebook Will Hire 3,000 Staffers to Review Violent Content, Hate Speech," *Variety,* May 3, 2017, http:// variety.com/2017/digital/news/mark-zuckerberg-facebook-violent-hate -speech-hiring-1202407969/. See also this interesting proposal for a mix between regulation and self-government: Robinson Meyer, "A Bold New Scheme to Regulate Facebook," *Atlantic,* May 12, 2016, https://www .theatlantic.com/technology/archive/2016/05/how-could-the-us-regulate -facebook/482382/. For the model of media self-regulation in the United States, see Angela J. Campbell, "Self-Regulation and the Media," *Federal Communications Law Journal* 51, no. 3 (1999): 711–772.

5. Victor Luckerson, "Get Ready to See More Live Video on Facebook," *Time,* March 1, 2016, http://time.com/4243416/facebook-live-video/; and Kerry Flynn, "Facebook Is Giving Longer Videos a Bump in Your News Feed," Mashable, January 26, 2017, http://mashable.com/2017 /01/26/facebook-video-watch-time/#XvOsKlECZZqi.

6. @mjahr, "Never Miss Important Tweets from People You Follow," Twitter blog, February 10, 2016, https://blog.twitter.com/official/en_us/a/2016/never-miss-important-tweets-from-people-you-follow.html.

7. The rapid progress of artificial intelligence is likely to facilitate the automatic detection of such harmful content in the near future. In the meanwhile, it may be unrealistic—and undesirable—for moderators to read millions upon millions of Facebook entries every day. But they don't have to: Since a few viral memes account for a vast share of online traffic, moderators could focus on adjudicating a comparatively small number of posts. On Facebook, for example, users would still be able to display hateful messages or made-up stories to their own friends on their own wall. But to slow or halt their spread, Facebook should stop accepting advertising dollars to boost such posts and change its algorithms to stop them from being displayed in a prominent position in the news feeds of other users. On the continued ability of hate speech groups to make money through advertising on platforms like YouTube, see Patrick Kulp, "Big Brands Are Still Advertising on YouTube Vids by Hate Groups—Here's the Proof," Mashable, January 26, 2017, http://mashable.com/2017/03/23/youtube-advertisers-hate-groups/#gqeCW7JsAOqk; and Charles Riley, "Google under Fire for Posting Government Ads on Hate Videos," CNN Money, March 17, 2017, http://money.cnn.com/2017/03/17/technology/google-youtube-ads-hate-speech/index.html.

8. Gideon Resnick, "How Pro-Trump Twitter Bots Spread Fake News," *Daily Beast,* November 17, 2016, http://www.thedailybeast.com/how-pro-trump-twitter-bots-spread-fake-news. See also S. Woolley and P. N. Howard, "Political Communication, Computational Propaganda, and Autonomous Agents," introduction to special section on Automation, Algorithms, and Politics, *International Journal of Communication* 10 (2016): 4882–4890; Philip N. Howard and Bence Kollanyi, "Bots, #StrongerIn, and #Brexit: Computational Propaganda during the UK-EU Referendum," Working Paper 2016.1, The Computational Propaganda Project, Oxford Internet Institute, University of Oxford, June 20, 2016, www.politicalbots.org, http://dx.doi.org/10.2139/ssrn.2798311; and Bence Kollanyi, Philip N. Howard, and Samuel C. Woolley, "Bots and Automation over Twitter during the Second U.S. Presidential Debate," Data Memo 2016.2, The Computational Propaganda Project, Oxford Internet Institute, University of Oxford, October 19, 2016, http://comprop.oii.ox.ac.uk/2016/10/19/bots-and-automation-over-twitter-during-the-second-u-s-presidential-debate/.

9. Private communication.

10. According to one poll, for example, half of New York City residents believed that the US government had intentionally failed to stop the 9/11 attacks. Alan Feuer, "500 Conspiracy Buffs Meet to Seek the Truth of

9/11," *New York Times,* June 5, 2006, http://www.nytimes.com/2006 /06/05/us/05conspiracy.html. See also Peter Knight, "Outrageous Conspiracy Theories: Popular and Official Responses to 9/11 in Germany and the United States," *New German Critique* 103 (2008): 165–193; and Jonathan Kay, *Among the Truthers: A Journey through America's Growing Conspiracist Underground* (New York: Harper Collins, 2011). For information about people's belief that the moon landing was faked, see Stephan Lewandowsky, Klaus Oberauer, and Gilles E. Gignac, "NASA Faked the Moon Landing—Therefore, (Climate) Science Is a Hoax: An Anatomy of the Motivated Rejection of Science," *Psychological Science* 24, no. 5 (2013): 622–633; and Viren Swami, Jakob Pietschnig, Ulrich S. Tran, I. N. G. O. Nader, Stefan Stieger, and Martin Voracek, "Lunar Lies: The Impact of Informational Framing and Individual Differences in Shaping Conspiracist Beliefs about the Moon Landings," *Applied Cognitive Psychology* 27, no. 1 (2013): 71–80. Regarding the Elders of Zion, see Stephen Eric Bronner, *A Rumor about the Jews: Antisemitism, Conspiracy, and the Protocols of Zion* (New York: Oxford University Press, 2003); and Esther Webman, ed., *The Global Impact of "The Protocols of the Elders of Zion": A Century-Old Myth* (New York: Routledge, 2012).

11. For illuminating analyses of the causes of conspiracy theories, see Cass R. Sunstein and Adrian Vermeule, "Conspiracy Theories: Causes and Cures," *Journal of Political Philosophy* 17, no. 2 (2009): 202–227; and Jovan Byford, *Conspiracy Theories: A Critical Introduction* (New York: Palgrave Macmillan, 2011). For the loss of trust in government, see Chapter 3 as well as "Public Trust in Government: 1958–2017," Pew Research Center, May 3, 2017, http://www.people-press.org/2017/05/03 /public-trust-in-government-1958-2017/.

12. See Adam M. Samaha, "Regulation for the Sake of Appearance," *Harvard Law Review* 125, no. 7 (2012): 1563–1638. The same idea is expressed by the famous judicial maxim given by Lord Chief Justice Hewart: "Not only must justice be done; it must also be seen to be done" (*R v Sussex Justices, Ex parte McCarthy* [1924] 1 KB 256, [1923] All ER Rep 233). See also the fascinating discussion in Amartya Sen, "What Do We Want from a Theory of Justice?" *Journal of Philosophy* 103, no. 5 (2006): 215–238.

13. See Gregory Krieg, "14 of Donald Trump's Most Outrageous 'Birther' Claims—Half from after 2011," CNN, September 16, 2016, http:// edition.cnn.com/2016/09/09/politics/donald-trump-birther/index.html; Jana Heigl, "A Timeline of Donald Trump's False Wiretapping Charge," Politifact, March 21, 2017, http://www.politifact.com/truth-o-meter /article/2017/mar/21/timeline-donald-trumps-false-wiretapping-charge/;

and Michael D. Shear and Emmarie Huetteman, "Trump Repeats Lie about Popular Vote in Meeting with Lawmakers," *New York Times,* January 23, 2017, https://www.nytimes.com/2017/01/23/us/politics /donald-trump-congress-democrats.html.

14. McKay Coppins, "How the Left Lost Its Mind," *Atlantic,* July 2, 2017, https://www.theatlantic.com/politics/archive/2017/07/liberal-fever -swamps/530736/; and Joseph Bernstein, "Louise Mensch Has a List of Suspected Russian Agents," Buzzfeed, April 21, 2017, https://www .buzzfeed.com/josephbernstein/menschs-list?utm_term=.jiKJEZoZmj# .ix3w2BMBnj.

15. "What should we make of this bizarre constellation of facts?" the re-nowned *Lawfare* blog asked in May 2017. "The honest answer for any-one who wishes to avoid speculation," they at first responded, "is that we don't know." But in an attempt to set out the range of possible expla-nations for Trump's links to Russia, the authors then went on to moot a range of scenarios—including one according to which Trump might be a Russian agent. "We consider this scenario highly unlikely," they empha-sized. "It simply strains credulity to imagine that a president would be in service of an adversary nation. That said, it is an interpretation at least consistent with the known facts. And a lot of people are saying . . ." Jane Chong, Quinta Jurecic, and Benjamin Wittes, "Seven Theories of the Case: What Do We Really Know about l'Affaire Russe and What It Could All Mean?" *Lawfare,* May 1, 2017, https://www.lawfareblog.com /seven-theories-case-what-do-we-really-know-about-laffaire-russe-and -what-could-it-all-mean.

16. "Transcript: Read Michelle Obama's Full Speech from the 2016 DNC," *Washington Post,* July 26, 2016, https://www.washingtonpost.com/news /post-politics/wp/2016/07/26/transcript-read-michelle-obamas-full-speech -from-the-2016-dnc/?utm_term=.8f6c82a2525f.

17. See Chapter 2.

18. For some recent proposals, see Lawrence Lessig, *Republic, Lost: The Corruption of Equality and the Steps to End It,* rev. ed. (New York: Twelve, an imprint of Grand Central Publishing, 2015); Zephyr Teachout, *Corruption in America: From Benjamin Franklin's Snuffbox to Citizens United* (Cambridge, MA: Harvard University Press, 2014); Lee Drutman, *The Business of America Is Lobbying* (Oxford: Oxford University Press, 2015); John P. Sarbanes and Raymond O'Mara III, "Power and Opportunity: Campaign Finance Reform for the 21st Cen-tury," *Harvard Journal on Legislation* 53, no. 1 (2016): 1–38; and Ta-batha Abu El-Haj, "Beyond Campaign Finance Reform," *Boston Col-lege Law Review* 57, no. 4 (2016): 1127–1185.

19. See Tony Blair Institute for Global Change, "The Centre in the United

Kingdom, France and Germany," June 2017, http://institute.global/sites
/default/files/inline-files/IGC_Centre%20Polling_14.07.17.pdf. For some
recent proposals on how to democratize the European Union, see Stéph-
anie Hennette, Thomas Piketty, Guillaume Sacriste, and Antoine Vau-
chez, *Pour un traité de démocratisation de l'Europe* (Paris: Seuil, 2017);
Agnès Bénassy-Quéré, Michael Hüther, Philippe Martin, and Guntram
B. Wolff, "Europe Must Seize This Moment of Opportunity," Bruegel,
August 12, 2017, http://bruegel.org/2017/08/europe-must-seize-this
-moment-of-opportunity/; and Cécile Ducourtieux, "Europe: Macron
livre une feuille de route ambitieuse tout en ménageant Berlin," *Le
Monde,* September 27, 2017, http://www.lemonde.fr/europe/article
/2017/09/27/europe-macron-livre-une-feuille-de-route-ambitieuse-mais
-menage-berlin_5191974_3214.html.

20. On congressional capacity, see Lee Drutman, "These Frightening New
Survey Results Describe a Congress in Crisis," *Vox,* August 8, 2017,
https://www.vox.com/polyarchy/2017/8/8/16112574/cmf-congress-survey
-crisis; Lee Drutman and Steve Teles, "Why Congress Relies on Lobbyists Instead of Thinking for Itself," *Atlantic,* March 10, 2015, https://
www.theatlantic.com/politics/archive/2015/03/when-congress-cant-think
-for-itself-it-turns-to-lobbyists/387295/; as well as Kevin R. Kosar et al.,
"Restoring Congress as the First Branch," *R Street Policy Study,* no. 50,
January 2016, http://www.rstreet.org/wp-content/uploads/2016/01
/RSTREET50.pdf.

21. See Jon S. T. Quah, "Controlling Corruption in City-States: A Comparative Study of Hong Kong and Singapore," *Crime, Law and Social
Change* 22, no. 4 (1994): 391–414.

22. George Washington, "Eighth Annual Address to Congress," December
7, 1796, available at the American Presidency Project, http://www
.presidency.ucsb.edu/ws/?pid=29438.

23. James Madison to W. T. Barry, letter, August 4, 1822, in *Writings of
James Madison,* ed. Gaillard Hunt, vol. 9 (New York: Putnam, 1910),
103–109, quotation on p. 103; available in *The Founders' Constitution,*
ed. Philip B. Kurland and Ralph Lerner (Chicago: University of Chicago
Press and the Liberty Fund, 1986), vol. 1, ch. 18, document 35, http://
press-pubs.uchicago.edu/founders/documents/v1ch18s35.html.

24. For the famous "Schoolhouse Rock" video, see "Schoolhouse Rock—
How a Bill Becomes a Law," season 3, episode 1, September 18, 1975,
American Broadcasting Corporation, available at https://www.youtube
.com/watch?v=Otbml6WIQPo.

25. See Allan Bloom, *Closing of the American Mind* (New York: Simon and
Schuster, 1987).

26. See American Bar Association and YMCA Youth in Government, "Part-

ners in Civic Engagement," 2010, p. 2, https://www.americanbar.org/content/dam/aba/migrated/publiced/YouthInGovtYMCA.authcheckdam.pdf.

27. James W. Fraser, *Reading, Writing, and Justice: School Reform as If Democracy Matters* (Albany: SUNY Press, 1997), 55.

28. *Bethel School District No. 403 v. Fraser* 478 US 675 (1986).

29. For a data-driven critique of how little college students actually learn on most American campuses, see Richard Arum and Josipa Roksa, *Academically Adrift: Limited Learning on College Campuses* (Chicago: University of Chicago Press, 2011); and Richard Arum and Josipa Roksa, *Aspiring Adults Adrift: Tentative Transitions of College Graduates* (Chicago: University of Chicago Press, 2014).

30. For an excellent run-down of the most concerning trends, see Campaign for the Civic Mission of Schools, "Civic Learning Fact Sheet," http://www.civicmissionofschools.org/the-campaign/civic-learning-fact-sheet.

31. See Max Fisher, "Americans vs. Basic Historical Knowledge," *Atlantic,* June 3, 2010, https://www.theatlantic.com/politics/archive/2010/06/americans-vs-basic-historical-knowledge/340761/; and Jonathan R. Cole, "Ignorance Does Not Lead to Election Bliss," *Atlantic,* November 8, 2016, https://www.theatlantic.com/education/archive/2016/11/ignorance-does-not-lead-to-election-bliss/506894/. See also William A. Galston, "Civic Education and Political Participation," *PS: Political Science and Politics* 37, no. 2 (2004): 263–266; and William A. Galston, "Civic Knowledge, Civic Education, and Civic Engagement: A Summary of Recent Research," *International Journal of Public Administration* 30, no. 6–7 (2007): 623–642.

32. As far as I am aware, there is little systemic research on this particular question. But since Americans of parenting age are much less interested in politics, and have much less knowledge of civics, than they did a few decades ago, it seems very likely that the anecdotal evidence does indeed point to a larger pattern in this particular case.

33. On the pedagogy of education schools, see David F. Labaree, "Progressivism, Schools and Schools of Education: An American Romance," *Paedagogica Historica* 41, no. 1–2 (2005): 275–288; and David F. Labaree, *The Trouble with Ed Schools* (New Haven: Yale University Press, 2004). For the push to educate more teachers in the context of research universities, see Arthur Levine, "Educating School Teachers," report of the Education Schools Project, Washington, DC, September 2006, http://files.eric.ed.gov/fulltext/ED504144.pdf.

34. See David Randall with Ashley Thorne, "Making Citizens: How American Universities Teach Civics," National Association of Scholars, January 2017, https://www.nas.org/images/documents/NAS_makingCitizens

_fullReport.pdf; as well as the response by Stanley Fish, "Citizen Forma-
tion Is Not Our Job," *Chronicle of Higher Education,* January 17, 2017,
http://www.chronicle.com/article/Citizen-Formation-Is-Not-Our/238913.

35. David Brooks, "The Crisis of Western Civ," *New York Times,* April 21,
2017, https://www.nytimes.com/2017/04/21/opinion/the-crisis-of
-western-civ.html?mcubz=0.

Conclusion

1. On Athens, see Sarah B. Pomeroy, *Ancient Greece: A Political, Social,
and Cultural History* (Oxford: Oxford University Press, 1999); and Rob-
ert Waterfield, *Athens: A History, From Ancient Ideal to Modern City*
(New York: Basic Books, 2004). On Rome, see Mary Beard, *SPQR: A
History of Modern Rome* (New York: Norton, 2015); and Marcel Le
Glay, Jean-Louis Voisin, and Yann Le Bohec, *Histoire romaine* (Paris:
Presses universitaires de France, 1991). On Venice, see the classic Fred-
eric Chapin Lane, *Venice, a Maritime Republic* (Baltimore: Johns Hop-
kins University Press, 1973); and John Julius Norwich, *A History of
Venice* (London: Penguin, 1982).

2. See Adam Easton, "Analysis: Poles Tire of Twins," BBC News, October
22, 2007, http://news.bbc.co.uk/1/hi/world/europe/7057023.stm; and
Choe Sang-Hun, "Park Geun-hye, South Korea's Ousted Leader, Is Arrested and Jailed to Await Trial," *New York Times,* March 30, 2017.

3. On Turkey, see Dexter Filkins, "Erdogan's March to Dictatorship in Turkey," *New Yorker,* March 31, 2016; and Soner Cagaptay, *The New Sultan: Erdogan and the Crisis of Modern Turkey* (London: I. B. Tauris,
2017). On Venezuela, see Rory Carroll, *Comandante: Hugo Chávez's
Venezuela* (London: Penguin Press, 2015); and "Freedom in the World
2017: Venezuela," Freedom House website, https://freedomhouse.org
/report/freedom-world/2017/venezuela.

4. See Kanchan Chandra, "Authoritarian India: The State of the World's
Largest Democracy," *Foreign Affairs,* June 16, 2016, https://www.foreign
affairs.com/articles/india/2016-06-16/authoritarian-india; Anne Applebaum, "It's Now Clear: The Most Dangerous Threats to the West Are
Not External," *Washington Post,* July 16, 2016, https://www.washing
tonpost.com/opinions/global-opinions/its-now-clear-the-most-dangerous
-threats-to-the-west-are-not-external/2017/07/16/2475e704-68a6-11e7
-a1d7-9a32c91c6f40_story.html; and Richard C. Paddock, "Becoming
Duterte: The Making of a Philippine Strongman," *New York Times
Magazine,* March 21, 2017, https://www.nytimes.com/2017/03/21/world
/asia/rodrigo-duterte-philippines-president-strongman.html.

5. Michael S. Schmidt, "In a Private Dinner, Trump Demanded Loyalty. Comey Demurred," *New York Times,* May 11, 2017, https://www .nytimes.com/2017/05/11/us/politics/trump-comey-firing.html; Sharon Lafraniere and Adam Goldman, "Guest List at Donald Trump Jr.'s Meeting with Russian Expands Again," *New York Times,* July 18, 2017, https://www.nytimes.com/2017/07/18/us/politics/trump-meeting-russia .html; Rosie Gray, "Trump Defends White-Nationalist Protesters: 'Some Very Fine People on Both Sides,'" *Atlantic,* August 15, 2017, https:// www.theatlantic.com/politics/archive/2017/08/trump-defends-white -nationalist-protesters-some-very-fine-people-on-both-sides/537012/; and @realdonaldtrump: "So why aren't the Committees and investigators, and of course our beleaguered A. G., looking into Crooked Hillarys crimes & Russia relations?" tweet, July 24, 2017, 9:49am, https://twitter .com/realdonaldtrump/status/889467610332528641?lang=en. (Note that, though Trump repeatedly refused to distance himself from white supremacists in clear terms, he has disavowed them on other occasions.)

6. See Tim Marcin, "Donald Trump's Popularity: His Approval Rating among His Base Voters Is Back Up," *Newsweek,* July 12, 2017, http:// www.newsweek.com/donald-trumps-popularity-approval-rating-base -voters-635626.

7. See David Leonhardt, "G.O.P. Support for Trump Is Starting to Crack," *New York Times,* July 24, 2017, https://www.nytimes.com/2017/07/24 /opinion/republican-support-donald-trump.html.

8. The best aggregate of Donald Trump's approval polls, including a useful comparison to past presidents, is run by FiveThirtyEight. See "How Popular Is Donald Trump?" FiveThirtyEight.com, https://projects .fivethirtyeight.com/trump-approval-ratings/.

9. Note that, at this point, a second term for Donald Trump seems unlikely—but not, by any stretch of the imagination, impossible. For a convincing scenario of how Trump could still win in 2020, see Damon Linker, "Trump Is Toxically Unpopular. He Still Might Win in 2020," The Week, August 30, 2017, http://theweek.com/articles/721436/trump -toxically-unpopular-still-might-win-2020.

10. Beard, *SPQR,* 232.

11. For an engaging popular history of the late Roman Republic, see Mike Duncan, *The Storm before the Storm: The Beginning of the End of the Roman Republic* (New York: Public Affairs, 2017).

12. Epictetus, *The Discourses,* Book 1, Chapter 1.

Credits

34   Vote share for anti-establishment parties in the European Union
          (EU15). *Source:* Timbro Authoritarian Populism Index 2017; https://
          timbro.se/ideologi/timbro-authoritarian-populism-index-2017–2/.
          Andreas Johansson Heinö, Giovanni Caccavello, and Cecilia Sand-
          ell, Timbro Authoritarian Populism Index 2017. TIMBRO, Stock-
          holm/EPICENTER (European Policy Information Center), Brussels.

80, 81   Cost of winning a House election; Cost of winning a Senate elec-
          tion. *Source:* Federal Election Campaign data processed by the Cam-
          paign Finance Institute; http://www.cfinst.org/data/historicalstats
          .aspx. Campaign Finance Institute (CFI) analysis of Federal Election
          Commission (FEC) data.

85   Lobbying expenditures in the United States, 1998–2016. *Source:*
          Center for Responsive Politics (CRP) analysis of Senate Office of
          Public Records (OPR) data (CC BY-NC-SA 3.0); https://www
          .opensecrets.org/lobby/

100   US respondents who express interest in politics, by decade of birth.
          Data source: World Values Survey (WVS), Wave 6 (2010–2014),
          World Values Survey Association; http://www.worldvaluessurvey
          .org.

101   Share of French voters who "fully" or "mostly" have faith in the
          president to "solve the problems France currently faces," 1995–
          2017. *Source:* Kantar TNS (formerly TNS SoFres) Baromètre/*Le Fi-
          garo* Magazine; https://www.tns-sofres.com/cotes-de-popularites.

105   "How important is it for you to live in a country that is governed
       democratically?" Ranking living in a democracy as "essential" is de-
       fined as any respondent who ranks the importance of democracy as a
       10 on a scale of 1 ("not at all important") to 10 ("absolutely impor-
       tant"). *Data source:* World Values Survey (WVS), Wave 6 (2010–
       2014), World Values Survey Association; http://www.worldvalues
       survey.org.

106   This figure examines survey responses in countries ranked as "free"
       by Freedom House and "high income" by the World Bank. It in-
       cludes all countries with populations over a million for which there
       are data on this question. Respondents were asked: "How impor-
       tant is it for you to live in a country that is governed democrati-
       cally?" Ranking living in a democracy as "essential" is defined as
       any respondent who ranks the importance of democracy as a 10 on a
       scale of 1 ("not at all important") to 10 ("absolutely important").
       Data source: World Values Survey (WVS), Wave 5 (2005–2009) and
       Wave 6 (2010–2014), World Values Survey Association; http://www
       .worldvaluessurvey.org.

107   This figure examines survey responses in countries ranked as "free"
       by Freedom House and "high income" by the World Bank with pop-
       ulations over a million for which there are data on this question. It
       shows the share of respondents who consider "having a democratic
       political system" to be a "bad" or "very bad" way to "run this coun-
       try," by country. Uruguay is omitted from this graph because no re-
       spondents born in the 1930s ranked democracy as a "bad" or "very
       bad" way of governing the country. *Data source:* World Values Sur-
       vey (WVS), Wave 5 (2005–2009) and Wave 6 (2010–2014), World
       Values Survey Association; http://www.worldvaluessurvey.org and
       European Values Study (Wave 4), European Values Study; http://
       www.europeanvaluesstudy.eu/page/surveys.html.

110   Percent change, per year, in worldwide respondents who think that
       "having the army rule" is a "good" or "very good" political system.
       Data source: World Values Survey (WVS), Wave 3 (1995–1998),
       Wave 4 (1999–2004), Wave 5 (2005–2009), and Wave 6 (2010–
       2014), World Values Survey Association; http://www.worldvalues
       survey.org.

111   This figure examines survey responses in countries ranked as "free"
       by Freedom House and "high income" by the World Bank with pop-
       ulations over a million for which we have time series data on this

question from either WVS or EVS. The rate of change is calculated per year between the first survey and the last available survey. For some countries the first survey in which this question was asked is WVS Wave 3 (1995–1998) while for others it is EVS Wave 3 (1999). Similarly, for some countries the last survey in which this question was asked is WVS Wave 6 (2010–2014) while for others it is EVS Wave 4 (2008–2010). *Data sources:* World Values Survey (WVS), Wave 3 (1995–1998), Wave 4 (1999–2004), Wave 5 (2005–2009), and Wave 6 (2010–2014), World Values Survey Association. European Values Study (EVS), Wave 3 (1999) ZA3811 and Wave 4 (2008) ZA4800, GESIS Data Archive, Cologne.

112   This figure examines survey responses in countries ranked as "free" by Freedom House and "high income" by the World Bank with populations over a million for which we have time series data on this question from either WVS or EVS. The rate of change is calculated per year between the first survey and the last available survey. For some countries the first survey in which this question was asked is WVS Wave 3 (1995–1998) while for others it is EVS Wave 3 (1999). Similarly, for some countries the last survey in which this question was asked is WVS Wave 6 (2010–2014) while for others it is EVS Wave 4 (2008–2010). *Data sources:* World Values Survey (WVS), Wave 3 (1995–1998), Wave 4 (1999–2004), Wave 5 (2005–2009), and Wave 6 (2010–2014), World Values Survey Association (www .worldvaluessurvey.org). European Values Study (EVS), Wave 3 (1999) ZA3811 and Wave 4 (2008) ZA4800, GESIS Data Archive, Cologne. Data for more recent, as yet unpublished, surveys on strongman leaders in the United Kingdom, France, and Germany available by request from the author.

121   This figure includes survey responses in countries ranked as "free" by Freedom House and "high income" by the World Bank with populations over a million for which we have time series data on this question. The percentage change for each country is the difference in participants who positioned themselves as either "1" (far left) or "10" (far right) on the political spectrum, from Wave 2 of either WVS or EVS to the most recent survey. Since countries' participation in WVS and EVS shifts over time, the dates for the initial survey ranged from 1989 to 1996 and the date for the last survey ranges from 2006 to 2012. *Data sources:* World Values Survey (WVS), Wave 2 (1990–1994), Wave 5 (2005–2009), and Wave 6 (2010–2014), World Values Survey Association; http://www.worldvalues

survey.org. European Values Study (EVS), Wave 2 (1990) ZA4460, Wave 3 (1999) ZA3811, and Wave 4 (2008) ZA4800, GESIS Data Archive, Cologne.

155   Percentage of children whose household income at age thirty is bigger than their parents' household income was when they were thirty years old, by decade of birth, for the United States. *Source:* Raj Chetty, David Grusky, Maximilian Hell, Nathaniel Hendren, Robert Manduca, and Jimmy Narang, "The Fading American Dream: Trends in Absolute Income Mobility since 1940," The Equality of Opportunity Project, December 2016; http://www.equality-of-oppor tunity.org/assets/documents/abs_mobility_summary.pdf.

167   Foreign-born population in the United States. *Source:* US Census Bureau, "Historical Census Statistics on the Foreign-Born Population of the United States: 1850–2000," https://www.census.gov/popula-tion/www/documentation/twps0081/twps0081.html; and Pew Research Center tabulations of 2010 and 2015 American Community Survey (IPUMS) in Gustavo López and Kristen Bialik: "Key Findings about U.S. Immigrants," Pew Research Center, Washington, DC, May, 3, 2017, http://www.pewresearch.org/fact-tank/2017/05/03 /key-findings-about-u-s-immigrants/.

Acknowledgments

At the end of "The End of History?," Francis Fukuyama revealed that he had some doubts about whether history would really end:

> The end of history will be a very sad time. The struggle for recognition, the willingness to risk one's life for a purely abstract goal, the worldwide ideological struggle that called forth daring, courage, imagination, and idealism, will be replaced by economic calculation, the endless solving of technical problems, environmental concerns, and the satisfaction of sophisticated consumer demands. In the post-historical period there will be neither art nor philosophy, just the perpetual caretaking of the museum of human history. I can feel in myself, and see in others around me, a powerful nostalgia for the time when history existed. Such nostalgia, in fact, will continue to fuel competition and conflict even in the post-historical world for some time to come. Even though I recognize its inevitability, I have the most ambivalent feelings for the civilization that has been created in Europe since 1945, with its north Atlantic and Asian offshoots. Perhaps this very prospect of centuries of boredom at the end of history will serve to get history started once again.

Does this passage help us understand our current predicament?

The parallels are obvious. Many of the most fervent, and most effective, adversaries of liberal democracy have enjoyed very comfortable lives—and now make full use of the freedoms our political system affords them. It does, at times, feel as though their hostility to a system that has treated them exceptionally well is, as much as anything else, driven by a desire to alleviate their boredom.

But the differences between our reality and Fukuyama's prediction are also considerable. For while some populists merely hope to show off their daring, their ability to attract so much support can only be explained by more structural factors. A lot of the discontent that is driving opposition to liberal democracy is founded in real grievances. Unless we commit ourselves to addressing those grievances, the coming decades will turn out to be rather too exciting.

Writers experience the tension between boredom and excitement in their own peculiar way. For decades, they have enjoyed the freedom to write whatever they want. Instead of cherishing this privilege, all too many secretly wished for a time in which their freedom would be more embattled, and they might more easily find opportunities for bravery and heroism.

That moment has now come. Reared in ordinary times, we have entered extraordinary ones. What writers do suddenly matters. And doing the right thing may take much more courage than we could have imagined a few short years ago. Instead of falling into the trap of romanticizing this situation, we must do what we can to return to the boredom of times in which the stakes of politics were, at most, medium-high.

But that doesn't mean that we can't enjoy the few consolations this moment brings with it. For me, a new sense of purpose and community has been foremost among these. There are the people whom I once saw as broadly aligned without feeling a real affinity for them; now, they seem like comrades. And then there are the people whom I considered my political adversaries until the early morning hours of the 9th of November, 2016; now, I recognize that our common commitment to liberal democracy goes much deeper than our disagreements about public policy.

So it is to this motley community of comrades and allies that I would like to express my gratitude first of all. My sincere hope is that, sometime in the not-too-distant future, the purpose that has united us will no longer be so urgent. Our sense of comradeship shall fade. With a little bit of luck, we might even live long enough to experience political times so ordinary that we can once again see each other as adversaries.

This broad community, one that includes people I know well just as much as it includes people I have only ever encountered in their writing, has given me a lot of succor over the past months. At the same time, a much more specific community of friends, colleagues, and collaborators has helped to make this book a reality in innumerable, more concrete ways.

Molly Atlas believed in this project back when my worries about the stability of democracy seemed a lot more far-fetched than they do now. She has been the best advisor, the most ferocious advocate, and the most incisive critic one could wish for, even at times when she shouldn't have been anywhere near her phone. I sincerely hope that she will still be hatching book plans with me once Donald Trump is but a distant memory, and the idea that liberal democracy could be in danger once again seems far-fetched.

Populism is a global phenomenon. So I have, from the beginning, been very keen for this book to make a small contribution to starting a truly global conversation about how to resist it. That is why I am all the more grateful to Roxane Edouard and Sophie Baker, who have been tireless (and amazingly successful) in their efforts to ensure that this book sees the light of day in many countries and in many languages.

John Kulka has helped to shape this project from the very start. Whenever I struggled to figure out how to make this project both serious and accessible, both analytical and passionate, he was at hand with a perfectly calibrated word of advice. So I was very sad when he changed jobs and handed over the reins on this project. As his parting gift, he made sure that the book would profit from the guidance of another extraordinary editor.

Ian Malcolm helped me conceive of the third part of *The People vs. Democracy*, and has significantly improved every other page of it. The effort he expended in ensuring that this book would turn into the best possible version of itself was, frankly, astounding. Academics often thank various people for advice, only to point out that any remaining shortcomings are completely of their own making. The long list of distinguished thinkers who have worked with Ian will readily attest to the fact that this cliché is, in his case, indisputably true.

Over the past months, Harvard University Press has put me in a very difficult position. Every author I know likes to whine about their publisher. So whenever friends of mine started on their inevitable litany of complaints, I baffled and annoyed them by raving about mine. Susan Donnelly, Richard Howells, Gregory Kornbluh, and Rebekah White have done a phenomenal job in getting the word out about the book and placing it in stores. Jill Breitbarth designed a striking cover. Kate Brick has done heroic work in editing and getting the book into print on a very tight timeline. Anne McGuire has worked wonders in cleaning up the bibliographical section and formatting notes.

The most inspired decision by the press has been to bring Angela Bagetta on board. When I heard what books she had helped to publicize in the past, I suspected that we would see eye-to-eye. Now that I have been working with her for a few months, I realize that I would never have heard of these books in the first place if she hadn't worked on them.

My biggest intellectual debt in this book is undoubtedly to Roberto Foa. When we started to look at some of the worrying data in the World Values Survey over the course of a beautiful summer week in Montelaterone and began to discuss the article that would turn into our work on democratic deconsolidation, we couldn't have known just how relevant our findings would prove, or how widely they would be discussed. Chapter 3 of this book is little more than an attempt at a definitive restatement of our co-authored articles. Without a doubt, our work to date is only the start of a long collaboration.

Three anonymous reviewers gave very detailed and overly charitable comments on the manuscript. They have made a big contribution to making the argument more tight and more complete. If the process of peer review was always as helpful and constructive as it has been in this case, our universities would be much more interesting places.

Monica Hersher has been of immeasurable help. She produced most of the graphs in this book and, at this point, probably knows the public opinion data on attitudes to democracy better than just about anybody else. She has also been a great interlocutor on other parts of the book; if I could convince her ever-skeptical mind of an argument, I knew for sure that I was on firm ground.

At twenty-one years of age, Sam Koppelman is without a doubt the most talented young writer I know. I was incredibly lucky to profit from his help on everything from big picture edits to finding supporting quotes. When he writes his first big book, as he inevitably shall, I hope that he'll let me return the favor.

The discussion of policy solutions in Part Three of the book has profited immensely from my basement debates with David Adler, Eleni Arzoglou, Sheri Berman, Ben Delsman, Limor Gultchin, Monica Hersher, Shashank Joshi, Sam Koppelman, Hans Kundnani, Harvey Redgrave, and Chris Yiu. I owe them, and the wonderful people who made our conversations possible, profound gratitude—for their intellectual contributions to this project, and for much else.

Dan Kenny and Jesse Shelburne provided very helpful research assistance on specific questions, from the history of judicial review in the 1920s to the finer points of international trade law. Leo Kim, Teoman Kucuk, Ted Reinert, Susannah Rodrigue, Dylan Schaffer, and Elena Souris provided patient bibliographical and research assistance.

Years ago, Jan-Werner Müller organized a conference on populism at the Center for Human Values at Princeton and had the bizarre idea of inviting a no-name graduate student to tag along. Gideon Rose had the even more bizarre idea of asking that student to turn his workshop paper into an article in *Foreign Affairs*. Both should be held responsible for the unintended consequences of their generosity.

It goes without saying that Larry Diamond and Marc Plattner have helped me improve my thinking on democratic deconsolidation. But my conversations with them, both over email and in person, have been nearly as important in shaping every other part of the book. I am very grateful to them, both for their intellectual companionship and for according the debate over democratic deconsolidation so much space in the *Journal of Democracy*.

One of the most valuable things Larry and Marc have done is to invite critical engagement with our argument. Though I continue to disagree with Amy Alexander, Pippa Norris, Erik Voeten, and Christian Welzel on important points, I have learned much from their responses to our work.

Over the past years, I have had the good fortune of writing pieces on democracy and populism for a large number of extraordinary editors. Sewell Chan deserves special thanks for championing my writing very early on and teaching me so much about what makes an effective op-ed. Since then, I have had the chance to work with Carla Blumenkranz, Jane Carr, Manuel Hartung, Giles Harvey, Laura Marsh, John Palattella, Max Strasser, and Elbert Ventura, among many others. Their insights are contained in many parts of this book, and their stylistic guidance in all of them. Brief passages from some of the articles I wrote for them have made it into these pages unchanged.

I wrote much of this book while on a fellowship at the Transatlantic Academy of the German Marshall Fund. Politically speaking, the year I spent with Frédéric Bozo, Stefan Fröhlich, Wade Jacoby, Harold James, Michael Kimmage, Hans Kundnani, Ted Reinert, Mary Elise Sarotte, and Heidi Tworek could not have been more depressing; personally speaking, it could not have been more fruitful and enjoyable. There is one, and only one, statement I would ever dare to make on behalf of the whole group: the fellowship year could only have been so pleasant and so productive because of the kindness and leadership of Steve Szabo.

One of the benefits of spending more time in Washington was that, after many years of being affiliated with New America, I finally got to be a more active part of its wonderful community. The Political Reform program, in particular, does extraordinary work; my approach to reshaping political institutions in the United States has been deeply influenced by Mark Schmitt and Lee Drutman; I also learned a lot from Hollie Gilman, Heather Hurlburt, and Chayenne Polimédio. Fuzz Hogan has been incredibly generous with his time, his advice, and his resources over the years. Peter Bergen and Anne-Marie Slaughter took a risk on me early on, and have been consistently generous since.

Slate has, for the past year, been an amazing publishing home, and I owe enormous gratitude to Jacob Weisberg and Julia Turner for giving me such a great platform for my ideas. John Swansburg was a wonderful ally and co-conspirator in conceiving of my weekly column, which allowed me to experiment with many of the ideas that fill the pages of this book; I hope to work with him for many years to come. Over the past months, Josh Keating has been an incisive, imaginative, and astoundingly patient editor (as has Allison Benedikt during his paternity leave).

In November 2016, I offhandedly raised the possibility of starting a podcast about "the ideas, policies, and strategies that can beat authoritarian populists like Donald Trump" to Fuzz Hogan. He turned my nascent idea into reality much better, and much more quickly, than I dared imagine. Since then, Steve Lickteig and June Thomas have done a great job transitioning "The Good Fight" over to *Slate*. But the fact that the podcast has found a ready listenership—and has been such a fun and productive way of testing and questioning the ideas in this book—is in very large measure due to the extraordinary skill, and even more extraordinary cheer, of John Williams.

Without the advice of Eric Beerbohm, Sheri Berman, Grzegorz Ekiert, Tom Meaney, K. Sabeel Rahman, Nancy Rosenblum, Michael Sandel, Richard Tuck, and Dan Ziblatt this book wouldn't exist. There are many others with whom I have discussed the themes of this book over the years, and who added valuable insights or offered incisive comments on parts of the book. They include Liaquat Ahmad, Jonathan Bruno, Aleksandra Dier, Martin Eiermann, Johann Frick, Art Goldhammer, Sam Goldman, Antara Haldar, Peter Hall, Alia Hassan, Michael Ignatieff, Dan Kehleman, Madhav Khosla, Alex Lee, Steve Levitsky, Michael Lind, Pratap Mehta, Guillermo del Pinal, Rachel Pritzker, Jed Purdy, Emma Saunders-Hastings, William Seward, Dan Shore, Ganesh Sitaraman, Dan Shore, Justin E. H. Smith, Dan Stid, and Don Tontiplaphol. It is inevitable that many will be missing from this list, and for that I sincerely apologize.

Heartfelt thanks for keeping me sane, and making sure that I have some fun, goes to Thierry Artzner, Eleni Arzoglou, Alex Drukier, Helena Hessel, Sam Holmes, Carly Knight, Tom Meaney, Nat Schmookler, Carl Schoonover, Shira Telushkin, William Seward— and of course to my mother, Ala (who also helped immensely with the German edition).

As I remark in the Conclusion, I feel very ambivalent about Stoicism. It can help to give us the resolve to do the right thing in this perilous political moment. But its exhortation to be indifferent toward things and people is a recipe for an impoverished life. Nobody has taught me this lesson more beautifully than Hanqing Ye. I could not have written this book without the strength she gives me. Had I not met her, I would not begin to understand just how rich life becomes when you decide to enmesh your happiness with that of the person you love.

Index